The Press
in the
Arab Middle East

Studies in Middle Eastern History

Bernard Lewis, Itamar Rabinovich, and Roger Savory
GENERAL EDITORS

OTHER VOLUMES ARE IN PREPARATION

The Press
in the
Arab Middle East

A History

AMI AYALON

In cooperation with
THE MOSHE DAYAN CENTER FOR MIDDLE EASTERN AND
AFRICAN STUDIES

New York   Oxford
OXFORD UNIVERSITY PRESS
1995

Oxford University Press

Oxford   New York
Athens   Auckland   Bangkok   Bombay
Calcutta   Cape Town   Dar es Salaam   Delhi
Florence   Hong Kong   Istanbul   Karachi
Kuala Lumpur   Madras   Madrid   Melbourne
Mexico City   Nairobi   Paris   Singapore
Taipei   Tokyo   Toronto

and associated companies in
Berlin   Ibadan

Library of Congress Cataloging-in-Publication Data
Ayalon, Ami.
The press in the Arab Middle East : a history /
Ami Ayalon.
p.   cm.
Includes bibliographical references and index.
ISBN 0-19-508780-1
1. Press—Arab countries—History.
I.   Title.   PN5359.A93   1995
079'.17'4927—dc20   94-9482

1 3 5 7 9 8 6 4 2

Printed in the United States of America
on acid-free paper

For my mother, Sara
and to the memory of my father, Moshe

Contents

II   ASPECTS OF DEVELOPMENT

Abbreviations

BSOAS	Bulletin of the School of Oriental and African Studies
EI^2	Encyclopaedia of Islam, 2nd edition
IJMES	International Journal of Middle East Studies
JA	Journal Asiatique
JQ	Journalism Quarterly
MEJ	Middle East Journal
MES	Middle Eastern Studies
MW	Muslim World
RMM	Revue du Monde Musulman
WI	Die Welt des Islams

Preface

This study is not a comprehensive history of the Arabic press. No single volume can tell the multifaceted story of the Arabic press and Arab journalism during the long period of their existence without leaving out far too many essential components. Broad as an ocean, the story invites explorers to wander and discover almost endlessly. What I have tried here is, more modestly, to chart the main phases in the evolution of the Arabic press and consider some of the major issues that shaped its role in state and society between 1800 and 1945. This work, then, is no more than an introduction to the history of that important institution in the Arab countries, leaving ample room for much further exploration, inquiry, and appraisal.

The undertaking, however, is somewhat ambitious in its span of time and geography. It examines developments in a sizable portion of the Arab region, the eastern Arab lands, including Egypt, the countries of the Fertile Crescent and the Arabian Peninsula, and to some extent the Ottoman capital—with whose history I am better familiar. Yet a glance would seem to indicate that quite a few of the findings discussed here—and their social, political, and cultural implications—largely typified the evolution of the press in the western Arab countries of the Maghrib as well. The story spans a long stretch of time, from the onset of the nineteenth century to the end of World War II—the formative era in the evolution of the medium, its infancy and adolescence, during which the political, social, and cultural roles of the Arab press were molded. The post–World War II period ushered in a new era when, under changed circumstances, the press began to play a different role, so different indeed as to justify another study altogether.

The term "Arab press" implies an all-embracing generalization, yet in different parts of the region, the press, like other institutions, developed in distinct ways and varying rhythms. Decades sometimes separated the starting point of press development in one locality from that of another; many years of journalistic trial and error elapsed in some places before the occupation emerged elsewhere for the first time.

Nor were the phases of evolution equal in length and intensity every-where. Still, the generalization is not altogether invalid. As we shall see, despite broad variance, society in the region responded to the idea and assimilated it in so like a fashion as to render local differences secondary in importance.

Our inquiry focuses on the written Arabic political press, that is, newspapers and other periodicals of political reportage and discussion. The broadcast media were excluded from this study, for although radio did appear in certain places in the 1930s, it clearly belonged to a later era in the relationship between journalism and society (television was not introduced into the region until the late 1950s). A related subject, which remained outside this study as well, was the simultaneous emer-gence of the non-Arabic press in the Arab countries. Newspapers and periodicals in languages other than Arabic were read by a small sector of society whose needs and outlook were generally different from those of the writers and readers of the Arabic press; those publications merit treatment in a separate study. Arabic journals devoted primarily to nonpolitical matters — literary magazines, specialized professional jour-nals, women's periodicals, juvenile publications, and so forth — al-though occasionally dealt with in the context of the journalistic scene generally, were not explored systematically in this study and are best treated separately as well. As will be amply evident, however, the line between political and other types of journalism was seldom clear-cut.

Within these confines, the study focuses on a relatively small num-ber of leading periodicals, both because they represent the essence of the development of the Arabic press story and because they are the most fully extant. We know far less about the myriad "ephemeral" publications (a recurring adjective in any study of the Arabic press), which generally left little impact on the community and which often disappeared without leaving a trace. Since initiating a journal was far easier than sustaining it, the records of periodicals that appeared in the region indicate hundreds of publications that died out as swiftly as they emerged, about which we know practically nothing. These anonymous publications constituted a large proportion of the fabric of the Arabic press, but, for the most part, will have to remain unexplored.

A considerable body of literature exists on various aspects of the Arabic press, most of it by Arab authors. This includes both studies of the history of the press in specific Arab countries and surveys covering the entire region. Countries in which the press had a relatively long history, primarily Egypt and Lebanon, are covered in detail by scores of works dealing with particular periods, specific newspapers, and the careers of individual journalists. A great many of these studies, often inspired by Philip di Tarrazi's pioneering *Ta'rikh al-sihafa al-'Arabiyya* (1913, 1914, 1933, in four volumes), follow a somewhat mechanical pattern of chronological enumeration of the appearance and disappear-ance of the many periodicals in one place or another. Seldom do they conceptualize the press as being a novel social institution whose evolution reflected complex political and cultural developments. A few works, however, are more analytical — notably Juzif Iliyas' study of the Syrian press; several of Ibrahim 'Abduh's, and Ramzi Mikha'il Jayyid's work on the Egyptian press; and 'Imad al-Sulh's biography of the writer and journalist Ahmad Faris al-Shidyaq. The sociopolitical and cultural roles of the Arabic press have only begun to be explored by Arab as well as Western scholars in recent years, most typically in studies devoted to individual newspapers or journalists (a favorite topic for doctoral dissertations). Notable among such studies are Tom McFadden's work on daily journalism in several Arab countries (by now over four decades old, yet still highly illuminating); the collection of essays on Arab journalists and writers edited by Marwan Buheiry; William Rugh's general survey that focuses on the post–World War II Arab press; and Beth Baron's study of the women's press in Egypt. In all that has been published so far there is no paucity of information and detail. Indeed, the abundance of detail is sometimes so overwhelming as to blur the story's main contours. The first part of the present study, therefore, is devoted to portraying the overall picture, followed by an examination of social, political, economic, and cultural aspects in the second part.

A few technical points should be noted. The terms "Arab" and "Arabic" ("Arab society," "the Arabic press," etc.) are used to denote the entire community that spoke, read and wrote in Arabic, including Egyptians. Although admittedly somewhat problematic, especially in the pre–World War I context, the terms are preferable to more cumbersome, if more accurate, alternatives. The terms "journal," "paper," and "newspaper" are similarly inaccurate, as they are applicable to periodicals that are diverse in nature and frequency. Here, the first two are used loosely and interchangeably to denote any publication issued periodically, while the third is employed more specifically to depict periodicals devoted primarily to news and political opinion, often, though not always, dailies. Every publication title is translated in parentheses, whenever translatable, the first time it is cited in the text. These, and all other renditions of names and passages quoted from Arabic, are the author's own translation. Sources in the footnotes are given in an abbreviated form, with full bibliographical references appearing in the References. Arabic is transliterated according to accepted practice in the field of Middle Eastern studies, but simplified by the omission of diacritical marks so as not to scare away the nonprofessional reader.

There remains the pleasant duty of thanking the many friends and colleagues who assisted me in so many ways during the various stages of this project. Much of the research and almost all of the writing was accomplished while I was a fellow at the Woodrow Wilson International Center for Scholars in Washington, D.C., between August 1991 and June 1992. The extraordinary scholarly atmosphere of this splendid institution and the superb cooperation of the entire staff constituted an inestimable contribution to this study. The staff of the Center's library, under Dr. Zdenek V. David's leadership, deserve special thanks for their devoted efforts on my behalf. Of the other fellows at the Center that year, the late Professor Elie Kedourie (whose premature death in June 1992 was a painful blow), Dr. Sylvia Kedourie, and Professor Pierre Cachia availed themselves for frequent discussions on matters presented in this book and offered invaluable suggestions and inducement. I am profoundly grateful to them.

Professors Bernard Lewis and Sasson Somekh read parts of the manuscript and provided many important comments. I am indebted to them for fruitful discussion of ideas and detail, as I am to Professor L. Carl Brown, Mr. Richard Harwood, and Professor Charles Issawi. Ms. Nancy Fischer, Ms. Vered Greenberg, and Ms. Michal Margalit rendered research assistance with remarkable efficiency and grace. Professors Beth Baron and Thomas Philipp, Dr. Yigal Sheffy, and Mr. Joshua Teitelbaum were generous enough to put at my disposal some of the fruits of their own search in the archives; my debt to them is acknowledged separately in the relevant places. Ms. Judy Krausz, an exceptionally keen reader of text and a master of style, saved me from many errors and markedly improved the presentation of the material. I am beholden to my friends and colleagues at the Moshe Dayan Center for Middle Eastern and African Studies and at the Department of Middle Eastern and African History of Tel Aviv University for their unfailing encouragement. Finally, I wish to thank Musa J. of Benghazi, Libya, without whose help I would never have brought this project to completion. His unique friendship will always be a precious asset.

The research for this study was supported by grants from the Israel Foundations Trustees, the Basic Research Foundation administered by the Israel Academy of Sciences and Humanities, and the Lucius N. Littauer Foundation. I acknowledge their help with much gratitude.

My wife Yael and my sons Yaron and Gil shared much of the burden this work entailed with admirable forbearance, as well as some of the joy. As they know best, their unflinching support was the indispensable mainstay of the entire project.

Tel Aviv   A.A.
May 1994

The Press
in the
Arab Middle East

Introduction

Communication is the cement that holds a community together. The community's viability as a whole, as well as that of its individual components, depends for its functioning on the ability to transmit and receive messages. Vital in the normal course of events, effective communication is even more crucial in times of crisis or rapid change, when a society is subject to unusual pressures and the threat of disruption. In such exigencies, normal communication modes may have to be modified, supplemented, or supplanted by other means so as to meet new needs, if the community is to retain its cohesion. Effective communication, while in itself not sufficient to guarantee a society's proper functioning, is undoubtedly indispensable in achieving that goal.

In the pre-twentieth century Muslim Middle East, an effective communications system existed that was in harmony with society's needs and facilitated the existence of a cohesive political, social, and cultural order. Two basic factors contributed to this harmony. One was the prevalence of the Islamic ethos, which dominated every sphere of the society's life. Rulers and subjects, the educated and the illiterate, townspeople, villagers, and nomads alike all subscribed to this ethos, so that there was a collective acceptance of the same values and a common approach to all major issues. The prescribed precepts of the faith dominated the principles of government, the fundamentals of law, social relations, moral conduct, and rules of personal behavior and family relationships, as well as the community's view of the world beyond Islam. A related unifying component was the recognition of one language, Arabic, as the medium in which activities related to the faith were performed, even in those parts of the region were other vernaculars were in use. The second factor facilitating communication was the dominance over the region by a single state during extensive periods in Islamic history, including the four centuries preceding World War I. The Ottoman Empire, which held sway over the Arabic-speaking provinces beginning in the early sixteenth century, was governed by a sophisticated hierarchical network of institutions ultimately subservient to the will of one sovereign. This long dominance produced institution-alized modes of dialogue between rulers and subjects that enabled the latter to be aware of what to expect from their potentates. The Islamic principles underlying the work of government further eased its commu-nication with the subjects.

The government had a variety of means at its disposal for announ-cing its positions and demands, both to its own subjects and to the governments of other states. Major events, such as the transfer of power, victories in battle, or the extension of state rule to new terri-tories were most commonly proclaimed through coins and stone in-scriptions on public buildings, city gates, public fountains, and the like. Military triumph was, in addition, declared through a *fathnameh*, literally a "victory announcement," a written document dispatched to state officials throughout the empire and to other rulers beyond its borders.[1] These were special devices whose solemn nature befitted the importance of the events they made known.

But there were myriad other matters, less dramatic in nature, whose communication required means to convey messages effectively to the state's subjects on a routine basis. This need was met largely through two channels. One was the mosque, where prayer leaders (*imam*, pl. *a'imma*) and preachers (*khatib*, pl. *khutaba'*), who were under government control, transmitted official notices to all males gathered for the weekly Friday prayer. The sermon preceding the prayers (*khutba*) was normally devoted wholly or in part to conveying political information emanating from or associated with the sovereign. This was the accepted method of announcing accession to power, the deposition of rulers, or rebellion by local potentates. A similar role was also played by roving preachers who were likewise in the employ of the govern-ment.[2] The other channel was a network of public criers or announcers (*munadi*) employed by the authorities to deliver official notifications of the imposition of new taxes, the anticipated arrival of a new governor, dates of religious holidays, the demise of important personalities, the arrival and departure of caravans and ships, and more common matters such as lost and found items and the names of escaped convicts. Such criers were employed in every town during the Ottoman period. They used to position themselves prominently on highways, in the market-place, or near public buildings, calling for attention of the public and, after making an announcement, enjoining those present to inform the rest of the neighborhood. "On that day," ran a typical account of this practice in 'Abd al-Rahman al-Jabarti's chronicle of Egypt for the Is-lamic year 1200 (1785 A.D.), "Salim Agha Mustahfizan rode [his horse] and announced (*nada*) in the markets that the Greeks, galleon-men (*qalyunjiyya*), and Turks should go back to their country. Those of them who failed to do so within three days would be put to death."[3] Anti-government rebels often used the same means for publicizing their positions.

News and opinion of unofficial nature circulated within society through a variety of channels. Again, the mosque, with its daily prayer sessions and weekly public gathering on Friday, was a major conduit for the regular communication of information, rumors, and ideas. So were the city bazaar, the cafe, the neighborhood barbershop, and similar traditional gathering places in the towns and villages. The caravansary — the merchant convoy inn — was a key source of foreign news, as was the annual pilgrimage to Mecca, when international information was exchanged and then transmitted to fellow countrymen back home.[4] All of this communication was oral, having roots in a period when reading and writing were uncommon and printing unknown. Not only official announcements and news were thus conveyed, but literary works, stories, and poetry as well. People were accustomed to conveying and receiving messages of any kind, even very long ones, orally rather than visually, a tradition that reflected the high rate of illiteracy in most of Arab society until the twentieth century. This tradition, of course, was not unique to the Middle East; it was paralleled in many other societies. In Europe and the European colonies abroad the cultural scene was quite similar until the late eighteenth century.

The general political stability under Ottoman rule and the prevalence of age-old sociocultural conventions guaranteed that these channels of communication sufficed for society's needs. Both the state and its subjects were satisfied that they received all the intelligence they required. Such, too, had been the case in premodern Europe, but with the close of the Middle Ages, vast changes in every sphere of life there affected communications as well. Growing individualism and the emergence of capitalism, the gradual pluralization of political systems, private economic enterprise and, consequently, the emergence of new sociopolitical ideas created a new hunger for information. The individual's subordination to the state and to rigid sociocultural conventions began to give way to free competition in commerce as well as in politics, and those who took part in this new movement needed the compass of reliable news to help them navigate in unfamiliar and often dangerous waters. The invention of the printing press in the mid-fifteenth century was the major breakthrough in the quest for the means to meet these needs, eventually leading to the emergence of periodicals of news and opinion — in Venice in the sixteenth century, in England, France, Germany, and various other European countries in the seventeenth century, and in North America in the early eighteenth century — all devoted primarily to satisfying the hunger for intelligence.

The early evolution of these publications in Europe and America was arduous, beset by technological, economic and, above all, political difficulties, for governments were not prone to allow such potentially dangerous tools to be wielded by their subjects uncontrolled. Struggling and paying a price that was sometimes painful, the press in the Western countries nevertheless made significant strides, establishing itself as a vital medium of popular enlightenment and public political debate and acquiring recognition as an indispensable guide to the rapidly changing landscape. By 1800, the press in Britain, the United States and, to a large extent, France had succeeded in freeing itself from governmental control and attaining nearly complete freedom of expression, which enabled it to become a growing enterprise with an expanding constituency of consumers. By then it had come to serve as a major vehicle for commercial advertising, which, in turn, became the economic mainstay of many newspapers. Although the press in the West still had a long distance to traverse before acquiring the power and prestige it would enjoy in the twentieth century — newspapers were still a luxury commodity in 1800, and journalism a less than respectable vocation — by the turn of the nineteenth century, after two centuries of evolution, the direction of the Western press was clear.

John Walter, founder of *The Daily Universal Register* (later to become *The Times* of London), characteristically laid out the paper's objectives in its opening edition in January 1785:

> Such, it is intended, shall be the UNIVERSAL REGISTER, the great objects of which will be to facilitate the *commercial* intercourse between the different parts of the community, through the channels of *Advertisement*; to record the principal occurrences of the times; and to abridge the account of debates during the sitting of Parliament.

In a lengthy discussion in several densely printed columns, Walter examined the benefits and flaws of other newspapers, then described his intention to produce a "paper that should blend all these advantages, and by steering clear of extremes, hit the happy medium" so as to offer "something suited to every palate."[5] Had a copy of the *Register* reached an Arab land, the reader there would have found it odd and probably quite unintelligible. The systematic coverage of major domestic and international events, records of the proceedings of parliamentary debates, and organized commercial advertisement, which were the *raison d'être* of the rapidly proliferating journals of the West, were for the most part alien to Arab society of that time. While business promotion was familiar and events of state and in society were recorded in chronicles, neither of these, let alone the work of government, had much to do with organized communications or the public's "palate." To the extent that the public was interested in such matters, it did not require channels of transmission other than the available traditional ones. In the year 1785, the Middle Eastern counterpart of *The Daily Universal Register* was a combination of the official *munadi* (as seen in Jabarti's account of that year, quoted above), the mosque preacher, and the exchange of intelligence in public gatherings. Newspapers did not appear in the Arab countries prior to the nineteenth century; they were unnecessary.

Nor was Arab society particularly interested in events in Europe, which for the most part remained beyond the horizon. This disinterest applied to the European press as well; the existence of newspapers in Europe is hardly ever referred to in Arabic sources prior to the nineteenth century. One rare exception is a report in 1690 by a royal Moroccan emissary to Madrid which contains a brief remark about Spanish journals, dismissing them as "full of exaggerations and lies."[6] In the empire's capital, Istanbul, there was considerable curiosity about events abroad, which was translated into informed foreign policy during the second half of the eighteenth century; the ruling leadership, aware of the European press, began to monitor a portion of it fairly systematically by the last quarter of that century. It is, however, quite unlikely that such knowledge by Ottoman officials was conveyed, or was of interest, to their Arab subjects. European newspapers might have occasionally reached the Arab provinces via foreign merchants and travelers, but if they did they left no noticeable impact. As late as 1831, the Egyptian writer and educator Shaykh Rifa'a Rafi' al-Tahtawi, relating his impressions of a five-year sojourn in Paris, dealt with French newspapers — "the daily sheets (*waraqat*) known as 'journals' and 'gazettes' (*al-jurnalat wal-kazitat*)" — as a novelty and deemed it necessary to explain their purpose and functioning. He too found them "full of countless lies."[7] As far as awareness of the institution of the press is concerned, then, Arab society at the onset of the nineteenth century started from *tabula rasa*. Large parts of the region remained ignorant of it for many decades thereafter as well.

This study, however, is not designed as a comparison between the Arabic press and the European prototype. While the institution of the press and the vocation of journalism were undeniably imported, the process of borrowing and the degree to which the Arab press replicated the foreign model are not the focus of this exploration. Rather, its aim is to shed light on the evolution of the Arab press in itself as a modern institution shaped by the region's political, social, economic, and cultural realities and exerting an influence on these realities in turn. The study examines the Arabic press during its formative first hundred years, a period of great change in Arab society materially, culturally, and in relations with other societies. The press will be seen as both reflecting and contributing to those changes, a mirror and a beacon at once.

I

HISTORICAL
PHASES

1

State Bulletins: Pronouncing the Official Truth

As with so many modern innovations in the Middle East, launching newspapers was, at first, the exclusive prerogative of governments. In the Ottoman capital, in Egypt, and in several other provinces, official bulletins were the only indigenous periodicals for several decades. Only governments had the motivation and the resources to adopt this foreign idea and employ it for their specific ends. Rudimentary sheets with limited objectives, the early newspapers were never in popular demand, nor did they play significant social or cultural roles, as would the private press at a later period. Yet, because they were the first, and for a while the only, enterprise of this kind, their role was vital in laying the conceptual and practical foundations for the assimilation of the idea in the region.

The dramatic landing of French troops on the beach of Alexandria in the scorching summer of 1798, and the swift conquest of Egypt that followed, had an impact on the Egyptians more dramatic than that which the gradual exposure to Europe had had on the Ottomans during the entire preceding century. Bonaparte's troops had reached the area in order to open a new front in their battle against England, but the effect on the front itself proved more far-reaching. Like the other Arabic-speaking provinces of the Ottoman Empire, Egypt had been isolated from events in Europe, complacently unmindful of the rapid pace of technological, political, and cultural developments there. The French invasion thus came as a shock potentially powerful enough to trigger a profound change. That change did not come immediately, but only some time after the French left, when the country was blessed with a gifted ruler, Muhammad ʻAli, who had the vision and vigor to turn the shock into a source of inspiration.

The trauma of the encounter with the might of modern Europe, Muhammad ʻAli's talent, and Egypt's convenient sociopolitical cohesion all combined to put Egypt on a course of change more rapid than in any other part of the Ottoman Empire, including its Turkish-speaking center. This was evident in myriad ways, not least in the development of modern communications: Egypt had an official printed bulletin several years before the Ottoman capital did, despite Istanbul's earlier awareness of that useful medium. The implications of Bonaparte's modern, skillfully directed propaganda machine were not lost on Muhammad ʻAli. Some time later, he would make Egypt apparently the birthplace of the first Arab paper.

Why "apparently"? The infancy of the Arab press is murky. One of the questions typically open to controversy is, which was the first Arabic-language paper? Everyone agrees that the first periodical to appear in an Arabic-speaking land was in French: *Le Courier* [*sic.*] *de L'Egypte*, first published by Bonaparte in August 1798, a mere two weeks after the conquest of Cairo. Designed for circulation among the French military and administrative personnel, it was printed every five days and carried official notices, local news, and other reports. Two months later, another French paper appeared, *La Décade Egyptienne*, a quarterly published by the French scientific expedition in Egypt.[1] Both publications were in a language that the native Egyptians could not read, printed with a non-Egyptian audience in mind.

But what of a paper for the Arabic-speaking public? Testimonies by Egyptian contemporaries of the French occupation contain vague references to a bulletin printed in Arabic at that time. The French, historian ʻAbd al-Rahman al-Jabarti related, "were eager to record daily developments in their various departments and courts." They ordered Ismaʻil al-Khashshab, secretary of the *diwan* (council) convened by Bonaparte, to prepare such accounts, which were entitled *al-Hawadith al-Yawmiyya* ("Daily Events"), then had them translated into French for circulation among the troops in the capital and the countryside. Jabarti neglected to mention what was done with the original Arabic texts of these accounts. Based on this somewhat ambiguous report, Philip di Tarrazi, the celebrated historian of the Arabic press, concluded that *al-Hawadith al-Yawmiyya* was "undoubtedly . . . the mother of all Arab newspapers."[2] Other contemporary reports in Arabic and French make similarly obscure references to a periodical sheet called *al-Tanbih* ("Notification"), published by order of General Menou, the French governor of Egypt from June 1800.[3] There is no evidence to show that such a paper did in fact appear, or to support other accounts about Arabic-language periodicals at that time, all of which seem to be based on erroneous readings of the mostly nebulous sources.[4] Nor can French proclamations in Arabic, which were issued from time to time, be regarded as periodical publications, although since they were printed frequently and widely circulated, they were a novelty. In the final account, however, whether or not an Arabic periodical was actually published in Egypt under the French is of little import. More significant is the fact that the French did publish printed notices in Arabic, even if irregularly, providing a model for the organized circulation of announcements. It was an appealing example of a control mechanism that would soon be emulated.

Similarly enigmatic reports tell us about the appearance in Baghdad of a paper called *Jurnal al-ʿIraq*, presumably issued in 1816 at the initiative of the local vali. Certain Western travelers to the Iraqi province mentioned a bulletin by that name printed in Arabic and Turkish, carrying reports on local and other affairs alongside official announcements. It was distributed, they reported, among army commanders, senior officials and notables, and was affixed to the walls and fences of the governor's residence for public notice. If such a *jurnal* was indeed printed and distributed, it might well have been the first Arabic newspaper. Iraqi scholars, although eager to identify the oldest paper in the annals of their country's press, have, nevertheless, found these reports highly dubious.[5] Still, once again, whether or not such a paper did exist is of lesser importance than the evidence that by the first quarter of the nineteenth century a venture of this kind was possible: Paper and the technique of printing existed both in the Ottoman capital and in the provinces, along with the European example of using such a medium as an effective means of communication. Furthermore, the government's target audience included people who could read, making the idea of a newspaper beneficial not only to the population but also to the state. All that was needed was a perceptive leader who would recognize the great potential inherent in this medium, adopt it, and develop it.

"Egyptian Events"

The French, who had brought with them the modern device of printing, demonstrated its capabilities in Egypt for over three years. If the two French journals were in a strange tongue, their proclamations to the public were issued in Arabic, which some Egyptians could read. When they left the country, in the fall of 1801, the invaders took their equipment with them, leaving the province without a printing press or many of the other innovations they had brought. But the demonstration had made an impression. Muhammad ʿAli, the Ottoman officer of Albanian extraction who soon afterward became Egypt's ruler for over four decades (1805–1848), fully appreciated the promise of this novelty. In 1809 he dispatched a close aide, ʿUthman Nur al-Din, to Europe with instructions to procure books on every conceivable subject. In 1815, having taken a few years to consolidate his rule, he sent another emissary, the fifteen-year-old Syrian-born Niqula Musabiki, to Milan to study the craft of printing and acquire printing equipment. Upon Musabiki's return in 1819, the cornerstone was laid for the first printing house, in the Cairo neighborhood of Bulaq, which was inaugurated apparently two years later. Other printing shops were soon built elsewhere in Muhammad 'Ali's capital. Shortly thereafter, the country began to produce its own ink, a commodity hitherto imported from Leghorn and Trieste. By 1835, Egypt, the cradle of papyrus, was producing its own modern paper. At that stage the state's printing presses had a near-complete monopoly over the new trade[6] — in Muhammad 'Ali's Egypt it could hardly have been otherwise. By the end of his reign, these presses had produced hundreds of printed books, mostly translations of European texts but also original works, in hundreds of thousands of copies (over 400,000 copies had been verified by 1846),[7] as well as innumerable public notices, administrative circulars, diplomatic documents, and the first official newspapers.[8]

Shrewd and ambitious, Muhammad 'Ali was quick to realize that traditional methods of communication were unsatisfactory in running his rapidly evolving government apparatus. Handwritten circulars and verbal commands were inadequate to instill the new standards of performance he sought for his state. A key component of the new administrative network he devised was a bureau (*diwan*) that regularly screened reports arriving from the country's different departments and the provinces and abstracted them into a single document. This document was submitted to the pasha and was then returned to the relevant offices with his comments — a procedure that seems to have begun as early as 1813. The document was known as *jurnal*, at that stage not yet a "journal," as it would later come to mean, but rather a register or report, and the office handling it was called, accordingly, *diwan al-jurnal* — "register bureau." Printing the register and circulating it in multiple copies could attain far better results than the old, inefficient methods: It would be speedier and clearer, and the texts would be available for repeated consultation. In 1821 or 1822, upon establishing a press in the Cairo Citadel, Muhammad 'Ali ordered the register to be printed under the title *Jurnal al-Khidiw*, a name whose two parts accurately reflected the foreign, Euro-Ottoman roots of the idea. "The Khedive's *Jurnal*" thus became the first printed Arabic periodical.[9]

The *Jurnal*, a bilingual Turkish-Arabic bulletin, was little more than a domestic circular intended for official consumption. With a run as small as 100 copies, it was designed for no other purpose than to keep the vali himself and his chief aides informed of state affairs. Handwritten at first, it was subsequently printed lithographically, appearing irregularly for a while before it became a weekly and later a daily publication. The paper included official notices, reports on developments in the capital and in the provinces, and, to alleviate the rigor of official business, stories from the *Thousand and One Nights*, a charming measure that would later become a feature of many Arabic papers. It was undoubtedly a success, for before long the vali ordered a larger print run and a streamlined format, so that it became a still more effective tool under a different name.

The first issue of *Waqa'i' Misriyya* (later *al-Waqa'i' al-Misriyya*, "Egyptian Events") was published on 25 Jumada al-Ula 1244, that is, 3 December 1828, succeeding *Jurnal al-Khidiw*. It was a small-format, 36 × 24 cm. paper in four austere-looking pages. Save for a rather low-key masthead composed of the paper's name, date (properly, according to the Islamic calendar only), and an unpretentious design of a vase of flowers, it contained nothing that would attract the eye, not even headlines or titles for the various news items. Immediately below the modest masthead came the text, running in two columns throughout the four pages, with Turkish on the right side and an approximate Arabic rendition on the left. The print, it has been observed, was characterized by "total disregard of the Oriental idea of beautiful calligraphy."[10] Later issues would continue to adhere to this simple format, with small modifications.

The paper's spartan appearance, no doubt a result of technological limitations, befitted its objectives as well. *Al-Waqa'i' al-Misriyya* did not aim to entertain. Rather, it was conceived as a serviceable tool in the governmental machinery of the efficiency-hungry pasha. Its main objective was "to improve the performance of the honorable governors and other distinguished officials in charge of [public] affairs and interests."[11] Beyond the small circle of high executives and army officers (for whom the paper's Turkish segment would have sufficed), the pasha also wanted to inform local notables, senior 'ulama', and the teachers and students of the new schools he had established, all of whom he hoped to integrate into his ambitious plans for state-building, which accounted for the paper's Arabic section. A total of 600 copies of each issue of *al-Waqa'i'* were printed during Muhammad 'Ali's reign. The paper was not sold on the street, nor was it produced for the man in the street; the public at large — the pasha's simple subjects — had no need to be informed on such matters.[12]

The contents of the paper also reflected this strictly utilitarian concept. It included mostly practical information, primarily state news and other details that could be of use to those effectively or potentially involved in the pasha's development plans. First came the vali's orders, notices of personnel changes, reports on the launching and progress of state projects, commendations of devoted officials, and reports on the punishment of those who deviated. Proceedings from the Consultative Council (*majlis mashwara*), formed in September 1829, became a regular item in the *Waqa'i'* from then on, as were routine reports from the other departments of government. This information was followed by news of events in the Ottoman capital and of the empire's international relations insofar as there was relevance to Egypt, which was included, however, only when Muhammad 'Ali was on good terms with Istanbul. News from other places—the empire's other provinces, Europe, even America—was sparse, haphazard, and generally incidental; it was considered largely irrelevant.[13] Only rarely did the paper deal with matters other than government-related reports. According to one count, "impractical" items occupied less than 2 percent of the space between 1828 and 1841.[14] These included amusing curiosities apparently designed to ease the paper's sober tone somewhat, such as a story about a Bulaq man who, slaughtering his mad cow, was shocked to find a live calf with two heads, four eyes, and four ears in her womb.[15]

Muhammad 'Ali never ceased to be fascinated by the immense possibilities of printing. Even before he issued his own publication, he received newspapers from Europe and ordered them read to him. This practice was important enough to warrant a note to Boghus Bey, the pasha's chief translator, warning that a delay in the dispatch of the newspapers to the palace would result in severe punishment "and no excuse will help."[16] Having invested in training personnel, acquiring equipment, and developing the basis for the extensive use of printing, he became directly concerned with every detail of the operation of the presses in Cairo once they began to roll. Foreign visitors to Egypt were taken by the proud pasha on a tour of the various presses and presented with copies of every book published there as a gift.[17] He regarded printing as a mark of progress and, more important, as a vehicle for advancing other projects. The official bulletin was a major component of this enterprise, and Muhammad 'Ali took it under his close personal care: He allocated ample resources to it, chose the best of his men to run it, involved himself in molding its format and style, and supervised its reporting policy directly, often demanding that the paper be read to him prior to its distribution. "It is not to be issued before we see it," he warned. Whoever was negligent in following his guidelines risked the awesome punishment of 300 blows of the cudgel. The pasha required all high officials who could afford it—those paid the substantial sum of over 1,000 qurush monthly—to subscribe to the *Waqa'i'* at their own expense, while others were allowed to receive it free of charge. The paper, he stated, should be distributed not by coercion but gently, "for it is a graceful and delicate product."[18]

An imported item transplanted to alien ground, the Egyptian official bulletin was at first afflicted with all kinds of maladies. It appeared irregularly, sometimes twice a week, at other times fortnightly. There were longer intervals as well: For about two years, between May 1834 and March 1836, no issue of the paper was published, and during the following five years, only 58 issues were printed, an average of one issue per month. Publication was often interrupted when Muhammad 'Ali was preoccupied with wars, revolts or urgent diplomatic matters. Eventually, like many of his other projects, the paper came to an almost complete halt under his successors, 'Abbas (1848–1854) and Sa'id (1854–1863).[19]

Another mark of initial difficulty was the rather unorganized and tardy reporting of events. News traveled slowly from the various administrative departments to the bulletin office and from the provinces to the capital, as it was brought by messengers on foot or by camel-riders. This, coupled with a cumbersome editorial process and the irregular appearance of the paper, often resulted in domestic news being published weeks or months after the event. While it should have been relatively easy to obtain up-to-date reports from the *majlis*, especially since the bulletin's editor was a member of it,[20] a report on the completion, in August 1828, of works to expand the army's artillery depot appeared in the bulletin a full year later, in August 1829.[21] If this was the case for domestic information, foreign news inevitably fared worse. Almost the only source of foreign intelligence was European newspapers arriving by sea — in 1830 about a week's voyage by sailing vessel from Cyprus or Antioch to Alexandria, and 49 days from England; in the mid-1840s about a week by steamship from Marseille.[22] Reports on events abroad always took months to be printed in *al-Waqa'i'*. The freshest foreign item that the paper published during this period appears to have been a decision by France, on 24 July 1847, to grant Egypt a loan, published in the issue of 2 September of the same year, that is, 40 days later.[23]

There were other difficulties. No one in Muhammad 'Ali's Egypt had prior knowledge or experience in editing an informative, widely circulated periodical of this kind, nor were there standards or even a sense of need for organizing and presenting the material according to rules. From the vantage point of the twentieth century, *al-Waqa'i'* issues during the early years of the nineteenth century look like raw drafts of unprocessed material, with administrative, economic, and personal items, as well as home and foreign reports, hopelessly intermixed without any categorization and often without headings. To pick a random example, the first two pages of issue no. 130 (March 1830) carried the following items, in this order: a detailed report by the *majlis* on the state of public food reserves on the eve of Ramadan; a brief extract from an Izmir newspaper dealing with Ottoman-Russian relations; a brief report from a French newspaper on the purchase of European uniforms for the Ottoman troops; a report from another French journal on the appointment of King Leopold of Belgium as ruler of Greece; two detailed reports on civilian cases tried by the Khedivial court; and a lengthy translation of a French article discussing Franco-Russian relations. The language, never before used for this kind of writing, was badly deficient, and the unavoidable resort to Turkish, European, and colloquial Arabic terminologies produced awkward texts that were not always readily comprehensible. An absence of punctuation, frequent typographical errors, and poor printing quality added to the amateurish nature of *al-Waqa'i' al-Misriyya* during this period.

These limitations characterized the official bulletin throughout

Muhammad 'Ali's reign, as well as the small number of issues printed under 'Abbas and Sa'id later on. Occasionally, certain modifications in format, arrangement of material, and linguistic style were introduced. The naive vase in the masthead, for example, gave way after several issues to a somewhat more symbolic design of a rising sun over a pyramid and a palm tree. Between 1842 and 1850 the paper was edited by the gifted Shaykh Rifa'a Rafi' al-Tahtawi, who made valiant efforts to ameliorate it, among other things by including literary and poetic pieces.[24] Such improvements, however, were of limited scope. By mid-century, *Al-Waqa'i'* was still a drab government organ featuring dry state communiques and dated news in a sober format for a small group of readers, some of them forced subscribers. This was the case as well for two other publications printed by the state during the same period. One was *al-Jarida al-'Askariyya* ("Military Bulletin"), first appearing in 1833 during the Egyptian campaign in Syria and continuing, intermittently, for several years thereafter, which was distributed to the troops and informed them on offenses, trials, and punishments within the ranks.[25] The other, an economic-commercial paper entitled *al-Hawadith al-Tijariyya wal-I'lanat al-Malakiyya* ("Commercial News and Royal Decrees"), was issued by order of Ibrahim, Muhammad 'Ali's son, in October 1848, and lasted for several months "for the benefit of merchants, farmers, and the public at large."[26] Both were of necessity bound by the same conceptual and technological handicaps that made *al-Waqa'i' al-Misriyya* the limited bulletin that it was. Yet, with all the difficulties, these official publications enjoyed an important advantage that private papers would not have: They were virtually unhampered by financial constraints. Attractive or not, skillfully or poorly executed, they continued to survive so long as the state found them of service.

The accession of Isma'il, grandson of Muhammad 'Ali, to the Egyptian throne (1863–1879) marked a new chapter in the country's history, and in that of the Egyptian press as well. Isma'il's reign was characterized by rapid change, especially pronounced after long years of sluggish progress, or even stagnation, under his two predecessors. In part this change was a result of the inexhaustible zeal of Egypt's "impatient modernizer," as he was termed by one scholar,[27] but it also reflected developments in the country's international position. A growing presence of Westerners in Egypt—missionaries, merchants, consuls, and travelers—entailed an increased flow of information into the area, greatly facilitated by current technological developments. By the time Isma'il came to power, the dissemination of printed information had become widespread in the region. Several private and semiofficial Arabic papers existed in other Ottoman provinces, as well as one in Istanbul that was distributed throughout the empire and beyond. In Egypt itself six journals in French and a comparable number in Italian had appeared during the 16 years prior to Isma'il's accession to power, all of them based in Alexandria,[28] and in 1857 there had been an attempt, apparently sponsored by the sultan and ultimately unsuccessful, to publish an Arabic paper in Cairo. Under the new khedive, the country would soon turn into a stage for lively journalistic enterprise and eventually become the leading center of Arab press activity.

Isma'il was quick to realize the importance of an effective information policy for his country. No sooner did he accede to the throne, at age 33, than he sent his confidant (later prime minister), Nubar Pasha, to France with orders to purchase shares in the leading Paris paper, *Le Temps*. The paper, hitherto a sharp critic of Egyptian policies, soon became pro-Egyptian. Similarly, Isma'il installed agents in Istanbul assigned to bribe local papers to give him favorable coverage. But his concern with the press as a powerful medium was not satisfied merely by manipulating foreign journals; it was complemented by an active press policy at home. Like his grandfather, but perhaps more sophisticatedly, Isma'il was eager to and capable of putting publishing to good use in his various modernization efforts. Reopening the royal press in Bulaq, which had been closed by Sa'id, he revitalized *al-Waqa'i' al-Misriyya* under an able editor, Ahmad 'Abd al-Rahim, and ordered the injection of additional financial and human resources into the bulletin's emasculated operations. "It is indisputable that journals have merits and benefits for people and government alike, hence I wish to make *al-Waqa'i' al-Misriyya* one of the most esteemed papers," Isma'il stated. Like Muhammad 'Ali, he seems to have concerned himself personally with his officials' execution of their duties at the paper, ordering that the reporters and editors be provided with hot coffee in the winter and fresh drinks in the summer "so as to keep them comfortable and content."[29]

Al-Waqa'i' al-Misriyya under Isma'il was a better product than before in various ways. Its publishing schedule was more orderly—it became a weekly in 1865 and a biweekly thereafter—its format was larger, it used better quality paper, and there were fewer typographical errors. Technological developments, primarily the expansion of the railway and telegraph systems, permitted a faster flow of information and an improvement in the pace of reporting. In 1866 Reuter's international news agency opened an office in Alexandria (which also serviced Havas, the other large agency), a vital two-way information conduit that allowed for the prompt publication of domestic as well as foreign news, sometimes on the same day it was received. There were also marked changes in style and language, which became more functional and accurate, although even in their improved version these official bulletins were in need of further refinement in editorial standards.

Isma'il also encouraged the establishment of specialized journals. Two such publications appeared in 1865: *Ya'sub al-Tibb* ("The Leader [literally: Drone] of Medicine"), a medical monthly for the use of students in the state schools of medicine, veterinary medicine, and pharmacology; and *al-Jarida al-'Askariyya al-Misriyya*, a monthly military bulletin published for the armed forces and for cadets in the military academies. Somewhat more significant was *Rawdat al-Madaris* ("School Garden"), a journal started in 1870 by the Ministry of Education, with Rifa'a Rafi' al-Tahtawi as its first editor, which appeared biweekly for eight years. It reflected the rapid expansion of educational activity and was a model of literary achievement. Another two state publications were established in 1873: *Jaridat Arkan Harb al-Jaysh al-Misri*, a magazine for the army general staff; and a French equivalent of *al-Waqa'i' al-Misriyya* called *Le Moniteur Egyptien*, reflecting Isma'il's concern with international public relations.[30]

The same political and technological changes that led to the improved standards of *al-Waqa'i' al-Misriyya* and prompted the government to expand its publishing enterprise eventually led to the relegation of these official organs to a secondary position. By the late 1870s, privately owned periodicals, benefiting from advanced technology, dominated the communications arena. These papers were mostly foreign-language journals protected and often financed by foreign powers, together with a few private Arabic ones that the Ottoman government licensed. The latter were to mark a new phase in the evolution of Arab journalism, which we shall examine later on. Under the new circumstances, as Isma'il was the first to realize, official bulletins could not compete adequately: Their identity as state organs undermined their effectiveness in ongoing propaganda battles against unofficial papers that were backed, often clandestinely, by diverse adversaries during the last decades of the nineteenth century. The new rules prompted the government to join the contest by sponsoring new publications that were privately owned but secretly supported and controlled from above, as well as by seeking to manipulate existing papers. *Al-Waqa'i' al-Misriyya* and the other state publications became less vital in the increasingly important press arena, their role restricted to the broadcasting of official notices and predictable commentary on current events by a government that simultaneously explored other propaganda channels. Increasingly, the official state organs came to resemble dry and unexciting official gazettes in the West, a role they would continue to play henceforth.

The Official Ottoman Press

At the time Muhammad 'Ali became governor of Egypt, the Ottomans had had several decades of experience in monitoring the European press and in utilizing it to shape their diplomacy. Like the Egyptians, they had also encountered the phenomenon of French newspapers published in their own capital—a brief experience in the late 1790s during the stormy years of the French Revolution, and another brief venture in 1811. Of more consequence and somewhat longer duration was a journalistic endeavor begun in the 1820s in Izmir by a Turcophil Frenchman named Alexandre Blacque, when the Ottomans were preoccupied with the Greek revolt against their rule. Blacque's paper, *Le Spectateur de l'Orient*, defended Ottoman interests and attacked Russian policies with such fervor that it evoked repeated Russian protests. Ribeaupierre, the Russian ambassador to the empire, warned Sultan Mahmud the Second against the dangers of a free press: "In France and England journalists can express themselves freely, even against their kings," he told him, "so that on several occasions . . . wars broke out between France and England because of these journalists." It was therefore wise to silence the aggressive French paper, the ambassador advised. For the sultan, however, this was a vivid illustration of what the printed word could achieve. He became convinced that such a powerful instrument had best be kept alive under the ownership, or at least the control, of the state.[31]

The Ottoman sultan and his governor in Egypt shared a similar view regarding the potential value of printed texts, but there were differences in emphasis. While both attached importance to newspapers as tools of domestic control, Sultan Mahmud, more so than Muhammad 'Ali, was concerned with the international position and image of his empire, and regarded newspapers primarily as useful implements in this area. This sensitivity to foreign affairs, the result of centuries of continuous contact with Europe, was at the root of all the modernization projects undertaken by the empire during the final hundred years of its existence. Even before the incident involving the Russian ambassador, Sultan Mahmud had approached the Austrians with a request that they establish a newspaper in Istanbul, hoping to gain control of it.[32] When this initiative proved unproductive, he initiated an organ of his own—*Le Moniteur Ottoman*, the first official Ottoman bulletin, which appeared in 1830, two years after Muhammad 'Ali's *Waqa'i'*. Published in French by none other than Alexandre Blacque, it was intended for international consumption. "Hitherto the relations of the Turks to the other nations of Europe remind one of the fable of the painter and the lion," observed a sympathetic American visitor to Istanbul. "All the painting has been on one side, and the character of the Turk and the acts of his government have been uniformly painted in dark and gloomy colors. Now the case is altered, and Mustapha can make his voice heard [in] the remotest corners of Europe."[33]

Other considerations, however, soon grew in importance. The percolation of foreign ideas into the empire was potentially dangerous, even if still on a small scale. It could make people "apt to interpret governmental acts in ways which are not even dreamed of or imagined by the authors," and this might lead to "attacks and misunderstand-

ings." It had become necessary, the sultan felt, "to check" these undesirable trends at home, an objective that could best be attained through
the publication of papers in the local vernaculars. On 25 July 1831,
the official Turkish-language *Taqvim-i Veqayi* ("Calendar of Events")
appeared, with the declared aim of giving "the people rest of mind
and satisfaction," by making them "acquainted with the real nature of
events."[34] The first issue of the paper included a promise of future
versions in other languages, so that "the usefulness of the work" could be
extended to the empire's non-Turkish subjects and "all friendly powers."
Indeed, according to registers found in the Ottoman archives, editions
in several other languages were distributed in the provinces, among
them, notably, an Arabic edition that apparently was published irregularly from 1839.[35] Like *al-Waqa'i' al-Misriyya*, the *Taqvim* was a monoto-
nous news periodical comprising imperial decrees, announcements of
official appointments, and reports on governmental activity. The paper's reported 5,000 copies were distributed to state officials, who were
required to buy them, dignitaries, 'ulama', and foreign consular personnel. Again, like its Egyptian counterpart, it was not meant to be read
by the man in the street.[36]

   Taqvim-i Vekayi was the empire's only Turkish-language paper until 1840, and not until the Crimean War in the mid-1850s was its
paramount standing seriously challenged by other Turkish publications
in the capital. In the Arab provinces, however, that challenge presented
itself earlier. The Egyptian *al-Waqa'i' al-Misriyya*, which preceded the
Istanbul gazette by some three years, was the mouthpiece of a foe
who defied his Ottoman masters and posed a genuine threat to their
sovereignty. Moreover, after the Egyptian occupation of Syria in 1831–
1832, Muhammad 'Ali was in a position to air his views in additional
provinces of the empire, which he controlled for the rest of the decade.
Later, in 1847, the French authorities in occupied Algeria started a
French-Arabic journal, *al-Mubashshir* ("The Announcer"), another public voice in the language of the sultan's subjects. In 1855, at the height
of the Crimean War, the challenge moved closer to home when an
Arabic newspaper called *Mir'at al-Ahwal* ("Mirror of Events") was published in Istanbul by a Syrian emigré, whose pro-Russian views were
revealed shortly afterward. The war also brought another innovation,
the telegraph—a problematic medium, as the Ottomans were soon to
discover, for it transmitted reports that were not always compatible
with their own announcements. Once the war was over, additional
Arabic papers began to appear both within and outside the empire—in
Beirut, Marseille, Paris, and, in 1861, once again in the Ottoman
capital. This last was Ahmad Faris al-Shidyaq's *al-Jawa'ib* ("Circulating
News"), a more important and durable paper than *Mir'at al-Ahwal*.
Later that year, the governor of another Arab province, the Tunisian
Bey Muhammad al-Sadiq, emulated his Egyptian colleague and his
Ottoman master by launching his own official organ, *al-Ra'id al-Tunisi*

("Tunisian Leader").[37] Some of these papers were circulated beyond the confines of their home base. More ominously, all made use of foreign journals, which were flowing into the empire at an alarming rate. In addition, in many cities — Beirut, Damascus, Aleppo, Baghdad, Mosul, Kazimiyya, Jerusalem — presses established to publish holy books printed other materials as well. In some of these places missions of the various foreign Christian denominations were using print in their frequent squabbles with each other and with local Christian communities over religious issues that had obvious political implications. By the mid-1860s, the independent dissemination of published views in the Arab provinces had become a serious problem for the empire.

Confronted with such a rapid spread of uncontrolled intelligence, the Ottoman government instinctively responded by trying to muzzle these voices, at least within its own territory. Shortly after the Crimean War, in January 1857, the first "Printing and Publication Law" was decreed, requiring licensing for publishers and prepublication censorship of all printed materials. In January 1865 the authorities went a step further by enacting a law dealing specifically with periodicals, prescribing various publishing limitations.[38] Meanwhile, pressure to curb criticism and promote support for the regime through warnings and punishment on the one hand, and generous subventions on the other, was exerted on owners of Arabic-language and other newspapers. These measures soon brought the Arabic papers in Beirut and Istanbul under the wing of the Ottoman Foreign Ministry. Apparently there was also an attempt in Egypt as early as 1857 to launch a pro-Ottoman organ disguised as a private enterprise under the name al-Saltana ("The Sultanate"), which lasted for several months only.[39] All these efforts, however, left something to be desired from the government's point of view: There was a palpable need for more organized channels to enlighten the key sectors of the community about Ottoman truths. It was important, in the Arab provinces as well as in the capital, to combat rumors and dangerous ideas by making public "the true nature of events and . . . the real purport of the acts and commands of the government."[40]

As was the case with many Ottoman reforms, establishing state papers in the provinces often stemmed from the initiative of local officials who were more aware of changing conditions and potential dangers than their superiors in Istanbul. In the early 1860s the authorities in Damascus, capital of the Vilayet of Syria, had to contend with a growing influx of publications from Cairo, Beirut, Istanbul, and Europe which often carried irritating reports and views that conflicted with their own stated positions. In late 1864 the vali Shirwani Muhammad Rushdi Pasha requested and was granted government permission to establish a state press in Damascus. The following year, Khalil al-Khuri, by then an experienced editor of a privately owned Beirut weekly, Hadiqat al-Akhbar ("Garden of News"), was brought to Damascus to establish an official gazette, run it for a while, and train a group of workers to continue operating it later on. The paper, a Turkish-Arabic weekly, was festively inaugurated at the governor's house in the autumn of 1865 under the name *Suriya*—a title as dry as the journal itself would soon prove to be. The utilitarian name and the bilingual format would become standard features of future state publications in the Arab provinces.

Two years later, another official paper appeared in similar circumstances in Aleppo, slightly closer to the heart of the empire. As with *Suriya*, the Aleppo paper also resulted from the initiative of the governor, Ahmed Jevdet, an administrator, historian, and man of letters who personally edited the paper and for a while wrote some of the articles. It too had an unpretentious name, *Ghadir al-Furat* ("Euphrates River"), which two years later became simply *al-Furat*. In concept, content, and format it was all but identical with its southern predecessor. These two publications were the only local papers in the Syrian vilayets for about a decade, when private newspapers and journals began to appear. Printed, by one estimate, in some 1,500 copies, *Suriya* and *al-Furat* continued to bring the imperial word to the Syrian region — more precisely, to the state officials who were required to buy it and to a minuscule number of other readers — until the fall of the empire in 1918.[41]

Meanwhile, additional state periodicals were started elsewhere. In 1867, Da'ud Pasha, governor of Mount Lebanon, ordered the publication of the official *Lubnan* in Bayt al-Din, his administrative center. This area had witnessed a certain amount of press activity for over a decade, and there seemed to be a demand for more. Reflecting the cultural situation in Lebanon generally, *Lubnan* was a unique paper: It was bilingual, but the language alongside Arabic was not Turkish — it was French. Da'ud Pasha, a Catholic Armenian with some European education and a high regard for Western culture, allocated considerable resources to the paper and, to supplement the standard official announcements, encouraged the reprinting of reports from European journals and permitted the publication of relatively liberal articles. He was thereby responding to the reality of growing cultural and intellectual ferment in Lebanon. A change of governors, however, brought a change in government attitude: In 1868, a year after it first appeared, *Lubnan* ceased publication by order of the new vali, Franco Pasha, who responded to another aspect of the same reality — the need for economy. The new governor found it more expedient to take control of the leading local private paper in Beirut, *Hadiqat al-Akhbar*, and turn it into a fully official organ. *Hadiqat al-Akhbar* served the official objectives for a while, until it was decided that *Suriya*, the bulletin published by the province of Syria, which also incorporated Mount Lebanon, could fulfill these objectives even more effectively. In 1888, the formation of the separate vilayet of Beirut prompted the establishment of yet another local organ, under the predictable title *Bayrut*, an additional link in a long chain of standard government gazettes. In Beirut of that time—a venue of spirited journalistic enterprise—this official paper went all but unnoticed.[42]

If the voice of the official papers in Lebanon was overpowered by the lively chorus of numerous private publications there, the situation was quite different in the more remote provinces—in Mesopotamia, Yemen, and Tripoli—where exposure to foreign ideas and the effect of Ottoman reform efforts were more limited. Inspired vision and resourcefulness were needed to modernize these provinces, traits that Midhat Pasha brought with him to the post of vali of Baghdad in 1869. In three brief years as governor, Midhat not only established the first Arabic-Turkish paper there, but also introduced a telegraph network, developed postal services, improved transportation, and expanded the education system—all vital contributions to the evolution of the press later on. Apart from a limitless zeal for reform, Midhat, previously the Ottoman ambassador in Paris, also brought in printing machines from France and newspaper editors from Istanbul.[43] In June 1869 the official *al-Zawra'* ("The Curved," a popular appellation for the city of Baghdad) appeared, a replica of its counterparts elsewhere in the empire. The governors of the two other Iraqi provinces eventually followed suit, launching *al-Mawsil* in Mossul in 1885, and *al-Basra* in Basra in 1889. These were the only domestic periodicals in the Iraqi provinces until the end of the century (and, with the exception of two religious journals published by missionaries, until the Young Turk revolution of 1908).[44] Similar publications were initiated in other parts of the empire to serve similar ends: *Tarablus al-Gharb* ("Tripoli of the West") in Tripoli (1871); *al-Quds al-Sharif* in Jerusalem (1876); *al-San'a'* in San'a (1877); and, after the Young Turk revolution, *al-Hijaz* in Mecca (1908).

Geared to attain similar objectives and produced under the same guidelines, the official journals in all of these provinces looked and read as if they were crafted by a single hand. They were normally four-page medium-sized publications printed by rather primitive machines on coarse paper, with ink that stained the reader's fingers. Besides routine segments glorifying the sultan—an indispensable feature—they normally carried, first and foremost, state decrees and official news. Then came news from the provinces, reports on the empire's international relations, and, occasionally, other foreign news. Sometimes they featured articles on major issues of the day adapted from the official press in the capital. Occasionally, to inject some life into the tedious text, there were reports on scientific developments, such as on "The Era of Electricity" and "The Benefit of Fruit and Vegetables."[45]

Much of the information was dated, since for the most part the officials who produced the journals relied on reports supplied by their colleagues in the other provincial departments and on the Istanbul press. The functionary in charge of the Iraqi *al-Zawra'*, for example, used to make a weekly tour of the government offices in Baghdad, namely, the police department, the postal and telegraph offices, and the bureau of river navigation. It was an easy task, for the city was small then and the other officials were accessible to him. The majority of news items — over 70 percent, according to one study — were gathered in this way, with the proportion of telegraph reports growing in time. The rest of the news was culled from journals that arrived from the capital, from the other provincial centers, and, occasionally, from the foreign press; reports sent sporadically by informants in the various provinces; and the international news agencies. This last source, which provided items for a section called *tilighrafat azhans rutir* (Reuter's Agency Telegrams), was used sparingly: It was safer not meddling with independent intelligence of this kind. *Al-Zawra*'s frequent tardiness, and its coverage of events weeks or even months after they occurred, were also due to the slow operation of the postal services — news received in the Baghdad office sometimes took a week or more to be delivered to the paper — and the often-languid performance of the translator and printers employed by the journal. These practices were typical of the entire field.[46]

Since the officials who produced the journals had a more limited command of Arabic than Turkish, their publications were marked by poor Arabic style and inferior language, sometimes so much so that the text was comprehensible only by consulting the parallel Turkish version. The editorial standards were scarcely any better, and only infrequently was the material arranged methodically. Arab historians discussing these journals commonly use adjectives such as "shoddy," "frail," "dull," and "wretched" to depict their appearance and contents.[47] In many ways, it would seem, these uninspiring bulletins mirrored the general attitude of the Ottoman officials to the Arab provinces under their control during this period.

Unlike most private Arabic papers in the nineteenth century, however, the official bulletins had long lives. Nearly all of them joined the exclusive list of papers that, by the eve of World War I, could boast a "silver" or "golden" jubilee.[48] Quality and size of readership had little to do with their impressive endurance: They lasted so long as the government that published them lasted. These state publications played no more than a secondary, or even more marginal, role in the Ottoman political and cultural milieu of the time. As far as the government was concerned, they constituted only one of many, generally more effective, vehicles for improving domestic control and enhancing its image abroad. To their readers, of whom we know little, they must have been less attractive than the private press, which was invariably more vivid. Since many of the private papers regularly ran official notices in any case, these state organs had little appeal and were practically redundant. While *al-Waqa'i' al-Misriyya* was a lone voice in Egypt for several decades, and therefore achieved some status at least as a vehicle for news, this was not the case with its Arabic counterparts elsewhere in the Ottoman Empire that appeared during the second half of the century, when information of all kinds flowed into the area at an ever-increasing pace and through many channels. These channels reached massive proportions by the eve of World War I; the flow of official messages, however steady, was merely a trickle in this current.

2

Enthusiastic Beginnings: The Private Press, 1855–1882

Lebanon in the mid-nineteenth century was the scene of growing intellectual ferment. An educated group with a command of foreign languages, and inspired by Western ideas, was eagerly shaking the dust off the old treasures of local culture. Their small circle was growing slowly but continuously thanks to an expanding network of new schools that competed with each other in introducing pupils to modern thought and technology. Printing was advancing: As against one active press in Lebanon in 1800, there were four in 1850 producing holy books but also, notably, other texts. Cultural and literary societies were being formed, following the lead of the Syrian Scientific Society (*al-jamʿiyya al-ʿilmiyya al-Suriyya*), founded in Beirut in 1847 by Protestant missionaries and their students. Five years later, the first volume of the society's yearbook, a mirror of this energetic endeavor, contained articles on scientific issues such as copper smelting, social questions such as women's education (a striking idea at the time), daily household matters such as modern methods of child rearing, and historical, geographic, and literary subjects. Soon Beirut would boast dozens of bookstores; presses that printed classical works, modern dictionaries and a modern universal encyclopedia; numerous scientific societies with substantial memberships; and two important colleges. Lebanon would blaze the trail for the cultural, and later nationalist, awakening of Middle Eastern society, while Lebanese intellectuals in Beirut, Cairo, Istanbul, and Paris would pioneer the revival of language and literature and the establishment of theater and the press.[1]

Why Lebanese? Two interrelated factors were responsible for their early leadership: A tradition of resourcefulness and creativity, en-

hanced by the markedly diverse composition of Lebanese society; and
the incentive provided by Christian missionaries based there since the
early 1820s. Lebanon, a Christian island in a Muslim sea, had been a
focus of European attention—more specifically, that of the Catholic
Church—as far back as the early seventeenth century. A printshop was
set up there at that time, the first in the Arab lands.[2] Intermittent
contact between Catholic Europe and the local Christians, especially
the Maronites of Mount Lebanon, continued until the early nineteenth
century, although it was too meager to have a significant impact on the
Lebanese cultural scene. The arrival in Lebanon of American Protestant missionaries in 1821, however, prompted competition between the
various missions there, which became a powerful vehicle for change.
The contest for winning converts focused on quality of education, pro-
voking the indigenous Christian communities to join the race lest they
lose members to the missionaries. The result was accelerated progress
in the schooling system, a development that appeared in Lebanon long
before it did elsewhere in the region.

The Christian Lebanese responded eagerly to the riches offered
them by the emissaries of the modern world. Having none of the Muslim qualms about borrowing from Westerners, they sought to benefit
from their newly acquired skills in order to improve their lot as a
minority while pushing the entire society forward. Such improvement,
they believed, was ultimately attainable by resurrecting indigenous
Arab cultural treasures and reviving the Arab genius in language,
literature, art, and science. Meanwhile, they immersed themselves in
learning new methods and adapting foreign ideas. Printing and scientific societies were two such innovations. Periodicals were another.

Christian Lebanese, along with coreligionists from northern Syria,
not only pioneered journalism in the Arab countries but dominated it
for the rest of the century, even when the center of Arab journalism
shifted from Beirut to Cairo in the late 1870s. It was a Syrian Christian,
Rizqallah Hasun (1823-1880), who started the first private Arabic
newspaper. The son of an Armenian Catholic merchant, Hasun grew
up in Aleppo and was educated in a mission. He joined the family
business, which brought him to Paris and London. At age 17, restless
and enterprising, he settled in Istanbul, where he continued in commerce, joining other Aleppines who formed a sizable immigrant community there. Fifteen years later, during the Crimean War, Hasun
launched his journalistic project, motivated both by business concerns
and intellectual ardor. The war provided two essential ingredients: the
public's hunger for news, and the telegraph, which the British brought
with them to the Ottoman front for the first time. Sometime in 1855
Hasun began publishing a news weekly, *Mir'at al-Ahwal*, which featured
battlefield reports as well as accounts of other developments mainly in
the Syrian cities. This was the second private paper to appear in the
Ottoman capital—it was preceded by a Turkish journal published by

an Englishman[3] — but the very first in the Arabic language. *Mir'at al-Ahwal* seems to have lasted for about a year (no copies are known to be extant), after which Hasun joined government service. Later, his Russophil views forced him to escape abroad.[4]

Hasun's Christian compatriots followed his example, turning journalism into an exciting field. One of them, Ahmad Faris al-Shidyaq, duplicated Hasun's move to the Ottoman capital and began publishing there. A Maronite convert to Protestantism and then to Islam, Shidyaq (1801–1887) had an unusually kaleidoscopic career that took him from Beirut via Cairo and Malta to Oxford and Paris. In each place he translated, adapted, and produced original Arabic literary works with great skill, acquiring a reputation as a gifted writer and a master of the Arabic language. He also engaged briefly in journalism in Cairo as editor of *al-Waqa'i' al-Misriyya* during 1833–1834. Shidyaq landed in Istanbul as the protégé of an old friend, Minister of Education Sami Pasha, apparently in 1859. Two years later, on 31 May 1861, he launched a weekly newspaper, *al-Jawa'ib*, which became one of the most influential Arabic papers of the century.[5]

For the Ottoman government, the publication of an Arabic paper in the capital by someone of Shidyaq's acumen was a development not devoid of advantageous potential. Shidyaq was allowed to run his paper on his own, under the eye of the authorities, but within a few months, as he ran into financial difficulties, the government willingly rescued his project and took it under its protective wing. Shidyaq was invited to print his paper at the state press and accept a royal subsidy, which he did for the next nine years, in return for which he defended the imperial point of view in his columns. "It has been decreed," the paper informed its readers, "that the expenses of *al-Jawa'ib* from now on be covered by the Ministry of Finance and that it be printed at the imperial press. Under these circumstances, we must pledge loyalty to our master, the great Sultan."[6] Shidyaq's prestige and editorial skill made *al-Jawa'ib* a more effective tool than the largely discredited official bulletins published in the provinces. He served the government by producing reports and analyses that were sympathetic to, or at least did not contradict, official policy, along with official government notices. The paper also contained detailed news about the ruling elite and about events in the capital, in the provinces, and abroad, for which Shidyaq had enviable access to sources. In addition, it carried original articles by the editor; texts of speeches by world leaders, international treaties, and diplomatic documents; discussions of social, cultural, and literary issues; and responses to critics from other papers. Despite its reputation as a semiofficial organ, *al-Jawa'ib* did maintain a degree of independence, for which it was even punished occasionally. In 1879 it was suspended for six months because of the editor's refusal to publish an article critical of the Egyptian khedive, who was another of Shidyaq's benefactors, and for printing a sympathetic piece instead.[7]

Shidyaq was at once an authority on Arabic literature and grammar and well-versed in European culture. This expertise, combined with government backing, made *al-Jawa'ib* what appears to have been the most popular Arabic paper of its time. According to contemporary accounts, it was read by Muslim rulers and intellectuals from Morocco to India and from Aleppo to Zanzibar ("I have found it in the Nejd merchants' houses at Bombay," reported a traveler in central Arabia in the 1870s[8]). It was also monitored by foreign observers who, quite logically, considered it to be a mouthpiece of the Ottoman government. Manifestly a one-man operation, *al-Jawa'ib* was in effect much more: a major institution in the cultural and political life of its time until its closing in 1883.[9]

The Private Press in Lebanon

Shidyaq, a conspicuous product of the cultural ferment in Lebanon of the nineteenth century, had transplanted himself outside the country. Others chose to express their creativity without leaving Lebanon. Among them were men of letters such as Nasif al-Yaziji and his son Ibrahim, Butrus al-Bustani and his son Salim, Tannus al-Shidyaq (Ahmad Faris's brother), Mikha'il Mishaqa, Nakhla Mudawwar, and Mikha'il Shihada, to mention only a few prominent names, all of them pupils of the missionaries in one way or another. Sensing an enormous cultural and educational challenge, they were eager to meet it by using the tools with which the missionaries had equipped them, displaying an endless appetite for knowledge and a remarkable capacity to absorb it.

Absorbing knowledge, however, was only the first step. No less vital was disseminating it. "There is no doubt that newspapers (*al-jurnalat*) are among the most important vehicles in educating the public," Butrus al-Bustani, secretary of the Syrian Scientific Society, stated in his famous *khutba* (public address) of 1859, discussing the cultural state of the Arabs.[10] Bustani was congratulating his colleague, Khalil al-Khuri, who a year earlier had established the news weekly *Hadiqat al-Akhbar* in Beirut. Khuri (1836–1907), a Greek Orthodox employed in a commercial firm, wrote poems that attested to a certain literary talent and had sound knowledge of both Turkish and French. These attributes made him an appropriate candidate to head the first journalistic undertaking in Lebanon. Wealthy Christian businessmen assisted by purchasing a defunct printing press that belonged to the Greek Orthodox metropolitan and securing a government permit to publish a newspaper. At first, Khuri favored a poetic name for it—*al-Fajr al-Munir* ("The Shining Dawn")—a seemingly innocuous name yet not entirely devoid of political connotations. In the end, however, he chose instead the safer *Hadiqat al-Akhbar* ("Garden of News"), a neutral title with a distinctly traditional flavor. Such caution was a valuable asset; it

enabled Khuri to publish his paper for the next 50 years, notwithstanding the many changes in the empire's government.[11]

With the appearance of the first issue of *Hadiqat al-Akhbar* on 1
January 1858, the educated elite in Lebanon had a periodical of their
own that in format, makeup, and regularity of publication resembled
the modern newspapers they received from Europe. Respectable-
looking, the paper was published exclusively in Arabic on four large
pages, with an aesthetic masthead and section headlines. It was available through agents listed on the front page, and the stated price for
subscribers was 120 qurush in Beirut and Mount Lebanon and 144
qurush elsewhere. Merchants and businesses were invited to advertise
at a cost of 5 qurush a line.

From the first issue, the paper carried detailed reports on developments in Beirut, the Syrian cities, Istanbul, and Egypt, as well as
Europe and America. This coverage was drawn from official Egyptian
and Ottoman organs, the international press, and reports sent by the
paper's agents and other acquaintances of the editor in the provinces.
Issue no. 20 of 10 May 1858, to pick a random example, offered reports
on the Paris conference concerning the future of Wallachia and Mol-
davia; a British parliamentary move to rephrase the members' inaugu-
ral oath; and rumors of an impending Spanish-American war, all of
which appeared on the paper's first two pages. The third and fourth
pages were devoted mostly to news within the empire, including accounts of the sultan's bestowal of ranks and titles upon several Egyptian
princes; a banquet held in Beirut by the head of the Ottoman Bank;
and the arrival of several European diplomats in Damascus. One item
contained segments from the proceedings of the dramatic trial of an
Italian named Orsini who had attempted to assassinate the French
emperor. Local and provincial news was two to three weeks old, while
foreign news, which was undated, referred to events that had taken
place up to two months previously.

Prudence required editorial distancing from religious issues, an
especially sensitive area in Lebanon of the late 1850s, as well as caution
in handling political issues, in particular foreign matters. Khuri wisely
followed the lead of the official bulletins coming from Istanbul, confin-
ing himself strictly to the factual reporting of events so as not to irritate
the authorities. He had more freedom in other areas: economic and
commercial affairs, both domestic and international, for which there
was much demand in the business-oriented milieu of Lebanon; and
perhaps more important, cultural, scientific and literary matters, for
which the local elite had a large appetite. Businessmen were offered
reports on the state of European markets, currency fluctuations, foreign
tenders and lotteries, and the arrival of ships at the port of Beirut. The
intellectuals were attracted by accounts of new books and theatrical
presentations, another novelty. An idealist, the 22-year-old Khuri saw

himself as a missionary bringing modern civilization to his community. He sought to enlighten his readers by including columns, however rudimentary, on modern science and technology, such as on electricity, barometric pressure, printing, and photography, and on other fields of general knowledge, for example, on the world's navies or the idea of *habeas corpus*.[12] He also wrote editorials — a new genre — on such issues as the need to expand education, including education for women; the need to modernize the Arabic language; and, most important, the need to learn "from the peoples and communities which have attained command of arts and sciences," to wit, "learning the sciences of Europe."[13] A literary supplement was also added from time to time, in which Khuri serialized classical Arabic works, translated foreign literature, and published original stories and poems by himself and other writers. *Hadiqat al-Akhbar* was Khuri's personal voice, but beyond that it became a lively forum for public discussion, and sometimes controversy, on issues that engaged the Lebanese intelligentsia of the time. As such it was a vivid mirror of the country's cultural life.

The mission that Khuri took upon himself was indeed enormous. As he and his colleagues saw it, informing and edifying society were only a means toward the larger end of rescuing society from its appalling, if temporary, backwardness. There was so much to do: inculcate modern science, redefine social values, revive the national cultural heritage, adjust the language to new needs. Khuri and his colleagues were convinced that newspapers and periodicals were an effective means of attaining these formidable goals. *Hadiqat al-Akhbar* styled itself a "civilian (*madani*), scientific, commercial, historical journal," an all-embracing formula that reflected its editor's ambitious vision. This intense focus on news and enlightenment as necessary agents for the improvement of society would characterize Lebanese journalists until the end of the century and beyond.

Hadiqat al-Akhbar seems to have been a success story. Three months after it appeared, it boasted some 400 subscriptions (with additional copies sold on the street), no small achievement considering the novelty of the institution.[14] Another mark of its success was the decision in 1860 by Fu'ad Pasha, the Ottoman foreign minister, to "adopt" the paper and provide it with a monthly subvention of 20 Ottoman pounds, thereby turning it into a semi-official organ.[15] The paper continued as a government mouthpiece until 1865, when its official role was assumed by the state bulletin *Suriya*, which appeared that year in Damascus. Later, in 1868, it was again turned into an official organ by Franco Pasha, the vali of Mount Lebanon, but resumed its independent status after a while. These changes in status, and the fact that Khuri himself was employed as state censor in Beirut in the 1870s and 1880s, would later prompt a debate among Arab historians of the press about whether *Hadiqat al-Akhbar* should be classified as an official publication.[16] *Hadiqat al-Akhbar*, along with *al-Jawa'ib*, which was published in Istanbul, dominated Syrian-Lebanese journalism with no significant competition throughout the 1860s.

There were several other attempts at publishing papers in Lebanon by missionaries and by private individuals during that decade. Protestant proselytizers, who were leaders in the cultural sphere, were particularly active in this field, providing an example to their local followers while angering the Catholics. As early as 1851, that is four years before Hasun launched his *Mir'at al-Ahwal*, Eli Smith, head of the American mission in Beirut, started a publication for his mission entitled *Majmu' Fawa'id* ("Collected Useful Lessons"), an annual compilation of essays on religious, historical, and cultural matters. It turned out to be a disorganized effort with little impact that died out after four issues, and merits mention only because it is sometimes considered "the very first and earliest of all Arabic-language periodicals."[17] The Protestants renewed their initiative with more gusto in the early 1860s, launching several new journals consecutively, each under a different name. By 1871 this energetic Protestant effort took on a more organized form with the publication of *al-Nashra al-Usbu'iyya* ("Weekly Bulletin").[18] Concerned, the local Catholics and their religious allies, the Jesuit Fathers, responded with their own weekly paper, *al-Bashir* ("The Herald"), which was begun in September 1870.[19] Both *al-Nashra al-Usbu'iyya* and *al-Bashir*, backed by their respective churches, proved impressively enduring, appearing in an orderly fashion throughout the rest of the century and on into the next. They carried on bitter debates with each other, often in harsh language, sometimes drawing other journals into the conflict. This kind of heated encounter, endemic to the Lebanese scene, had constructive results in generating a seminal educational and cultural contest of ideas in the nineteenth century. In the twentieth, however, the encounter would become less beneficial, spawning painful intercommunal political friction.

One other publication during the 1860s, put out by an individual, deserves consideration. Between September 1860 and April 1861, in the wake of the bloody factional clashes in Syria and Lebanon, Butrus al-Bustani, a prominent Lebanese intellectual, addressed a passionate call to his countrymen for restraint and unity, choosing as his medium a series of bulletins (*nasharat*, as he named them), which he issued irregularly under the title *Nafir Suriya* ("Syrian Clarion"). Apparently 11 issues of this broadsheet, one or two pages in length, appeared altogether, containing variations on the themes of patriotism, religious freedom, and communal coexistence written by Bustani.[20] While there was little journalistic merit in this series of fervent appeals, there was a certain novelty in the fact that an individual with no official standing would publish his views on social and political issues. The novelty turned out to be a portent for the future, for it was Bustani who published the next significant periodical a decade later.

With the painful events of 1860 over, and political and administrative stability attained, Lebanon again became the scene of feverish cultural activity. The Syrian Protestant College, later to become the American University of Beirut, opened in that city in 1866. The Syrian Scientific Society, all but moribund for several years, vigorously resumed activity in 1868, attracting a membership three times larger, and considerably younger, than formerly. In another celebrated speech to the society that year, Bustani addressed the need for more schools, more printing presses, and more newspapers. In an age of great spiritual advancement, he stated, "We must have . . . more books fit for educating and entertaining those who can read and for kindling the desire for education among the illiterate," as well as more "reading rooms for books, commercial magazines (*kazitat*), and professional journals (*jurnalat*)."[21] Soon thereafter a spate of journals sprang up in Lebanon, no less than seven in 1870 alone. Bustani, together with his son Salim, again led the way. In January of that year they began to publish the biweekly *al-Jinan* ("Gardens"), and six months later the weekly (later semiweekly) *al-Janna* ("Garden," or "Paradise"), which became two mainstays of the enlightenment effort of the time.

Butrus al-Bustani (1819–1883), a Maronite won over to the Protestant church, was an impressive product, and later leader, of the Lebanese cultural awakening. He founded the National School (*al-madrasa al-wataniyya*, 1863), published the first modern Arabic dictionary (*Muhit al-muhit*, 1870–1871), and launched the first modern multivolume Arab encyclopedia (*Da'irat al-ma'arif*, 1876–1900), editing its first six volumes before he died. In *al-Jinan*, an educational, historical, and literary journal, Butrus and his son made a systematic effort to acquaint their fellow Arabs with the fruits of Western achievement while reviving their own rich legacy. "Thanks to our magnanimous rulers," he stated in an opening note, the country already had several Arabic-language papers that provided news and information. But it was still in need of a means "to spread universal knowledge — scientific, cultural, historical, industrial, commercial . . . and the like — as in the foreign countries where their benefits have become evident."[22] Summaries of current events in Europe, chapters from its history, and translations from the European press and its literature were presented along with Arab literary and historical pieces. To pick an example at random, the issue of 15 December 1870 included a lengthy article on the idea of politics, past and present; an analysis of aspects of the Franco-Prussian war of that year; a report on Russia and the Black Sea adapted from an Istanbul paper; a segment of a serialized biography of Napoleon III; an article on moral values; an essay on translation; a segment of a serialized Arabic novel; and a set of anecdotes. The biweekly was an ambitious enterprise that won high esteem on the part of the educated community throughout the Arab lands during the 16 years of its existence. The other project, *al-Janna*, was a weekly and later a semiweekly, and hence primarily a news medium, its lifespan identical to that of its biweekly counterpart. In 1871 the third in this "botanic" series appeared under the name *al-Junayna* ("Little Garden"), edited by Salim al-Bustani and his father's cousin Sulayman. *Al-Junayna* came to be regarded as the first Arab daily, although it was published only four times a week.[23] Like most of the early Arabic papers, it did not last long, expiring after four years.

Other intellectuals, similarly stimulated by the new horizons they had discovered and the old ones they rediscovered, and anxious to spread the light, also utilized the potent new device of printing. In January 1870, at the same time that *al-Jinan* appeared in Beirut, another literary journal, *al-Zahra* ("Flower," or "Venus"), was started there by the Catholic writer and poet Yusuf al-Shalafun, who later published several other papers as well. In May that same year, the literary monthly *al-Nahla* ("The Bee") appeared, the first in a long series of periodicals published by an eccentric Catholic priest, Luis Sabunji. Both *al-Zahra* and *al-Nahla* turned out to be short-lived, but once they died out, their owners joined forces in a typical example of Christian journalistic collaboration and produced another paper in Beirut under the optimistic name *al-Najah* ("Success"), a semiweekly devoted to politics and science. Their cooperative effort, however, proved as short-lived as their previous papers.[24] The next journal to appear was far more important, the scientific and literary monthly *al-Muqtataf* ("Selections"). Begun in May 1876 by Ya'qub Sarruf and Faris Nimr, it became one of the leading Arabic-language publications, a prominence it would retain for the next 75 years. Yet another notable venture was the semiweekly (later daily) *Lisan al-Hal* ("Voice of the Present"), published by Butrus al-Bustani's nephew Khalil Sarkis in October 1877, which would play a distinguished role as a source of news and commentary for a full century. By the end of the decade, Beirut had become the birthplace of no less than 25 newspapers and journals,[25] divergent in frequency and focus but having similar objectives.

Conspicuously, all of these papers were established by Christians, who led the cultural awakening. Muslims were not involved in the early phase of this endeavor; most of them, in fact, regarded it with suspicion. This was an anomalous situation that could not persist for long, for the zeal of the Christians in spreading their innovative message was bound to provoke a Muslim reaction. In 1873 a group of educated Muslims convened in Beirut to establish the Society of Arts (*jam'iyyat al-funun*), with the twofold objective of disseminating knowledge and, more traditionally, helping the poor. In April 1875, apparently concerned about the growing assertiveness of some of the Christian journalists, the society began to publish a weekly organ, *Thamarat al-Funun* ("Fruits of Knowledge"), edited by one of its members, 'Abd al-Qadir al-Qabbani. The paper, which acquired a mostly Muslim readership, was manifestly pro-Ottoman and strongly traditional in cultural orientation and literary taste. *Thamarat al-Funun* lasted until 1908, in large part due to the backing of wealthy Muslims, during which time it was the leading Muslim publication. It was a less attractive product than many of its Christian counterparts, reflecting an odd dissonance between the novelty of the medium and the conservatism of its message.[26]

Thamarat al-Funun was a group project that was run as a share company, and in that, too, it differed from Christian papers. Christian journalists often collaborated with each other and contributed to each other's papers, but usually disbanded their partnerships after a while and moved on to the next project. Theirs was typically an enterprise of independent individuals, sometimes idealistic, often gifted, always ambitious. Their individualism and sense of competition was the product of their experience as a minority whose skills in survival generally and in commerce in particular were channeled into an aggressive missionary drive. The press, like other commercial areas, involved competing for a limited market and entailed rivalry and even conflict; more than other commercial enterprises, it engaged in ideological and religious issues, which often rendered the contest highly passionate. Considerable space and energy were devoted to internecine squabbles — such as between the Maronite-turned-Protestant Bustani and the Greek Catholic Sabunji;[27] between Bustani, along with Ibrahim al-Yaziji, and the Islamized Shidyaq;[28] or between Shidyaq and the Greek Catholic Hasun[29] — over political, cultural, linguistic, and invariably personal issues. Muslim papers such as *Thamarat al-Funun* were also involved in controversies with Christian papers,[30] but these were generally less acrimonious than the intra-Christian encounters.

For all its ambition, and the impressive progress that it generated, the Lebanese press of the 1860s and 1870s was still in its infancy and faced difficulties of all kinds. Idealistic motivation to educate the community, however fervid, was in itself insufficient. Setting up a paper and running it required financial resources, especially as the market was not yet prepared to absorb this novelty. Publishers who were not wealthy could not afford to sustain a paper at a loss for long, and they were usually forced to abandon these projects. The technological conditions necessary for running a newspaper — gathering news, printing it, and distributing the final product — were primitive and developed slowly. The flow of information was sluggish: Unlike in Egypt, where the telegraph had been inaugurated in 1866, Lebanese journalists remained without access to this innovative source of information until the end of the century and had to rely on reports sent by agents and informants through the mail and on foreign (including Egyptian) journals for news. An issue of *Hadiqat al-Akhbar* from June 1861, for example, featured a "telegraphic messages" section on events in Europe which quoted cabled reports that were 10 weeks old or older.[31] Sixteen years later, in 1877, the opening issue of *Lisan al-Hal*, whose owner made special efforts to gather and print news faster than his competitors, still drew on Egyptian and European papers and quoted telegrams that were up to four weeks old.[32] Printing was likewise slow, with machines that produced one to three newspaper copies per minute.[33] All these difficulties discouraged the publication of daily newspapers (with the partial exception of al-Junayna)[34] and limited the number of other news journals to a handful. Newspapers of the period clearly reflected these hardships in their poor physical quality, sloppy layout, and mostly irregular publishing schedule.[35] Technically, it was much easier to publish scientific or literary periodicals, where production could be handled by a single individual who would gather or write the material, print it, and even distribute it all by himself.

There was another, rather obvious reason why Lebanese journalists should choose to invest their efforts in non-news journals and, more generally, nonpolitical writing. The Ottoman government viewed any active interest in politics by its subjects with unmistakable distaste. In previous centuries such activity would have been inconceivable. But even in the second half of the nineteenth century, when various reforms were being introduced, the printing of news and views on public affairs by anyone other than the authorities was still suspicious. We have already seen that the government under Sultan 'Abd al-Majid decreed licensing and censorship of all publications. Actually, Ottoman policy under both 'Abd al-Majid (1839–1861) and his successor, 'Abd al-'Aziz (1861–1876), is known to have been relatively liberal in these matters compared with what was to follow. During their reigns, so long as journalists respected the rules, the government showed reasonable tolerance. Nevertheless, caution was in order; it was safer to praise the achievements of scientists than of political rebels. No one was more aware of, and sensitive to, this need than the Christians of Lebanon, with their millennium-old experience as a minority in an Islamic land.

Economic, technological, and political factors, then, constricted the development of the Lebanese press during its infancy. The typical product of these circumstances was the majalla, a weekly or monthly scientific and literary magazine with an emphasis on expounding rather than on reporting, on long-term enlightenment rather than day-to-day information. Political matters were also discussed, but to a limited extent and within the framework of the kingdom's rules. If these journals waged a battle, it was against ignorance and backwardness. "All we seek," wrote the editor of al-Zahra in an opening article in 1870, is "to attract our compatriots, above all the common people, to the pleasure of habitual reading, to the joy of acquiring scientific and cultural books."[36] Political struggle was rarely a part of the endeavor at this stage; it would become so at a later time and in another place. This pristine journalistic quest, however limited in focus, was a promising beginning in its sincerity of purpose.

The government's attitude changed markedly when 'Abd al-Hamid the Second acceded to the sultanate (1876–1909). The new sultan resorted to harsh domestic measures following the Ottoman de-feat in the war against Russia (1877–1878), suspending the constitution (which he himself had earlier promulgated), dissolving the parliament, and enforcing stringent press censorship, which became even more rigid in time. No new papers were permitted to appear for five years after the war, with the exception of the Maronite *al-Misbah* ("The Light," 1880) and the Greek Orthodox *al-Hadiyya* ("The Gift," 1883) which undertook to limit themselves to domestic communal affairs only. Later, publication permits were granted sparingly, entailing ex-tensive bureaucratic difficulties, and the few periodicals that appeared were subject to harassment of all kinds. This harsh atmosphere, replete with punishments for deviations from the rules, was a major factor in the strangulation of the nascent Lebanese press and in prompting its practitioners to look elsewhere for a more hospitable environment.

From the early 1860s onward, Syrians and Lebanese, mostly Chris-tian, began to emigrate in large numbers as a result of several factors: intercommunal strife, which reached a bloody peak in the Damascus massacre of 1860; economic pressures largely due to the gap between rapid educational advancement and slow economic development; and the pull exerted by Egypt under Isma'il's animated leadership for the Syrian intellectuals' skills, alluring them with options that their country could not offer. Another factor that encouraged the exodus from Leba-non was the limitation on freedom of expression imposed by the new sultan in the late 1870s. Between 1860 and 1915, fully a quarter of Lebanon's population—the great majority of them Christians—emi-grated, primarily to Egypt and the Americas. Egypt now presented itself as a more suitable venue for writers and journalists, and would become still freer a decade later. The Christian Syrians and Lebanese who came to Egypt, mostly young unmarried men, joined the state administration, worked as physicians, pharmacists, and teachers, and opened businesses in Cairo and Alexandria.[37] Among the educated immigrants who moved there were those who brought journalistic expe-rience, zeal, and sometimes their periodicals, thereby shifting the base of the incipient Arab press from Lebanon to Egypt.

Egypt: The Focus Moves West

Isma'il's Egypt was a dynamic milieu. Throughout most of his reign, until around the mid-1870s, it was also marked by a striking purpose-fulness. Resolved to make Egypt "a part of Europe," the spirited khe-dive invested his vision and talent in the reformation of every aspect of the country, from the economy to education and from the legal system to the urban architecture of the capital. The call of the day was modern-ization, the model for emulation Europe, primarily France. Egypt's integration into world trade, begun under Muhammad 'Ali, was inten-sified, and the country reaped the fruits of this effort when it became a

major cotton supplier to Europe as a result of the halt in American
exports during the American Civil War. The opening of the Suez
Canal in 1869 a decade after digging had begun further enhanced the
country's international importance. Other projects, more domestic in
nature, were less spectacular but also had decisive effects. Isma'il, con-
scious that education was essential in order for the country to reach the
desired European level, invested vast resources in expanding both the
traditional and modern sectors of the school system.[38] He also sought
to modernize the governmental bureaucracy by forming *majlis shura
al-nuwwab* in 1866, an elected council of provincial notables with deliberative and advisory authority which was meant to function as a tentative counterpart to European parliaments. Isma'il expanded and beau-
tified Cairo, built an extended railway system that connected the capital
with the provinces, installed a telegraph network linking Egypt's towns,
and introduced modern state postal services. By the end of his reign,
the country, though still far from realizing the objectives that the restless khedive envisaged for it, was clearly making great strides toward
this goal.

Quite likely, Egypt in the second half of the nineteenth century
would have attracted Western interest even without Isma'il's deliberate
efforts. It was perhaps inevitable that Europe, at the height of its impe-
rialistic age, would seek deeper involvement in that strategic territory.
Undoubtedly, however, the khedive's policy accelerated the process.
The economic momentum generated by his development projects and
the relatively liberal atmosphere that he fostered allured foreigners to
settle in Egypt, especially Greeks, Italians, and Frenchmen, who led a
vibrant communal life there. The foreign population increased seven-
or eight-fold under his rule, reaching some 70,000 by the end of his
tenure.[39] This momentum also drew foreign capital investment and,
more significantly, loans to the Egyptian government. The foreigners
enjoyed the legal and political protection of European states, a status
that gradually became a pressing constraint on the government. Eventually European powers, exploiting Egypt's financial indebtedness, invaded it after removing Isma'il from office.

The process of exposure to the West had other facets as well. The
expansion of the foreign presence in Egypt brought with it an increase
in missionary activity and the educational endeavors that went along
with it. As in Lebanon, missionaries played a role in educating Egyptian society that was far more significant than their limited presence
might have suggested. Missionary schools, along with those established
by the foreign communities, offered quality instruction and training in
practical skills, primarily foreign languages, and attracted a sizable
share of the country's student body. A local class educated in Western
mores was slowly emerging, the product of modern institutions and
exposure to ideas transmitted to the country through a variety of channels: the large community of foreign settlers; the educated Syrian

Christian immigrants; translations of Western books and travel journals; periodicals that arrived from Europe or that were published by the foreign communities in Egypt; and, eventually, the newspapers that they themselves established. This last development was facilitated by the introduction and expansion of railways and telegraph, the establishment of international news agency offices, and the accelerated development of printing, with many private presses set up to serve growing literary activity.

Perhaps more than any ruler in the Middle East of the nineteenth century, and surely more than any ruler before him, Isma'il appreciated the power of the press. He understood how to manipulate it and make it work for him. Journals in Europe as well as in the empire, foreign-language papers in Egypt, and the Reuter and Havas news agencies all enjoyed generous Egyptian government subsidies, as Egyptian archives reveal. Foreign journalists visiting Egypt received royal treatment at the state's expense.[40] Isma'il revived the official journal that had become paralyzed under his predecessors and initiated several other official organs. Upon his instruction, *al-Waqa'i' al-Misriyya* was transformed from an interior circular for state officials only to a publication that engaged in public debate with the foreign-language papers and was sold on the streets of Cairo and Alexandria.[41] Yet this ardent believer in the power of the printed word soon became convinced that a more subtle and incisive press strategy was needed based on the manipulation of newspapers that would have an independent image but would be unreservedly loyal to him.

Such was the semiweekly *Wadi al-Nil* ("Nile Valley"), started in Cairo in July 1867, a small-format (16 × 22 cm) publication that looked more like a booklet than a newspaper. Its subtitle, printed below a fancy masthead embellished with a drawing of pyramids, palm trees, and camels, defined it as a "popular paper" (*sahifa ahliyya*). Claiming "popularity," it would often be depicted, somewhat fancifully, as the first private Egyptian paper. In fact, it was comfortably under the government's protection, assured of a regular flow of information and an equally reliable subvention. The editor, 'Abdallah Abu al-Su'ud, was a veteran translator in the state service, a writer of school textbooks, a poet, a pupil of Shaykh Tahtawi, and one of Isma'il's protégés. Much of the paper's reportage and commentary focused on defending Isma'il's policies against his critics, so that *Wadi al-Nil* read rather like *al-Waqa'i' al-Misriyya*. There were also up-to-date reports on foreign affairs and commercial developments— *Wadi al-Nil* was the first Arab paper to use Reuter's telegrams — as well as a literary section. As would often happen in later years in Egypt and elsewhere, Abu al-Su'ud's son, Muhammad Unsi, joined the venture and became a journalist in his own right. The paper ceased publication in 1874, to be replaced by *Rawdat al-Akhbar* ("Meadow of News"), another professedly "popular" publication with Unsi in the role of editor and his father in charge of the political and literary sections. *Rawdat al-Akhbar* differed from *Wadi al-Nil* in name only; sources, political point of view, and editorial style were all but identical. When Abu al-Su'ud died in 1878, the project died with him.[42]

Isma'il's relatively liberal attitude, however, encouraged the emergence of a truly private press as well. Educated Egyptians, as impressed as the khedive with the importance of periodically printed texts, began initiating their own publishing projects. The first attempt of this kind was made in 1869 by two men: Ibrahim al-Muwaylihi, a printer and a close acquaintance of Isma'il, who would later become his private secretary, and 'Uthman Jalal, a translator and writer. The two were granted a permit to put out a political weekly called *Nuzhat al-Afkar* ("Promenade of Thoughts"), but it must have been too dangerously assertive, because Isma'il closed it down after only two issues.[43] Four years later, in 1873, two Syrian Greek Orthodox emigrants, the brothers Salim and 'Abduh al-Hamawi, began a political and literary weekly in Alexandria entitled *al-Kawkab al-Sharqi* ("Oriental Star"). It was the first Arabic paper in the city, where several foreign-language journals had previously appeared, but it met the same fate as *Nuzhat al-Afkar*. "Circumstances do not call for the publication of Arabic journals at this time," Isma'il explained to the brothers, and ordered the paper closed.[44] At that stage, the khedive was still vacillating between his desire to encourage cultural activity — he offered the Hamawi brothers reimbursement for their losses — and the necessity to contend with the political implications of such activity. But before long he agreed to permit additional ventures of this kind. The next journalistic undertaking, likewise by Syrian immigrants in Alexandria, would prove far more significant and durable.

The Greek Catholic brothers Salim (1849–1892) and Bishara (1853–1902) Taqla moved from Beirut to Alexandria in the early 1870s, bringing with them new ideas and high aspirations. Well educated, and possessing a keen business sense, they would start a newspaper that would set new standards in Arab journalism. Like many of their countrymen, they valued the transmission of Western knowledge to their own society. But perhaps more important, they were particularly interested in the process of obtaining and marketing the latest and most accurate news, which, they felt, was in demand in Egypt. In 1875, still in their twenties, the Taqlas applied for and were granted a license to open a press in Alexandria and publish a weekly paper. They decided to call it *al-Ahram*, "The Pyramids," an innocuous name, possibly appealing subtly to the popular sense of regard for anything ancient, although not to any political position.[45] They conscientiously pledged to limit themselves to printing "telegrams, [and] commercial, scientific, agricultural, and local" news, as well as cultural and literary items, namely, only "the things whose printing is permissible." The khedive, disposed to encouraging the enterprising Syrians but still cautious, granted the permit, but not without reiterating these restrictions.[46]

Al-Ahram began and remained above all a conveyor of news. From the first issue (5 August 1876) on, it offered its readers a wealth of reliable, up-to-date information on local and foreign political and economic issues, accompanied by a fair measure of analysis. The Taqlas' financial situation, which apparently was solid from the start, allowed them to subscribe directly to Reuter's and Havas news agencies, as well as to retain agents of their own who acted both as informants and sales representatives throughout Egypt and in the main cities of the region from Baghdad to Istanbul.[47] The necessary degree of caution and political discretion enabled them to successfully navigate the paper through the troubled waters of domestic and international politics, a strategy that required praising the khedive occasionally as well as acquiring the patronage of a foreign power, namely France, a clever choice. With this investment, the brothers were able to produce a high-level publication that showed continuous improvement in reporting techniques, editorial standards, and linguistic style. The Taqlas, however, were not indifferent to the powerful sociopolitical forces at play in Egypt in the late 1870s. They expressed their views, favoring greater political freedom and opposing foreign intervention, in two other papers that they published, *Sada al-Ahram* ("Echo of the Pyramids," 1876–1879) and *al-Waqt* ("Time," 1879–1880). Both papers were issued warnings for expressing "subversive" views, suspended, and eventually shut down.[48] *Al-Ahram*, on the other hand, adopting a more neutral tone, was not restricted by the authorities.[49] In January 1881 it became a daily, maintaining the same guiding principles and continuing to improve its professional standards. It operated from Alexandria until November 1899, and thereafter from Cairo.

In many ways, *al-Ahram* was a unique species in the garden of Egyptian journalism. From the first, it stood apart by putting reportage before political ideology. For most other papers in the late 1870s, political confrontation was the key word and the *raison d'être*. Egypt's recent exposure to international politics, combined with the emergence of a modern Egyptian elite with keen political awareness reinforced by educated Syrian arrivals, engendered a new phenomenon: a demand on the part of the governed, articulated by an intellectual leadership, to be involved in matters of government, to be informed, and to be consulted on questions relating to their future. It was becoming apparent, during the second half of the 1870s, that Egypt was in grave economic and political trouble, and there were growing doubts about Isma'il's ability to rescue it. To those with modern education, the new ideas of political rights, a constitution, and popular representation seemed not only attractive but vital to the country's situation. Inspired by such views, the *majlis*, the quasi-modern advisory body set up by the khedive in 1866, had become by the end of the 1870s a forum for criticizing the government for its failures. Echoing this criticism, periodicals conveyed popular discontent and became a major vehicle for the expression of public sentiment. The journalists believed that at that stage Egypt could not afford the evolutionary pace of educational development that would gradually invigorate the community and eventually lead it to repel its adversaries, sensing that circumstances demanded a more immediate political response. This sense of urgency molded the nature of the early private press in Egypt with far-reaching effects.

Several of the leading papers of the period were inspired by Jamal al-Din al-Afghani, the Iranian-born, charismatic politico-religious agitator who resided in Egypt from 1871–1879. Afghani's international experience had exposed him to the power of the press, and he urged his eager adherents to raise a cry against the government's tyranny as well as its feebleness in the face of the threat of foreign onslaught. The situation, he argued, called for action of the most effective kind — making use of the traditionally mighty weapon of the word through a powerful new means, print. Responding, his followers initiated a lively movement of political writing, producing periodicals and books. Among them was the Greek Catholic Syrian Adib Ishaq, an impatient activist who arrived in Egypt in 1876 at the age of 20. Ishaq had an intensive if brief career: In his short life of 28 years (1856–1884), he published and edited half a dozen papers in Beirut, Cairo, Alexandria, and Paris — notably *Misr* ("Egypt," weekly, published in Cairo and Alexandria, 1877–1879), *al-Tijara* ("Commerce," daily, Alexandria, 1878–1879), *Misr al-Fatah* ("Young Egypt," weekly, Alexandria, 1879), and *Misr al-Qahira* ("Egypt the Victorious," monthly/weekly, Paris, 1879–1880), along with producing literary and theatrical works. Ishaq aimed to acquaint the Arabic-reading public with the ideas of the French revolution — political freedom, civil rights, free speech, and opposition to despotism — and to demonstrate the relevance of these ideas as a remedy to the ills of Arab society.[50] He collaborated in some of the papers with the Syrian Christian Salim Naqqash, who also published his own journals: the daily *al-Mahrusa* ("The [divinely] Protected," a popular epithet used mostly for Egypt) and the weekly *al-'Asr al-Jadid* ("Modern Era"), both in 1880. A third Syrian, Salim 'Anhuri, founded the semiweekly *Mir'at al-Sharq* ("Mirror of the Orient") in Cairo in 1879, edited it for a few weeks, and then passed it on to another fervent disciple of Afghani's, the Egyptian Muslim Ibrahim al-Laqqani.[51] Another paper that was launched during this period, the Coptic weekly *al-Watan* ("Homeland"), founded in 1877 by Mikha'il 'Abd al-Sayyid, aimed primarily to provide the Coptic minority with an outlet for its communal views and grievances rather than fight a national battle. But under its bold editor, *al-Watan* soon joined the protest movement, calling for greater popular representation in government and an end to tyranny, and enduring punishment for its outspokenness.[52]

More original and colorful, and subsequently more famous, was the Jewish Egyptian Ya'qub (James) Sanu' (1839–1912), another member of this highly charged political-ideological band. Commonly known by the title that he used for several of his many papers, *Abu Naddara* ("The Bespectacled One"), he published the first version of his satirical journal in early 1877, and it became popular overnight. Sanu' was friendly, at first, with Isma'il, but managed to upset the khedive with his biting criticism and was deported a year after his journal was launched. Settling in Paris, he continued to publish papers, which were smuggled back into Egypt, harshly attacking Isma'il and later his successor.[53] One of Sanu''s prominent colleagues who also merits mention was the Egyptian 'Abdallah Nadim (1845–1896), an eloquent orator and an aggressive critic of the government. Nadim, who at first wrote for several of his friends' papers, later established two journals of his own in Alexandria, the biweekly *al-Tankit wal-Tabkit* ("Mockery and Reproach") and the daily *al-Ta'if* ("The Rover").[54] Nadim's papers in fact belonged to a second wave of nationalistic publications that made their appearance in 1881, the stormy year preceding the British invasion. Other papers in this group included Hamza Fathalla's *al-Burhan* ("The Proof"), founded in May 1881; Ibrahim Siraj al-Madani's *al-Hijaz*, begun in July of that year; and Hasan al-Shamsi's *al-Mufid* ("The Informer"), established in October 1881, and *al-Safir* ("The Traveler," or "Mediator"), begun in August 1882.[55]

Young, restless, most of them Christians, these writers waged a passionate battle for reform. Their publications were conceived as weapons, the best the country could produce at the time. Many of the titles of their periodicals attested to this spirit: "Young Egypt," "Modern Era," even simply "Homeland," or "Egypt"—more than just names, they were battle cries. They lashed out at Isma'il, expressing the discontent of the small educated class with his autocracy and inadequate performance and helping create the atmosphere that, along with other factors, brought about his dethronement in June 1879. Warning against the growing European encroachment on their country, they avidly supported the rebel Ahmad 'Urabi, the Egyptian officer who defied Isma'il's successor, Tawfiq, and later led the vain military effort to prevent the British occupation of Egypt. The government met this outspoken challenge with bribery, warnings, and punishment. Newspapers were suspended and closed down,[56] and journalists were forced out of the country. When this proved insufficient, the new government of landed notables, formed in September 1881, issued a prohibitive press law in November of that year imposing licensing and *a priori* censorship and prescribing heavy penalties for offenders.[57]

Egyptian political journalism was thus molded in its infancy by circumstances that evoked intense struggle. The atmosphere was tumultuous, characterized by an unprecedented variety of political options, with the press mostly on the protest end of the battlefield. Professionally still immature, newspapers aspired to higher standards. But format and style were of secondary importance: It was the political message that mattered. Nearly all of the papers that were born during that fateful period became casualties of the contemporary turmoil and perished early, having had only limited bearing on the forces that shaped Egypt's destiny between 1878 and 1882. They did, however, play a lively role as a forum for debate among social and intellectual leaders and as a means of involving the public more actively in events. Eventually, these publications of protest were overwhelmed by powerful forces, and the press arena became silent for several years. But the lesson of the potential contained in newspapers was not lost in Egypt, and news journals would be vigorously revived by other intellectuals toward the end of the 1880s.

Europe, the Convenient Refuge

Lebanon and Egypt were the only two centers of independent Arab journalistic endeavor in the region up until 1908, to which may be added the important *al-Jawa'ib* in Istanbul — the privately published newspaper with strong governmental backing. A third center, however, existed outside the region, in Europe. Some of the earliest journals were founded there in the 1850s and 1860s by Arab immigrants, all of them Christians, who arrived in mid-century seeking a better life. Another wave of Arab immigrants, escapees, and deportees reinforced these expatriate communities in the European cities toward the late 1870s when the political atmosphere in the region became repressive. Among them were a group of journalists who pursued their occupation upon settling abroad.

Faced with economic, cultural, and political difficulties in its own homeland, Arab journalism moved from Beirut to Cairo and Alexandria, and when Egypt became less friendly, to Paris and London as well as New York. Europe offered a convenient environment, with an atmosphere of free speech and a technologically more advanced infrastructure for the publication of periodicals. Moreover, the immigrant Arab communities there, though not large, constituted a potential pool of avid readers. Papers could also be shipped, or if necessary smuggled, to the journalists' lands of origin, where they could have an impact. The constricting realities in the Ottoman Empire and Egypt lent Arab immigrant papers a significance beyond that which expatriate publications normally have when conditions at home are more comfortable.

As early as 1858, the year the first important Arabic journal appeared in Beirut, an attractive-looking Arabic publication titled *Birjis Baris* ("The Paris Jupiter") appeared in the French capital. Its owner and editor was the Lebanese Rushayd al-Dahdah (1813–1889), whose lively career contained many elements typical of other Arab writers abroad. Dahdah, a member of a prominent Maronite family from northern Mount Lebanon, had been employed in the early 1840s as advisor to one of the region's princes and was also a writer of poetry.

The political upheaval of these years in the province prompted him to emigrate and he settled in Marseille in 1845. There, while successfully engaged in commerce, he satisfied his literary cravings by setting up a printing press and publishing several classical Arabic works, meanwhile becoming, in the words of a contemporary observer, *"Français de coeur et d'âme."*[58] When *Hadiqat al-Akhbar* first appeared in Beirut in January 1858, Dahdah, then living in Paris, was convinced that his intimate acquaintance with European culture and ready access to its technology equipped him to produce an even better publication and render a more useful service to his compatriots in Lebanon and abroad. The result, in June of that year, was *Birjis Baris*, a large-format, handsomely printed Arabic biweekly. It was admirably rich in content, with reports and commentary both on local issues geared to the immigrant Arab community, and international affairs, especially France's relations with the empire and the Arab countries. Literature and historical essays were also featured. Dahdah made great efforts to adapt the Arabic language to modern usage, devising many new terms and rejuvenating old ones (he is credited with first using the word *sahifa* for newspaper). *Birjis Baris* seems to have won popularity quickly and, as the list of its agents would indicate, was sold extensively in Syria, Egypt, and North Africa. In 1860 it became bilingual — Arabic and French. In that year, following the paper's relentless assault on the Ottoman authorities' poor handling of the Lebanese crisis, the government banned it from its territory, a fate shared by many Arab publications thereafter. Dahdah edited the paper until 1863, when he retired, assigning this duty to a colleague, Sulayman al-Hara'iri, who carried on for another three years before the paper closed down. Dahdah himself moved to Tunis but later returned to France where he occupied himself with trade, writing poetry, and possibly also with another brief journalistic venture until his death.[59]

Dahdah's biography typified many Arab men of letters who left their distressed homelands for Europe during the nineteenth century and devoted themselves to journalism either as a mission or as a business. Such was the case with the Syrian Rizqallah Hasun, founder of the first Arabic paper, who, like Dahdah, fell out of favor with his patrons at home, left, and found his way to London. There he published several short-lived papers in the late 1860s and 1870s, including one that replicated the name of his Crimean War journal, *Mir'at al-Ahwal*.[60] Such was also the case with the Armenian Catholic priest Luis Sabunji, who left Beirut in 1874 or 1875 due to a religio-communal controversy. Moving to England, he published a series of periodicals intermittently during the 1870s and 1880s, the best known being the Arabic-English *al-Nahla*, and was also engaged in other business, cultural, and political activities.[61] The career of yet another Christian, Jibra'il Dallal, followed a slightly different pattern. An Aleppine like Hasun, Dallal arrived in London in the mid-1870s, motivated less by

pressure in his homeland than by an urge for an adventure. After
briefly collaborating with Hasun on one of his papers, Dallal moved on
to Paris where he published his own journal, *al-Sada* ("The Echo"),
which proved short-lived.[62] Dallal's place in journalism was insignificant, but he merits attention as an example of a notable phenomenon
that recurred throughout the century. As individuals, most of these
emigrants played a role as ephemeral as Dallal's, as did their numerous
periodicals, which rarely attained popularity. Together, however, they
represented a vital option for escape on the part of ambitious men of
letters. The importance of this option increased with the increase of
pressure at home, ultimately forcing the press to shift its base temporarily from within the region abroad. This was the case with the "Young
Ottomans," the Ottoman opposition writers who emigrated in the 1860s
in order to write in Paris and London, as well as with the Egyptian
opposition press the following decade.

As we have seen, growing numbers of Lebanese writers who were
oppressed by the distrustful sultan in the late 1870s moved to Egypt,
but in articulating their forward-looking ideas clashed with the authorities there as well, as did their Egyptian colleagues. The Egyptian government, if more liberal than the sultan's, was tolerant only up to a
point. Aggressive newspapers were shut down and defiant journalists
were muzzled or expelled. Sanu' was deported in 1878, and Adib Ishaq
was forced to leave the following year. In an odd twist of fate, the
khedive who drove them out was deposed in 1879 and was himself
deported to Naples. His own views, which ceased to be accepted in his
country, could now be expounded only outside it, a curious if not
altogether unique situation. Isma'il's friend and secretary, Ibrahim al-
Muwaylihi, who joined him in Italy, served for a while as the ousted
ruler's voice through a paper he published there, *al-Khilafa* ("The Caliphate"). Muwaylihi then moved to France, where he continued his
journalistic activity. Other intellectuals from Syria and Lebanon joined
the growing Arab emigrant community in Paris, most notably Khalil
Ghanim, a former delegate to the short-lived Ottoman parliament and
an outspoken critic of the government. Following the dissolution of the
parliament in 1878, Ghanim arrived in France and launched a journal
called *al-Basir* ("The Keen Observer"). Shortly thereafter, the community welcomed an even more eminent figure, the mentor of so many
young activists in Egypt, Jamal al-Din al-Afghani, who was deported
by Tawfiq, the new khedive, when he acceded to power in 1879.

Europe, the new home of so many Arab political activists, became
an important base for the ideological struggle for political freedom.
From Paris, Ya'qub Sanu' continued to lash out at the Egyptian rulers,
first Isma'il and then, even more venomously, Tawfiq, conducting his
offensive through a series of innovative illustrated papers with endlessly
changing names designed to circumvent official attempts to thwart their
entry into Egypt. With their sarcastic style, vibrant colloquial lan-

guage, and witty cartoons drawn by Sanu' himself, these journals were received eagerly throughout the country. The ample evidence that they made their way to the educated readership and to the military (and even, inadvertently, to the khedive's own table) illustrates that they filled a real need.[63] Similarly, Adib Ishaq occupied himself with "stirring . . . oriental zeal and exciting . . . Arab blood" through his journal *Misr al-Qahira* under the motto: *hurriyya-musawa-ikha'*—"liberty, equality, fraternity."[64] Another important, and apparently influential, paper emanating from Paris was *al-'Urwa al-Wuthqa* ("The Firm Bond"), which Jamal al-Din al-Afghani published for several months in 1884 together with his most celebrated pupil, Muhammad 'Abduh. With Egypt occupied by Britain, *al-'Urwa al-Wuthqa* devoted its columns to impassioned assaults on British imperialism and to exposing the roots of Muslim weakness. Although banned by the authorities, in this case the British, the paper found its way to many eager readers in Egypt and elsewhere, setting the imagination of such young thinkers as Rashid Rida "in a blaze."[65]

Shortly afterward, under Lord Cromer's more liberal administration, Egypt once again became an arena of free speech and consolidated its position as the capital of Arab journalism. It retained this status until after World War II, despite moments of tension with the authorities at home, providing a haven for journalists from various Arab countries who faced obstacles in writing in their homeland. During these later years, expatriate Arab writers would continue to publish in Europe and elsewhere but with a different objective: They would cater mainly to the ever expanding communities of Arab emigrants abroad rather than to the readership in their lands of origin. Their journals, in Arabic as well as in other languages, would reach their home countries and find a market there, but their role in the region's sociopolitical affairs and in the development of its press would be all but negligible. They are therefore excluded from the rest of this survey. Only in the second half of the twentieth century, with the political rules in the region once again rewritten, would bases outside it again become an important front for journalistic opposition and political involvement.

3

The Private Press, 1882–1918

By the beginning of the 1880s the hub of Arab journalistic activity had shifted west, from Lebanon to Egypt. Economic pressures at home, restrictions on freedom of expression under 'Abd al-Hamid, and the lure of more promising opportunities in Egypt both financially and intellectually motivated many writers to make a new start there, first under Isma'il and Tawfiq, then under the British. They came from the communities of Mount Lebanon and Beirut, as well as (though in lesser numbers) from elsewhere in the Syrian provinces—and will henceforth be referred to, generally, as Syrians. Statistics clearly reflect this shift in the center of gravity of the Arab press: From 1852–1880, 25 nonofficial periodicals appeared in Beirut, compared with 13 in Cairo and 10 in Alexandria. From 1880–1908, a period equal in length, Beirut produced 42 private papers—an increase of some 60 percent over the previous period—but Cairo and Alexandria together yielded an astonishing 627 newspapers and journals (514 and 113 respectively), a 21-fold increase.[1]

Arriving in Egypt, the Syrians promptly became a catalytic force in the press, as in many other areas of Egyptian life. Educated Egyptians, both Muslims and Copts, reacted to the challenge of the Syrian example by joining the journalistic field in growing numbers. Political and economic stability under the British occupation, and the occupiers' liberal attitude toward the press throughout most of the period, led to a flowering in this field that was unparalleled elsewhere in the region. New papers also appeared in other places; indeed, quite a few cities in the Middle East witnessed the birth of their first periodicals during this period. But for the most part, such activity outside Egypt was sluggish, hampered by difficulties of all types. Only with the Young Turk revolution of 1908 and the concomitant change in the political atmosphere did a surge of feverish journalistic action sweep through the Ottoman Arab provinces of Syria, Lebanon, Palestine, Iraq, and even the Hejaz. But Egypt, by then the center of a highly dynamic press industry, continued to lead the way with its ambitious, colorful, and constantly improving newspapers.

Egypt, the Capital of Arab Journalism

The guns of the summer of 1882 set Alexandria ablaze, defeated Ahmad 'Urabi's troops at al-Tall al-Kabir, and opened a new chapter in Egyptian history. The country was brought under foreign control, which would be in effect for the next four decades, to be followed by an ongoing alien military and political presence for decades longer. Nominally Egypt remained an Ottoman province and the khedive the semi-autonomous ruler on its behalf, but the British were the real masters of the land, with the head of their administration the final authority on all important matters, domestic and foreign, despite his modest title "agent and consul-general."

The immediate impact of conquest was shock. The failure to check the British despite valiant efforts, the evident impotence of the country's leaders, and the direct contact with massive contingents of foreign occupiers were deeply disconcerting, inducing an intellectual paralysis in Egypt that lasted until the end of the decade. When Egyptian thinkers finally began to face the challenges, they discovered that the issues were more complex than they had seemed at first, and that solutions were anything but obvious. In one sense, the situation was clearer than before: The Westerners were no longer a vague potential menace but rather occupiers—a distinct target for attack. The struggle for liberation from foreign occupation was thus a clear focus for the community's energies. But the British also provided a model of political stability, good economic management, and efficient administration at a time when the Islamic state was manifestly declining. Egypt, so it seemed to some members of the educated class, could benefit from the British presence by adopting the administrative example and rebuilding the domestic infrastructure on more modern foundations. The British, then, were both a target for nationalistic rage and a model for emulation—a problematic blend that entailed an uneasy dilemma. This was further complicated by the ambiguous formal political situation: The foreigners ruled the country in effect, while the Islamic-Ottoman suzerainty remained in force. Moreover, the occupation itself was declared only "temporary," an indefinite status that added to the ambiguity. These tensions—between the curses and the blessings of the occupation, between identification with the Ottomans and disappointment with their weakness, and, more broadly, between traditional values and the attractions of modernity — created a problem in orientation for Egyptian intellectuals that would haunt them in various ways for many years. Debate over these questions rose to the top of the agenda for thinkers and writers, spurred by the liberalistic input of the Syrian Christian newcomers. The major medium for this debate was the press.

Lord Dufferin — the special British envoy sent to Egypt after the conquest to recommend policy and whose report provided the initial guidelines for the British administration there — pointedly emphasized that "a free press" would be "necessary to render vital and effective" the functioning of other institutions that he proposed.[2] Lord Cromer, the British official who was to implement this precept for most of the period (1883–1907), was a firm believer in the humanistic mission of British imperialism as well as an efficient administrator. He believed in freedom of expression both as a principle and as an instrumental safety valve for releasing pressures. He was prepared to leave the press alone, interfering only when its conduct was excessively aggressive. However, in the few instances when the Egyptian government at his instruction did react to press attacks with punishment, Cromer discovered that silencing the papers was a difficult and indeed impractical task, since other foreign powers offered many of them protection. Cromer therefore chose to let the Egyptian press develop unimpeded, and after 1894 he no longer invoked the rigid 1881 Press Law, officially still in force. He tended to overlook attacks by journals opposed to the occupation, convinced that such talk was inconsequential. This freedom was bound to be less than complete, given domestic and foreign sensitivities on the part of both the British and the khedive; yet, while warnings and suspensions remained realities,[3] on the whole it was a relatively happy period for the press, a "golden age" in the definition of one of its historians.[4]

Syrians, mostly Christian, who arrived in Egypt in a steady flow, bringing with them high literary standards and refined business skills, continued to lead the way in journalism, playing a parallel role among Arab employees of the civil service. For the Syrians, who along with the Armenians were "the intellectual cream of the Near East" in Cromer's view,[5] journalism and publishing in general were natural and attractive vocations, second only to commerce. The Syrians were highly visible in the Egyptian press, where they were represented more heavily than in any other occupation. By one count, about 15 percent of all the papers established in Egypt between 1873 and 1907 were founded by Syrians, although they comprised less than a third of one percent of the population in 1907.[6] Their qualitative contribution was even more impressive: Syrians owned two of the five most influential daily newspapers of the period and had exclusive control over the most popular cultural periodicals. An Egyptian challenge to their dominance began to emerge toward the end of the century, but the Syrians continued to retain a prominent position in the field until after World War I.

Non-news periodicals, initially the undisputed domain of the Syrians, consumed much of their journalistic energy. Their literary and scientific journals, aimed at enlightenment, played an important role in fostering reading habits among the people and training them to assimilate modern knowledge of every kind. In Beirut of the 1870s, this genre had been saliently represented by *al-Jinan* and *al-Muqtataf*. The transfer of the latter journal to Cairo in the 1880s, and the appearance of another emigré publication, *al-Hilal* ("The Crescent"), in the following decade, marked a shift to Egypt in this branch of the press as well.

The monthly *al-Muqtataf* had been founded in Beirut in 1876 by two young instructors at the Syrian Protestant College, Ya'qub Sarruf (1852-1927) and Faris Nimr (1857-1951), with Shahin Makaryus as a third partner. When intellectual and political horizons in Beirut became too narrow for them,[7] the three moved to Cairo in 1884 and restarted the journal. For several years, *al-Muqtataf*, "a magazine for science, craft, and agriculture," was the only periodical of its kind. It popularized science, from anatomy to astronomy and from physics to veterinary medicine, discussed social and philosophic issues, and translated extensively from European literature, thus contributing immensely to the edification of its readers — that is, of the small but crucial nucleus of urban educated men who could read and benefit from such knowledge. Starting off with a readership of some 500 in Beirut, the journal was reported, eight years after it moved to Cairo, to have reached a circulation of about 3,000 throughout the region.[8] Sarruf and Nimr were the paper's leading spirits, but many other intellectuals contributed as well, including Shibli Shumayyil, Iskandar Ma'luf, Farah Antun, Jurji Zaydan, Muhammad Kurd 'Ali, and later Salama Musa. *Al-Muqtataf* provided them with their earliest training in writing, after which they moved on to publish their own journals. Many readers whom *al-Muqtataf* exposed for the first time to the systematic presentation of modern, basically secular knowledge gratefully acknowledged the benefits they derived from it. "I felt as if I owned all the treasures of earth" when leafing through the pages of *al-Muqtataf*, recalled Jamil Sidqi al-Zahawi, the leading Iraqi poet of the late nineteenth century.[9] Salama Musa, another devoted reader of the journal around the turn of the century, later an eminent writer and journalist, noted: "I owe *al-Muqtataf* the scholarly drive that has engaged me all my life, just as I owe it the 'telegraphic' style in which I write."[10]

Although its message was universal, *al-Muqtataf* was a Syrian Christian product par excellence. Most of its writers were Syrian (including some who resided outside Egypt), as were, in all probability, most of its readers. A broader audience was sought by *al-Hilal*, the monthly founded by Jurji Zaydan (1861-1914) in 1892.[11] A Beiruti like Sarruf and Nimr, Zaydan likewise moved to Egypt, in 1886. Several years earlier, he had submitted his first article to *al-Muqtataf* for publication. It was rejected, and the author was advised to learn more before trying to buy fame by appearing in print.[12] A fervent reader and autodidact, Zaydan heeded the advice. When he felt ready, he started his own journal, which soon became a keen competitor of *al-Muqtataf*. He was less interested than they in pure science and more concerned with the human condition: sociology, history, literature, and language. These predispositions were reflected in his own impressive output of works on Arab history, culture, and language, along with a sizable number of historical romances. His interests were also reflected in the contents of his journal: *al-Hilal* focused on popularizing the Arabic and Islamic heritage (despite its owner's Christian origin) rather than the sciences. More than his colleagues in *al-Muqtataf*, Zaydan was deeply involved in the Egyptian intellectual debate on the question of communal orientation, advocating Arabism as a framework for identity and a blend of Islamic values and modernity as cultural guidelines. His captivating writing style, aesthetic editorial sense, and exceptional business instincts made *al-Hilal* a success story. The journal's focus on Arab and Islamic matters accounted, at least in part, for the fact that it lived longer than *al-Muqtataf* (which closed following Nimr's death in 1951) and, in fact, longer than any other periodical, still thriving after it marked its centennial in 1992.

The success and influence of these periodicals were, of course, relative. The Arab press at this early stage catered to a privileged few, those who could read it and learn from it. There was a palpable appetite for information among the educated: By its third year, *al-Hilal* was offering to buy back copies of first-year issues from subscribers because of considerable "pressure" by readers for them.[13] In 1897, within five years of its establishment, the journal was said to be selling some 10,000 copies in Egypt, the Arab provinces, and abroad, an impressive figure by any standard if true.[14] A readership in the thousands for the two leading journals was evidence of newly developed regular reading habits in a public which until recently had none. Interest in this medium was also evidenced by the proliferation of other periodicals, and even more so by the success of several of them. No less than 90 new magazines on diverse topics appeared in the 1890s in Cairo alone,[15] all stemming from the same cultural impetus. Most of them turned out to be ephemeral, an inevitable result of large supply and a limited reading market, but several made a certain impact — notably Farah Antun's *al-Jami'a* ("The Community") and *al-Jami'a al-'Uthmaniyya* ("The Ottoman Community"), Muhammad al-Najjar's *al-Arghul* (a kind of musical wind instrument) and Salim Sarkis' *al-Mushir* ("The Counselor") — even though these periodicals too were short-lived.

Rashid Rida's *al-Manar* ("The Lighthouse," or "Minaret") met a better fate than most of the periodicals that appeared during this period.[16] Like the founders of *al-Muqtataf* and *al-Hilal*, Rida (1865–1935) was Syrian, born in a village near Tripoli. Unlike them, he was a Muslim and an ardent advocate of Muhammad 'Abduh's reformist

Islamic ideas. Immigrating to Cairo in 1897, Rida founded his journal shortly thereafter, in March 1898, having received his mentor's blessing and promise of support. His aim was to join the intellectual debate over the issue of Islamic society's cultural and political orientation. After some initial difficulties (*al-Manar* started as a weekly but was forced to become a monthly in its second year), the journal became a success, continuously expanding its body of readers — mostly Muslim — both in and out of Egypt. By 1909, the journal's 12th year, back issues of the first volume were reportedly selling at four times the original price, and a second printing of that volume was issued.[17] *Al-Manar* became a voice for the movement that held that Islam, properly interpreted in light of modern developments, was the only response to the challenges of the day, an ideology known as *salafiyya* (adhering to the forefathers). For Rida, this view was also the cornerstone of Arab nationalism, of which he was the first important exponent. For a period of 37 years, until his death in 1935, Rida's journal voiced a relatively consistent massage — relative, since authentically it also reflected a measure of the confusion and even the occasional contradictions born of the perplexing vicissitudes of the time.

Weeklies or monthlies, rather than dailies, were the preferred medium for reportage and intellectual debate during the early decades of the Arab press. This was so because of technological limitations, which dictated the slow gathering, printing, and dissemination of news, and possibly also because the traditional Arabic literary style was better suited to periodicals. But by the late 1880s, dailies had begun to play a more important role, reflecting both technological and literary changes. By the turn of the century, daily papers offering news and commentary had moved to center stage, relegating other types of journals to a secondary status.

Al-Ahram, Egypt's first important news journal, had become a daily even before the British occupation. Briefly paralyzed during the conquest, it soon reappeared, providing reports and analysis of the new scene. Its owners' instinct for political adaptability led them at first to voice support for the occupiers. But after a while this same instinct, combined with their Francophile education, resulted in a somewhat more critical line. In the more liberal atmosphere prevalent in Egypt under the British, they felt, such a policy did not jeopardize their paper, while it contributed to their relations with the French and pleased the Egyptian public. The Taqla brothers attacked Britain for its inability "to hold to its promise [of quick evacuation] any more than a sieve can hold water,"[18] and in the early 1890s they opened the paper's columns to the person who would become the leader of the anti-British nationalist movement, Mustafa Kamil. This attitude led the British to suspend the paper for a month, in August 1884, a move that drew a strong French protest. Such open foreign protection of the paper enhanced its image as a "French mouthpiece," which, in the political circumstances, was not altogether unwelcome. Retrospectively, *al-Ahram* would sometimes be depicted as "the standard-bearer of Egyptian nationalism" during the early years of British occupation,[19] a description that might be exaggerated in relation to the conservative paper. The Taqlas were probably more interested in the business of reporting than in bearing standards of any kind. Strong nationalistic emotions which began to be articulated unequivocally in Egypt in the 1890s were for the most part voiced through channels other than *al-Ahram*.

If *al-Ahram*, though pro-French, professed to be independent and objective, Sarruf and Nimr, the two Protestant editors of *al-Muqtataf*, who were Anglophiles, were prepared to commit themselves more openly to a political cause and to a patron. "The lowliest British sergeant is higher than the most exalted Egyptian," remarked Nimr, who had been educated in an English school and was married to the daughter of a British consul.[20] The British, occasionally upset by *al-Ahram*'s unfriendly stance, encouraged the two partners to publish a new daily, *al-Muqattam* ("The Broken," the name of a range of hills to the east of Cairo), with their financial support—a timely offer, as *al-Muqtataf* was then struggling with financial difficulties.[21] Nimr undertook to edit the new paper, while his colleague continued to run *al-Muqtataf*.

Al-Muqattam, begun on 14 February 1889 as a weekly, became a daily within six weeks. From the first, it was a qualitative publication, carrying up-to-date political, military, economic, and commercial reports, both domestic and foreign, drawn directly from Reuter and Havas, from the paper's own agent-reporters in the provinces (who were "using the telegraph as freely as their English and American brethren do"),[22] from informants in the empire and in Europe, and from the international press. The paper also offered extensive news analysis and commentary that was often sophisticated. Its layout was logical and coherent, with a systematic arrangement of sections, headlines, and subheads. The language was elegant and effective, a far cry from the awkwardness of earlier publications. By the second issue, advertised notices, both official and private, filled a full page of the paper's four, and within three months they were spilling over into a second page,[23] an impressive mark of the paper's impact. *Al-Muqattam* offered unmistakable journalistic quality which paid off. An English traveler visiting Egypt in 1892 saw it "in all the *cafes* from Alexandria on the Mediterranean to Wady Halfa on the frontier of the Soudan."[24]

Al-Muqattam, however, also articulated a controversial political position that drew considerable fire. "The British are partners of [our] government, whether by advising it on foreign affairs and foreign relations or by working to perfect [the country's] irrigation, organize its army, and improve public order," Nimr stated, reflecting a conviction that the stability and reforms brought by the Europeans were in Egypt's best interest. The paper exhorted against "sowing hatred between them [the British] and the people, [which would] lead to a break between the

government and the governed," an objectionable circumstance.[25] Such
open sympathy with the alien occupiers by Christian emigrants who
were at the same time outspokenly critical of the Ottoman sultan and,
moreover, secularists in outlook, was bound to be viewed with suspicion by many Egyptians and with animosity by exponents of independence. *Al-Muqattam* was attacked by papers advocating a nationalistic
line, its editors were bitterly denounced, and its premises were occasionally targeted for assaults by nationalist demonstrators. One of these
assaults, in January 1893, was led by none other than Mustafa Kamil,
then a fiery 19-year-old student, who would later play a pivotal role in
the country's politics and press.[26] Later, on the eve of World War I, not
only Sarruf and Nimr but the entire immigrant community that they
represented would become an object of Egyptian anti-European sentiment intensified by the occupation.

In mid-1889, the two leading newspapers in Egypt were both
owned by Christian immigrants and backed by foreign powers, one of
them an avid supporter of the occupiers. This anomalous situation was
as unacceptable to educated Egyptians as was the British presence itself.
At the end of the year, a new daily appeared in Cairo, *al-Mu'ayyad*
("The Strengthened," or "Victorious"), the first powerful voice of anti-
British protest. It was initiated by 'Ali Yusuf (1863–1913), an ascetic
Muslim from a humble family in Upper Egypt with some experience in
journalism, with the tacit backing of Egyptian Prime Minister Mustafa
Riyad Pasha.[27] Having no financial resources, Yusuf established the
daily together with a richer partner, but his associate departed shortly
thereafter and Yusuf continued to edit the paper alone for the next 23
years. Displaying unusual writing ability and an unwavering faith in
the Islamic solution to the country's national problem, he gained the
support of many Egyptian thinkers. More significant, Yusuf gained the
support of Khedive Tawfiq and of his son, 'Abbas Hilmi, who succeeded Tawfiq in 1892 and who backed Yusuf's paper as consistently as
the British supported *al-Muqattam*. Unlike his Christian counterparts,
Yusuf was attracted to journalism less by financial considerations than
by ideological passion, a motivation that would typify other Muslim
writers as well. The Islamic, anti-British cause — which Yusuf advanced
with much eloquence, as did other articulate participants in his paper,
including Mustafa Kamil, Muhammad Farid, Ahmad Lutfi al-Sayyid,
and Sa'd Zaghlul — turned *al-Mu'ayyad* into the country's most widely
circulated newspaper toward the turn of the century. The pan-Islamic
aspect of its message also generated demand for it, as well as considerable support, outside Egypt's borders, "from Fez to Peking."[28] Like its
Christian competitors, *al-Mu'ayyad* provided its readers with detailed
news reportage and commentary. Unlike them, however, by focusing
on the powerful Islamic theme, it also provided a voice for the views
and emotions of a large segment of the public.

Al-Mu'ayyad gained momentum during the 1890s in a milieu of growing political effervescence in Egypt, somewhat reminiscent of the period leading up to the British conquest. Yusuf's paper voiced the Islamic community's protest not only against the European presence but also against the sympathy shown by the foreign community in Egypt for it. *Al-Muqattam*'s Anglophile editors challenged *al-Mu'ayyad* with some zeal and much skill, and as the decade progressed, many other thinkers and activists entered the fray, issuing their own papers and turning the press into an aggressive combat arena, its style often brazen. *Al-Ra'id al-Misri* ("The Egyptian Leader"), established in 1896 by Niqula Shihada and edited by Muhammad Kurd 'Ali from 1901, echoed *al-Mu'ayyad*'s criticism of *al-Muqattam*'s point of view. The Syrian Christian editor of *al-Ra'y al-'Amm* ("Public Opinion"), on the other hand, joined his compatriots Sarruf and Nimr in lashing out both at *al-Ra'id al-Misri*, with its "lowly and base editor," and at Yusuf—*kalb al-Mu'ayyad* or *himar al-Mu'ayyad* ("the dog, or ass, of *al-Mu'ayyad*"), who "in each and every line of his paper provides the reader with ample evidence of ignorance."[29] *Al-Mushir*, a bilingual Arabic-English weekly published by the Lebanese emigré Salim Sarkis, another Anglophile, also devoted articles and cartoons to attacking "the donkey-teacher (*al-himar al-mu'allim*) 'Ali Yusuf" for his "anti-Christian fanaticism, especially [his incitement] against British soldiers."[30]

The unambiguous tone of the debate did not necessarily indicate that the national problems, let alone the solutions, were defined clearly. On the contrary, the British occupation created a perplexing situation. The British presence, at once a provocation and a model, put certain traditional identities and loyalties in question and brought others into focus. One result of this dilemma was the deepening rift between Syrian Christians and Egyptian Muslims, who found themselves on two opposing sides of the issue. The Egyptians, waging a battle against the occupation through "the press, the only weapon that the occupier has left in the hands of the nationalists to repel that which is objectionable," in Yusuf's words,[31] felt that the Syrians, mere guests in Egypt, were displaying ingratitude and even treachery. The Syrians, for their part, did nothing to discourage growing anti-British xenophobia aimed at themselves. Under the circumstances, their hopes for assimilation in Egypt were dashed, a failure that would lead to the end of their centrality in the country's press, and in other areas, by World War I.

The twentieth century dawned on an agitated political arena in Egypt, with the press both reflecting and stimulating heated controversy. By then, the leading newspapers, *al-Ahram*, *al-Muqattam*, and *al-Mu'ayyad*, were selling thousands of copies daily, with *al-Mu'ayyad*, the most popular, boasting an estimated circulation of 6,000. These papers, combined with a score of others, reached an audience of perhaps 200,000 readers in Egypt, according to one assessment,[32] a figure that still represented a small segment of society but that marked immense progress compared to the past. The press, as 'Ali Yusuf noted, was indeed the only weapon that the British had left in the natives' hands, as Cromer assumed it would be basically harmless. Cromer may have been wrong. The newspapers' sting at first seemed slight and was conveniently disregarded, but its cumulative effect proved dangerous. By aggressively projecting political messages to its readers and generating active political debate among an expanding reading public—by "spread[ing] an enormous mass of explosive matter amongst the people," as one contemporary observer noted[33]—the press helped create a climate for political action that would eventually undermine the British hold on the country. Developments over time gave Cromer's successor, Sir Eldon Gorst, a different perspective: "The virulence of the vernacular press" and "the intemperate criticism of the actions and motives of the government . . . have gravely added to the difficulties of administering the country," he complained in 1908. From his vantage point after a quarter of a century of occupation, the damage "this species of literature and . . . violent nonsense" was causing not only to British interests but also to Egypt itself was palpable. It "demoralized" the youth, "terrorized" the "respectable middle classes," and stirred up "fanaticism, either between native Christians and Moslems or between Egyptians and Europeans."[34] The press was no longer benign, then, but rather an effective means for galvanizing the public to become involved in and respond to national issues.

By the time Gorst wrote his memorandum, Egypt's political-journalistic horizons had expanded far beyond exchanges between *al-Muqattam*, *al-Mu'ayyad*, and their lesser satellites. In January 1900 Mustafa Kamil, who was soon to become an outspoken leader of the Egyptian nationalist movement, began publishing the daily *al-Liwa'* ("The Banner").[35] Kamil (1874–1908) had received a modern Egyptian education, had graduated from a French law school, and had been politically active as a student leader and orator. In 1893, at age 19, he founded his first paper, *Majallat al-Madrasa*, a students' organ. Thereafter he wrote spirited political pieces mainly for *al-Mu'ayyad* and *al-Ahram* before launching his own daily. *Al-Liwa'* was conceived by Kamil as the mouthpiece of a popular movement that he had initiated, that sought British evacuation and an independent nationalist Egyptian state. The precise nature of that state, and its position on such cardinal issues as the role of Islam or relations with the suzerain Ottoman Empire, was somewhat inconsistent in Kamil's thinking. But this was secondary to the significance of a struggle articulated for the first time in Egyptian rather than Islamic terms, as in 'Ali Yusuf's ideology. Kamil was a magnetic leader, and the country's educated class, profoundly dissatisfied with the political reality, was ready for his call. His paper was received enthusiastically, especially among young people. "*Al-Liwa'* haunted our souls, and we rushed to buy it immediately after classes," a high school student of the time later recalled.[36] Kamil, primarily an activist rather than a journalist, used journalism as one of several

means to effect political action, along with oratory, intense correspondence with foreign leaders, and writing books. Sensing that Egypt's fate
was shaped as much by forces abroad as by its own countrymen, he
launched two foreign-language counterparts to *al-Liwa'* in March 1907,
The Egyptian Standard and *L'Etendard Egyptien*. Shortly thereafter, he went
a step further and founded the Nationalist Party (*al-hizb al-watani*),
which the paper then represented.

Chronologically, the Nationalist Party, established in October
1907, was the second political party to appear that year. It was preceded
in September by the People's Party (*hizb al-umma*), formed by a group
of well-to-do notables who were followers of Muhammad 'Abduh.
Prominent among them was Ahmad Lutfi al-Sayyid (1872–1963), a
thinker and writer who would later play a central role in the country's
cultural life. Sayyid was appointed editor of the group's organ, *al-Jarida*
("The Newspaper") — a "solid, middle class, Egyptian-gentry oriented"
product, in one scholar's words — which had been started six months
previously. A third party to spring up at this time was the Constitutionalist Reform Party (*hizb al-islah al-dusturi*), founded by 'Ali Yusuf in
November. The background to this political trend was growing tension
between the British and the educated Egyptian class, manifested dramatically in two incidents in 1906 in Taba and Dinshaway. All three
parties demanded independence, the differences between them being in
how they sought to attain it and their respective visions of Egypt's
political future.[37] Hitherto, the main vehicle for nationalist activism
had been the dissemination of printed sheets containing reportage,
commentary, and debate, but this had given way to a more formal
framework of organized activity, for which the press had prepared the
ground. Loosely organized parties dominated Egypt's intense political
life until World War I, vying for public opinion through their newspapers and debating with passion. In fact, the prevailing political rules
did not permit political parties to do much beyond expressing their
views; contesting parliamentary seats and mobilizing mass popular
support were still in the future for Egypt. The press, therefore, was the
main battlefield, and journalists enlisted themselves as soldiers in what
they regarded as a national struggle. Significantly, many of the approximately 250 new papers that appeared between 1900 and 1914, the vast
majority in Cairo, bore such names as *al-Jihad* ("Holy War"), *al-Hurriyya*
("Liberty"), *al-Nahda* ("Renaissance"), *al-Istiqlal* ("Independence"), *al-
Indhar* ("Warning"), and *al-Ahrar* ("The Freemen," or "Liberals").[38] Publishing in such a highly charged political environment was to have a
decisive effect on the fate of both the medium and the profession.

Freedom of self-expression, which the various political groups exploited fully, and which certain groups and individuals no doubt also
abused, alarmed both the British and members of the Egyptian government. Gorst, troubled by this reality ever since he replaced Cromer in
May 1907, pushed through a cabinet decision in March 1909 to renew

the rigid Press Law of 1881.[39] His aim was to place the press under
stricter state control and force it to tone down its style. The press,
however, displayed remarkable resilience. "We say to the authorities
that the policy of pressure and oppression is useless and has no impact
on a nation in quest of freedom," declared the Nationalist Party organ,
appearing under a new name only a day after it had been suspended.[40]
Issuing a suppressed paper under a different name, a common maneuver (the Nationalist Party's paper used four different titles within five
days),[41] was one of many stratagems to circumvent the barriers put up
by the government to restrict the press. The authorities were to learn
that battles waged by governments against free speech were hard to
win, especially when the quest for freedom of expression was part of a
national struggle for independence, and in fact constituted its primary
means.

While waging a nationalist battle, the Egyptian press also served
as a lively channel for airing and debating other issues that preoccupied
the educated class: political and social reform, communal identity, cultural orientation, and problems of linguistic modernization. Muslim-
Coptic relations was an important issue. The Copts, Egypt's indigenous
Christians, who viewed themselves as deprived and largely estranged
within their own society, undertook the defense of their interests by
entering the press arena with several papers, the most important of
which were Mikha'il 'Abd al-Sayyid's al-Watan, published in Cairo from
1877, and Misr ("Egypt"), begun in Cairo in 1895. Their lackluster
appearance and style—the Coptic press was "easily recognizable by its
crudeness of form and its insignificance of matter," an observer noted
in 1899[44]—reflected both the Copts' inferior position in Egyptian society and perhaps also the low priority their problem had on the national
agenda. Periodically these relations flared into open confrontation that,
from the beginning of British occupation, focused primarily on the
issue of representation in civil service employment. In 1908–1909, and
again in 1910–1911, these tensions came to a head, with the press
serving as the main arena for mutual accusations, pitting al-Watan and
Misr against al-Liwa', al-Mu'ayyad, and several other Islamic newspapers.[45] The social status of women was another issue that engaged the
Egyptian press in the late nineteenth century. A journal published by
and for women first appeared in Alexandria in 1892—Hind Nawfal's
al-Fatah ("The Young Woman"). It was followed by about a dozen
similar periodicals, published in Egypt until World War I, by women
liberated from the bonds of traditional conventions who set out to serve
the interests of their gender.

Fueled by a spirit of combat, the Egyptian press made significant
progress in other areas as well. These were years of rapid technological
development. By the mid-1880s, many papers were capable of running
reports based on telegrams received the previous day or even on the
day of publication. By the turn of the century, some papers had their

own telephones,[42] which had been introduced into Egypt in 1881. Printing became faster and better. 'Ali Yusuf was the first publisher to introduce an electric printing apparatus (rotative), in 1906, to replace the more primitive hand- or steam-powered machines, and other major papers quickly followed suit.[43] Typeface became more aesthetic and elegant. The November 1894 issue of *al-Ra'y al-'Amm*, for example, ran the paper's name in handsome Arabic calligraphy only. By September 1896 it had added a heading in Latin script and additional information in a variety of typefaces and continued to improve the graphic presentation in later issues. The number of pages in the leading papers also increased during this period, from four to six or eight. Periodicals, and occasionally newspapers as well, began to use illustrative graphic material, although it was rather rudimentary and often hand-drawn at this stage. The large papers gradually adopted a more specialized editorial policy, abandoning the one-man-show tradition and hiring staffs. The establishment of political parties prompted another innovation: Papers published on behalf of institutions were organized as share companies based on the European model, as was the case with the organs of all three parties. Most of the papers that appeared during this period folded quickly because of economic constraints but were soon replaced by others, so that the press remained a lively industry, impressive in quantity and showing steady if modest improvement in quality.

The Fertile Crescent and the Hejaz: Beginnings

"As the twentieth century sun rises over the Nile Valley, its press shines in the dress of independence and freedom," the proud owner of a new Cairo journal noted enthusiastically in 1902. This press, he declared, was "the envy of other papers in the east — those wretched sheets whose hands are shackled by the chains of tyranny, whose tongues are bound by the fetters of slavery, whose pens are smashed by the axes of despotism."[46] The depiction, if somewhat florid, was fairly accurate. Poor economic conditions, a dearth of trained writers, a low level of education, detachment from the stimulus of the European example, and, last but by no means least, the rigidity of Hamidian censorship from the late 1870s onward, effectively left the provinces of Syria and Palestine, Iraq, and the Hejaz without a press worthy of the name until 1908. The government continued to print dull Arabic-Turkish weekly bulletins in the central cities of the region — Damascus, Aleppo, Baghdad, Mossul, Basra, and Jerusalem — a sad mirror of the unproductive cultural panorama in these provinces. Occasional local attempts to put out private periodicals were strictly and narrowly circumscribed by suspicious authorities.

The situation was slightly brighter in Lebanon, the cradle of Arab journalism. Better educated, more resourceful, and more experienced, the Lebanese continued to produce more newspapers and periodicals than elsewhere in the area. But the best sons of Lebanon had gone abroad, investing their talent elsewhere — in Egypt, Europe, and North and South America. According to one meticulous survey, Lebanese publishers founded as many as 297 papers between 1880 and 1908, but only 68 of them (23 percent) were based in their homeland.[47] With the most gifted journalists abroad, and with government restrictions increasing, journalism in Lebanon remained a dispirited domain. The Christian *Hadiqat al-Akhbar* and *Lisan al-Hal* and the Muslim *Thamarat al-Funun* were the most important publications of the previous generation to remain, reporting events and offering commentary as best they could while keeping a low profile to avoid being swept away by the wrathful Hamidian storms. Of the new papers begun during this period — at a rate averaging less than three per year — about half were high school student newsletters that could not have had more than a limited local circulation. Some were handwritten. Three new papers in this period, however, deserve mention: Khalil Badawi's daily *al-Ahwal* ("Circumstances"), started in 1891 in Beirut and soon gaining recognition in Lebanon and even abroad for its reliable news reportage and commentary; Philippe and Farid al-Khazin's *al-Arz* ("The Cedar"), appearing in Junya in October 1895 and for 16 years thereafter serving as a fervent exponent of Maronite views and Lebanese patriotism; and the monthly *al-Mashriq* ("The Orient"), founded by the Catholic priest Luis Shaykhu in January 1898, an important cultural and literary journal comparable, in many ways, to *al-Muqtataf* and *al-Hilal*. Religious organs founded previously — the Protestant *al-Nashra al-Usbuʿiyya*, the Jesuit *al-Bashir*, the Maronite *al-Misbah*, and the Greek Orthodox *al-Hadiyya* — continued to be as popular among their respective communal constituencies as nonreligious papers. Dealing with factional affairs, and carrying on disputes with each other and, somewhat more cautiously, with their Muslim counterparts, they signaled the pitiful deterioration of the Lebanese press from a vital pioneer of Arab revival to a vehicle for clannish particularism.

The situation elsewhere was bleaker still. Only four political papers, all weeklies, were published in the Syrian cities of Damascus and Aleppo up until 1908, two in each city. *Al-Shahba'* ("The Grey," an epithet for Aleppo) was the first to appear there, in May 1877, edited by ʿAbd al-Rahman al-Kawakibi, who would later gain a certain amount of fame elsewhere. Kawakibi (1849–1903) was previously the editor of the official *al-Furat* for several years. Motivated to undertake this initiative by the advent of the Russian-Ottoman war in 1877, Kawakibi castigated the government for its repressiveness, denouncing the rigidity of its provincial administration. Although *al-Shahba'* was launched before ʿAbd al-Hamid's censorship took on its most rigorous form, the local vali was quick to suspend the paper after its second issue, and an additional suspension and closure followed after a third offense. Upon the replacement of the vali, in July 1879, Kawakibi published a second journal, *al-I'tidal* ("Moderation"), but it met a similar fate. With its closure Aleppo was left with only an official gazette up until the Young Turk revolution.[48]

The Damascus experience was similar. The official *Suriya* was the only newspaper in the city for 13 years before the first private paper, the weekly *Dimashq*, was issued in 1878 by Ahmad 'Izzat Basha al-'Abid. It appeared intermittently for nine years, then closed for economic reasons. Another nine years elapsed with only the official bulletin in circulation, when in 1896 another private journal appeared, Mustafa Wasif's *al-Sham* (a name denoting the geographic entity of Syria), which lasted until 1908. Both of these private papers were published by men who simultaneously held positions as state officials—'Abid was the editor of *Suriya* as well as chief of intelligence in the provincial administration; Wasif headed the state press and the local fire brigade. Both were supported by the authorities and both advocated a line consonant with that of the government. Focusing mostly on local news, they dealt "with matters that do not enrich the mind nor do they inspire anything good," in the words of a contemporary reader, and could barely have been more exciting than their official counterpart, reflecting a sterile, or perhaps sterilized, intellectual spirit.[49] Literary and scientific journals, which in Lebanon and Egypt had pioneered the emergence of the press, first appeared in the cities of Syria more than 20 years after the earliest political papers were founded. When they did emerge they were limited in number and frail: Only two came out in Damascus and one in Aleppo before 1908, and none lasted more than several months.[50]

If papers in Syria were shoddy, they were virtually nonexistent in the Iraqi provinces, except for two literary-religious journals printed by missionaries: *Iklil al-Wurud* ("Flower Garland"), which the Dominicans published in Mossul from 1902, and *Zuhayrat Baghdad* ("Baghdad Blossom"), initiated by the Carmelites in Baghdad in 1905.[51] Technological and educational backwardness, and the remoteness from European inspiration, which partly accounted for this depressed state of affairs, were more severe here than in Syria, and the government's hand was heavier. "Iraq is at the farthest end of God's land" and distant from "the advanced nations," a contemporary Iraqi writer noted in dismay. Furthermore, he observed, Iraqis had particularly unproductive mindsets: They were skeptical and passive, and "would not start on a project, would not set up a company, would not establish a plant and the like, until after they had seen the benefits with their own eyes, even if this keeps them far behind." Yet there was hope: A successful project initiated by their Egyptian or Syrian brethren could prompt the Iraqis to wake up and demonstrate their talent and stamina.[52] The situation in the Hejaz was similar, and no periodical appeared there until 1908. These places were marginally exposed to journals that arrived sporadically from Istanbul, Beirut, and Cairo, and occasionally even from Europe after having transcended the barriers of Ottoman censorship, but there was limited demand for this commodity among the largely uninterested public.

On 1 August 1908, after months of political agitation throughout the empire, the Ottoman constitution of 1876 was restored and the Young Turks became the effective rulers in Istanbul. Their rebellion soon turned into a revolution, sweeping away the sultan's autocracy and replacing it, at least for a while, by resounding pluralism. This event marked a new era for the press in the Arab provinces of Syria and Palestine, Iraq, and the Hejaz, and it surged forward with a burst of vigor.

The journalistic reaction to the change in the capital was immediate and powerful, like the rush of a great river upon the collapse of a large dam. Before the year was over, no less than 44 new Arabic papers had appeared in Lebanon, Syria, Palestine, and Iraq, as well as in Istanbul,[53] and the massive flow continued unabated. By World War I, these countries, along with the Hejaz, witnessed the founding of 355 additional newspapers and journals, an average of one new paper every six days. Lebanon led the way with 165 new periodicals, more than 40 percent of the region's total. Damascus and Aleppo, which on the eve of the revolution had only one nonofficial and two official journals between them, produced as many as 62 newspapers and journals during this brief period. No less than 70 new papers appeared in the Iraqi provinces, hitherto an almost total desert in terms of press activity. Palestine and the Hejaz also took advantage of the new opportunities: The former produced 34 papers (15 of them in a spontaneous outburst in 1908), the latter a more modest six. Finally, the Ottoman capital itself, where less than 20 Arabic papers had appeared during the entire half century prior to 1908, now became the base for 27 new newspapers and journals launched in six feverish years. These remarkable figures testify to a unique chapter in the story of Arab journalism.

Quantity was one aspect of this explosion. Another was the choice of themes and editorial style. The fledgling periodicals gave full expression to their elation with the new era of freedom. "It is well known that our Ottoman community lagged behind the other advanced nations only by the ruinous forces of tyranny, which had devastated its body and oppressed its mind," ran a typical editorial in the first journal ever to appear in Sidon. Now that this affliction was removed, the editorial went on, papers could engage in "enlightening the minds and . . . educating the people whom past despotism had kept in such an abyss of ignorance."[54] The Damascus journal *Dimashq*, which had previously defined itself in its subtitle as "a paper in the service of all Ottomans," demonstratively changed the subtitle to "a paper in the service of the nation, the homeland, and public interests."[55] The Beirut daily *al-Watan* adopted a dramatic masthead featuring a pen and an arrow, a winged angel with a trumpet and the scales of justice, an Ottoman flag flying over such symbols of progress as sailing ships and a rushing train, and a string of inspirational mottos, among them "Liberty, Equality, Fraternity" and "Freedom of the soul is the source of bliss."[56] Like their Egyptian counterparts previously, the new publications in the Ottoman provinces took on such bold titles as *al-Inqilab* ("Revolution"), *al-Hurriyya* ("Liberty"), *al-Nahda* ("Renaissance"), *al-Wataniyya* ("Patriotism"), *Shams al-'Adala* ("The Sun of Justice"), and, somewhat curiously, *Brutistu* ("Protesto," or protest).

Symbolic graphics and passionate statements of intention were indeed telling. But even more significant was the active involvement of the new papers in politics. The closing years of the Ottoman Empire were a stormy period, with many crucial questions on the public agenda both at the center and in the provinces: the very survivability of the empire, its form of government, relations between Turkish rulers and non-Turkish subjects, issues of political and cultural identity, and foreign policy orientation. Ideological movements and parties formed to advance various causes, confronting each other through their journals. The ruling party in Istanbul, the Committee of Union and Progress (CUP), faced opposition from the start, especially in the Arab provinces, where criticism was daringly expressed in print. Most important of the opposition papers were *al-Muqtabas* ("Acquired Learning"), the first daily in Damascus, begun in 1908 by Muhammad Kurd 'Ali, one of the country's *savants*; and *Bayn al-Nahrayn* ("Mesopotamia"), published in Baghdad from 1909 by Ahmad Kamil. The CUP, for its part, induced several papers to support it and issued its own organs— *al-Mishkah* ("The Lamp") in Damascus, *Baghdad* in Iraq's main city, and *Shams al-Haqiqa* ("The Sun of Truth") in Mecca.[57] In addition, a number of papers were devoted to promoting the nascent ideas of Arab nationalism as well as other more local ideologies; no less than 36 such papers in Syria, Lebanon, and Palestine have been listed in a recent study.[58]

In Palestine, Zionist settlement constituted an additional incentive for the emergence of Arabic publications, many of them, although not all, opposed to the new Jewish presence. Three leading papers voiced Palestinian Arab emotions in this period, all of them published by Christians: Jurji Habib Hananya's *al-Quds* ("The Holy," an epithet for Jerusalem), appearing in that city from 1908; Najib Nassar's *al-Karmil*, begun in Haifa the same year; and the Jaffa paper *Filastin*, established by the cousins Yusuf al-'Isa and 'Isa al-'Isa in 1911 (the last two papers outspokenly anti-Zionist in their position). Jewish immigration to Palestine also began to evoke antagonistic emotions among Arabs elsewhere, which was likewise articulated in print.[59] Expressing political views in writing was one of several options for activists during this turbulent period, along with engaging in parliamentary activity in Istanbul and joining new political associations (some of them secret) that were forming throughout the region. In the post-1908 Fertile Crescent, as in Egypt sometime earlier, the nature of the press in its formative phase was largely dictated by the considerations of political struggle.

Was the journalistic explosion of 1908 an instance of suppressed energy suddenly let loose? It was, but only to some extent. For many this was indeed a long-awaited opportunity to propound repressed views, air complaints, and openly debate the burning issues of the day. Others, however, entered the field without having felt such a longtime urge, drawn like moths to the heat generated by public debate. This sudden blossoming occurred, however, on ground that had hardly been prepared. The technological and economic realities, and the vastly illiterate population, were far from capable of sustaining such an ambitious endeavor. Even the public's growing interest in news, a consequence of the activation of the political environment, was inadequate to support the scores of publications established with such dazzling speed. The swift proliferation of papers was premature. It was one thing to secure a license and print an issue or two of a journal with a particular political view; it was another to sustain the journal as an effective medium that could elicit public support and make an impact. Moreover, lack of experience was clearly reflected in the crude form of many of the papers, especially in places where they were an innovation. The great majority of publications initiated during this period perished quickly. Although they constituted an impressively long list, no more than a handful were ever published simultaneously. A typical phenomenon was that of journals presenting themselves as "a daily paper, appearing temporarily once a week."[60] The transitory nature of the papers in terms of frequency of publication and location of their offices or printshop was a characteristic of the time. "The majority of [Arabic] newspapers," one disheartened journalist complained, "are like water bubbles, rising to the surface once, then dying out, or like the rooster's egg, appearing once in a lifetime."[61] Such swift appearances and disappearances of publications following a sharp shift from repression to freedom, and so large a gap between quantity and quality, were not unusual historical phenomena. They had occurred in similar situations elsewhere — in France during the revolution, in Russia following the death of Nikolai I, in Hungary with the fall of the Hapsburgs, in post-Franco Spain, and in other times and places. Typically, many misfits joined the rising tide of periodical printing — "anybody who can put two phrases together and even those who cannot" — creating a state of "journalistic anarchy" (*fawda sihafiyya*) which the few serious professionals loathed.[62]

The more solid papers that survived competed keenly for a share of the limited market. Leading journals in Syria and Palestine had a circulation at that stage of an estimated 1,000 to 1,500 copies each, in Iraq 500 to 1,000, and in the Hejaz even less. The Lebanese press fared somewhat better, with some papers reaching a circulation of 2,000 to 3,000. *Lisan al-Hal*, apparently the most popular Lebanese newspaper of the prewar period, seems to have sold about 3,500 copies daily in 1914.[63] Undoubtedly, this was an improvement over the pre-1908 situation. Yet the press of the region was still frail, vulnerable, and insecure, especially in contrast to its Egyptian equivalent.

Compared with the "dark age" of Hamidian oppression, the years following 1908 were an epoch of light and liberty. This emancipation, however, was only relative. The CUP, facing immense domestic and foreign challenges, adopted an increasingly hard line against its critics. Three acute domestic political crises, in 1909, 1912, and 1913, consolidated CUP rule but also heightened its distrust and rigidity. The press, lashing out at the authorities, supporting the opposition, and calling for Arab separation from the empire, was subject to government harassment and punishment. In this the Young Turks' methods differed little from those of 'Abd al-Hamid, relying primarily on a press law, devised in 1909 and amended no less than five times between 1912 and 1914,[64] that allowed for banning newspapers and the imprisonment and flogging of journalists. In his memoirs the Syrian Muhammad Kurd 'Ali, a biting critic of the CUP, vividly described incidents in which the authorities sent gendarmes to warn him, on several occasions attempted to capture him, and hired an assassin to do away with him. Assisted by friends, he always managed to escape. In April 1912, he slipped out of his office, which was surrounded by police, and fled on foot from Damascus to Palestine and from there to Egypt. Outraged, the authorities arrested his brother and imprisoned him in Istanbul.[65] Other journalists in Syria, Iraq, and Palestine had similar experiences. After the January 1913 events in the capital, harassment mounted to such an extent that, according to a contemporary testimony, "there is not a single journalist in the entire Ottoman Empire whom the government does not prosecute at least two or three times a year."[66]

Nonetheless, doing battle with the government was easier for the press during that period than under the Hamidian regime. The government's routine recourse to legal procedure allowed the papers to operate more or less according to rules, finding loopholes that facilitated ongoing publication while carrying on their political campaigns. They resorted to the tactic used by the Egyptian Sanu' a quarter of a century earlier, and by the Egyptian opposition early in the twentieth century, of changing the name of the newspaper frequently, a legal device that proved effective under the post-1908 rules. 'Abd al-Ghani al-'Uraysi's *al-Mufid* ("The Informer") in Beirut, for example, appeared under four different names between May and November 1912, each change prompted by the suspension of the previous version.[67] A report about papers in Istanbul having fictitious "prison editors" who were paid to get arrested so that the paper could carry on with the real editor under a new name, however fantastic-sounding,[68] reflected the atmosphere of the time both in the capital and the provinces.

The government's relatively tolerant attitude came to an abrupt end with the outbreak of the war when the empire mounted its last battle under a tough military leadership. Verbal assaults from within, tolerable in quieter times, became highly dangerous and unacceptable. Engaged in fateful battles against formidable enemies on many fronts, the Ottomans used an iron hand to keep the domestic arena docile so as not to impede the empire's overall effort, effectively silencing the Arab press in the provinces under their control and bringing its lively and promising beginning to a halt.

Wartime Exigencies

World War I, spilling over into the Middle East, brought political upheaval and economic hardship unprecedented in the region's recent memory. For the press this meant near-complete paralysis: Most of the existing papers collapsed, hardly any new ones were allowed to appear, and the few that survived faced tremendous difficulties. Political activity and the nationalist struggle, hitherto embodied by the press, were largely suppressed for the duration of the war, to reemerge only when hostilities ended.

In Egypt, the three leading party papers died out during this period. Lutfi al-Sayyid's *al-Jarida* ceased publication in October 1914, apparently because of financial hardship (its editor accepted an official appointment as director of the National Library). Two months later the Nationalist Party organ, then published under the title *al-Sha'b* ("The People"), shut down, reportedly because its editor, Amin al-Rafi'i, refused to print the news that Egypt had become a British protectorate. *Al-Mu'ayyad* closed in December 1915, following a period of decline without the spirited leadership of its founder, 'Ali Yusuf, who had died in 1913. Material and other troubles brought on by the fighting forced most other papers to close as well. One day, one publisher related, "as I was sitting and considering the newsprint problem, I was summoned to the Publications Office":

> Rumors abounded concerning the suspension of journals and newspapers. I sat before one of the Syrian officials who greeted me, ordered coffee for me, and began to flatter me with sweet words. He asked me about the journal, whether it was selling well or did I lose money on it. Then he sent to call for an Englishman. The man came and sat before me, listening without uttering a word. The [Syrian] official explained to me how critical the [economic] situation was, which required that some journals be stopped (namely suspended). Although, as I have said, I did not mind suspension, I was strongly reluctant to probe or discuss [the matter], especially in front of that Englishman. I therefore insisted that I was able to publish *al-Mustaqbal* whatever the difficulties. . . . Eventually, abandoning his politeness, the [Syrian] official started screaming, saying that the Publications Office was authorized to suspend [any publication], and that those defying the law under the existing circumstances

might be deported or arrested. That was what I wanted to hear. I got up, notified them I would suspend the journal, and left.[69]

Egypt was left with a handful of periodicals, most importantly *al-Ahram* and *al-Muqattam* in Cairo, 'Abd al-Qadir Hamza's *al-Ahali* ("The People," founded in 1910) and Rashid Shumayyil's *al-Basir* (founded in 1895), both in Alexandria.

Past wars, which took place away from home and involved Egyptians only marginally or indirectly, had usually generated increased interest in news and resulted in prosperity for the press. This time, however, the proximity of the fighting had a painful impact. The war produced a chronic shortage of newsprint resulting in a five-fold or more increase in its cost; hindered the supply of spare parts for printing presses; restricted economic activity, thereby aborting what little advertising had existed; and created general want, which severely limited public demand. The papers that survived had to use ingenuity in order to overcome obstacles: They cut the number of pages (*al-Ahram*, for example, reduced its size from eight pages to six, then four, and at times two), made do with low-quality newsprint, switched to smaller typefaces and headings in order to save space, and sacrificed sections of secondary importance such as literary columns. Focusing primarily on reportage and analysis of events in the battlefield, they relegated domestic issues to the sidelines.

Another development was the silencing of the nationalist struggle by the authorities, marking a different type of pressure. The state of war and the declaration of the British protectorate over Egypt (18 December 1914) brought wartime censorship in its wake, a new experience for the Egyptians that involved the direct intervention of the authorities in the daily production of newspapers. Censors became full members of the editorial staff, their task being to bar or limit the publication of information that could harm the British war effort. Empty white columns abounded in the press of the period, attesting both to the extensive practice of deletions by the censor and to the editors' mute protest against this policy. Still, although the Egyptian press was hit hard by the war, it continued to function and even to proliferate modestly: Some 15 newspapers and a similar number of periodicals were inaugurated in Cairo and Alexandria during this period. Several of them were short-lived, but nine were still operating 10 years after the war's end.[70]

The situation was even more difficult in the areas under Ottoman control. Upon the outbreak of hostilities, the authorities imposed stringent censorship on all publications printed in Syria, Lebanon, Palestine, and Iraq, as well as Istanbul, the capital. This, combined with economic realities that were harsher than in Egypt, quickly caused the great majority of newspapers in these areas to disappear. Jemal Pasha, commander of the Ottoman Fourth Army in Syria, was a notoriously ruthless administrator. Having seized documents in the French consulates in Beirut and Damascus incriminating Arab political activists as dissenters, he had scores of them tried and many of them hanged—11 in the Beirut police headquarters on 21 August 1915 at dawn, another 20 in public squares in Beirut and Damascus on the morning of 6 May 1916—as a warning. Among these victims were 16 journalists, early exponents of an Arab identity who became martyrs in the annals of Arab nationalism. They included Shukri al-'Asali, editor of *al-Qabas* ("The Firebrand"), 'Abd al-Ghani al-'Uraysi of *al-Mufid*, Ahmad Hasan Tabbara of *al-Ittihad al-'Uthmani* ("Ottoman Union") and *al-Islah* ("Reform"), 'Abd al-Hamid al-Zahrawi of *al-Hadara* ("Culture"), Philippe and Farid al-Khazin of *al-Arz*, and Sa'id 'Aql, editor of *al-Ahwal* and several other papers previously. Journalists, among many others, were also tried *in absentia* and sentenced to death or long prison terms, among them Rashid Rida, Faris Nimr, Shibli Shumayyil, and Rafiq al-'Azm.[71] The large proportion of journalists among the prosecuted "agitators" was not coincidental, for both the Arab nationalists and the CUP government were aware of the power and the danger that the press had come to represent, both potentially and in practice. Only a handful of papers were left in the towns of Syria and in Beirut, notably Kurd 'Ali's *al-Muqtabas*, which survived until 1917 because of its editor's rapport with Jemal. The situation was similar in Iraq, where all prewar journals perished save for two privately owned ones that persisted irregularly—*al-Zuhur* ("Blossoms") in Baghdad and *Da'wat al-Haqq* ("The Call of Truth") in Mossul. All the local publications in Basra, which had been under British occupation since the beginning of the war, were discontinued, while the British circulated their own daily and a weekly in Arabic. The heavy hand of the censor, along with the prevailing economic hardship, are clearly evident in the copies of newspapers that have survived from that period: Timid and shabby, with frequent changes in format, number of pages, and quality of newsprint, they featured mostly, and often solely, laconic news from the front.[72]

Another measure taken by the Ottomans was mounting a propaganda campaign to muster popular loyalty, a step strongly recommended by their Germans allies. The common denominator highlighted by the Ottomans in this effort was Islam: From the outset the sultan-caliph declared that the community of believers was waging Jihad against the enemies of Islam, which called for a consolidation of effort under Ottoman leadership. Any form of dissidence was tantamount to rejecting the foundations of the faith. To spread the message the government launched several newspapers under the direction of individuals with a distinguished reputation. One such journal was *al-Sharq* ("The East"), published in Damascus from April 1916 under the direction of Muhammad Taj al-Din al-Hasani (later prime minister of Syria) with such celebrated editors as Muhammad Kurd 'Ali and the Druze Shakib Arslan. Another was *al-'Alam al-Islami* ("The Islamic

World"), begun in Istanbul the following month, edited by 'Abd al-'Aziz Jawish, an aggressive fundamentalist exiled leader of Egypt's National- ist Party. Several other papers owned or controlled by the government appeared in the towns of Syria, Lebanon, Iraq, and Palestine, generally a single publication in each locality. These organs, beyond merely transmitting an appeal for loyalty to Arab readers, found themselves combatting publications that propounded opposing views to the same audience. Most important among the opposition voices was that of the Hashemite Sharif Husayn bin 'Ali, governor of the Hejaz on behalf of the Ottomans, who in the summer of 1916 issued his own call for Muslim unity without CUP or Ottoman leadership.[73]

With the rebellion by Sharif Husayn against his masters in June 1916, the Hejaz — except for an area around the town of Medina that remained in Ottoman hands — became an independent enclave in a vast territory that was under Ottoman or British domination. Two months later, on 15 August, Husayn issued a semiweekly organ, *al-Qibla* (the direction to which Muslims turn in prayer toward Mecca), backed by the British. The sharif's name appeared on the front page of the first issue as "editor in charge," signifying that the organ reflected his per- sonal views, although the paper was edited by the Syrian-born Muhibb al-Din al-Khatib.[74] That a potentate in the Arabian Peninsula, actually a tribal shaykh, should adopt this modern vehicle as a means of propa- ganda was in itself a striking mark of the power ascribed to the press in the region by then. With a background of many years in Istanbul and extensive exposure to international affairs, Husayn fully appreciated the potential of the medium and aimed his paper primarily at Arab and Islamic audiences outside the Hejaz.[75] Muslim, and especially Arab, backing was of crucial importance to him, as it was for the Ottomans, and he too adopted the legitimation of Islam, claiming that the CUP, "a reckless lot," had distorted the Islamic message.[76] Although Husayn waved the banner of the faith, by rejecting Ottoman leadership he also sought to encourage, if tacitly, the nascent sense of Arab identity that had emerged before the war, mostly in Syria. His confrontation with the government was total and multifaceted, with the press constituting only one front. The Ottomans, who continued to hold Medina until the end of the war, used it as a base both militarily and in the war of words, countering the sharif's message with their own local paper, *al-Hijaz*. This was produced with presses impounded from the Lebanese journal *Zahla al-Fatah* and appeared at first three times a week and then daily until 1918.[77] *Al-Qibla* and *al-Hijaz*, the only two newspapers in the peninsula during the war, were sponsored by the only powers able to undertake such ventures in the harsh conditions of the time and place, the British and the Ottomans.

4

The Arab States and the Press, 1918–1945

The disintegration of the Ottoman Empire following the war rewrote political rules in the Middle East and created a new reality for the press. The locus of power was diffused — no longer in Istanbul but in Cairo, Baghdad, Damascus, Beirut, Jerusalem, Amman, Mecca, and San'a. Governments in these places began to rule according to new formulas, sharing authority with foreign forces — Britain in Egypt, Iraq, Palestine, and Transjordan; France in Syria and Lebanon. Under the new and fluctuating terms of reference, these foreign powers had the final say in most important matters, and their relations with local governments therefore involved rivalry as often as cooperation.

For the press, this state of affairs entailed both difficulties and advantages. It was subject to harassment and suppression by either of two masters with their divergent priorities, or by both; but it also had two potential sources of material support, a circumstance especially convenient when contention between these masters was at high pitch. Thus, ubiquitous political rivalry created options for survival and even prosperity for newspapers that otherwise would have disappeared. The new political scene affected the press in other ways as well. Local potentates, experimenting with running a state along modern lines, sought to demarcate the parameters of private media activity constitutionally and legally, while the press, eager to test the limits of these rules, became involved in endless battles with the state. In addition, inter-party rivalry — an extension of past power struggles — generated intensified journalistic activity. These dynamic developments produced a politically zealous press throughout the region during the interwar period and provided a powerful incentive for its growth by enhancing public interest in news and opinion. Rapid technological developments were another major factor in the evolution of the press during this period, among them, notably, the appearance of the radio, which became an important complementary medium in some places from the 1930s onward.

Political argumentation — the essence of press activity in Egypt from the late nineteenth century, and elsewhere from 1908 — continued to dominate Arab journalism even though targets had changed. The political essay — the *maqal* (or *maqala*) — still had primacy over *khabar*, the reporting of news. Many papers came into being for no other purpose than to engage in controversy; informing was generally subordinate to the needs of the struggle. Typically, newspapers featured an editorial and other political essays on the front page, with news relegated to the back of the paper. The encounter with Europe, and the myriad cultural questions it evoked, heightened further by the absence of the caliphate, prompted writers to delve into issues of identity and orientation ever more intensively.

These developments were widespread in the region but did not prevail everywhere. The Arabian peninsula, where the war put an end to Ottoman sovereignty as well, was not subject to European control (except for small parts on its southern and eastern flanks). Independent states emerged there: Imam Yahya's Yemen, Sharif Husayn's Hashemite kingdom in the Hejaz, and the Saudi kingdom. These were countries with little or no journalistic tradition and whose cultural, educational, and technological state was far less conducive to the development of the press than in the other Arab countries. There was also little political impetus for the evolution of the press, as the political climate in these places nurtured traditional autocratic patterns and was scarcely affected by outside influences. The situation was similar in most respects in the newly carved out entity of Transjordan, a sparsely populated land under British tutelage until after World War II. The newspapers that appeared between the wars in these states were no more than embryonic experiments as compared to the Egyptian or Lebanese press at that stage, or even to the Syrian press, although they constituted an important first step in establishing a tradition for a local press.

The division of the region into separate states with defined borders and individual governments did not result in a press exclusively confined to separate national territories. On the contrary, the tradition of the region as a single pool of communication with roots going back to earlier times remained and even developed further, enhanced by improved means of transportation. The newspapers of one country were routinely read by audiences elsewhere, and were often composed with the readership abroad in mind. Newspapers from Egypt — politically freer than other countries, with a richer press tradition and the largest concentration of talent in the region — were most in demand among the educated population everywhere, who read the major Egyptian dailies and literary magazines extensively. According to an authoritative assessment in 1936, about 10,000 copies of Egyptian daily newspapers and some 15,000 copies of other periodicals were forwarded weekly to the Fertile Crescent countries,[1] and at times were as popular there as the local, normally less impressive press. Lebanese journals also circulated regularly in Syria and Palestine (and to a lesser extent vice versa as well). A part of the Lebanese and Syrian press was read regularly in Iraq. Such major political issues as the struggle against foreign domination and opposition to Zionism evoked similar emotions in many parts of the region and prompted a spirited intraregional dialogue in the press. Writers debated political and cultural matters with their colleagues across the borders, reproduced their colleagues' views that were of interest to local readers, and made use of their own papers to stage assaults on their colleagues' enemies. Governments, however, often blocked the free flow of publications between the countries by imposing sanctions, a commonly used weapon in the counteroffensive against aggressive newspapers. Ultimately, it was the radio that was to unify the countries of the region even further in terms of communications, as it could traverse boundaries more readily than written texts.

Still, the essence of the history of the press during this period reflected developments in each state separately, a sign of the course of the region's sociopolitical history generally.

Egypt

The interwar period was, arguably, the liveliest and perhaps happiest period in the history of the Egyptian press. For much of the time it was as free politically as it had been at the turn of the century. Moreover, it was greatly enriched by the vibrant spirit born of the new politically pluralistic milieu and the optimism of intellectuals projecting their society's future in an atmosphere of national struggle. Egypt had formally gained independence in February 1922, had its own king in March 1923, and, as of the end of that year, had a new constitution that permitted the election of a parliament. The replacement of autocracy by constitutional monarchy, however, generated tension and conflict between the monarch and other forces, as well as among these various forces themselves. The British military presence caused additional dissension. This setting produced a dynamic press which, grappling with a broad range of national and political issues, both consumed and generated vast amounts of energy.

Hundreds of papers appeared in Egypt during this period. A 1937 survey identified over 250 Arabic and 65 foreign-language papers in circulation. Of those in Arabic, about 200 were published in Cairo, the hub of anti-British and interparty contention and the center of cultural ferment. Each year during the interwar period saw the appearance of dozens of new papers.[2] A great many of these were devoted to news and political polemics and were small enterprises with a limited circulation, ultimately of brief duration. They were established privately by individuals seeking personal publicity or trying to make a profit by selling or leasing the publication. Other publications were nonpolitical — magazines devoted to the arts and literature, agriculture, health, education, household affairs, and other topics. Like many of the political newspapers, most of these were also short-lived. Still, the number of more substantial and more popular papers was remarkably large.

Increasingly, dispute over political issues was becoming the province of indigenous Egyptians, led by Egyptian nationalists and articulated by Egyptian writers. Foreigners, especially Christian Syrians, were gradually being pushed out of the scene. As far back as the turn of the century, Egyptian nationalists had been expressing anti-Syrian sentiments, and as the national struggle intensified, many Egyptians came to feel that their Syrian guests' sympathy for this cause was half-hearted, an impression the Syrians themselves may not have tried hard enough to refute. It was for Egyptians, not for aliens, to build their new state and define their future, the nationalists felt. By the early 1920s second- and third-generation Christian Syrians in Egypt were leaving mainstream journalism, as well as several other major fields, and shifting to other occupations. Culturally they were undergoing a process of de-Arabization, adopting the French language and style instead. This was reflected in their journalistic pursuits: They switched to French newspapers and soon dominated this branch.[3] The Syrian-owned dailies al-Ahram and al-Muqattam remained conspicuous exceptions, retaining their popularity because of their high standard of reportage. A third exception was the monthly al-Hilal, which opened its pages to Muslim Egyptian writers and editors and thrived. Other Syrian papers either perished or, like al-Mahrusa in Cairo and al-Basir in Alexandria, dropped to secondary importance. Previously, journalism had been viewed by the Syrians as both a business and a cultural-educational undertaking; now it became a business only, devoid of passion, avoiding sensitive issues and thus the wrath of the authorities. Indeed, Syrian papers during this period seldom angered the government and were seldom harassed by it, a cause of resentment on the part of their more bellicose Egyptian colleagues.[4]

Anti-British sentiment and the demand for British withdrawal from Egypt were voiced increasingly by political leaders in late 1918 and were echoed in the press, becoming a unifying issue for the country. The message at this early stage was communicated mainly by al-Ahram, which temporarily deviated from its cautious neutrality to express strong anti-British protest, indicating the direction the press was soon to take. Al-Ahram's lead was followed by the organ of the Nationalist Party which, having discontinued publication in 1914, reappeared in February 1920 under a new name, *al-Akhbar* ("The News"), edited by Amin al-Rafi'i. *Al-Akhbar* gained popularity for a while, but the Nationalist Party lost its leadership position in the national struggle to other groups.[5] The nationalist movement in Cairo was reinforced in 1921 when 'Abd al-Qadir Hamza, an able writer who had doggedly published his journal, *al-Ahali*, throughout the war years, moved from Alexandria to the capital to aid the new nationalist leader, Sa'd Zaghlul. Several lesser papers that appeared before the 1922 British declaration of Egypt's independence followed a similar line. But before long the national movement was rent by friction, and by the time the constitution was declared, in 1923, the political scene was divided into rival camps, each with its own journal. While in the decade preceding the war, newspapers had initiated the formation of political parties, political parties now launched newspapers. These party papers became the most widespread and in many ways the most important journalistic endeavors of the period.

The daily *al-Siyasa* ("Politics"), which appeared in October 1922, was the organ of the Liberal Constitutionalist Party, a group representing mostly landed and business interests that disagreed with what they regarded as Zaghlul's militant line. *Al-Siyasa* was edited by Muhammad Husayn Haykal, one of the most gifted and prolific Egyptian writers of the century, later minister of education. It was an impressive publication and functioned for a period of three decades as a forum for debate by the country's intellectuals on domestic and foreign policy, social issues, questions of national identity, literature, and other subjects. Despite its high quality, however, the paper's popularity was rather limited, like that of the party itself. The Wafd, the group that backed Zaghlul, did not publish its own official organ until much later, but several papers articulated its views explicitly during this period, most importantly *al-Balagh* ("The Message"), begun by 'Abd al-Qadir Hamza in January 1923. The rivalry between *al-Siyasa* and *al-Balagh* came to constitute a major element of the political scene until 1952. Both papers began publishing weekly editions in 1926 — *al-Siyasa al-Usbu'iyya* in March, *al-Balagh al-Usbu'i* in November — that dealt with broad national issues. Another paper expressing Wafd positions in the 1920s was *Kawkab al-Sharq* ("Star of the East"), begun by the veteran writer and journalist Ahmad Hafiz 'Awad in September 1924, which lasted until World War II. A third political group that appeared briefly on the political stage during this decade — a group of king's men calling itself "the Union Party" (*al-Ittihad*) — launched a paper by the same name in January 1925. Its duration was brief, even briefer than that of the party itself.

Political fragmentation intensified in the 1930s, with papers being born and expiring alongside the parties that sponsored them. One of the new political groups, the militant nationalist *Misr al-Fatah* ("Young Egypt"), formed in 1933, launched an organ by the same name in

1938. The Sa'dist Party, a splinter of the Wafd, started *al-Dustur* ("The Constitution") the same year. Among the many other new papers, several reflected the Wafd point of view, notably Muhammad Tawfiq Diyab's *al-Jihad*, during 1931–1938; *al-Misri*, published by Mahmud Abu al-Fath and Muhammad al-Tabi'i from 1936, which the party adopted as its official organ — and which soon broke all circulation records, becoming the most popular newspaper in any Arab country — until its closure in 1954; and *al-Wafd al-Misri*, inaugurated by the Wafd in 1937.

While newspapers linked to political parties were typical of the time, many periodicals contributed to the political dialogue without formal party affiliation. *Al-Kashkul* ("Scrapbook"), an illustrated satirical weekly started by Sulayman Fawzi in 1921, took a distinctly anti-Wafd line. Four years later, in October 1925, a popular actress, Ruz (Fatima) al-Yusuf, founded a journal bearing her name. *Ruz al-Yusuf* began as a weekly magazine devoted to art and culture, but within two years it shifted its focus to politics under Muhammad al-Tabi'i's editorship. Advocating the Wafd position, it soon became the country's best-selling periodical with a reported circulation of 20,000 copies by the late 1920s. Success prompted the daring lady to start a daily counterpart in March 1935, *Ruz al-Yusuf al-Yawmiyya*, with Mahmud 'Azmi as editor-in-chief and 'Abbas Mahmud al-'Aqqad as leading columnist. It too began to gain popularity, but Fatima al-Yusuf then broke ranks with the Wafd and became a sharp critic of it. The party, which rose to power in May 1936, forced her to close down the daily, although not the weekly journal. Meanwhile, Muhammad al-Tabi'i had left *Ruz al-Yusuf* in 1934 to initiate his own political weekly, *Akhir Sa'a* ("The Latest Hour"). There were also many nonpolitical magazines, the most prominent of which was the weekly *al-Musawwar* ("The Illustrated"). It was published from October 1924 by the owners of *al-Hilal* — Jurji Zaydan's sons, Emile and Shukri, who by the late 1920s had turned their father's enterprise into Egypt's leading publishing house. All four weeklies continued publishing until after the end of World War II, the last three still extant and prospering in the early 1990s.

The political writers of this period were preoccupied with four separate issues: ideological and political conflicts within and among political parties; the confrontation with the palace and its supporters, primarily over the question of press freedom; the battle against the foreign presence; and the long-standing but still intense debate over the desired cultural identity of the new Egyptian community. Party rivalries — ideological disagreements, factional disputes, and personal animosities — occupied the lion's share of space in many papers. Parties formed, splintered, and shifted from government to opposition in rapid succession, engaging all the while in aggressive and passionate mutual recrimination. The personal dimension was pivotal in these exchanges, and in the public mind papers were identified with particular writers even more than with parties. "We used to read the paper not because it abounded in news or pictures, but because X or Y wrote an article in it," related an avid reader and impassioned writer of the period.[6] Party leaders and their loyalists attacked their opponents with abandon for their erroneous attitudes, political impotence, and unethical style, as well as for corruption, treachery, and base character. Such clashes were marked by vivid linguistic imagery (which, as a contemporary journalist recalled, often "involved the mothers, wives, and sisters").[7] "These are not newspapers. These are hagglers' stalls," noted the contemporary thinker Mustafa Sadiq al-Rafi'i, deploring the waste of political and intellectual resources.[8] Journalists of a later generation would admire the freedom and vitality that marked this kind of activity, which they themselves did not have the fortune to enjoy, but they would lament the largely futile squandering of so much energy on intramural squabbling.

Another struggle, closely intertwined with the interparty melee, was waged by the papers against the palace and the government. The kings—Fu'ad until 1936, Faruq from 1937—were assailed for yielding to the British, for poor performance in domestic matters, and above all for their autocratic style and their encroachment upon freedom of expression. Articles 14 and 15 of the 1923 constitution guaranteed freedom of expression "within the limits of the law" and prohibited preventive censorship, suspension, and the banning of newspapers. The constitution did, however, permit such measures "when vital to the preservation of social order" (al-nizam al-ijtima'i).[9] Protecting the "social order" from the perils of an excessively free press was entrusted to the monarch and his government. When attacked, the king and his ministers fought back by using, and abusing, the constitution and the law to punish the aggressors with suspensions, fines, and imprisonment and by rewarding supporters with generous subventions. Slur and retribution were two basic ground rules in this combat. When Ihsan 'Abd al-Qudus, Ruz al-Yusuf's son, joined his mother's journal in 1942 as a correspondent, she remarked that only after he had been imprisoned could he become editor-in-chief, for only a writer who had served time in jail could be counted as a real journalist.[10] Ruz al-Yusuf, resuming publication in August 1931 after one of numerous suspensions, marked its seventh anniversary by noting that "it should have published about 360 issues [by that time], but this impressive number has shrunk [due to bans and suspensions] so the readers in fact have seen no more than 158."[11] An attack on the government by the daring columnist Mustafa Amin resulted in his father losing his job as a state official several times. Amin's daily routine was to write in the afternoon while spending the morning in police headquarters paying fines and undergoing interrogation.[12] Certain prime ministers, notably Muhammad Mahmud (1928–1929) and Isma'il Sidqi (1930–1933), became notorious for their rigid handling of the press and the mass punishments meted out to it.[13]

Yet, as in the past, the press found loopholes and bypasses. As the government was constitutional and the principle of press freedom was acknowledged, the press had considerable leeway and could evolve and progress despite the harassment. "My adversaries," prime minister Isma'il Sidqi lamented in his memoirs, "were able to fight me with the most powerful weapon, the press." Even after the massive punishments he meted out, Sidqi felt that the press remained quite capable of marshaling the readers' sympathy for its point of view: "Had I had a supportive press on my side, my enemies' offensive would not have succeeded."[14] Proven techniques from the past were reused: The owner of a suspended paper would immediately reissue it under a different name, for which he had secured a license earlier, and when the period of suspension was over he would rent the newly available name to someone else similarly in need. This practice partly accounted for the inflated number of newspaper titles listed for the period, many of which were merely straw names.[15] When unable to attack openly, newspapers conveyed their message between the lines, for example castigating "the rulers of China" for their misdeeds and relying on the readers' wit to grasp that it was their own government that was under fire.

Engrossed as it was in combatting rival parties and challenging the government and the palace, the press dealt with other issues as well. Newspapers served as an important means for opposing British domination by instilling a spirit of protest among the readers and arousing their ire. In particular, the press protested the presence of a British high commissioner and his patronizing meddling in Egypt's affairs, as well as the presence of British troops in their country. Once a treaty was signed with the British in August 1936, designed, among other things, to reduce Britain's role, the press called for complete British evacuation. "Who would enlighten the nationalist of his rights?" Amin al-Rafi'i pointed out in the Nationalist Party's al-Akhbar in 1924. "Who would instruct him about his duties? Who would lend him support in the battle into which he is throwing himself? . . . No doubt the press is one of the finest means for fulfilling the nationalist's commitment."[16] Ahmad Husayn, in a newspaper that sought to heighten anti-British emotions, a decade later urged the young generation: "Youth of 1933 – be the youth of 1919!"[17] Nevertheless, the issue of relations with Britain rose to the fore only periodically, especially during times of critical Anglo-Egyptian negotiations as in 1922, 1924, and 1935–1936. Otherwise it remained in the background, as the political community and its press were generally preoccupied with domestic politics. The British, whose hold on Egypt was more restricted than before World War I and was limited to certain specific interests, tended to overlook the periodic outbursts by the press, and perhaps even welcomed them as a harmless channel for Egyptian political zeal, seldom interfering with the journalistic protest against their presence.

Yet another area in which the press made a major contribution to the community was by constituting a platform for the discussion of issues of national identity and culture. Since the political aspect was integral in these issues, it was not only the literary monthlies but also the daily and weekly political journals that dealt with them. The press opened its columns to thinkers and essayists, for whom newspapers — faster, cheaper, and simpler to produce than books — served as a preferred medium. These writers debated the issues of religion vs. secularism, Egyptian identity ("Pharaonicism") vs. Arabism, territorial vs. pan-regional nationalism, and democracy vs. dictatorship, reacting to developments in other countries in the region and elsewhere and examining possible implications for their own society. The major newspapers played an important role in these debates, along with new journals that were founded during these years of intellectual ferment to meet the need for such a dialogue. Most important among the latter were Ahmad Khayri Sa'id's *al-Fajr* ("Dawn," 1925–1927), Isma'il Mazhar's *al-'Usur* ("Epochs," 1927–1930), and Salama Musa's *al-Majalla al-Jadida* ("The New Journal," 1929–1944), all of which advocated a secularist "Egyptianist" orientation; and Ahmad Hasan al-Zayyat's *al-Risala* ("The Message," from 1933) and Ahmad Amin's *al-Thaqafa* ("Culture," from 1939), articulating a more traditionalist view, both of which continued publishing through World War II.[18]

As elsewhere in the region, the intense involvement of the Egyptian press in politics gave priority to the political essay over reportage. Polemics and diatribe were the *raison d'être* of many papers. Still, progress in the mechanics of news gathering and cumulative experience in production methods contributed to a gradual improvement in reportage. The older, more serious papers, such as *al-Ahram*, *al-Muqattam*, and *al-Basir*, which favored profitability over outspokenness, had long since developed up-to-date standards of reporting drawn directly from the international news agencies and foreign correspondents. A growing number of newspapers began running photographs, which became common in the early 1920s. Newer politically orientated publications also devoted more attention to reporting in response to an increasing public hunger for news during the 1930s, a decade of momentous international developments. Primarily an urban phenomenon, the interest in news was turning into an addiction, as the growth in newspaper circulations showed. If in 1928–1929 the circulation of Arabic papers in Egypt was assessed at about 180,000 daily, with the leading paper, *al-Ahram*, selling an estimated 30,000 copies, by the second half of the 1940s total circulation apparently reached well over 500,000 daily, with *al-Ahram* selling some 80,000 copies, and at least two weekly journals selling even more. The size of the audience directly or indirectly exposed to the contents of these publications was, of course, even larger.[19] A fighting press, a lively diversity of periodical literature, and steadily improving standards of reportage combined to produce a remarkable journalistic output which, despite certain serious flaws, showed considerable promise for the future.

From the early 1930s onward, part of the hunger for news was satisfied by a service of a new kind, radio. Haphazardly operated in Egypt by private individuals in the 1920s, radio came under government control in 1931 and official broadcasting was initiated in May 1934. Possessing a radio receiver, at first fashionable among upper-class Egyptians and the foreign community in the cities, gradually became popular, and by 1939 the number of receivers in Egypt was estimated at no less than 86,000, of which many were installed in such public places as cafes and restaurants.[20] The audience of the broadcast message, though still a small part of society, was rapidly expanding, unhampered by the obstacle that hindered newspaper reading — illiteracy. Radio played a key role in instilling the habit of regular news consumption among the public, primarily among city dwellers, generating a growing appetite for information which, in turn, enhanced the demand for newspapers. The increased popular demand for news eventually resulted in the institutionalization of the study of journalism as a profession: The first academic department of journalism in the Middle East was inaugurated at the American University in Cairo, in 1936; and, three years later, an "institute of editing, translation, and journalism" was opened by royal decree at Fu'ad I University (later Cairo University).[21] A new era was dawning in the history of communication in Egypt, in which the media were to play a role quite different, and often more important, than hitherto, socially, culturally, and, not least, politically.

Syria and Lebanon

The entry of Faysal bin Husayn through the gates of Damascus in October 1918 kindled high hopes for a brighter future in Syria and the Muslim parts of Lebanon after an era that had been difficult for all residents of the area. Many of these hopes, however, were dashed quickly, and others would be disappointed later on. After a period of international haggling, the French became masters of the area with a League of Nations mandate to "guide" the communities of Syria and Lebanon toward independence. Imposing new borders and a new political order, the French remained in the area until the end of World War II. The rules they introduced had a profound impact on every aspect of life in these countries, including the role of the press.

The feverish journalistic outburst of the post-1908 period notwithstanding, Syria's experience in journalism was far more limited than Egypt's. Beyond obvious economic and cultural causes for this gap, the Syrian press was also a victim of bad historical timing, beset by the war just as it was emerging, and then by the imposition of French occupation. Between these two troubled periods, however, there was a brief happy interval. On 14 October 1918, only a fortnight after the Allies' occupation of Damascus, the first newspaper of the new era made its appearance under the name *al-Istiqlal al-'Arabi* ("Arab Independence"). Published by one Ma'ruf al-Arna'ut, it was a frail publication whose two small pages still evinced material wartime hardship. Its title, however, reflected lofty aspirations, as did its columns, which echoed the hopes of the prewar Arab nationalists. Syria now witnessed a journalistic surge reminiscent of August 1908. Another paper appeared the following day, and before the year was over the country had ten new publications: five in Damascus, three in Aleppo, one in Homs, and one in Hama. In the 22 months until the arrival of French troops, a total of 42 newspapers and 13 periodicals were started—23 and 11 of them, respectively, in Damascus. An official biweekly, *al-'Asima* ("The Capital"), appeared in Damascus in February 1919, featuring official announcements alongside impassioned essays supporting Faysal's independent government. From August 1919 it was edited by Muhibb al-Din al-Khatib, previously the editor of Sharif Husayn's *al-Qibla*, who moved to Damascus to join the journalistic struggle in what was, for a while, the Hashemite's main battle front. Among the new popular publications was, notably, Muhammad Kurd 'Ali's *al-Muqtabas*, whose owner eagerly accepted Faysal's invitation in 1919 to return from his self-imposed exile in Istanbul. The optimism generated by the formation of an Arab kingdom in the Syrian capital backed by Great Britain was clearly reflected in these papers, many of which carried such evocative titles as *Suriya al-Jadida* ("New Syria"), *al-Fajr* ("Dawn"), *al-Nahda* ("Renaissance"), *al-Raya* ("The Banner"), and *al-Watan* ("Homeland"). *Al-Istiqlal al-'Arabi*, its editor announced, "is edited by the rising Arab youth. . . . Oh Arabs! This is your independence, guard it. This is your banner, have passion for it. This is your king, support him."[22]

The enthusiasm of publicists anxious to appear in print after a long silence did not necessarily herald progress in press standards. In Syria, a community still accustomed to the politics of notables, with popular participation as yet an oddity, the zeal of the few could not push journalism forward very far. Newspapers remained at an immature stage during the brief era of the Arab kingdom in Damascus, and, though outspoken, their message elicited little public response. Papers sold 500, and at the very most 1,500, copies each. Moreover, the Syrians were permitted to show "passion for their banner" and "support for their king" for a brief time only. On 24 July 1920 their forces were defeated at Maysalun by a French army, and, with the dream of a sovereign kingdom shattered, most of the newspapers expired or were banned. For the next quarter century the Syrian community and its press would have to contend with French domination.[23]

The typical Syrian newspaper during the French mandate was poor in appearance, stridently vocal, and short-lived, sometimes suppressed by the French or the local government but more often simply unable to hold its own financially. The list of journals published in Syria from July 1920 until the end of World War II contains an impressive total of 128 newspapers (71 of them in Damascus) and 129 other periodicals, mostly literary, scientific and professional (80 of them in the capital) — an average of some ten new newspapers of all kinds each year. Yet, as the great majority promptly perished, in reality the statistics at any given moment were far more modest. For example, about 80 newspapers were started in Syria between 1920 and 1931, but at the onset of 1932 only six or seven of them were, reportedly, still in circulation.[24] Demand was scarce: Until the mid-1930s the most popular Syrian papers seem to have sold no more than 3,500 copies daily, while second-rank papers distributed 1,000 to 2,000 and other periodicals sold far less. Later, during the turbulent events at home and abroad, circulations increased somewhat, with a handful of leading papers in Damascus reaching a peak of 7,000 to 8,000 copies on exceptional occasions. The market, however, was much smaller than that of Egypt, where, according to a reasonable estimate, twice as many papers were sold per 1,000 persons, despite a higher illiteracy rate.[25]

The Syrian press, if less mature and weaker than its Egyptian counterpart, was confronted with political challenges that were often more intricate. French involvement in every sphere of life was deeper than that of the British, reflecting the aim of achieving closer integration of the overseas territories. Consequently, French officials were more concerned than their British opposite numbers about what the local population did, said, and published, and were less accommodating toward the press. Anti-French sentiment, evident in Syria prior to the war, turned into open resentment after the defeat at Maysalun, expressed in various ways, from ongoing verbal assaults to a violent revolt in the mid-1920s that lasted for two years. Newspapers served as a vital medium in this battle. "The pens wielded by Syrian journalists were mightier than the guns and machine guns brought by the French army to eliminate the Arab government," a Syrian author commented in a somewhat wishful but typical assessment.[26] The press, through impassioned editorials, endeavored to stir public animosity against the foreigners, called upon the people to resist the mandatory government's attempts to divide and rule, and lashed out at Lebanese newspapers, which for reasons of their own showed sympathy for France. This effort was led by Muhammad Kurd 'Ali's celebrated *al-Muqtabas* during most of the 1920s, run at the time by his brother Ahmad. With the closure of the paper in 1928, its leadership role was assumed by *al-Qabas*, edited by Najib al-Rayyis, with his cousin Munir serving as senior columnist. Other outspoken newspapers in the nationalist cause included *Al-Sha'b* (from 1927) and *al-Ayyam* ("Days," from 1931) in Damascus, and *Suriya al-Shimaliyya* ("Northern Syria," from 1921) in Aleppo.[27]

Anxious to preserve calm, the French tried to keep the press under control through manipulation and, when needed, punishment. They resorted to the familiar, but only partly effective, methods of licensing, censorship, suspension, imprisonment, and reward for complacency. Censors in the French high commissioner's office busied themselves with expunging improper material — "*considérés comme de nature à troubler l'ordre public*" was the standard formula — from local publications. When papers came out with white spaces where articles had been excised, an act of protest against the censor, the French demanded that the editors fill in the gaps or face suspension, aware that "too many white spaces in papers feed conjecture and doubt."[28] The mandatory authorities also prohibited the entry of publications from other countries that could generate trouble, most commonly papers from Lebanon, where there were fewer restrictions than in Syria. The Ottoman Press Law was nullified in April 1924 and immediately replaced by an equally rigorous law, to which additional restrictions were added periodically.[29]

In the Syrian national memory, the period has remained as, largely, one of consensual struggle for independence — a joint national effort against foreign domination. Indeed many, perhaps most, newspapers during these turbulent years were established to wage this battle. Still, the French occupiers and their Lebanese "lackeys" were not the only targets of these papers' fire. Like Egypt and other neighboring countries engaged in a struggle for independence, the Syrian community faced the challenge of building a new state and new political institutions, objectives that necessitated new terms of reference within society. Thus, quarrels among traditional local antagonists, a familiar phenomenon, were at times as bitter as the enmity toward the French. Loyalties and rivalries now found expression in political parties, a new institution in Syria. These, for the most part, were not ideological organizations but rather bands of supporters of various urban notables and prominent families. Newspapers, by now a popular means for expressing opinion and attacking enemies, were often issued as party organs. The leading political grouping during most of the mandate was the Nationalist Bloc (*al-kutla al-wataniyya*), an ad hoc heterogenous coalition of dignitaries mostly from Damascus and Aleppo, two historically antagonistic centers that temporarily halted their rivalry. Several newspapers voiced the views of the Bloc on the anti-French struggle, primarily *al-Muqtabas*, *al-Qabas*, and *al-Ayyam*. This last journal was founded in 1931 as a joint venture by such Bloc leaders as Hashim al-Atasi, Ibrahim Hananu, Sa'dallah al-Jabiri, and Lutfi al-Haffar, but, facing financial difficulties, it was sold a year later to a private individual, Nassuh Babil, a Bloc loyalist with some journalistic experience. Other journals were started by Bloc members as a result of personal conflicts within the party, such as Lutfi al-Haffar's *al-Insha'* ("Creation") in Damascus and Ahmad Qanbar's *al-Nadhir* ("The Herald") in Aleppo, both begun in 1936; and Munir al-'Ajlani's daily *al-Nidal* ("The Struggle"), established in the capital in 1939 following a dispute between 'Ajlani and other leaders, and carrying on despite many vicissitudes into the 1950s. Other splinter parties and their newspapers appeared and disappeared: the Aleppine Syrian Progress Party, which issued a newspaper bearing its name, *al-Taraqqi al-Suri*, in 1923; the League of National Action (*'usbat al-'amal al-qawmi*), a small pan-Arab group that published the short-lived *al-'Amal al-Qawmi* in 1938; and the tiny Communist Party, which circulated several bulletins, some of them handwritten. Unofficial individuals also published newspapers, the most important being the daily *Alif Ba'* ("ABC"), published by Yusuf al-'Isa (previously one of the founders of the weekly *Filastin* in Jaffa). Begun in Damascus in September 1920, it became one of Syria's most respected journals and lasted for a half century.

The newspapers were fervidly contentious toward each other and there was little general consensus on any issue. Even the question of independence, the central item on the public agenda, elicited less than universal agreement. Several local French and Arabic papers, among them *al-'Umran* ("The World") in Damascus and *al-Umma* ("The Nation") in Aleppo, apparently subsidized by the French, even advocated the continuation of the mandate and were bitingly attacked by the nationalist press. Disputes were also carried on between the Bloc's radical papers and journals endorsing a more moderate, "submissive" line, primarily *Alif Ba'* in Damascus and *al-Taqaddum* in Aleppo. A typical front-page article in *al-Qabas* charged: "You donkeys of imperialism (*mataya al-isti'mar*)! . . . You who preach moderation, who . . . give away your honor in exchange for official appointments. . . . What is this moderation you take for your slogan? Can there be moderation in the quest for freedom, independence, life?"[30] Debate on other issues was often equally heated, such as on the sensitive question of borders, in view of the unacceptable French-imposed delineation; questions relating to the optimal type of regime, whether republican as in France or monarchical as had been instituted under Faysal; problems of religion and state; questions of regional orientation and foreign policy alignment; and issues concerning the country's economy, society, and culture, all of which preoccupied the thinkers and writers of the young state.

While grappling with these issues, the press also had to fight for its very freedom and survival. Local dignitaries now ensconced in ministerial positions, long accustomed to being obeyed — and hence sometimes more prone to taking their cue from the high commissioner than from lower-rank compatriots — restrained the press through warnings and punishments. Syrian premiers, ministers, and officials, when attacked by the press for their "oppression" and for "selling their honor," responded with harsh measures designed to "protect freedom against such abuse by reckless elements." Press-state tensions came to a head during the second half of the 1930s under the Bloc's "national" government, a period of conspicuous maladministration and public malaise. "Certain

papers write things which transcend the limits of national interests,"
Prime Minister Jamil Mardam asserted in November 1937, echoing
counterparts in many different times and places. "[Their assertions]
are based on calumnies and vanities. . . . This cannot be tolerated or
overlooked."[31] By the end of the year, Mardam's government had issued
no less than 17 suspension orders to various newspapers, some of them
punished twice or three times, and the same number of suspensions —
mostly of indefinite duration — the following year as well.[32] Temporary
closure was the device most commonly used by the government, and at
any given moment one or several newspapers were likely to be suspended. The outspoken al-Qabas was closed for more than a third of the
mandate period, while other Syrian papers were closed for an average
of 10 to 20 percent of the time during the period.

These tribulations molded the Syrian press during the period of its
adolescence, honing it primarily as a combat weapon. While news
reportage was integral to its self-definition — vital, in fact, during a
period of so many rapid developments of consequence — reportage was
subordinate to the nationalist cause and hence selectively presented.
More often than not, the front pages of Syrian daily newspapers consisted primarily, or solely, of political editorials, as did their Egyptian
counterparts. But unlike the Egyptians, Syrian journalists had very
little experience of any other kind. Their press was born into a storm of
political controversy over cardinal national issues and evolved as part
of this development. The battle was harsh, taking its toll and leaving
victims behind. "We are tormented, we are suffering spiritually and
materially. We are no longer able to bear it, being on the brink of
bankruptcy and terminal despair," complained Najib al-Rayyis, a leading nationalist advocate, in 1928, reflecting a gloom that sometimes
beset his colleagues.[33] Indeed, many journalists yielded after repeated
suspensions, prosecution, and economic penalties, quitting "this waste-
land that would grow nothing but thorns."[34] But others stayed on,
tenaciously challenging the alien occupiers, the governments, and the
politicians. In the midst of this struggle they also made efforts to improve professional and technical standards, expanding newspapers
from four pages to six, eight, and even (as al-Qabas in the 1930s) twelve
pages per issue. A sense of professional solidarity began to emerge, and
there were several brief attempts in the late 1920s to form a journalists'
union, eventually resulting in a durable syndicate in 1942.[35] In the
process, however, Syrian journalists developed and retained a rough
style that they deemed essential for survival. By the end of the period
they were a group of bruised warriors, at odds with the government
and with each other and winning only limited public recognition.

The history of journalism in mandatory Lebanon resembles that
of Syria in many respects. There too the press continued to evolve amid
a struggle for national independence coupled with efforts to build new
political institutions, becoming an integral part of these developments.

Lebanon's problems, however, were more complex than those of its eastern neighbor, as the development of its press clearly reflected.

Lebanese journalism had passed its early peak by the eve of World War I. Many of the country's leading intellectuals had moved abroad — the outcome both of sociopolitical tribulations and an enterprising spirit — and continued to write and publish in Cairo, New York, and Rio de Janeiro. Of those who had chosen to stay, many perished on the gallows during 1915–1916 under Jemal's forbidding regime. The war brought additional afflictions to the country — hunger, want, and destruction — weakening the press further. Later, the postwar political arrangements portended new dilemmas. The former tiny province of Mount Lebanon, predominantly Christian Maronite, found itself fused into a larger state along with other, mostly Muslim, regions. Local political patterns, long characterized by sectarian quarrels and rivalries between dignitaries (zu'ama'), were infinitely complicated with the formation of this larger entity and the introduction as well of new political institutions. The Muslims harbored profound resentment against the French, who had turned them into a minority in a non-Muslim state, but were divided among themselves regarding their community's future. The Christians, still a majority but no longer predominantly so, were also split over differing political options. Many of the Maronites, historical allies of France, valued the patronage of the great power as a shield against Muslim assertiveness and wanted a continuation of that patronage, while others aspired to national sovereignty and freedom from French occupation. The picture was further complicated by the grievances and demands of other minorities such as the Greek Orthodox, the Armenians, the Druze and the Shi'ites. From the end of World War I onward, these conflicts dominated the new state's political and intellectual scene and had a fragmentizing effect on the press as well.

The political passion generated by these developments was reflected in the growth of the interwar Lebanese press. Between 1918 and 1939, no less than 250 new Arabic journals and over 30 French and Armenian papers appeared[36] — a strikingly energetic development for such a small community (750,000 people at the outset of the period, 1.2 million at its conclusion), though not quite matching the exceptional outburst in the post-1908 era there. The high level of education, a traditional interest in world affairs, keen business instincts, and the intensity of the country's pluralistic politics all contributed to this journalistic flowering. Newspaper presses began to emerge in places that had no experience with journalism hitherto, including such small towns and villages as Ba'albak, 'Amshit, Salima, Bikfaya, and Anfa. The familiar transitory pattern, however, was at work here as well. For example, of the 148 journals that appeared in Lebanon during the 1918–1928 period, 102, or over two-thirds, had expired by the end of 1929.[37] Initial backing by interested groups and individuals was available, but it was not always sufficient to sustain a newspaper for long.

The small market, and the multitude of competing publications, worked against the newspapers' survivability, causing most of them to "quickly disappear into oblivion" in the words of a French consular report.[38] These factors also gave rise to what came to be identified as a typically notorious Lebanese phenomenon: newspapers renting themselves out for a fee to serve as exponents of the views of individuals, groups, or even governments. The Lebanese press, beset by bitter factional division but blessed with many talents, became the archetype of the "hired press" (sihafa ma'jura), an institution that evolved integrally with it.

Lebanon's dilemmas of communal and political identity were complex and pressing. The country's political mosaic precluded the emergence of a broad-based leadership body that could articulate a national program and attract widespread popular recognition, such as the Egyptian Wafd or even the Syrian Nationalist Bloc. Instead, numerous small political groupings formed around individual leaders and families, perpetually at odds with each other. The press mirrored this divisiveness, marked as much by partisan fragmentation as by ideological conviction. There were no large or dominant newspapers but rather myriad small ones with circulations of several hundred or a few thousand at most. Often, personal interests lay at the root of disputes between newspapers, disputes ostensibly over ideological or political issues. The daily Bayrut would "defend Moslem interests," but only "where the cause does not interfere with the personal ends and ambitions of its owners," a 1944 British consular report noted typically.[39] Illustrative of the convoluted ideological situation, the two most important political groups of the time, Emile Ede's Unionist Party and Bishara al-Khuri's Constitutional Bloc—both Maronite—published their main organs in French: the former the pro-French L'Orient, founded in 1923, the latter the anti-French Le Jour, founded in 1934. This reflected a specific Lebanese quandary—the problematic and multifaceted relationship with the occupier.

A few papers did, nonetheless, acquire more popularity than others. One was the daily al-Ahrar, published in Beirut from 1924 by the Greek Orthodox Jibran Tuwayni along with two partners. Tuwayni, a gifted journalist and an active politician, left the paper in 1932 to become minister of education, then returned to the field and established another daily, al-Nahar ("The Day") in 1933, which soon became even more popular than its predecessor. Both of Tuwayni's journals gained a reputation as reliable and professional conveyors of information comparable to older respected publications such as Lisan al-Hal and al-Ahwal. Tuwayni's papers consistently voiced anti-French and pan-Arab sentiments. A similar nationalist line was followed by 'Awni al-Ka'ki's daily al-Sharq, begun in 1926, which was blatantly anti-French; the daily al-Nida' ("The Call"), published during 1932–1935 by Taqi al-Din al-Sulh and his brothers Kazim and 'Imad; the daily al-Masa' ("Evening"), published by 'Arif al-Ghurayyib and Ahmad al-Saba' from 1934–1939; and Muhyi al-Din al-Nusuli's popular daily *Bayrut*, which was launched in the capital in 1936 to air Muslim views under the motto "Arabism above all" and lasted until the late 1950s. Alongside these private initiatives were newspapers sponsored by the diverse political groups that emerged during the interwar period, including Pierre Jumayyil's Maronite Phalanges (*kata'ib*), organized in 1936, whose weekly *al-'Amal* ("Action") was launched two years later; the Saviors (*najada*) Party, a Muslim group, which published *al-Hadaf* ("The Goal") from 1942; and the Lebanese Communist Party, whose semi-clandestine *al-Insaniyya* ("Humanity") in 1924 was the first in a long series of ephemeral bulletins under various titles (the last of these, *Sawt al-Sha'b*, or "Voice of the People," was begun in 1937 and was somewhat longer lasting). Not all that was published was rigorously austere: Lebanon, like Egypt since an earlier time, produced satirical journals whose messages were no less biting than those of their more sober counterparts. Notable among these were the weekly *al-Dabbur* ("The Wasp"), founded by Yusuf Mukarzal in 1923, and Sa'id Furayha's weekly *al-Sayyad* ("The Hunter"), established in 1943, both of which lasted for decades.[40]

The Lebanese press, weakened by fragmentation, had to contend, in addition, with control by the state authorities — both the mandatory power and the local government — aimed at curbing journalistic expression. The restrictive press law of May 1924 introduced in Syria applied in Lebanon as well, and the mandatory authorities employed the same tactics in enforcing it everywhere. The Beirut newspapers, normally containing more information and generally better edited than their Damascus and Aleppo counterparts, were read in Syria and throughout the region and participated actively in the controversies over France's position there too. Accordingly, they were punished by the high commissioner in Lebanon for obstructing the mandatory efforts not only in Lebanon but in Syria as well.[41] Yet the French found their task in Lebanon far easier than in the other territories they controlled: The intense intra- and inter-factional wrangling facilitated the enlistment of local political loyalists, journalists, and others who were prepared to support their rule, with or without bribes. Moreover, the introduction of a constitution into Lebanon in 1926 and the beginning of parliamentary activity fomented additional factional turmoil, leaving less antagonistic energy to devote to the French. The authorities could afford to absorb the relatively minor challenge posed by the Lebanese press, and thus refrained from interfering with it excessively.

Developments during the early 1930s, especially the suspension of the constitution in 1932 and the subsequent formation of Bishara al-Khuri's anti-French bloc, generated increased tension between the French authorities and large segments of the local political leadership. Press criticism became more aggressive than previously, eliciting warn-

ings and occasional suspensions. Simultaneously, newspapers representing political and personal opposition to the local government challenged it, while the government, for its part, sought to silence them.
This conflict was more intense from the very start than that between
the press and the French. As debate on the future of the new national
entity grew excited and the press more outspoken, the politicians in
power reacted more harshly toward their critics, while the French could
afford to show more lenience. "Distribute official positions justly!" Muhyi al-Din al-Nusuli admonished the newly formed government early
in 1937. "Note that . . . the people are shaking off the dust of idleness
and apathy, concerning themselves with national affairs more than in
the past, getting organized, and demanding their rights." Al-Nusuli's
militant daily *Bayrut* was just resuming publication following a period
of suspension imposed on it by the government.[42] "Suspensions are
more and more the work of the local government," France notified the
League of Nations in a 1927 report. This trend continued, so that
by 1937 the high commissioner made do with suspending merely five
Lebanese papers that year, as against 16 that were shut down by the
president of the Lebanese Republic.[43]

Lebanese journalists, however, also concerned themselves with
matters other than intercommunal grievances and political battles:
Business and commercial interests were often deemed equally, or more,
important. Advertisements for consumer goods—the space allocated to
them constantly increasing—were as typical of the interwar Lebanese
newspapers as were news reportage and political essays.

The press thus mirrored Lebanon's unique spirit, that of a small
community with a highly volatile social and political fabric, threatened
by mightier forces, but also possessing enough ingenuity to exploit
whatever advantages its vulnerable situation entailed, and thrive. Its
problematic makeup and adverse political circumstances notwithstanding, Lebanon would continue to prosper for several more decades after
World War II, with its press once again attaining a leading position in
Arab journalism.

Iraq

Iraq's postwar press was characterized by personal and political confrontation played out before a largely apathetic audience. Once viewed
as located "at the farthest end of God's land,"[44] Iraq had acquired some
economic and strategic status prior to the war and became increasingly
important in these respects thereafter. Upon the formation of the new
state after World War I, traditional personal rivalries were translated
into national politics. Political leaders in Baghdad, Basra, and Najaf
devoted most of their energies during the postwar period to trying to
end British control. Once formal independence was attained in 1930,
they directed much of their activity inward against the government

(when they were out of power), against rapidly proliferating rival groups, and against personal adversaries, thereby preparing the ground for the intervention of the army in politics in 1936. Newspapers played only a minor role in these embroilments and had marginal impact, although they were utilized as vehicles for articulating viewpoints to the few who could, and cared to, read them.

The period between the end of World War I and the appointment of Faysal I as king of Iraq some three years later was tumultuous. British troops, in control of Basra since the outset of the war, occupied Baghdad in March 1917 and the rest of the country by November 1918. In some seven or eight of the places they occupied they issued newspapers in Arabic to announce and explain their presence, a practice they would continue to follow.[45] The League of Nations decision in April 1920 to accord Britain a mandate over Iraq ignited a revolt in the country's central and southern regions during July–October of that year, fanned by mosque sermons that induced violent attacks against British troops. The rebels viewed the propaganda printed by the British as a key to their power and were anxious to counter it by comparable means. "We are grieved by the absence of national newspapers in the country and the indifference of writers in these fateful days," declared *al-Istiqlal*, a new paper begun in Najaf in October 1920 that pledged "to respond to the occupiers' deception, to disquiet them, to reveal their barbaric misdeeds."[46] A similar message was expressed by *al-Furat* ("Euphrates"), launched in Najaf in June 1920, and by *al-Istiqlal* of Baghdad three months later. Once the revolt was quelled, the immediate questions of the kind of regime the country should adopt — republican or monarchical, and, if the latter, who would be king — prompted a spate of new publications (three of them within one week in June 1921) that engaged in heated exchanges over these issues.[47] The British, however, resolved the matter without much heed to these views, and in August 1921 Faysal I, ousted from Syria, became Iraq's first modern king.

Iraqi politics under the monarchy, and the evolution of the press as a reflection of it, was marked by a progression of sudden and often violent shifts, illustrating what Elie Kedourie has depicted as "a wretched political architecture and constitutional jerry-building of the flimsiest and most dangerous kind."[48] Until 1930, opposition to the existence of the British mandate and to British interference in the country's affairs constituted a unifying cause among diverse forces that would agree on nothing else. British officials were the target of these repeated attacks launched personally by Iraqi politicians, in speeches in the constituent assembly, and in most of the press. Some 20 new newspapers emerged during the 1920s, poorly executed four-page products bearing rousing names that contrasted sadly with their unimpressive quality and short life-span. Some were organs of the tiny parties that sprang up with the foundation of the monarchy, bickering among themselves and with those in power. Two papers, however, were of

somewhat better quality and lasted longer: the Baghdad *al-Istiqlal*, begun in September 1920 by ʿAbd al-Ghafur al-Badri, owner and editor
of several other newspapers; and the six-page daily *al-Bilad* ("The Country"), founded in October 1929 in the capital by Rafaʾil Batti, a Christian lawyer and "beyond all comparison the ablest newspaper man in
Iraq," according to one knowledgeable source.[49] A small number of
journals undoubtedly financed by the mandatory power voiced pro-
British positions, supporting the various versions of treaties proposed
by Britain to the antagonistic nationalists. Most conspicuous among
these was Razzuq Daʾud Ghanim's *al-ʿIraq*, published from June 1920
until the end of the decade.

With the conclusion of the Anglo-Iraqi treaty of June 1930, Iraq
became formally independent, although an extensive British military
presence remained, and Iraq's politicians shifted their attention to other
issues. Like the Syrian pattern, and perhaps to an even greater extent,
Iraqi politics were based on personal, family, and tribal loyalties. Hastily created political parties that disbanded just as quickly, and even
parliament itself, were forums of secondary consequence, for it was
clan alliances that were of primary importance, whether forged in or
out of parliament or the parties. The group of older-generation politicians who made up the ruling establishment and formed the rapidly
changing cabinets, and who normally found it expedient to cooperate
with the palace and with London, faced a heterogenous array of forces
strongly resentful of the government, of the Hashemite monarch, and
of the British presence. Old-style plotting involving local Shiʿite religious leaders, tribal chiefs, and the military proved infinitely more
effective than the modern modes of political activity, including elections
and the press. Newspapers remained secondary instruments, although
they had become fashionable enough to motivate most political groupings to acquire one of their own. The fate of these publications was
determined by the fluctuations of the political kaleidoscope, and they
usually existed only as long as the coalition of politicians that produced
them.

Perhaps the most stable extra-parliamentary grouping during the
1920s was the Nationalist Party (*al-hizb al-watani*), founded in August
1922 under Jaʿfar Abu al-Timman's leadership. Its views were articulated by *al-Istiqlal* of Baghdad during the decade of the 1920s, but in
September 1930 the party launched its own daily, *Sada al-Istiqlal* ("Echo
of Independence"). This organ was soon suppressed by the government, but the party replaced it with a succession of journals under
different titles, each of them quickly banned in turn. An opposition
faction existed inside parliament as well, the People's Party (*hizb al-
shaʿb*), which contested the British presence. Established in July 1925
under Yasin al-Hashimi, it published a newspaper that bore the party's
name. By the end of the decade, however, Hashimi had formed a
different alliance with several other politicians (Rashid ʿAli al-Kaylani,

Hikmat Sulayman, Naji Suwaydi, and ʿAli Jawdat al-Ayyubi) to begin
the Nationalist Fraternal Party (*hizb al-ikhaʾ al-watani*). This group
sponsored Batti's *al-Bilad* and, when that newspaper was suspended,
established a series of other journals with different names under the
same editor. Other politicians within the ruling establishment who
formed "parties" of supporters, as was fashionable, likewise thought it
useful to be represented in the press. Notable among these was the
Progressive Party (*hizb al-taqaddum*), which in June 1925 grouped
around ʿAbd al-Muhsin al-Saʿdun, then prime minister, initially relying
on papers published by supportive individuals—*al-ʿIraq*, *al-ʿAlam al-
ʿArabi*, and *al-Liwaʾ*. In October 1928 it launched its own organ under
the party's name, *al-Taqaddum*, but seven months later the party disinte-
grated and its paper expired. One of its former members, Nuri al-Saʿid,
who served his first term as prime minister starting in 1930, also organized a party, the Commitment (*al-ʿahd*), in order to muster support for
his policies in parliament and for the treaty with Britain that he was
about to sign. This reverse procedure—creating a party after having
attained the premiership or some other governmental position—had by
then become customary in Iraqi politics. Saʿid backed the move by
publishing a paper, *Sada al-ʿAhd*, like its counterparts a disposable
means for a short-term end. Another group that merits mention, although it did not call itself a party, was formed in late 1931 by a few
younger politicians under Husayn Jamil and ʿAbd al-Qadir Ismaʿil, and
came to be known as the *Ahali* ("People") group, based on the name of
its newspaper which appeared in January 1932. This was a coalition of
left- and right-wing oppositionists who allied themselves with a group
of dissatisfied army officers headed by General Bakr Sidqi. In October
1936 Sidqi staged the first of many military *coups d'état* Baghdad was to
witness. As the resort to military force plainly showed, communicating
the group's ideology to the public through the medium of the press was
of little practical import. By the time the coup had taken place, all of
the parties formed previously had dissolved, and new parties were not
to appear until after World War II.[50]

Relations between the press and the government in Iraq followed
a pattern that was familiar elsewhere in the region. The rigid Ottoman
Press Law remained in effect until as late as 1931—repealing it was
hardly an urgent matter—when it was replaced by a new Publications
Law with similar provisions.[51] The government suspended and banned
any critical press as a matter of course, and the newspapers just as
routinely resorted to standard maneuvers for bypassing these obstacles,
most commonly frequent changes of name. As elsewhere, Iraqi journalism evolved as a craft of confrontation and controversy: "The press,
when sincerely fighting for God and the homeland, is the best weapon
the people can use," asserted the editor of *al-Istiqlal*, expressing a common view.[52] Incentives to engage in any other kind of journalism were
limited, for nonpolitical journals met with meager success. Accord-

ingly, reportage was of secondary importance and was marked by ama-
teurishness, while technical standards were, on the whole, equally poor.
One conspicuous exception to this rule was the daily *al-Zaman* ("Time"),
established in May 1937 by Tawfiq al-Sam'ani, a Christian. *Al-Zaman*
presented balanced news reports, gaining popular respect and even a
circulation abroad. A reliable survey in 1950 found *al-Zaman* "just about
the only Arabic paper in Iraq which was generally agreed to be a
completely honest newspaper."[53] There were also a few satirical journals, notably Nuri Thabit's *Habazbuz*, as well as several modest literary
and professional magazines.[54] But the main thrust was political, with
the inevitable result that the Iraqi press hardly fared any better than
Iraqi politics of the time, which were arguably the most brutal and
chaotic in the region.

In many ways the lot of the Iraqi press was among the worst in the
Middle East. Not only was the political background unfriendly but,
moreover, the Iraqi public was among the poorest and least educated.
As late as 1947 only 11 percent of all Iraqis above the age of five could
read.[55] If at mid-century demand for newspapers in Syria was half that
of Egypt, in Baghdad, according to the same survey, the figures were
half those of Damascus—an estimated 5 copies for each 100 inhabitants, as against 10 in Damascus and 20 in Cairo. Thus, only a tiny
fraction of the Iraqi public was exposed to the press.[56] But the size of
the audience mattered little to the publishers. Judging from the assumption of transience underlying the publication of Iraqi papers, and
the newspapers' intrinsic vulnerability to swift political change, it seems
obvious that the advancement of professional standards, let alone ethics
and a regard for public expectations, were marginal considerations for
most papers. The educated class that was interested in quality reportage and debate had to content itself with the small handful of good local
papers and, just as often, with imports from Egypt and Lebanon.

Palestine

The case of Arab Palestine was unique in several ways even within the
checkered political scene of the Middle East during the interwar period.
Vigorous Zionist settlement, which threatened to compromise the
country's Arab character, posed a major challenge that had an overwhelming effect on every facet of the Palestinian Arab community. It
preoccupied the Palestinian Arabs in addition to, and beyond, the more
familiar problems of the struggle for independence and the search for
communal identity. Unlike the public in some of the neighboring
states, the Palestinians had no opportunity to gain experience with
representative political institutions: There was no constitution, no local
body with legislative or executive authority, no parliamentary elections. The rivalry between Arabs and Jews, as well as within the Arab
community itself, effectively thwarted the formation of such institu-

tions. The British, who held the League of Nations (and later United Nations) mandate for Palestine from 1920 to 1948 were the true masters of the land, safeguarding their strategic interests while allowing — or not preventing — the emergence of a Jewish political entity in the midst of the Arab population.

For the country's small Arab community — some 650,000 in 1922, about 1.3 million in 1945 — the mandatory period was one of intensive political flux. The issues at stake, imbued with fateful implications, called for an urgent response. The Palestinians, however, confronted this challenge with a tradition of polarizing rivalries among the notable families and a rift between Muslims and the small but better-educated Christian community. This meant a diffusion of the community's efforts among several fronts rather than a focus on attaining common goals. Palestine's Arabs combated the British occupiers and the growing Jewish presence while simultaneously quarreling with each other over control of municipal councils and influence in the countryside, with the press playing a lively role in this dynamic picture.

Even before World War I, rage over the Zionist intrusion prompted and nourished the publication of newspapers in Palestine. Arab press activity was halted by the Ottomans throughout most of the war. But once hostilities came to an end, the old opposition to Jewish settlement, now coupled with resentment against British occupation, spurred the reemergence of an energetic press. First to appear was the Jerusalem semiweekly *Suriya al-Janubiyya* ("Southern Syria," alluding to the concept that Palestine was part of Syria), which was published in June 1919 by two political activists, Hasan al-Budayri and 'Arif al-'Arif. Various difficulties compelled them to close down the paper within less than a year. More important was the reopening of two of the leading prewar journals upon their owners' return from exile: Najib Nassar's *al-Karmil*, which reappeared in Haifa in January 1920, and *Filastin*, which 'Isa al-'Isa revived in Jaffa in March 1921. ('Isa's cousin and former partner, Yusuf, remained in Damascus where he published the daily *Alif Ba'* for the next three decades.) By the early 1930s, 'Isa and several other ambitious colleagues would make Jaffa the uncontested capital of Palestinian Arab journalism.

In the 1920s, however, there was no definable press center in Palestine. Some 20 papers were established in Jerusalem, most importantly *Mir'at al-Sharq* ("Mirror of the East"), which Bulus Shihada, a Christian, founded in September 1919, and *al-Jami'a al-'Arabiyya* ("Arab Union"), the organ of the Supreme Muslim Council, which appeared in December 1927, edited by Munif al-Husayni. Some five or six papers were founded in Jaffa in the 1920s, in addition to *Filastin*, notably *al-Sirat al-Mustaqim* ("The True Path"), launched by the outspoken religious Shaykh 'Abdallah al-Qalqili in September 1925, and *Sawt al-Haqq* ("The Voice of Truth"), another Islamic organ, begun by Fahmi al-Husayni in October 1927 and relocating in Gaza the following year.

Additional papers appeared elsewhere: approximately a dozen in Haifa, with *al-Karmil* the most prominent, in Tulkarm, and in Bethlehem. It was a variegated press scene, mirroring a multipolar polity. Most papers appeared twice or three times a week; dailies were to emerge only during the following decade.[57]

The 1920s were formative years for the Palestinian Arab national movement, during which standards of political activity as well as patterns of press involvement took shape. Opposition to Zionism—to the very idea of a Jewish "national home" in Palestine, Jewish settlement, immigration, and acquisition of land—was from the start a matter of broad consensus (with a few marginal exceptions).[58] The gravity of the Zionist menace and the need to confront it forcefully was a central theme in political discourse and in the press. "Danger" (*khatar*) was a recurrent term, reflecting a sense of communal harassment. "We are facing a threat which in itself is rather simple, yet it is of the utmost severity," stated a typical editorial in the first issue of a Jerusalem paper in 1920:

> We say "simple," for [the Zionist drive] is based on a false foundation. It is vain and futile. If we meet it from a just and truthful position, truth will surely prevail over falsehood. We state earnestly: If we desist from facing [the peril] and defending our rights . . . deceit will triumph. By this formidable danger we mean the Zionist threat.[59]

Much indignation was also directed toward the British, who were perceived not only as depriving the country of its independence but, worse yet, permitting the growth of an alien entity in it according to the principles of the Balfour Declaration. "In the era of freedom and enlightenment, as all peoples and nations are arising and recovering their lost freedom and independence, the English inflicted upon us the Balfour Declaration—the offspring of oppression and stepchild of tyranny," charged another paper. "Let us make it plainly clear to the High Commissioner that opening the gates wide to the Jewish vagrants and the Bolsheviks of Europe only increases [our] nation's agony and ire."[60]

The reiteration of these themes in most journals lent the Palestinian press of the time an appearance of unity, further enhanced by recurrent appeals for communal solidarity. But despite this apparent unanimity, the press was rent by conflict reflecting the division of the community into two political camps during the early 1920s: supporters of the Arab Executive and the Supreme Muslim Council, who were known as *majlisiyyin* ("[supporters of the] council") under the leadership of the mufti of Jerusalem Hajj Amin al-Husayni; and their rivals, led by Raghib al-Nashashibi and other members of his family, the *mu'aridin* ("opponents"). This division split the Palestinian community along family lines locked in bitter confrontation, which included pitting their respective papers against each other. *Al-Jami'a al-'Arabiyya* served as the chief mouthpiece for the former camp during the 1920s, while the opposition expressed itself mainly through *Mir'at al-Sharq* and, somewhat later, *Filastin*. That both of the latter papers were owned by Christians was not coincidental: Many Christians were driven into the opposition out of concern over the growing Islamic tone of the national movement under the mufti's leadership. Several other Christian papers, among them *al-Karmil*, joined this camp later on.[61] Yet the line separating the political camps, as well as their printed organs, was not necessarily religious. Islamic papers such as *al-Sirat al-Mustaqim* and *al-Quds al-Sharif* backed the opposition, a result of close relations between their owners and the Nashashibis. The struggle would become more acrimonious and violent in the following decade, but it already consumed much of the community's energy and that of its press in the 1920s.

Palestinian society's response to the impassioned messages of its journalists was, at that early stage, lukewarm if not indifferent. As elsewhere where newspapers were a novelty and the educational infrastructure undeveloped, newspaper-reading in Palestine was still a limited pursuit. Owners complained of the paucity of readers: "Another 50 years will elapse before the press becomes a profitable trade in Palestine," one editor predicted pessimistically. The journalist, meanwhile, would have to toil "not for himself but for others, like a candle which slowly expires while illuminating its surroundings."[62] Palestinian papers typically sold 1,000 to 1,500 copies per issue each during the 1920s. *Filastin*, the most popular newspaper, had a circulation of some 3,000 copies per issue in 1929, while the total circulation per issue of the leading papers that year was assessed at 12,700. Compared with Lebanon, a similar-sized community, where circulation amounted to 68,000 copies in 1930, the Palestinian press was in a rather pitiful state.[63] But this is an unfair comparison, given Lebanon's longer journalistic tradition. More significantly, newspaper consumption in Palestine was on the ascent: Between 1914 and 1929, the country's Arab population grew by some 50 percent, while total press circulation was estimated to have increased by at least 150 percent,[64] a trend that would continue to accelerate in the 1930s.

The attitude of the British authorities, the temporary masters of the land, to the vociferous and often-hostile Palestinian press was benign. During the early years of the mandate, the British realistically assessed the public impact of newspapers to be minimal. With the political atmosphere relatively calm, they left the press to its internecine squabbles as the publishers pleased. They also saw no need for new legislation regarding printing and publishing and retained the old Ottoman Press Law until 1933. Consequently, Palestinian journalists enjoyed more freedom of expression during the 1920s than their colleagues in some of the other states in the region where the foreigners in charge were more rigid and local governments more sensitive to criticism. There is no denying, one editor acknowledged in 1926, that "the

[British mandatory] government has one advantage which puts it above the other neighboring governments, namely, that it allows full freedom of speech and writing."[65] This too was to change in the following decade.

The dramatic events of the summer of 1929 marked a turning point in the modern political history of Palestine, ushering in a stormy period of violent encounter between Arabs and Jews, between the Arabs and the British, and between rivals within the Arab community. From the early 1930s, the potential for political activity was broadened by the emergence of Palestinian political parties. Encounters on all three fronts reached a peak in April 1936 with the eruption of the Palestinian revolt, which continued intermittently until early 1939. Deeply involved in these battles, the press adopted an increasingly aggressive stance and was often punished for it.

A mark of change in press activity was the appearance of daily newspapers following the 1929 crisis. The Jaffa-based *Filastin* became a daily in September of that year, as did *al-Jami'a al-'Arabiyya* in Jerusalem and a number of other newspapers shortly thereafter.[66] From the early 1930s onward, there were at least three Arabic dailies in Palestine at any given time, though many of them were short-lived. The most important newspapers launched during this decade were *al-Difa'* ("Defense"), founded in Jaffa in 1934 as an organ of the Istiqlal Party (which split from the *majlisiyyin* coalition in 1932), edited by Ibrahim al-Shiniti; and *al-Jami'a al-Islamiyya* ("Islamic Union"), also published in Jaffa by Shaykh Sulayman al-Taji al-Faruqi from 1932 to 1937. Daily newspapers responded to the public demand for news and opinion bred both by the intensity of current events and by the rapid expansion of education, which spurred an increase in press consumption throughout the decade. Jaffa emerged as the country's press center and was the base of the two leading dailies — *Filastin* and *al-Difa'* — until the end of the mandate. The latter newspaper was the more popular of the two, its daily circulation assessed at 3,500 copies in 1935, a year after it was established, as against 2,000 for *Filastin*. By 1946, *al-Difa'* sold 6,000 to 10,000 copies daily, compared with *Filastin's* 3,000 to 4,000.[67] One reason for *al-Difa's* greater attraction was that it was edited by a Muslim, unlike its competitor. Muslims, rather than Christians, had gradually come to set the tone in the community's battles. The relatively wide popularity of the Christian-owned *Filastin* was, in fact, a peculiarity in the changing reality. Far more typical was the decline of the Christian-owned, Haifa-based *al-Karmil*, which exhausted its public appeal and was forced to close in 1942.

If communal struggle was the focus of the press in the 1920s, it was all the more so after 1929. The consensual opposition to Zionism deepened during the 1930s, as did Arab anger with the British as protectors of the Jewish entity (though on this there was somewhat less of a consensus). With the Palestine problem becoming an all-Arab issue, Palestinian papers embarked on an animated dialogue with the press and readership of the other Arab states. Shared enmities continued to produce routine appeals for unity, domestic as well as pan-Arab. Yet beyond these nationalistic slogans, Palestinian papers carried on tenacious intramural quarrels. None of the papers (save those of the communists) functioned strictly as a party mouthpiece but, rather, oscillated in their support for individuals and political groupings (whose own positions were seldom consistent) according to economic and familial considerations.[68] This conduct evoked the familiar specter of newspapers backing the same objectives while attacking each other bitterly. "What a pity," one journalist lamented, "our newspapers in Palestine are like a woman who is afraid of her husband's other wife, hence she harbors for her nothing but rancor, malice, and ill will."[69]

The contribution of the press to the mounting agitation prompted the mandatory government to react by issuing a new Publications Law in January 1933, formalizing the government's authority to deny or withdraw publication permits, suspend and close down papers, and punish journalists. The law was amended several times during the decade, and twice, in 1936 and 1939, emergency regulations were introduced by the British limiting press freedom still further. Enforcing legal measures maximally to restrain the press, the government issued no fewer than 20 suspension orders against newspapers in 1937 — more than in any other Arab state that year — and 14 such orders in 1938. In the same vein, the authorities frequently prevented the entry of newspapers from neighboring countries into Palestine, especially during the latter half of the decade.[70] If Palestinian newspapermen had enjoyed the authorities' benign disregard during the 1920s, the more bellicose journalists in the 1930s suffered harassment much as their colleagues under the French mandate did. With the outbreak of World War II and the enforcement of emergency laws, the British ordered the closure of all but three papers — *Filastin*, *al-Difa'*, and *al-Sirat al-Mustaqim* — which they retained as channels for conveying closely censored news and commentary.

Professionally, the Palestinian press in the interwar period was not a particularly impressive medium. Newspapers invested the better part of their efforts in dispute over domestic issues and in economic survival rather than in journalistic self-improvement. Perseverance was a goal unto itself, the quality of editorial opinion and reportage a secondary priority. Many, perhaps most, of the newspapers in the 1920s, and several in the 1930s, utilized publications from other countries and even local Arab and Jewish papers as a main source of news, plagiarizing at will. With the appearance of dailies, however, the press gradually shifted to relying on news agencies, on reporters based throughout the country and sometimes even abroad, and on a new convenient source — radio, which transmitted from Cairo from 1934, and from Jerusalem (the government "Palestine Broadcasting Service") from 1936.[71] In terms of technical standards, the Palestinian press resembled the weaker output of Syria and Lebanon, and, like them, was unable to reach the level of the more experienced and wealthier Egyptian press, which operated under less restrictive conditions (and which, in Palestine as elsewhere, constituted competition for the local press). Yet, if "feeble and destitute" in comparison to the Egyptian press, as one Jewish journalist in Palestine recalled, "we nevertheless felt the pulse of life in each and every section of it, from the editorial article to the simple reporting of news."[72]

The Journalistic Periphery:
Transjordan and the Arabian Peninsula

Remote from the region's main urban centers and from the impact of Western culture, sparsely populated Transjordan and Arabia remained marginal to the development of the Arabic press until World War II, when the press in these areas began to catch up with the rest of the region. Until then, political, social, and cultural conditions relegated it to a rudimentary state.

Across the Jordan River from Palestine, a new political entity was forged in March 1921 by British interests and Hashemite aspirations in a land that had never before been a separate political unit. The small Transjordanian emirate had a population of about 300,000 when it was established (and about 400,000 by the end of World War II), half of it nomadic or seminomadic; Amman, which would become its capital, was a tiny town of no more than 2,500 inhabitants. No newspapers had existed in Transjordan before 1920, and although the country's small urban population may have been aware of the existence of Arabic and other papers elsewhere, it is unlikely that they had been exposed to them more than marginally. For the next 25 years, under an imported prince and the close supervision of a foreign British "resident," Transjordan would gradually take shape as a state and would expose itself to many innovations, among them the press.

Amir 'Abdallah, son of the Hejazi Sharif Husayn, provided the new country not only with its first royal house but also with its first newspaper. Like his father, 'Abdallah was aware of the importance of political propaganda, especially under such fateful circumstances as prevailed after the war. While still in Ma'an on his way north to avenge his brother Faysal's defeat at Maysalun, he issued a primitive handwritten sheet entitled al-Haqq Ya'lu ("Truth Shall Prevail") to disseminate his views on the crisis. Five issues apparently came out, four in Ma'an during the winter of 1920 and the fifth in Amman, which 'Abdallah entered in March 1921.[73] Two years of press silence followed before the next paper appeared—an official government organ, al-Sharq al-'Arabi ("The Arab East"), which published official notices along with some local and international news for about three years. From June 1926 it limited itself to state announcements only, its name appropriately altered to *al-Jarida al-Rasmiyya* ("The Official Gazette").

The emirate's small capital witnessed the publication of its first private paper in 1927, *al-Urdunn* ("The Jordan"), in 1927 a news weekly that had been transferred to Amman by Khalil Nasr, a Christian from Haifa who had started it there in 1923. *Al-Urdunn* proved remarkably durable, becoming a daily in 1949 and lasting well into the second half of the century. Three other weeklies that also appeared in Amman in 1927 — *Jazirat al-'Arab* ("The Arab Peninsula"), *Sada al-'Arab* ("Arab Echo"), and *al-Shari'a* ("The Holy Law") — did not fare as well and expired within a year. Only six or seven other periodicals were launched during this period, of which two proved more enduring: Subhi Zayid al-Kaylani's news weekly *al-Wafa'* ("Loyalty"), published between 1938 and 1947; and Taysir Zabyan's political and cultural daily (later weekly) *al-Jazira al-'Arabiyya*, which relocated from Damascus to Amman in 1939 and lasted until the mid-1950s. An attempted cultural and scientific journal, *al-Hikma* ("Wisdom"), survived for ten months (July 1932 to April 1933), and a military bulletin entitled *al-Jaysh al-'Arabi* ("The Arab Army)" lasted from 1940 to 1949.

The new state was small and poor, its population overwhelmingly uneducated: only about 1 percent of the population attended schools in 1921, about 2.5 percent in 1939, and by mid-century the illiteracy rate was still estimated at about 85 percent.[74] The few existing papers probably had circulation figures measurable in the hundreds; as late as 1950–1951, the two dailies published in Amman were thought to be selling only 1,500 copies apiece.[75] With such limited sales, and with minimal advertising and marketing activity, sustaining a paper in Transjordan must have been all but impossible. There were also political obstacles, for the government monitored the papers closely. When found to be too independent for the taste of the patriarchal monarch, newspapers were punished by suspension according to the Ottoman Publications Law, which remained in effect, with minor changes, until as late as 1953.[76] From the viewpoint of the British authorities, the incipient Transjordanian press was as yet too insignificant to be of concern, while the institution of political parties, elsewhere a source of vigorous press activity, was still in the future for that country. Politically timid, technically poor, featuring rudimentary essays on such topics as world geography and "The Arabs' Contribution to World Civilization,"[77] Transjordanian newspapers during the second quarter of the twentieth century were reminiscent of the Lebanese and Egyptian press half a century earlier.

At the time 'Abdallah issued Transjordan's first periodical in Ma'an in 1920, the Hejaz under his father's reign had had over a decade of experience with journalism, including the regular publication of an ambitious weekly newspaper in Mecca, Sharif Husayn's *al-Qibla*. A product of British wartime propaganda effort, however, this paper was designed from the start primarily for foreign consumption. With an economic and cultural milieu akin to Transjordan's, the Hejaz itself as well as the rest of the Arabian Peninsula had a very limited potential readership for a newspaper at that stage. Sharif Husayn continued to publish his weekly organ in Mecca until the onslaught of the advancing Saudis forced him to close it down in September 1924. For a while thereafter he supported another paper, *Barid al-Hijaz* ("Hejaz Mail"), published from November 1924 in Jidda, then still under Hashemite control. A year later, however, that paper disappeared as well with the downfall of the Hashemite kingdom.[78]

Two months after occupying Mecca, in December 1924, the Saudis launched their own official weekly organ, *Umm al-Qura* ("Mother of Towns," an epithet for Mecca). It appeared simultaneously with its Hashemite opposite number for about a year, until the latter vanished. *Umm al-Qura* continued to appear well into the second half of the twentieth century, gradually abandoning its official character and dealing with cultural and literary matters as well. Two more newspapers were published under the Saudis until World War II: *Sawt al-Hijaz* ("Voice of the Hejaz"), a weekly (later semiweekly) forum for cultural debate among the educated elite that appeared in Mecca in April 1932; and the semiweekly (later daily) *al-Madina al-Munawwara* ("Shining Medina"), which appeared in Medina in April 1937. Like *Umm al-Qura*, both continued into the second half of the century. Three cultural-religious periodicals also appeared during this period, of which only one, the monthly *al-Manhal* ("Water Spring," Medina, from 1937), lasted through World War II and beyond.[79] On the whole, it was "an idealistic press," assessed 'Ali Hafiz, one of the founders of *al-Madina al-Munawwara*—a press "that asked for goodness, not destruction, a press that called for unification, not separation, a press that served Islam and truth, a press for the faithful."[80] Given the country's technological and educational backwardness, however, such good intentions were hardly sufficient to advance these incipient journalistic efforts beyond the most elementary stage. By mid-century, according to a reasonable assessment, only 7,500 copies of daily newspapers circulated in the kingdom, a meager rate of 1 to 2 copies per 1,000 inhabitants.[81]

In Yemen, at the peninsula's southwestern flank, the Zaydi Imam Yahya, having gained independence following the collapse of the Ottomans, at first felt no need for printed communication and continued for a while to use traditional channels to address his subjects. In 1926, however, inspired by foreign examples, the paternalistic ruler launched an official monthly organ, *al-Iman* ("The Faith"), designed for domestic consumption. Yahya must have deemed it a useful means of control and a success, for in 1930 he turned it into a daily and increased the print run from the original 800 copies per issue to 1,500. Another journal, a political and literary monthly entitled *al-Hikma al-Yamaniyya* ("Wisdom of the Yemen") appeared in San'a in January 1939 at the initiative of an official in the Ministry of Education. Published in the ministry's press and supervised by the government, it was shut down about two years later for expressing views that differed from the imam's.[82] Kuwait briefly had a privately owned literary journal, *Majallat al-Kuwayt* ("Kuwait Magazine"), published from 1928 to 1930, while in Bahrain, a private political and literary weekly, *al-Bahrayn*, had a slightly longer life-span, from 1939 to 1944.[83] In these places, as in Saudi Arabia, primitive imported equipment was utilized to produce embryonic sheets that circulated locally among a tiny minority of educated males and probably had a negligible impact.

'Ali Hafiz, who together with his brother 'Uthman founded the Saudi newspaper *al-Madina al-Munawwara* in 1937, shed light on the circumstances into which the press in these peripheral regions was born at that stage:

> There weren't any presses in Saudi Arabia at the time, and we knew we should have to bring one from Egypt. So, first we asked His Majesty the late King Abdul Aziz for permission to start a newspaper and to bring a press into the Kingdom. After His Majesty approved our request, my brother Osman traveled to Egypt to find the press needed. He left with the few dollars we had and I stayed in Medina, trying to obtain the rest of the financing we would need. That included selling the family jewelry and borrowing money from my father and two friends. Then we had to bring the press from the port to the city of Medina and, of course, there were no paved roads in Saudi Arabia at that time. But we got the press to Medina and with the help of Osman, who had been trained in Egypt to work the old flatbed press, and Sharif Afendi, the engineer for the Harem al-Sharif mosque, we put it together and started printing.[84]

The End of an Era

The impact of World War II on the Arab countries of the Middle East was not nearly as traumatic as that of the previous world war. Only limited parts of the region, mainly in Syria and Iraq, were directly affected by actual fighting, and even then rather briefly. The effects on the press were, accordingly, less severe as well. Nevertheless, a crisis did occur. War brought economic hardship and a shortage of supplies because of difficulties in transport. Arab countries under the control of European powers or tied to them by treaties experienced economic pressure by mid-1940 following the fall of France in Europe, and even more so in the spring of 1941 when the Allies were on the defensive on the various fronts. For the press, once again, this meant shortage and rationing of newsprint and the necessity to streamline. In Egypt, *al-Ahram* — which in World War I had cut back from 8 pages to 6, 4, and eventually 2, and which by the eve of World War II had expanded to 20 pages — announced a cut to 12 pages when the war broke out, but material hardship and government decrees forced it to cut back further, to 8 to 10 pages in July 1940, 6 in October, and 4 in April 1942. The weekly *Ruz al-Yusuf* cut back from over 60 pages before the war to 36 in 1940, 28 in 1941, and 20 in 1942. In Syria and Lebanon, the French authorities in May 1940 ordered all papers to cut their size by half. Some papers ventured to use low-quality wrapping paper as newsprint, but this initiative was curbed by a high commissioner's order limiting the use of that material as well. Economic exigencies resulted in the shrinking of local commercial and advertising activity, leading the papers to raise their prices, but the French inhibited that move too by setting limits on newspaper prices. The smaller and weaker papers were the first to suffer, and most of them disappeared for the duration of the war. Those that survived used all their ingenuity to balance news with advertising within the limits of their few pages and to maximize technical and editorial efficiency. Another sort of resourcefulness was reflected in illicit trafficking in surplus newsprint, a widespread practice in other commodities as well.[85]

Another aspect of wartime adversity was experienced in the political realm — censorship. Upon the outbreak of the war, rigid censorship rules were imposed everywhere in the Middle East, requiring prior approval for all copy. Such measures were considered essential by Britain and France because of the antagonistic popular mood of many Arabs, the result of two decades of foreign domination and national strife. Even prior to the war there were unconcealed, and sometimes rather organized, displays of sympathy with Germany and Italy fostered by well-orchestrated German and Italian propaganda efforts; during the war, various Arab personalities and groups maintained active ties with the Axis states. Such feelings were implicitly or overtly echoed by the press, sometimes "rather encouraged than restrained by the Prime Minister," as one observer in Iraq noted.[86] Local governments, undergoing frequent changes in composition during the war, struggled with the dilemma of Allied pressures, on the one hand, and the Anglophobia and Francophobia felt by large segments of the public, on the other. In Egypt and Iraq, both formally independent, the press was freer to maneuver and to express opinions; while in Syria and Lebanon, where the French imposed stricter rules, especially prior to the arrival of the Free French troops in the summer of 1941, the press was more restricted. The British, the French, and the local governments all used punishments and rewards through the selective supply of newsprint, official advertisements, and subsidies more relentlessly than in peacetime. The French also confiscated radio receivers from the public in Syria and Lebanon in an effort to prevent exposure to Axis propaganda and arrested several outspoken journalists, including Najib al-Rayyis of *al-Qabas* and Ahmad Qanbar of *al-Nadhir*, whom they detained in a camp in south Lebanon. They also launched a political and cultural monthly, *Dimashq*, in January 1940, which supported their policies.[87] These measures, generally quite effective, had an even more corrupting effect on the press than in peacetime. Yet, even though the war period was a difficult one for the Arabic press, the result was not the profound paralysis of World War I, when the press had been less mature and had been subjected to far more formidable pressures. Courage and sophistication acquired through years of encounters with both local and foreign governments helped it sustain debate on political issues and air opposition views.

Once the war was over, the press resumed its former momentum relatively quickly. It was more experienced, enjoyed broader popular recognition than after the previous war, and had a significant record of professional achievement in reportage, editing, linguistic style, and technological proficiency. After nearly a century in which much of its vitality was spent on establishing itself as a legitimate, vital institution, the Arab press was on the verge of a new era. Many of the old obstacles seemed to have been removed. Shortly, complete national independence would be attained throughout the region and the road would be open to professional self-improvement and growth. The Arab press at that point, Tom McFadden has suggested, was reminiscent of its American counterpart after the American Revolution, which was likewise dominated by "the numerous, tiny enterprise, highly partisan, political party press." This situation contained great promise, for as the American experience had shown, the road winding through that stage could lead to a significant raising of standards. "It can be predicted confidently that similar developments will occur in Arab journalism," McFadden stated in 1953. "This day appears to be approaching on the Arab scene."[88]

II

ASPECTS OF DEVELOPMENT

5

Press, State, and the Question of Freedom

"I'm told that . . . provided I do not write about the government, or about religion, or politics, or ethics, or people in power or with influence, or the Opera, or other theatres, or about anybody connected with something, I can print whatever I choose under the supervision of two or three censors," said the Barber of Seville, mocking the situation in eighteenth-century Madrid. Arab writers in the nineteenth and twentieth centuries often made similar observations about the state of affairs in their own countries. Their complaints, like Figaro's, were sometimes overly gloomy but never too far from the mark. Beaumarchais' hero, "lured" by circumstances, launched a newspaper which he named "The Useless Journal," but before long he saw "a thousand poor devils of hacks" rise against him, and his paper was suspended.[1] In this, too, the experience of the Arab press offered many analogical examples, strikingly similar in detail.

The concept of government prevalent in the Middle East on the eve of modern times, sanctioned by age-old tradition and Islamic law, posited a division between rulers and ruled. The ruler was expected to govern effectively, and it was desirable that he be just; the ruled were required to obey him, regardless of the quality of his justice. The basic principle underlying this concept was that effective government was essential for the stability and proper functioning of the community, and obedience was vital in assuring such effectiveness. This principle predominated over every other, to the extent that obedience was regarded by rulers and ruled alike as much more than a political obligation; it was seen as a religious duty. This, of course, did not mean that the principle was always followed: Revolt and rebellion recurred in the history of Islam as often as in any other society. Nevertheless, obedience and respect for authority remained broadly revered principles of the community's political life until the second half of the nineteenth century. According to this system, expressing a view on state or public matters was an official function reserved for the ruler, his aides, and the leading 'ulama', a group of religious sages with spiritual authority whom rulers sought to keep under their control. The rest of the subjects remained outside the circle of state and politics, nor were they expected to take an active interest in such matters, explore them, or seek intelligence.

It is easy to see why journalistic initiative was inconsistent with such precepts and could sometimes be diametrically opposed to them. The appearance of newspapers in Arab countries posed a threat to the old principles and was bound to involve conflict with government, whose power rested largely upon these traditional and popular beliefs. The conflict of the press with authoritarian regimes was not unique to the Middle East, of course — it marked much of the history of journalism in the West as well. Yet, as we shall see, the press in the Middle East was forced to fight harder for its freedom, and against more difficult odds, than its counterparts in Europe and America. How this struggle was viewed by the state whose authority was thus challenged by the press, and how it was seen by journalists — who were also part of a community that traditionally would not consider questioning the authority of its rulers — will be discussed below.

State and Press: The Stick and the Carrot

The first contact that Middle Eastern rulers had with the press was as readers of European newspapers. The Ottomans became aware of this Western innovation around 1780 at the latest, and shortly thereafter set up a special bureau at the office of the grand vezir in which European papers were regularly received and translated. In Egypt, Muhammad 'Ali, who was impressed with the French publishing policy during the occupation of that country, made it a habit to acquire European newspapers and study them personally. Both governments subsequently decided to adopt this vehicle for the benefit of their own states. The first issue of *Taqvim-i Veqayi*, the official Ottoman journal which was begun in July 1831 under Sultan Mahmud, defined the concept that underlay this enterprise succinctly. The paper, it stated, represented a natural extension of the role of the *vakanüvis*, the traditional imperial historiographer. Just as the government had hitherto attended to the recording of events in their "true nature" and had published that record periodically for the public good, so it was doing now by another means for similar ends. No real novelty was seen in this project, which simply signified the implementation of an old practice through a different mechanism, better suited to the needs of the time. Similarly, the adoption of this tool in Egypt was in no way viewed as a departure by the government from its traditional tasks or its relations with its subjects.

If there was nothing problematic about introducing the publishing of periodicals into the government apparatus in Istanbul and Cairo, putting the newspapers into the hands of subjects was another matter. A century earlier this would have been inconceivable, let alone permissible. But in the nineteenth century the region's leaders, resolved to face new international perils with the help of imported tools, were forced to tolerate this and many other novelties as part and parcel of the strategy of modernization. At first the new practice seemed harmless, easily controllable and hence ignorable. But the rulers soon found themselves involved in an irritating battle against the press. Papers began by issuing benign accounts of events at home and abroad along with seemingly innocent discussions of cultural questions, yet these reports also conveyed new concepts and ideas. Journalists described situations where freedom of expression was a popular right and where their counterparts could openly air views about the government and even criticize it. Their positive impressions of these realities augured something dangerous that might infiltrate through this channel—a menace that the authoritarian rulers felt obliged to check.

The governments in the region encountered the phenomenon of freely published opinion from a position of strength. However shaken they may have been by confrontations with powerful foreign forces, their authority at home was still firm, perhaps even firmer than before since it was fortified by modern means to which they had easier access than their subjects. They could set the rules, punish and reward, permit or prohibit publishing at will. When exposure to Western culture generated a demand for newspapers, they responded by introducing restrictive legislation and by setting up an apparatus to enforce it, which became increasingly rigid as the medium grew more dangerous. Muzzling and suppression was one aspect of the response. Another was manipulation and co-option through selective subsidization.

The earliest legislation affecting the press came soon after the feeble beginnings of Turkish and Arabic publishing, and before the appearance of the first important private paper. The Ottoman "Law of Printing and Publications" of January 1857 required anyone wishing to start a press to obtain permission from two separate authorities: the Council of Education and, notably, the Ministry of Police. It also obliged those who were granted a license to submit all texts intended for publication to the same council for prepublication approval. A Penal Code enacted the following year fixed punishments of closure and fines for printing unapproved matter or any material "harmful to the sultanate, its government, and its subject peoples."[2] If the 1857 law and the ensuing code did not specifically mention journals, which at that stage were of little import, they revealed the empire's cautious approach to permitting the introduction of private printing, immunizing itself against potential harm. The local potentates in the largely autonomous Ottoman province of Egypt took similar precautions: An individual's request, in 1858, for a license to establish a press in Cairo's Khan al-Khalili quarter would be granted on condition that he submit all material intended for publications for prior inspection by a special council at the Ministry of the Interior. A similar rule applied to anyone wishing to publish journals (*jaranil*), gazettes (*ghazitat*), and notices, the council announced, while pledging to prevent the production of "books and messages offensive to the faith, politics, cultural values, and ethics."[3] Licensing, prepublication censorship, and prescribed punishments — a set of preventive measures — would become the cornerstone of government control of printed self-expression by individual subjects.

The first law dealing expressly with the press, the Ottoman "Law of Journalistic Publications" of February 1865, reiterated these principles and prescribed additional penalties for offenders. Typically, it fixed a punishment of six months to three years imprisonment and a fine of 25 to 150 golden pounds for offending the sultan or members of his family, a useful shield to protect the ruling house.[4] The law remained in effect throughout the empire until the Young Turk revolution. Later ordinances provided for an elaborate mechanism of censorship under the supervision of provincial censors (*mektupcu* or *maktubji*). With the expansion of the press, a control system developed involving a daily routine of reluctant collaboration between newspapers and censors.[5] The government, however, had no illusions that this mechanism alone would contain the possible damage caused by publishing. In March 1867 it announced its intent to act against deviating newspapers "as often as the interests of the country required it, through administrative channels and independent of the existing press law."[6] This step, too, portended the future attitude of governments in the region toward the press: Laws were important in regulating the conduct of the press, but if proven insufficient, other means were readily available to the authorities.

Mild legal measures, however, seemed quite adequate during the early years of the press. The first journalists were intuitively cautious and adhered to a policy of self-censorship. If they reported about political matters, they were careful to follow a line that was in harmony with that of the government. The government, for its part, found it easy to show tolerance. The Lebanese *Hadiqat al-Akhbar*, for example, was allowed to print a serialized report in 1858 on the trial of the Italian nationalist Felice Orsini, who had made an attempt on the lives of Emperor Napoleon III and Empress Eugenie. Later, describing similar events, or any rebellious act abroad, would become impossible for papers published in the empire. Even at that stage, under the relatively tolerant Sultan 'Abd al-'Aziz, reportage was prudent: The series on Orsini, published several months after the event, left out sensitive details and condemned the assault explicitly.[7] The authorities did not

need to resort to drastic measures to control journalists until the late
1870s. Only three cases of suspensions of newspapers are known to
have taken place under 'Abd al-'Aziz (1861–1876), and only two private
papers in Egypt were closed by Isma'il (1863–1879) who, if apprehen-
sive of the phenomenon, was somewhat uncertain as to how to handle
it. In both places the government displayed a certain hesitation in
licensing new papers but did not bar them. Yet, while direct confrontation between press and state was still far off at that early stage, viewed
retrospectively the press and the ruling power were on a collision course
from the moment the press was born, despite society's traditional compliance.

The encounter between government and press turned into an open
conflict during the second half of the 1870s. The beginning of this
process may be specifically pinpointed to 1878–1880, when both Istanbul and Cairo were in crisis. Sultan 'Abd al-Hamid, humiliated in the
recent war against Russia, was determined to preserve what was left of
the empire's independence with an iron hand. He dissolved parliament
in 1878, suspended the constitution, and imposed stringent restrictions
on self-expression of any kind. In his view, the menace was real, reflected in the dangerous power exerted both by the Young Ottomans,
the group of outspoken intellectuals who were partly responsible for his
own accession to power, and by the more aggressive delegates in the
first Ottoman parliament (1877–1878). For 'Abd al-Hamid, printed
materials, often the product of foreign inspiration and backing, were a
source of endless trouble — a conviction congruent with the traditional
rejection of popular interference in public matters. The sultan instituted a control system whose *ad absurdum* rigidity would become legend-
ary. Motivated by deep-seated suspicion, he used all the power of his
autocratic regime to castrate journals, and every other type of publication, with remarkable success. 'Abd al-Hamid would have been happier
without any press at all, but his state's international position, with the
growing involvement of the European powers in the empire and their
protection of sizable numbers of his subjects, apparently made such an
option unrealistic. It was politically undesirable to eliminate the press
entirely, nor was it possible to insulate the empire fully from the pene-
tration of alien publications (which arrived through the foreign postal
services that had concessions to operate in the empire). It was, however, possible to render the press impotent, a situation that prevailed
for 30 years.

Contemporary sources, texts from the post-Hamidian period, and
later memoirs vividly present a peculiar, almost incredible, portrait of
Hamidian censorship. Typical of the system were the famous lists of
forbidden topics and words, which grew ever longer with the passage
of time. Forbidden items included references to the murder of heads of
state anywhere (lest this inspire readers adversely); terms denoting
dangerous ideas such as revolt, revolution, freedom, independence,

constitution, and republic; terminology connected with risky devices such as dynamite; and using the sultan's titles and honorifics to describe someone else. The rules for what was permissible or prohibited were seldom consistent, and interpretation depended largely on the understanding, or ignorance, of the censors. This resulted in endless ridiculous situations. To quote an example, a private advertisement in a Lebanese journal concerning the rental of "the property (*mulk*) of Muhammad al-Tarabulsi" was altered by the censor, who disqualified the word *mulk* since it also meant "royalty," and only the sultan was deserving of that description. But in unvoweled script the word could also be read as *malik* (king). The overzealous official, therefore, replaced it by *imbaratur*—emperor, a title applying to foreign monarchs and hence permissible—so that the rephrased notice read: "the house of the *imbaratur* Muhammad al-Tarabulsi is up for rent."[8] Such absurd stories abound in the sources, and while they are sometimes patently exaggerated, they reflect the spirit of the time, which was inhospitable to journalists. Writers were guided by elusive rules that frequently left them not knowing what to expect. "What was difficult about [this] censorship," Muhammad Kurd 'Ali later recorded in his memoirs, "was its being based on no principle, no firm or known rule. You could write a piece assuming it would not please the censor, but he would approve it; or you could write another, in your view unblemished, and it would be deleted. There was no guideline in censorship, save for the censor's taste and whim."[9]

Censorship was not the only means of control. A tedious licensing procedure was designed to deter would-be owners of journals. Jurji Hananya of Jerusalem, for example, obtained a permit to publish *al-Quds* in 1908 only "after having paid a *baqshish* of 200 napoleons to the Porte and having waited for seven years."[10] Rashid Rida, who applied for a license to start a journal in Tripoli, prior to his emigration to Egypt, was another victim. Rida completed the necessary application procedure with the local authorities and, having been notified of his eligibility for a license, paid the required security, whereupon his application was forwarded to the vali of Beirut for approval. The vali, however, delayed the matter protractedly before announcing his decision: The request was denied, "for there already exists one newspaper in Tripoli, and if a second one were to be established the burden on the censor would be too heavy."[11] An incident recorded by the Lebanese writer Ramiz Khalil Sarkis sheds light on other aspects of the atmosphere during the period. His grandfather, the journalist Khalil Sarkis (founder of *Lisan al-Hal*), was summoned by the vali of Beirut, who expressed interest in the state of his press. The vali asked Sarkis if it was true that he had recently imported a large paper cutter. When Sarkis confirmed this information, the vali notified him of his intention to use the new device as a guillotine for beheading a convicted criminal. Sarkis' resourcefulness eventually prevented the utilization of his equipment for such a gruesome end.[12] In other instances, however, journalists themselves were the victims of violent punishments by the authorities. One of the most common penalties for offenders of every kind was the bastinado—flogging the soles of the feet—known as *falaqa* (after the device used to hold the legs during the beating). Journalists were often subject to this treatment at the censor's order, as, for example, was Khalil Sarkis himself, who was flogged thus in his own home.[13]

If the guidelines did not seem obvious to Muhammad Kurd 'Ali, they were clear enough in 'Abd al-Hamid's mind. Notwithstanding the excesses of his measures and the capricious image of his censorship— no doubt a result both of his peculiar idiosyncracies and poor performance by some of his officials—the sultan was consistent in what he wanted and, more to the point, in what he did not want. In this his thought was perhaps clearer than those of other rulers in the region: He did not want any of the troubles and risks inherent in the new ideas that printed materials conveyed, and he believed that it was both desirable and possible to emasculate the press. "The number of newspapers which stand on the side of truth and justice is indeed meager," he observed, referring to the European press but revealing his view of the medium in general, "and since obtaining true and precise intelligence from behind the scenes is difficult, [papers] rely on the market of lies where they find what they seek."[14] As pressures grew, the sultan's orders became more repressive, but this was only a change in degree, not in his basic approach, which remained consistent. In his attitude 'Abd al-Hamid upheld a traditional principle seldom contested in his society, while displaying the survival instinct of an autocrat. The majority of his successors would profess the same attitude.

The view of the press from 'Abdin palace in Cairo resembled the view from Yildiz palace on the Bosphorus in the late 1870s. Interested in fostering a supportive press, Khedive Isma'il had set up a special office in his Foreign Ministry to supervise both foreign and domestic papers in the mid-1860s.[15] After some early misgivings, he was prepared to tolerate nonhostile journals, such as *al-Ahram*, that explicitly pledged to deal with neutral topics only. But toward the end of his reign, the press grew increasingly critical and the khedive became irritated. Despite his policy of accelerated modernization, the opening of his country to the West, and the formation of a deliberative forum of representatives, he saw himself as a supreme ruler of the traditional type. Such gestures as he made to his subjects were his exclusive privilege and, as far as he was concerned, revocable at any time. When his critics—Ishaq, Sanu', Nadim, and their colleagues—became outspoken, he warned them that they should "accommodate their conduct to the place and time,"[16] then began punishing them by suspension, closure, and exile. Although Isma'il is known to have been considerably more open-minded than 'Abd al-Hamid, his tolerance did not extend so far as to permit public censure by his subjects. Such disobedience was no more acceptable to the khedive than to the sultan and had to be suppressed. That the fate of the Egyptian press was not similar to that of its Ottoman counterpart under 'Abd al-Hamid was due only to the country's weakness in the face of external pressures, the protection offered to many local journalists by foreign states, and domestic power struggles on the eve of British occupation.

The ancestral concept of governmental supremacy and immunity to criticism was upheld not only by the region's hereditary rulers but also by the aristocratic sociopolitical elite, known as the *khassa* (or *khawwas*), which continued to produce many of the leaders of the twentieth century as well. An incident that occurred in Mount Lebanon in 1864 will suffice to illustrate the prevalence of this view. A complaint by Yusuf Karam, a local popular Maronite leader, against the vali of Beirut for misconduct and poor performance was published in *al-Jawa'ib* that year. When the government in Istanbul demanded an explanation from the vali, he appealed to the Council of Delegates (*al-majlis al-niyabi*) of Mount Lebanon, consisting of local notables, for their backing. The *majlis* summarized its position in a letter, also published in *al-Jawa'ib*, that expressed the traditional view of government succinctly: In printing Karam's complaint, the *majlis* charged, the editor of *al-Jawa'ib* had "deliberately engaged in commentary which no one of his status is entitled to do (*ma la yahiqqu li-mithlihi*), which is [the prerogative of] the sublime [Ottoman] state alone. He thus indirectly compromised the well-being of our subjects." The *majlis* then demanded that both Karam and the editor be prosecuted. In the event, the case did not reach the court, because of intervention by the British and French ambassadors, and was eventually forgotten.[17] But the letter by the notables is illuminating. The dignitaries of Mount Lebanon would have had little problem in supporting the vali in the face of published criticism by one of his subordinates; they themselves would accept criticism from "no one of [the editor's] status." This view was shared as well by the Turco-Circassian elite in Egypt, whose members formed the September 1881 cabinet. Exposed to attacks by the press upon assuming power, they hastened to issue the first Egyptian press law, establishing rules that were even stricter than those imposed by the 1865 Ottoman law, which had been in effect in Egypt until then. The new law included a confirmation of the government's right to suspend and close down newspapers without prior warning.[18]

Twentieth-century rulers and members of the political elite in the region retained a profound belief in these authoritarian principles. Muhammad Mahmud, Egypt's prime minister in 1928–1929, was a prominent example of an exponent of these values. A landowner and dignitary, he despised members of the lower classes whom the constitution and recent laws allowed to enter state politics. As soon as he came to power he suspended the constitution, announced his intention to treat his opponents "with an iron hand," and issued a warning to journalists — "the critics who are ignorant about events" — that "slander, degradation, deception and . . . doubting the patriotism of the government will not be tolerated under any circumstances. We warn every newspaper against them. Any paper engaging in such acts will be banned conclusively."[19] Mahmud's successor, Isma'il Sidqi (premier from 1930 to 1933), similarly believed that "the press is a force capable of building as well as destroying, but its destructive capacity is greater than its constructive power, especially in a community that is still immature." Sidqi, an industrial baron and, like Mahmud, an aristocrat known for his autocratic style, replaced the suspended constitution by a markedly more conservative one. He charged that the press in his time, although "free of any shackles," wrongfully interfered with his efforts to provide Egypt with a more efficient government "devoid of past vices."[20] Jamil Mardam, Syria's prime minister between 1936 and 1939, voiced a similar view: "One of the Syrian government's greatest wishes," he stated in 1937, "is for the press in this country to enjoy the greatest measure of freedom, so it can fulfill its noble role of enlightening the public, guiding it, and articulating its hopes and desires." Such freedom, however, could not be allowed if papers abused it to "discredit the nation's honor" and, more tellingly, to "defile the sacredness of the state (*hirmat al-dawla*)."[21] Syria's prime minister in the 1940s and 1950s, Khalid al-'Azm, retained the same perception. Although he had nothing but praise for the courageous struggle that Syrian journalists had waged against the French, 'Azm, an old-style notable, viewed the attitude of the press toward his own and his colleagues' governments differently. "Poisonous articles were published, revealing their authors' evil intentions under a veil of patriotism," he asserted in his memoirs, a practice that undermined the government's authority and abused its image. Is it any wonder, 'Azm ruminated bitterly, "that the people lost confidence in their leaders and commanders and regarded them as leading the community to hell?"[22] For Mahmud, Sidqi, Mardam, and 'Azm, the act of questioning their patriotism, the "sacredness of the state," or the devotion of the state to the good of the community by ordinary subjects was no more tolerable than it had been for 'Abd al-Hamid and Isma'il the previous century.

Were the leaders who expressed such displeasure with the press unduly repressive? Were they unduly critical of a press earnestly engaged in legitimate political debate? Undoubtedly, the performance of many newspapers left more than something to be desired and gave the authorities ample cause for complaint. Yet it seems quite clear that many of the region's leaders, both in the nineteenth and the twentieth centuries, were irritated not only by the conduct of the press but by its very existence as well. Freedom of expression, a novel concept and a newly coined phrase in Arabic, was part of an alien system, and, as other components of that system, incurred opposition, particularly by those whose status and power depended on the perpetuation of the old rules.

The old, uncomplicated order based on a division between rulers and the ruled was giving way to a more complex scheme. The political scene in Egypt during the late nineteenth century, and elsewhere in the region during the twentieth, became more pluralistic, and rulers were confronted with demands for freedom inspired and protected by foreign interests. These demands intensified after World War I as the Arab provinces of the empire became states with governments and political structures of their own. Wholesale repression along the old lines gradually ceased to be the obvious option in dealing with the press. The situation called for a more sophisticated approach, one consonant, or appearing to be consonant, with the new principles to which Middle Eastern leaders had committed their society. These included, most conspicuously, manipulation of the press through legislation and economic control.

Where local rulers were forced to share governmental authority with foreign powers, the foreigners not only dictated and supervised the conduct of politics, they also served as an example for handling the press. There were certain differences between the British and the French approach in this area, the French being more deeply involved in the domestic arena than the British. But of greater significance was the gap between the attitude of both the British and the French governments toward the press in their own countries and their treatment of it in territories under their control overseas. Abroad, one observer has suggested, they were the embodiment of "a monarch with an absolute authority—even if only in the last resort of veto—long since discarded at home."[23] British and French colonial interests dictated that certain administrative considerations take priority over such principles as freedom of expression. Moreover, their experience led many of the foreign administrators to believe that such principles, far from universal, were perhaps not applicable to the societies under their tutelage. Accordingly, they introduced restrictive press regulations and penalized certain journals and writers while rewarding others, demonstrating to local leaders that a strong hand, bribes, and manipulation of the press were acceptable and even desirable. Foreign office records in London, Paris, and the capitals of other foreign states involved in the region contain ample evidence of the systematic manipulation of indigenous newspapers. A letter of 1921 from Gertrude Bell, secretary to Sir Percy Cox, the British high commissioner in Iraq in the early 1920s, sheds light on this policy:

> I am now turning very serious attention to the press, a job I hate, but it is necessary. I have arranged with the editor of the moderate paper (it's called *Iraq*) to come in and see me two or three times a week so that I

> may give him news and supply him with ideas. He is a good little man
> but not very brilliant — it's a pity that the rank and file of angels can never
> contrive to cut so striking a figure as Lucifer![24]

But the press policy of the British, the French, or the other foreign
powers is of limited relevance to our discussion. Local rulers, while
certainly reassured by the foreign example, proceeded according to
their own dictates, and it is primarily with these that we are concerned
here.

The constitutional and legal status of the press in the Arab countries during the post-World War I period vacillated endlessly. Laws
were pliant and open to varied interpretations, and their life-span was
strikingly short. Regulations invariably included an option for the government to bypass them and resort to whatever steps it saw fit to ensure
public order and its own survival. The Egyptian constitution of 1923,
the first constitution of an independent state in the region after the fall
of the Ottomans, illustrates this state of affairs well. Article 14 stated
that "freedom of opinion is guaranteed. Any person may express his
views in speech or writing or drawing or otherwise." The next article
referred specifically to the press, stating that it was free (*hurra*): "Censorship of the press is prohibited. Issuing warnings to papers, suspending
them, or banning them by administrative measures are likewise prohibited." However, there was a limitation on this freedom, explicitly prescribed in the document: Freedom of the press was allowed only "within
the limits of the law," and administrative measures against the press
were permitted "when needed for the protection of social order (*al-nizam
al-ijtimaʿi*)."[25] These limitations in effect stripped the constitutional
guarantee of free expression of practical meaning. The subordination
of freedom of speech to the somewhat nebulous principle of "social
order," with the palace and the government as guardians of that order,
perpetuated the age-old political game. Similarly, since the constitution
did not specifically abolish the harsh press law of 1881, the phrase
"within the limits of the law" could be interpreted as a reference to the
law of 1881. "*Cette liberté d'opinion certes ne serait qu'illusion, qu'un principe
vain*," a contemporary Egyptian student of law soberly observed.[26]

Events following the promulgation of the constitution revealed the
intent behind the phrase "social order." It was commonly interpreted as
the community's traditional sociopolitical structure, to wit, one in which
the final say in public matters was in the hands of whoever was in
power. All other views were of limited or no consequence and were best
unexpressed. While the new rules did give journals certain benefits as
compared to the situation in the past — by requiring the authorities to
deal with criticism through legal channels, and giving newspapers the
opportunity to argue, and even win, in court — such new options were
far less potent than the autocratic license retained by the government.

"I rushed to our press building," recalled Fatima al-Yusuf, owner

of the popular weekly *Ruz al-Yusuf*, after a police raid on her paper in
1928, "and saw the chief of the 'Abdin police, officers of the political
police (*al-bulis al-siyasi*), and two British constables rip up copies [just
published] of the journal." For the daring lady journalist this was the
first incident of its kind, one that was "odd and incomprehensible: how
can the government prevent a paper from expressing its view? I was
infuriated in the extreme."[27] For Premier Muhammad Mahmud, however, the incomprehensible and infuriating aspect of the affair was the
paper's audacity to attack him, in articles and cartoons, depicting him
as ruthlessly trampling on the law. What seemed inconceivable to Fatima al-Yusuf had become a government habit, not a new strategy but
rather a modern version of an old one. Nothing was easier than punishing papers that made undesirable noises by invoking the constitutional
article authorizing the state to defend social order. "There is no doubt,"
Prime Minister Isma'il Sidqi stated characteristically in 1930, while
banning three pro-Wafd newspapers, "that the assertions on public
affairs made by demagogues are shaking the foundations of social order, causing its structure to crack and stirring up anarchy in the country." The government, as the guardian of social order, decided in this
case to suspend the papers indefinitely.[28] The frailty of the rules dealing
with the status of the press was also reflected in frequent alterations by
the series of politicians who took turns heading the government in quick
succession during the period of the monarchy. In 1928 the constitution
itself was suspended, allowing Prime Minister Mahmud to cancel the
licenses of more than 60 papers by the end of the year without any legal
procedure. The document that replaced the suspended constitution two
years later, known as the 1930 constitution, was a set of stiff rules
tailored to suit the autocratic political convictions of Isma'il Sidqi, Mahmud's successor. Sidqi also issued a new press law in June 1931 that
prescribed the subordination of newspapers and other publications to
strict government control in no uncertain terms. Typically, this law
extended the scope of offenses, hitherto confined to verbal criticism, to
include "drawings, paintings, photographs, emblems, and other means
of representation." It also facilitated the massive punishment of newspapers and journalists, marking Sidqi's tenure in office as one of the
darkest chapters in the history of the Egyptian press.[29]

With the press identified for the most part with political parties or
groupings, and with party leaders alternating frequently in government
office, newspapers consistently paid the price of suspension, closure or
fines when the leader they opposed came to power. Their fate depended
on the shilly-shallying of cabinet formation—no less than 44 cabinets
were formed during the 29 years of Egypt's monarchy—with the premiers applying, adjusting, or ignoring the rules according to their own
interests. The royal house, however, a remnant of the Ottoman period,
had a more absolute hold on power than that of the cabinets and was

above party contest. Its regal status was hardly affected by press criticism, as the constitution and country's laws provided it with a shield against published assaults, with heavy penalties meted out to anyone who offended members of the royal family, let alone the king himself. The case of the cartoonist 'Abd al-Mun'im Rakha, who in the 1930s dared portray the king humorously in caricatures and was punished with four years imprisonment, was a striking illustration of these rules.[30]

The Egyptian scene was mirrored, with variations, elsewhere in the region. Nuri al-Sa'id's government in Iraq replaced the old Ottoman publication law in 1931 with one that was more rigid on many points: It prohibited any criticism of state officials and permitted the government to take administrative measures against overly vocal journals. An amendment in 1932 restricted the press still further. But the following year, with the rise to power of the anti-Sa'id party under Rashid 'Ali al-Kaylani's premiership, a new publications law was formulated abolishing many of the previous restrictions, although the government's prerogative of employing administrative measures was retained. The tide turned yet again several months later, in 1934, when a new government under Jamil al-Midfa'i revised the law once more and reinstated some of the old restrictions. Such swift fluctuations within a brief span of time were hardly exceptional in the history of press legislation in Iraq,[31] nor did they have much impact on the way governments, regardless of who headed them, dealt with newspapers that were critical of them. As in Egypt, the rapid alternation of cabinets — in Iraq an even more frequent and sometimes more violent process — meant a wave of punishments with each change, with the party in power suppressing the publications of its opponents.

The situation in Syria was similar, replicating the pattern of selective punishment, muzzling, and suppression made possible by a pliable law that could be interpreted according to need. This situation became most conspicuous after the formation of the nationalist government in 1936 following the signing of the draft treaty with France. The government, freer than before to manage domestic affairs, routinely applied administrative means to punish the press. The daily *al-Qabas*, for example, was suspended by Jamil Mardam's government three times within 10 weeks during the summer of 1937, and *al-Ayyam* and *Alif Ba'* were suspended twice. In the course of one week in mid-July, the government suspended all three of them, along with another paper, indefinitely.[32] Syrian leaders, elected under modern ground rules but acting upon traditional premises, consistently took the precaution of neutralizing those who questioned their leadership, and Syrian journalists were subject to professional and personal harassment and even violent attacks. Nassuh Babil described "one of those measures of terror" thus:

A young man knocked on the door of the owner of *al-Ayyam* [i.e., Babil himself]. The maid opened and he said he was looking for Mister Nassuh. I came out to meet him, and as soon as I opened the door he tried to beat me with a stick which he had brought with him. But I was quick to shut the door in his face, so he missed me, and the stick was left caught in the door. He left it behind and turned to flee, whereupon I hurried to chase him, still in my pajamas, eager to find out who that "hero" was. I failed to find him.

An uproar by Babil's colleagues following this incident prompted the government to set up an inquiry committee and to promise to find out who was behind the attempted attack, a reaction, Babil believed, that was merely a camouflage for the government's own involvement in the affair. Unsurprisingly, no one was found.[33] In Syria, as in Iraq and Egypt, most of the leading politicians during the first half of the twentieth century still subscribed to the old concepts, viewing what they considered their sociopolitical inferiors with contempt. They regarded newspapers that backed them as useful (though not altogether indispensable) tools, and those that disagreed with them as nuisances to be dispensed with.

In the more conservative countries of the Arabian Peninsula, at the periphery of the press, the old rules of politics continued to prevail, untainted by foreign-inspired demands for pluralism. In 1928, when 'Abd al-'Aziz Rashid of Kuwait wanted to publish his journal *Majallat al-Kuwait*, he prepared the first issue and sent it to the country's ruling shaykh for review—the only conceivable course of action. The shaykh approved publication, but not without appointing a supervisor (*muraqib*) for the journal. A Press and Publication Law in Saudi Arabia the following year stipulated procedures for licensing and censorship. The law did not specify what items could not be printed and only prohibited very generally the "publication of news that is false or essentially corrupt." In the Saudi kingdom prior to World War II, as in the Ottoman state a century earlier, further elaboration was hardly necessary.[34]

The suppression of outspoken publications was instinctive for the various governments. However, writers capable of expressing themselves with political effect could also be handled in other ways, with benefit to the government. Paying for panegyrics and bribing critics were neither alien nor novel in the region; here, as in other countries, they were centuries old and as natural as the muzzling of undesirable voices by force. Under the changing circumstances, with the proliferation of independently expressed opinion at home, such methods could be particularly useful.

Paying for favorable coverage was useful in dealing with attacks from outside, where financial manipulation was almost the only recourse. Both Khedive Isma'il and Sultan 'Abd al-Hamid were active in this area, regularly allocating resources to gain a sympathetic press abroad. Isma'il financed newspapers in Europe (especially France) and

Istanbul and generously supported various publications in Lebanon, incurring their gratitude. 'Abd al-Hamid followed suit.

> The French press cost us dearly ['Abd al-Hamid related in his memoirs].
> . . . The Greek journalist Nikolaides, who lived in Paris, was receiving
> large sums from us annually to publish his newspaper *Notre Organe*. . . .
> We used to give away medals of honor freely, as if they were ornaments,
> bestowing them upon journalists so as to draw them to our side. Receiv-
> ing our medals, they made our voice heard in all places.[35]

This method was applied not only to the foreign press, but also to papers published abroad in Turkish and Arabic by Ottoman subjects now beyond the government's reach. Such, for example, was the case with Ibrahim al-Muwaylihi, a former aide of Khedive Isma'il who had accompanied the khedive on his way to exile in Italy and later settled in France. A publisher of several papers in Arabic in these two countries, he repeatedly attacked the sultan for poor performance and corruption, thereby incurring his rage. 'Abd al-Hamid applied diplomatic pressure to silence Muwaylihi, with some effect, and eventually succeeded in buying his friendship with handsome subventions, persuading him to move to Istanbul and later even to publish a supportive paper in Egypt (*Misbah al-Sharq*). This practice seems to have continued in later times, although less effectively, for, as 'Abd al-Hamid observed, "after a while thousands of papers appeared on the opposite side" that, with or without subsidies, reported on the Islamic state as they saw fit.[36]

More important was the application of these tactics by the govern-ments of the region in controlling the press at home. The fact that both foreign and local private patrons extended support to journalists made it logical, and even necessary, for the government to engage all the more intensively in this practice and try to win an advantage. More-over, foreign powers with extraterritorial privileges offered newspapers not merely support but also immunity, thus making it difficult for the government to silence them, a further inducement for government investment in financial manipulation. One technique was to buy the talents of accomplished writers and mobilize them to work for govern-ment papers, or turn their publications into pro-government organs. Among many such cases were those of Ahmad Faris al-Shidyaq, whose financial difficulties with *al-Jawa'ib* were exploited by the Ottoman gov-ernment, which rescued the paper and turned it into its semiofficial organ; Khalil al-Khuri, editor of *Hadiqat al-Akhbar*, who was bought off several times during the 1860s and his journal made a government mouthpiece; Muhammad 'Abduh, who wrote extensively for *al-Ahram* and for the papers published by Afghani's disciples (*Misr* and *Mir'at al-Sharq*) and was then made editor of the official Egyptian gazette, *al-Waqa'i' al-Misriyya*; Muhammad Kurd 'Ali, owner and editor of *al-Muqtabas*, who was enlisted by Jemal Pasha during World War I to edit the pro-Ottoman organ *al-Sharq*; and Ibrahim 'Abd al-Qadir al-Mazini, the popular Egyptian essayist who was recruited by King Fu'ad to edit the pro-palace journal *al-Ittihad*. Another variation of this tactic was to launch pro-government publications that, edited by nonofficial individuals, were camouflaged as private ventures. Sultan 'Abd al-'Aziz used this method in 1857 when he induced Iskandar Shalhub to establish *al-Saltana*, as did Sultan 'Abd al-Hamid in 1891 when he set up *al-Nil*, both of which appeared in Egypt to counter the anti-Ottoman position of the Egyptian newspapers. Later, in 1925, supporters of King Fu'ad published *al-Ittihad* for a similar reason.[37]

The most widespread method of influencing the press, however, was through rewards and subsidies. In a way, this was a continuation of an old practice, whereby governments supported men of letters, poets, and artists, who in turn displayed gratitude to their patrons. Although journalism, a new occupation, may have required a shift in tactic, the strategy remained fairly useful and attractive to those in power. One form of reward was medals, a routine procedure as noted by 'Abd al-Hamid himself and as the photographs of many nineteenth- and twentieth-century journalists readily attest.[38] Titles and honorifics were another type of reward, conferred with equal ease. *Al-Ahram*'s editor Bishara Taqla, to cite one example among many, gained the title of pasha, and his son Jubran became Jubran Bey Taqla Pasha—both illustrating a quasi-feudal practice of signifying royal favor. The device was strikingly effective, for, as one journalist noted, people were "blinded by these delusions and would shamelessly humiliate themselves in order to receive a title or a medal."[39]

Above all, however, governments granted money. Ever since the press began, and consistently thereafter, subsidy was apparently the most common way for the authorities to elicit the support and the dependability of the press or, alternatively, to attain silence. Salim Sarkis, nephew of Khalil Sarkis, who in 1896 published the weekly *al-Mushir* in Cairo, described the following instance of such government tactics: An emissary of one of the sultan's advisers came to see him, knowing that Sarkis was "planning to publish, in the following day's issue, a caricature of [the man's master] Abu al-Huda, showing him in a repugnant way (as an octopus)."

> He said: "Withdraw the cartoon and I will pay you forty pounds." I sent my steward to the printer, and after a while he came back with the plate containing the drawing. I gave it to the man, who then paid me forty English pounds and left. So *al-Mushir* was published without a cartoon.

Sarkis did not see anything unusual about this bribe and felt, moreover, that his reaction was fully justified. "This money was earmarked for bribing the press. If I did not take the money, someone else would have."[40] The practice was carried on in the twentieth century by post-Ottoman Arab governments as well. The Syrian journalist Nassuh Babil, for example, claimed to have been approached repeatedly in the late 1920s by high officials acting on behalf of Prime Minister Taj al-Din al-Hasani, who came to him and to his colleagues at the aggressively critical *al-Qabas*, seeking to buy their acquiescence. One day, Babil related, a prominent public figure arrived at his press:

> When he showed up, I welcomed him and invited him to have tea, as a sign of friendship and hospitality. But he excused himself and asked that we get out of the press and away from the workers. We stopped in a place nearby . . . and started our conversation, which revolved around a new [bribe] proposal that the man conveyed to me on behalf of the prime minister. He said: "I beg you not to disappoint me and not to send me back to the premier in shame." I apologized for refusing to accept the proposition.[41]

Such arrangements were usually tacit by nature, and testimonies like Sarkis's and Babil's are scanty and not always reliable. Yet the weight of indirect evidence is so convincing that there can be no doubt that the phenomenon was widespread. Much of this indirect evidence concerns the financial situation of pro-government publications which, as will be shown in a later chapter, would not have been able to hold their own without state support.

Governments often financed the press directly through transfers of money to paper owners or editors on behalf of the palace, the government itself, or a particular minister seeking favorable coverage, with the funds granted either regularly or sporadically, according to need. Financial support could also be indirect, such as through the purchase of a significant number of subscriptions, thereby assuring a newspaper of a steady income, or payment for the publication of official notices. The use of this last method is particularly instructive, for it illustrates many aspects of the relationship between the state and the press. The practice grew out of the government's desire to take advantage of the medium to publicize its official and legal announcements. Initially, the authorities obliged journals to publish notices on their behalf without pay, as was stipulated, for example, in the Ottoman press law of 1865 (and, much later, in the Saudi press law of 1929).[42] After some time, however, rulers became aware of the political potential of this device. In Egypt in the late nineteenth century, and elsewhere after 1908, governments began to publish their notices in private papers for a fee, allowing newspaper owners to enjoy the financial reward and the promotional advantage of being a carrier of state announcements (papers sometimes advertised this fact on the front page, so as to underscore their multiple usefulness).[43] But apart from the benefit of maximum exposure there were also political considerations. Paid official advertisements could be given to friendly journals, inducing dependence on this income; denied to hostile papers, depriving them from of this source of revenue; or transferred from one journal to another. Governments profited thereby from the newspaper industry's endemic poverty, which greatly facilitated state control of the press. An example of the suspension of government advertising as a penalty was the case of *Ruz al-Yusuf* in the 1930s. Apparently the most popular weekly of its time, this journal had enjoyed government advertising for many years, a mutually beneficial arrangement. But following the paper's breach with the Wafd in 1936, the Wafdist government then in power punished it by withdrawing this support, dealing the paper a painful economic blow.[44]

Rich and powerful, and disposed to traditional values no less than to the imported ideas, governments in the Middle East used a variety of means to curb printed criticism. For the Ottoman sultans, the khedives, and kings, whose authority rested both on heredity and popular acceptance, freedom of expression was a necessary evil, a hateful but inseparable part of the process of modernization they had decided to adopt. As they were well aware, it was also a yardstick by which foreign powers assessed their performance as enlightened rulers. It was a tolerable evil, however, since it could be restricted and made largely ineffective, and sometimes even exploited to advantage. For political leaders who rose to power in the twentieth century under a new set of ground rules, freedom of expression was a central component of the modern system that was enshrined in constitutions and laws, and hence it had to be kept alive, at least in appearance. Still, like the hereditary monarchs, they were also irritated by the attacks of critics and likewise attempted to silence them. Perhaps it was inevitable, in that early phase of modern politics in the Middle East, that governments, hereditary or elected, should consistently regard the press as abusing the privilege of free speech that they had reluctantly granted it. During this first, formative century of the Arab press, most leaders in the region still believed that the press had to be contained and disciplined, by stick and carrot, so that political order, now sometimes called the "social order," could be maintained. Most of them did not accept Figaro's conclusion "that printed nonsense is important only in countries where its free circulation is hindered; that without freedom to criticize there can be no flattering praise."[45]

Journalists and Freedom

The newspaper arrived in the Middle East along with other new ideas that together stirred up a social and political storm. But since ancient values were so profoundly rooted in the community, it took the press a while before it became a serious challenger to the existing order. Private journalism began as an enterprise with very modest objectives, seeking not to defy authority but rather to serve it, to collaborate and coexist cordially with it. The demand for freedom of expression, as well as for individual political freedom, a true challenge to the existing order, came only later, and hesitantly at that, and was met by a public response that can best be described as faint.

For the individuals who first ventured to publish journals, dealing with political questions was a delicate and risky matter. Not only were these early journalists aware that the basic rules of society rejected such probing, but they themselves fully subscribed to the traditional belief that politics was the exclusive domain of the state, of *arbab al-dawla* and *ashab al-siyasa*, "masters of the state" and "lords of politics," as society's leaders were popularly known. This precept was shared by the non-Muslim journalists—a large proportion of the early writers—as well. They all felt they could contribute to the community in many ways without encroaching on the absolute prerogative of the ruler to engage in politics (and, preferably, without touching upon equally delicate issues of religion). It was not incidental that Khalil al-Khuri, owner of *Hadiqat al-Akhbar* in Lebanon, defined his paper as a "civilian, educational, commercial, and historical journal"—"civilian" (*madani*) rather than "political." Khuri's compatriot, Luis Sabunji, similarly announced on the cover of *al-Nahla*, in resounding rhyme, that the journal "will steer clear of discussing religion and politics, in deference to the prevalent faith and to the government." He advised his compatriots: "Leave religious matters to the men of guidance and politics to the leaders (*al-siyasa lil-riyasa*), and you will have peace of mind." Sabunji pledged to limit himself to other areas, which he enumerated on the front page, including culture, history, literature, and language. He also listed two potentially sensitive areas, home news (*hawadith wataniyya*) and foreign news (*hawadith ajnabiyya*), but the published items that fell into these categories were as innocent as the rest of the content. The domestic section in the first issue, for example, featured a lengthy report on the battle being waged against locusts in Lebanon with the generous and efficient assistance of the vali, while foreign news, safely adapted from the official *al-Zawra'*, consisted of a curiosity about the marriage of nuns in America. Yusuf al-Shalafun, another fellow countryman and colleague, subscribed to the same values. In his weekly *al-Zahra*, which was designed as a cultural and literary magazine, he pointedly declared that the paper "will absolutely avoid touching upon any religious matter or one pertaining to the state (*dawli*)." This cautious attitude was brought over to Egypt by the Lebanese brothers Salim and Bishara Taqla who, applying for a license for *al-Ahram*, solemnly pledged to limit themselves to "things it is permissible to print" and to "absolutely avoid dealing with political matters (*al-umur al-bulitiqiyya*)."[46]

Such statements of good intent did not in effect mean that writers refrained completely from reporting on state matters at home or abroad. All of the journalists mentioned above, and many others similarly committed, soon found themselves presenting news that had political implications, although they did not feel that such reporting compromised their pledge. Their stated commitment, more than a declaration

of loyalty to the ruler, was a sincere expression of belief in the old
principles: They would report on matters of a political nature if necessary, but without trespassing on the traditional territory of the government. As both writers and rulers were to discover, this approach, however honest in intent, was difficult if not impossible to follow.

A ubiquitous mark of the reverence for government authority was
the widespread habit of starting every text, handwritten or printed,
periodical or otherwise, with high words of praise for the ruler. This
was a time-honored tradition complete with standard formulas of
praise, just as lavishly polite cliches were used in ordinary daily communication.[47] But even if expressed in set formulas, profound respect
for the ruler in power was most often sincere. "Allah created for us the
throne of the House of 'Uthman," Yusuf al-Shalafun stated in the opening note of *al-Zahra*;

> It illuminates our time with the light of its Caliphate, with the rising sun
> of existence and the crown of good fortune, the great Sultan and glorious
> Khaqan, the Sultan son of a Sultan, Sultan 'Abd al-'Aziz Khan, may God
> perpetuate his throne of valor forever. His lofty thoughts and benevolent
> intentions have facilitated progress and success and have expanded the
> scope of learning and prosperity. . . .

And so forth. Shalafun knew the rules. Even if he may not have had
much esteem for the personal virtues of Sultan 'Abd al-'Aziz, he certainly believed in the propriety of showing esteem for authority. He
was also careful to add words of acclaim for the grand vezir, the vali of
Mount Lebanon and the governor of Beirut, before getting down to
explaining the paper's objectives.[48] Such embellished phrases can be
found in virtually every text published in the region in the nineteenth
century, with the sultan, khedive, and lesser men of authority the
objects of effusive exaltation. Often this material was formulated in
rhyme, sometimes as poems (*qasida*), elaborating the ruler's merits and
expressing gratitude for his generous care. At times such praise marked
a special event, most commonly the ruler's birthday or the anniversary
of his enthronement, but it was also offered without any particular
reason. "Every act in [the ruler's] beloved land must begin with words
of adoration for his grace," the editor of the Alexandrian *Lisan al-'Arab*
stated upon launching his paper in 1894. In addition, he produced a
lengthy versed treatise (*manzuma*) in honor of Khedive 'Abbas Hilmi.
The editor of *al-Zahir* in Cairo found it natural to dedicate the paper "to
the sublime throne of kings and princes of the East in general and of
the Muslims in particular." It was equally natural that publications
should bear names such as *al-Nur al-Tawfiqi* ("The Tawfiqian Light") in
Khedive Tawfiq's Egypt, and *al-Nur al-'Abbasi* under his successor, 'Abbas Hilmi. The Egyptian women's journal *Anis al-Jalis* ("The Intimate
Companion") aptly added, along with the standard praise for the sultan
and khedive, expressions of reverence for "his noble mother"—appar-

ently the sultan's.[49] The wording of these expressions, of course, was unimportant, as were the author's true sentiments about the specific ruler he happened to be praising. The significant aspect was the deep respect for governmental authority that these dedications conveyed.

Harboring this regard for authority, the early writers believed that it was possible to engage in journalism, and even write on matters with political content, without upsetting the equilibrium between government and the governed. Moreover, they thought, papers could contribute to the community's *maslaha* — its well-being and prosperity — by improving communications between the people and their leaders and thus actually help reinforce that equilibrium. Political issues could be discussed without departing from the basic conventions of society or calling into question the status or prerogatives of the rulers who were there to guarantee stability. "The foremost obligation of journals," Jurji Zaydan wrote in 1895 in a long article on "Papers, Their Duties and Ethics," is to try to contribute to "the community's *maslaha* and the advancement (*islah*) of its affairs." It was permissible and desirable to criticize the community's behavior, and even the acts of its leaders, but at the same time it was of the essence to retain "respect for the person of the sovereign, who is in charge [of the community] and appointed to protect it. He is the delegate of the Creator, the Great and Magnificent, in handling the affairs of His creatures."[50] Newspapers, the early writers believed, could be useful in fulfilling specific, traditionally important functions. For example, historically, the people had been permitted and even encouraged to bring their grievances and protests against injustice (*mazalim*) before the ruler in order to allow the ruler to govern more justly by providing him with first-hand evidence on the state of his subjects (the decision of how to act upon that evidence was left to his discretion exclusively). Journals could facilitate this process by serving as efficient channels for the people's complaints. Isma'il Abaza, who began publishing *al-Ahali* in Cairo in 1894, defined the paper's objective as "notifying the government of the people's wishes, desires, complaints of misdeeds and grievances (*ragha'ib al-ahali wa-amanihim wa-mazalimihim wa-shakawihim*)."[51] Likewise, Nimr and Sarruf described the goal of *al-Muqattam* as "bringing the hopes and desires of the governed to the government's attention." Both *al-Ahali* and *al-Muqattam* also articulated another, equally familiar objective: serving the government by conveying its message to the people. We wish to convey the word of the rulers, Nimr and Sarruf stated, "and interpret their good intentions" to the ruled, since "we are confident that the country's leader, his highness the great khedive, and the pillars of its edifice, the prime minister, ministers, and all the other officials, are concerned with the country's welfare and aspire to its good."[52]

Such notions were also consistent with the basic view of freedom as a collective attribute, attainable by the individual only as a member of the community. That such a view was prevalent during the formative phase of the press is evident from statements by writers in various places. One example is offered by Sulayman Faydi, an Iraqi journalist and politician who, during the exciting period following the Young Turk revolution, offered definitions of liberty, equality, and fraternity in an effort to enlighten his fellow countrymen. Freedom (*al-hurriyya*), Faydi suggested, meant that every person in the Ottoman kingdom may establish a commercial or industrial company, an office, or a school without interference. But it also meant the "obedience of the entire community (*milla*) to the Sultan's authority, for such obedience is a duty for every Muslim, according to His saying: 'Obey God and obey the Prophet and the men of authority among you.'" Freedom also entailed obligations on the part of the state: "It requires that the government be gentle with its subjects . . . and fully attentive to their complaints and grievances."[53] One need hardly point out that the inspiration for this definition did not come from the anti-despotic ideology of the Young Turks, nor from any other modern or external source.

Fascinated by the prospect of free speech, educated Arabs throughout the nineteenth century simultaneously retained their deep respect for authority—the very authority that had an interest in muzzling this freedom. News reports, political debate, and public criticism, they believed, were desirable only insofar as they did not compromise the government's supremacy. This problematic, ambivalent attitude may have been an obstacle in the path of turning the Arab press into a vigorous and independent enterprise.

Yet, as we have seen, there were journalists who did champion the use of newspapers as weapons in the struggle for individual and political freedom. Writers such as Adib Ishaq, 'Abdallah Nadim, Ya'qub Sanu', and 'Abd al-Rahman al-Kawakibi spoke up loudly, lashing out at what they saw as tyrannical and corrupt government, earning punishment but persisting. Sometimes they waged the battle against their rulers in the pay of those who had their own motives. At other times, however, they did so out of sincere personal conviction, the result of a seminal development: secularization—the embracing of secular political ideas so fully that the traditional reverence for authority was abandoned. If obedience to authority was all but an article of faith in Islamic tradition, secularization held up the struggle for political freedom as a primary virtue. The shift in values was easier for non-Muslims, even though they had hitherto shared their Muslim compatriots' basic cultural mindset. "Let my people know that they have a right that has been plundered, which they should restore, and stolen possessions which they should retrieve,"[54] wrote Adib Ishaq in 1879, expressing the shift in outlook from compliance to liberation. "Some of our newspapers," he charged, "are devoid of the markings of freedom and display a mentality of servility and bondage in their treatment of the 'circles of power.'"[55] In his view, the "mentality of servility and bondage" was a trait of the traditional, essentially religious frame of mind. Choosing the motto

"Liberty, Equality, Fraternity" for his Paris-based paper, Ishaq enthusi-astically absorbed new sources of inspiration and felt no reservations or ambivalence about taking the khedive to task, often in the most blatant terms.

As historical circumstances would have it, the battle for individual freedom in the region was inextricably bound up with the struggle for national independence, namely, for the liberation of the collective. When Jamal al-Din al-Afghani's disciples in Egypt began to publish their outspoken journals in the late 1870s, they were attacking first and foremost the enemies of the community (that is, of Islam, as Afghani saw it)—the Europeans, who were encroaching upon their country unopposed. The culprit in this battle against external foes was the khedive, who failed to halt the enemy's onslaught. For that alone he deserved to be called to order, condemned, and perhaps replaced. But as the battle against foreign adversaries coincided with the beginning of a struggle for a newer cause—the pursuit of political and civic free-dom—the khedive came under fire not only for his ineffective foreign strategy but also for the tyranny of his regime. This confluence of struggles for two distinct causes, which would henceforth preoccupy the political press, often blurred the precise objectives of those engaged in the battles. Clearly, however, the drive for national independence took precedence over the quest for political and individual freedom: Far more energy was devoted by the press to fighting against foreign ene-mies than to combating government oppression at home. 'Ali Yusuf and Mustafa Kamil, Muhammad Farid and Amin al-Rafi'i, Shukri al-'Asali and 'Abd al-Ghani al-'Uraysi, leading nationalist spokesmen of their communities, fought first and foremost to free their society from the domination of others. Later on, this was the case with the Egyptian Wafd as well: Although its various organs bore as a motto Sa'd Zaghlul's slogan "Justice Above Might, the Nation Above the Government," the party saw itself primarily as a standard-bearer in the struggle for national independence rather than for political freedom. Wafd leaders, like their nationalist predecessors, gained prestige chiefly because they articulated the community's desire for liberation from foreign rule. Their simultaneous campaign for individual political free-dom was of secondary import and may have been largely incomprehen-sible to a large portion of the public.

Still, freedom of expression was an important issue for journalists, who advocated it more boldly in the twentieth century than previously. This was so partially because they had acquired more experience in using their medium as a weapon, but also, more importantly, because governmental authority, which had been redefined under new rules, had lost much of its popular standing. Governments headed by an unending procession of alternating politicians could hardly elicit the popular reverence formerly accorded to the hereditary head of the Is-lamic Empire who was also the Prophet's caliph, or to the khedive who reigned on his behalf. The confrontation with the new power-wielders was thus less hampered by the ambivalence that had hindered the struggle against the old ones. Sharp criticism, rebuke, and disparagement of those in charge of the "social order" were an authentic reflection of the erosion in public regard for government. Some of the old reverence for the ruler in power was retained for kings, where they existed, who symbolized a more permanent authority. But presidents, premiers, ministers, and members of the newly formed legislative bodies were regarded as legitimate targets for censure by the public at large. "The Egyptian press . . . will not put up with Nero's tyranny," asserted the veteran journalist Muhammad Tawfiq Diyab, in a typical attack on the country's prime minister.[56] Still, in the twentieth century, as in the nineteenth, this kind of activity was largely overshadowed by wars of national independence, which preoccupied the press.

It is instructive to look at some of the difficulties that the press itself had in meeting the complex challenges of free speech. Freedom of expression, observed Rafiq al-Maqdisi, a Syrian author, was a sharp weapon that could be used either beneficially or destructively. He told the following story to illustrate its destructiveness:

> It happened in 1908, following the restoration of the Ottoman constitution, in the Banyas district of the province of Ladhiqiyya. An angel walking from the town to the country met a villager on his way to Banyas, who asked him:
> "What is new in town?"
> "Freedom has been declared."
> "How come?"
> "Our lord the Sultan has restored the constitution and has imparted freedom."
> Whereupon the villager shouted at the top of his voice: "The world is free then!" and immediately grabbed a stick and started beating the angel, for the world had become free!

"I suspect," the author added, "that some journalists understand the meaning of freedom the way the villager understood it, and shoot with their pens left and right, for the world, in their view, has become free."[57]

Maqdisi was referring, primarily, to the kind of behavior the main mark of which was unrestrained assaults on government, sometimes including rude personal slander, written in a manner that could serve no constructive end but merely reflected the writer's (or his patron's) pent-up frustration. "The rulers of the province of Beirut are all fornicators (*zunah*)," asserted Salim Sarkis in *al-Mushir* in a typical instance of brazen attack on authority.[58] Having moved from Beirut, where he had been repeatedly harassed by the Ottoman censor, to the freedom of Cairo, Sarkis seems to have felt he was no longer bound by restrictive rules of any kind at all. Many others took freedom of expression to mean a blanket license to malign the ruling authorities, deep-rooted social conventions, and basic cultural and moral values, abusing every-thing that was sacred to the community. This phenomenon — for conve-nience we may call it the "beaten angel syndrome" — was hardly unique to the Middle East. It appeared wherever even a limited degree of free speech was first allowed, let alone where self-expression had become unhampered. The tendency toward excess was only to be expected in a society in the process of moving from one value system to another. The new possibility of expressing views freely on any subject, even that which involved the government, and conveying them through a power-ful device such as mass printing, was exciting in itself, the more so after an age-old silence enforced by oppressive governments and social convention. It was even more appealing in a society that attached so much weight to verbal matters.

What was the scope of this phenomenon in the Arab press? The unsatisfactory state of extant press sources (and especially the near-complete disappearance of the weaker newspapers) does not permit a reliable assessment. The poor content and style of the ephemeral papers that have survived — just a few samples of an immense number of such publications, produced by individuals who had never before or after engaged in journalism — would tend to indicate that this kind of abuse was widespread. Even more convincing are the numerous complaints by the more serious writers. Rafiq al-Maqdisi, who wrote in the middle of the twentieth century, was by no means the only one to criticize the practice of "beating the angel": Journalists in Egypt from the late nineteenth century onward, and their colleagues elsewhere in the re-gion from 1908, railed against the phenomenon repeatedly.

In a detailed discussion of the ethics of the Egyptian press in 1895, Jurji Zaydan chided his colleagues for abusing freedom "to such an extent that one yearns for enslavement." Is it proper, he wondered, that the press, which regards itself as monitor of acts of government and advisor to the authorities, be a model of excess, carelessness, slander, and defamation? Journalists, he charged, exploit the freedom bestowed on them to attack the rulers wildly and vilify them personally; denigrate other nations disparagingly, maliciously, and unjustifiably; besmirch individuals and fabricate accusations against them; and worst of all, insult the various religions and sects, which "recalls the darkest days when blood flowed as a river." The situation had reached such a point, he wrote, that some writers terrorize others with threats of murder, challenges to duels, and legal suits. For such people, "freedom is like a sword in the hands of a baby, who flies with it at people's throats, striking blindly." Clearly, Zaydan concluded, "they have exceeded the prescribed laws of the press (*hudud al-sihafa*)."[59] The "prescribed laws of the press" was, of course, a meaningless phrase, for at that stage not even the most basic rules for the responsibilities of the journalist ex-isted. Such rules would have to be devised by writers based on their intuition and common sense, as well as on social conventions. Zaydan's acid criticism, however, was apparently valid and was echoed repeatedly by other writers equally frustrated by their colleagues' intemperance. "Too much freedom is no better than the absence of freedom," stated Rashid Rida in 1898. "It produces despicable acts, such as assault by the base on the notable, with or without justification, and the dissemination of immoral and fallacious views."[60] Rida, Zaydan, and others who voiced similar disapproval of the mishandling of freedom reluctantly came to a far-reaching conclusion: The only treatment of the syndrome was to impose governmental limitations on freedom of expression in the form of restrictive press laws. As Ibrahim al-Yaziji put it, "imposing limits in a situation like this is better than freedom."[61]

The problems generated by the shift from repression to freedom of expression were reflected in microcosm in the journalistic outburst throughout the Arab provinces of Syria and Mesopotamia following the Young Turk revolution. There, unlike in Egypt, the change in atmosphere was abrupt, a classic precondition for the "beaten angel syndrome." Almost no restrictions existed on publishing newspapers or on their contents, especially at first. This situation attracted many writers who had, in the words of a contemporary Arab critic, "emaciated pens and sick souls" and who attacked merely for the sake of exercising the rights of the newly emancipated. "Some five years have elapsed since the constitution was restored, and our papers are still at the stage of adolescence. They quarrel and slur, vilify and wrangle, and there is no telling when this juvenile behavior will end," an Iraqi journal noted with irritation in 1913.[62] Such charges continued to be leveled against the Arab press, attesting to the entrenchment of the syndrome. In a somewhat later period, Najib al-Rayyis, a highly respected Syrian journalist and editor of *al-Qabas*, bitterly attacked "the base writers and owners of impudent papers" of his country "who assail [parliamentary] delegates, insult them, and spread lies about these . . . legitimate representatives of the nation." Freedom of the press has been sought, he stated, "but we have demanded it within the limits of morality and logic (*hudud al-akhlaq wal-mantiq*). We have demanded it in order to express the nation's wishes regarding its problem [of foreign occupation] and its expectation from the government." Yet there are those who "plunder this honorable freedom and, rather than discuss political issues and the good of the community, seek to hurt people, thereby undermining the reputation of the press at large."[63]

Rayyis, Rida, Zaydan, and other serious journalists who criticized the performance of their less responsible colleagues were particularly grieved by the arbitrary attacks on authority that marked a breach with society's long-esteemed principles. But they were also hinting at other forms of unethical behavior, such as fabrication of news and massive plagiarism. Worse still was the indication of acts that violated basic social norms and that could be classified as blackmail. Journalists who resorted to such practices would induce their victims to subscribe to their newspaper, or, alternatively, pay a sum of money, in order to avoid or stop the publication of slanderous pieces. "Only two kinds [of journalists] profit from the press," a Lebanese writer noted in 1909, "the impudent, whose derogation the people dread and hence they subscribe to his paper, fearing his evil tongue, and the eminent, whose paper they buy out of respect for him."[64] A foreign resident in Egypt around the same time offered the following description of the practices of "impudent" journalists:

> Their tactics are somewhat like this: They write a very flattering article about some petty public official whom they think gullible. The article generally contains a most eulogistic poem to the honor of the victim. They show it to him and then beg for a photograph. The whole is then set up in type and again showed to him; he is gradually brought to understand that there is only one thing that now stands in the way of its publication, *i.e.*, a present! If, with patience, this is not forthcoming, a villainously slanderous article is shown to him about to be substituted for the laudatory one. One editor, who was notorious for this method of making a living, exhausted all possible Egyptian sources of revenues, so he toured round the whole coast of Arabia and victimized all the petty Arab chiefs.[65]

These practices were rarely documented, and all that we know about them comes from complaints by victims and accounts by contemporary critics, so that we can hardly assess the scope or frequency of the phenomenon. Yet repeated references to such foul play indicate that it was an integral part of the evolution of the medium—"a scene which recurred in every journalistic show," in the words of a veteran Egyptian writer—though apparently at different levels in different places.[66] An Egyptian journalist suggested in 1938 that those who engage in such acts "are, in any case, not quite as few as some people would think"; and, around the middle of the twentieth century, testimonies gathered throughout the region showed that such practices, in various versions, still went on.[67] Blackmail and other unethical acts were common enough to upset the more responsible writers and lead them to advocate the remedy prescribed half a century earlier by Rida, Zaydan, and Yaziji: restrictive legislation. They reckoned that "a certain minimum degree of control by the authorities is necessary" in order to check those "who do not understand the meaning of freedom."[68] It was imperative, members of the Syrian press union stated in a memorandum to the government in the mid-1940s, that a restrictive law be devised that "would guarantee for the press a just [process of] filtration, admitting those papers that deserve to remain for the country's good and shutting down the ones which harm rather than help . . . [and which] have made the press a tool of denigration, a weapon for threats, a blackmail device."[69] In the eyes of the more conscientious Arab writers in the mid-twentieth century, control from above, the traditionally legitimate way to manage public affairs, was still a better guarantee of freedom than the newer idea of entrusting it entirely to the journalists.

In view of this kind of performance by journalists, the attitude of governments to the press might be regarded in a somewhat different light from that frequently portrayed by the indigenous critics. Whether complying with the old rules of submission to authority, or, in a later period, viciously attacking those who exercised authority, journalists sometimes unwittingly contributed to the authoritarian approach of governments by giving them reason to be rigid. Complacent writers confirmed the ruler's autocratic convictions, while those who challenged him were viewed as attacking the hallowed values that legitimized the ruler's power, thereby inviting a counteroffensive of superior force. Governments acted sensibly, from their viewpoint, when they suppressed overly aggressive papers, as did the Egyptian Assembly before it reinstated the stringent 1881 press law in 1909, viewing journalists as *"une bande de gens sans scrupule."*[70] Often, the authorities used the poor conduct of certain journalists as an excuse for extensive suppression of the press. Equally often, however, they were truly alarmed by the damage caused them, and the community, by an abusive press. 'Ali Mahir, Egypt's prime minister in 1936, was apparently referring to a legitimate problem, which beset many other governmental officials at different times and places, when he implored his country's journalists: "Help me clear the press of its filth, and I will be ready to render any support that would assist the press in performing its noble duties."[71]

Why was the transition from self-imposed silence to the exercise of free speech so arduous? The question defies a simple answer, and we can do no more than briefly recall some of the factors associated with, and in some way responsible for, these difficulties. Clearly, the very novelty of freedom of political action had much to do with its abuse — and in that, we may again add, Arab society was no different from others in a similar phase. Misuse and abuse were natural aspects of acclimatizing to a fundamental change in basic values. Many historical reasons accounted for that in Arab society — primarily the rootedness of old beliefs, the weakness of educational systems that could have been the primary transmitters of the new views, and, not least, the repressive political conditions of foreign intervention or occupation under which these developments took place. Economic factors were another major cause in slowing down the process of adjustment to the concept of free self-expression: The region's chronic poverty forced newspapers to rely on subsidization from patrons whose concerns were essentially political, and such financial dependence often compromised professional standards and ethics. These patrons included local and foreign governments as well as individuals with influence who, by offering to subsidize journalists, contributed significantly to their corruption. In an environment of material want, the lure of subsidies was often too powerful to resist. While striving for free speech, therefore, the press also had to free itself from other constraints that were as powerful, and sometimes more harmful, than the political limitations imposed by governments. Prevalent traditional concepts, pervasive illiteracy, profound indigence, and inauspicious international circumstances all played a role in mitigating against the freedom of expression and slowing down its assimilation by the Arab press.

6

The Reader

"A community needs news for the same reasons that a man needs eyes," the famed British journalist Dame Rebecca West once observed. "It has to see where it is going." What kind of news a community needs and in what ways it is obtained are, of course, questions with less universal answers, which change with place and time. Arabic-speaking society, naturally, was interested in news. But the nature of the news that was demanded, and the methods used to communicate it, differed from the norms in the society that had first produced the press — Europe — and as such had a crucial bearing on the assimilation of the press in society.

Cultural Determinants

Traditional channels of transmitting information had served the needs of Middle Eastern society effectively. The official announcer and the mosque preacher, both of whom delivered official messages, and public congregation in the bazaar and coffeehouse, where these and other news items were spread further, had functioned as the community's eyes. They were effective and adequate because the pace of events affecting most of society in pre-modern times was relatively slow (which was not, of course, peculiar to the Middle East) and, more important, because the type of news in which the people were interested was somewhat limited. The basic view that matters of government concerned only the government, which should be trusted to lead the community rightly, was widely accepted by the governed. The individual did not have, or seek, a political status except as an anonymous member of the collective of the ruled, led and protected by the representative of God's will. This did not necessarily signify utter passivity and absence of any interest in state and public affairs. But it did entail a largely noninquisitive attitude toward the government. There was also the element of pervasive poverty, which forced the inhabitants of the region to focus on matters immediately relevant to their daily survival, to the exclusion of more remote issues. The community was still less concerned with developments in the non-Islamic lands, the outside wilderness: What happened there was intellectually uninteresting to a society that saw itself as spiritually superior, and politically irrelevant to one that felt protected by Ottoman might. Lack of interest was perhaps also attributable to a broader outlook that tended to view knowledge as finite, with clear limits, and whose fundamentals had been fully recorded in the books of the sages. Anything not included in the known texts would be useless and possibly even harmful. This pronounced orientation to the past and reverence for tradition resulted in a suspicion of novelties and generally limited curiosity until the outset of the modern era.

Traditionally, communication in Arabic-speaking society had been mostly oral. Messages were conveyed through the announcer and preacher in the mosque, in the market, and within the family, in speech rather than in writing. Writing was reserved for the holy books, for stating religious legal opinion, for official communication among the ruling authorities, for diplomacy, and for announcements of major events through stone inscriptions in public places. Less officially, it was used for chronicles, geographic and scientific treatises, literature, and poetry. In all of this, the act of writing was conducted by a limited number of trained individuals: the 'ulama', state officials, and men of letters. The rest of society, overwhelmingly illiterate, accepted this state of affairs and looked up to those who could read, and still more to those who could write, with respect. Those children who in premodern times were fortunate enough to attend school, in which the rudiments of reading were taught, learned almost exclusively to read the Qur'an or, more often, to recite it from memory. Reading for other ends was considerably less common, and writing was seldom regarded as a useful skill, except for religious purposes. When the option of widespread reading and writing emerged in the region, with the introduction of printing, these traditional views, and the inherent instinct against innovation, were bound to generate suspicion. "What is the use of putting words and phrases together and serving them to a community not inclined to that which is not holy nor related to a [religious] principle?" the founders of a cultural journal in Mecca were told upon launching their paper in 1932.[1] This attitude was typical. As we shall see later, it was primarily the 'ulama' who articulated this opposition to the novelty, for they understood best its dangers to the community's traditional values.

The adequacy of the old communication channels, limited interest in news, and prevalent sociocultural conventions inconsistent with widespread writing and printing hindered the introduction of newspapers into the Middle East. But these obstacles were whittled away by the impact of political, social, cultural, and technological developments in the nineteenth, and even more so in the twentieth, centuries. The changes to which Arab society was exposed in the modern era were different from those of the past: They were more profound and intensive, and had greater implications for all segments of society. Not only were the acts of domestic leaders and developments within the community relevant, but events abroad became relevant as well, with bearing on everyone. The outside world impinged upon the region, shaking society's benign confidence in the old order. Broad reforms in various areas, wars with non-Muslims at the doorstep of the local community, the percolation of new political ideas and practical trial with them, and the ever-growing influx of foreigners, primarily from Europe, all created a situation in which interest in news could no longer remain circumscribed. Nor could the traditional means of transmitting news satisfy the community's need for eyes. Under the circumstances, historic conventions had to give way to new concepts. This was a slow and difficult process, but its direction was abundantly clear.

The factor that most hindered the introduction of the press and its acceptance by the public, more than traditional concepts, was illiteracy. The inability of the great majority of Arabic-speakers to read was a crucial determinant in shaping the fate of the Arabic press during the nineteenth and the first half of the twentieth centuries.

Illiteracy was pervasive throughout Arab society at the beginning of the nineteenth century. Although no data are available, all assessments point to only a tiny, almost infinitesimal minority that was able to read. The percentage of literacy throughout the region was measurable in single-digit figures with only small variations between them, the situation being slightly better in Lebanon and Egypt and worst of all in Iraq and the Arabian Peninsula.[2] Most of the cultural and scientific achievements of Islamic civilization, a glorious chapter of a remote era, had long been abandoned and were in large part forgotten. Education at the *kuttab*, the local town or village school, was limited to an elementary level of reading and occasionally writing. Basic arithmetic was not taught at school; when acquired, it was from the *qabbani*, or owner of a scale in the market. Children attended the *kuttab* for two or three years, the main goal being memorizing the Holy Book. In any case, only a small percentage of boys attended at all, and girls rarely. There was also a second stage in the educational system—the *madrasa*, or mosque school, with its mostly theological curriculum, where a still smaller number of students were trained to become 'ulama'.

Early nineteenth-century descriptions portray a dispiriting picture of the system. "I was lately told," Edward Lane wrote from Egypt in the 1830s, "of a man who could neither read nor write succeeding to the office of a schoolmaster in my neighborhood. Being able to recite the whole of the Kur-'an, he could hear the boys repeat their lessons; to write them he employed the "areef" (or head boy and monitor in the school), pretending that his eyes were weak."[3] When the Bulaq press began producing school textbooks, the government at first tried selling them to the students, then gave them out free of charge, passing them on from grade to grade, and eventually decided to let the students keep them, for "it could not find readers for them except for those school students, and the books were piling up in the warehouses."[4] John Bowring, who visited and reported on Syria in 1838, was struck by the fact that "the demand for books is so small in Syria that I could not find a bookseller in Damascus or Aleppo. I was told no scribe could now get his living in copying MSS for sale." The situation in the schools was another aspect of this reality: "There are no elementary books of any kind for the instruction of Mussulman youth, and they chiefly learn by repeating altogether what the teacher reads to them."[5] Such was also the situation in Lebanon where, as Butrus al-Bustani observed in 1868, one would have to "wander in the markets of this town [Beirut], not to say throughout the country, which in old times had been the cradle of culture and birthplace of civilization, and search hard until one finds a person able to read or, as they say, decipher a name."[6]

Developments in the nineteenth century initiated a process that would slowly change this state of affairs. In Lebanon, with its small, enterprising, largely Christian population, the educational efforts of missionaries, subsequently taken over by the local communities, prompted the emergence of a literate, modern-minded sector of the population that began to participate in literary and journalistic life as readers and writers. By World War I, as much as half the population of Mount Lebanon or more were able to read. The number continued to grow, reaching some 60 percent in Mount Lebanon (a little less in other parts of the country) by 1932 and, according to one credible assessment, some 80 percent of the country's population by mid-century.[7]

Lebanon, however, was an exception. In Egypt, pioneering efforts made by the state under Muhammad 'Ali to establish a school system continued even more intensively under Isma'il and his successors, resulting in a gradual increase in the number of schools and students. In 1882, an estimated 160,000 students attended Egyptian schools. By World War II, the number had increased to 490,000. This last figure, however, still excluded some 83 percent of all school-age children from the educational system, reflecting the tremendous difficulties lying on the way to educational reform. In 1897, a startling 94.2 percent of the country's settled population was still illiterate, and by 1917 the illiteracy figure had changed only slightly, to 92.1 percent.[8] In Syria, with no such organized effort on behalf of the state but with a smaller community and some missionary educational activity, the situation was somewhat better: On the eve of World War I, illiteracy was assessed at 75 percent. The situation was gloomier in Iraq, which scarcely had any educational system at all. For example, in Baghdad in 1885, with a population of about 100,000, there were only four primary schools with a total of 362 students, a crafts school with 69 students, a high school with 30 students, and four small schools for children of religious minorities. A total of 261 books were printed in Iraq during nearly half a century, between 1856–1899 — an average of six books annually — most of them on religious topics. By World War I, at least 95 percent of the country's population was still illiterate.[9] The situation in the Arabian Peninsula could not have been any better than in Iraq.

The formation of Arab states after World War I led to a more energetic and organized effort in the field of education in some of the countries, with a greater investment of resources. Yet the low point of departure, and a variety of political, economic, and cultural difficulties, restricted progress. Throughout much of the region illiteracy remained as high as 80 to 85 percent in the interwar period (lower in Lebanon and Syria, higher in Iraq, Transjordan, and the countries of the Arabian Peninsula). A 1937 census in Egypt recorded an illiteracy rate of 82 percent, a significant decline from two decades earlier; a further decline to 77 percent was recorded by the 1947 census. In Palestine, the 1931 census showed an illiteracy rate in the Arab sector of 81 percent, and an assessment in 1941 put it at 73 percent. In Syria the rate reportedly dropped to 63 percent in 1932 and to an estimated 40 percent at mid-century. In Iraq, however, illiteracy remained as high as 90 percent even by the mid-twentieth century; in Jordan it was 85 percent; and in the Arabian Peninsula it was probably as high as in Iraq, or higher. A survey conducted by UNESCO in 1960 showed that the illiteracy rate in the Arab states as a whole was around 75 percent. A. L. Tibawi, a seasoned observer of Arab society, estimated that in 1972, about two-thirds of the aggregate adult population of the region was still illiterate. While illiteracy decreased slowly thereafter, it still remained high and has afflicted the majority of the region's population until the present.[10]

The figures regarding illiteracy are highly imprecise, as disparate definitions and methods of assessment of education and literacy do not permit more than an elastic picture (censuses conducted under European supervision had their own serious deficiencies). Phenomena such as relapse into functional illiteracy after attendance at school, a common occurrence, further blur the scene. The classification "literate" did not necessarily imply the ability to read a newspaper; often it was merely a designation for someone who had memorized certain sections of the Qur'an. "I was in Egypt in that year," related the French judge Pierre Crabitès, referring to the census year 1917, "and I was counted in the literate minority. And so was my Berberian *suffragy* [steward], who can barely scribble."[11] A precise and credible notion of the number of people who could read a newspaper at a particular stage in the evolution of the press in any country of the region is unobtainable. Yet an assumption can be made with certainty that the number was meager and, with the exception of Lebanon, comprised a small minority of any country's population. While literacy did increase steadily, in some places faster than in others, by the middle of the twentieth century the majority of the population of the region were still nonreaders.

That the bulk of society did not have direct access to written or printed texts is of pivotal importance in the history of the Arabic press. It meant a limited reservoir of potential buyers of journals, which entailed powerful economic constraints on the growth of the press. It also signified limits on the impact, political and otherwise, of the press on society. Yet the exclusion of the majority was, of course, only one side of the coin. The other was the emergence of a reading elite, a small but prominent class of educated people with the potential of becoming involved in the development of the press as consumers, as writers, and as patrons. The few percentiles that this class constituted in each of the Arab countries amounted to tens or hundreds of thousands of prospective readers; in mid-twentieth-century Egypt they numbered millions. They formed the target audience for the journals, a group more aware than the rest of the population of matters beyond their immediate surroundings and better equipped to appreciate the relevance of public, national, and foreign issues to their own situation.

What sectors of society did these educated segments comprise? First, they were overwhelmingly male. As late as the mid-twentieth century (and in many places thereafter as well), males received education while females, by sociocultural standards, remained ignorant, by and large. Women were not meant to be educated, and were left, in the sarcastic phraseology of an American missionary, with the "donkeys and camels [to] bear the burden throughout the East."[12] Nor did they expect to be edified: "This habit of reading is an ailment from which women of my generation did not suffer," an Egyptian woman brought up in the nineteenth century admonished her granddaughter, who had been exposed to modern instruction. "I never allowed my daughters enough time [during the] day to read."[13] In 1897, 5.8 percent of Egypt's settled population was defined as literate, but only 0.2 percent of the women (a total of about 18,000) could read, as against 8 percent of the men. Education for women, introduced on a minuscule scale in the late nineteenth century, expanded slowly in the twentieth. By 1917, 2.1 percent of Egyptian women could read. By 1937 the rate had grown to 9 percent, and the 1947 census indicated a figure of 13 percent female literacy.[14] Data from other areas in the region, while piecemeal, indicates a similar trend. For example, of 23 schools in Beirut in 1860, only four were for girls (none of them Muslim). In Transjordan in 1922, out of 3,316 children who attended school, 2,998 (over 90 percent) were boys, and only six out of 44 schools were for girls. In Palestine in 1931, 25 percent of Muslim males above 7 years of age could read, but only 3 percent of females could read. In Iraq in 1947, where 11 percent of the population above the age of 5 could read, only 3 percent of the women were literate, compared with 18 percent of the men.[15] The pattern recurred throughout Arab society, a mirror of its time-honored values. Consequently, during the entire period under review, the reading public everywhere in the region (again, with the possible exception of twentieth-century Lebanon) was preponderantly male. Women constituted at best one quarter of this group, and in most times and places far less.

Another characteristic of the literate population was, as in all societies, its concentration in urban areas. The peasant community in the countryside — the great bulk of Arab society — remained predominantly illiterate until the middle of the twentieth century and beyond. Literacy evolved mostly in the large cities — the capitals of provinces and later of states, and the loci of government and of links with the outside world — where the state and the missionary societies invested their main, if modest, educational efforts. Until very recently the rural areas were outside the reach of modern instruction. Typically, only one or two men in a village — normally the shaykh, sometimes the local teacher — could read. Peasants, ever preoccupied with daily survival in harsh conditions, were rarely free or prone to explore new horizons. For example, the Egyptian census of 1897 showed that 8 percent of all Egyptian men were literate, but as many as 21.6 percent of the men in the province of Cairo and 19 percent in the province of Alexandria were identified as able to read. In another example, a count conducted in 1932 by the French mandatory authorities in Syria indicated that the literacy level countrywide was 37 percent, with 45 percent in the province of Damascus but as little as 18 percent in the more rural Hama and 3 percent in rural Jazira.[16] Literary endeavors in the Middle East, including the press, thus developed primarily as an urban phenomenon, affecting the countryside only marginally. The gap between city and village in terms of exposure to the world outside was narrowed significantly only with the introduction of broadcasting, which required no literacy, toward the middle of the twentieth century.

Yet another mark of the educated class was the relatively high proportion of non-Muslims it contained, not merely in Lebanon with its Christian majority, but also elsewhere in the region. This was largely the result of the educational enterprise of missionaries, who for obvious reasons attracted mostly members of the minorities to their schools, and to some extent could also be attributed to the various kinds of ties that local non-Muslims had with Europeans. Of the 75 schools in Beirut in 1869, 61 were Christian and three Jewish. Muslim students formed a mere 13 percent of those who attended these schools. In Egypt in 1907, 4 percent of Muslims could read, as against 10.3 percent of Copts. In Palestine in 1931, while 25 percent of all Muslim males 7 years old or older and 3 percent of Muslim women could read, the rates among the Arab Christian population were 72 percent and 44 percent respectively.[17] When large numbers of Syrian Christians emigrated to Egypt in the late nineteenth century, they brought with them a high level of literacy and education, which made them an integral and even a leading segment of the local Arabic-reading intelligentsia. According to the 1917 census, more than 50 percent of the Syrian Christian immigrants could read, a six-fold higher rate than the Egyptian average at the time.

The nature of the reading public in a region as diverse as the Middle East during a period of accelerated change naturally varied extensively with time and place. Not only did the size of this public, and its relative proportion within the community, change, but also its composition. As a general rule, the reservoir of potential readers throughout the region during the period under study consisted mostly of men, although the proportions of women grew slowly, was mostly urban, and included a greater proportion of non-Muslims than their representative rate within the population. During the early decades of educational change in the late nineteenth century, with literacy expanding mostly among young people who attended and graduated from the new schools, the reading public was also characterized by relative youth. Literate children of illiterate parents was a typical mark of this process. The phenomenon naturally declined later on, but only in a very few places has it disappeared completely.

Circulation

The small literate community discussed above comprised the obvious potential consumers of newspapers. How many of them, however, were actually exposed to the press?

The question of press circulation in the Arabic-speaking countries is perhaps the most elusive issue in the history of the medium. The notion of a circulation audit would have been more novel (and perhaps odder) than that of the publication of periodicals itself in these countries, nor did any other mechanism evolve for systematically recording and publishing this kind of data. The circulation of an individual paper or of the press as a whole in any given country during the nineteenth century hardly concerned the authorities, who viewed the press as negligible. In the twentieth century, as the political importance of journals increased, governments became more interested in distribution, especially of the more influential papers, and devised such methods to monitor circulation as the registration of journals mailed by post, and police interrogation of press employees. However, such data as the authorities gathered, the credibility of which is in some doubt (it could readily be slanted to suit the interests of the officials involved), was rarely if ever published. Access to it is difficult, and the results of such a search may well be unworthy of the effort. In the absence of reliable official information, then, two sources of circulation data remain, neither of which is particularly reliable: the papers themselves, as well as journalists who reported on circulation at the time of publication or subsequently; and outside observers.

Newspaper owners sometimes published circulation data, even in the nineteenth century, for a variety of reasons: personal pride in reaching a large circle of readers, desire to show political influence, and, from the late nineteenth century onward, interest in encouraging advertising. It is reasonable to assume that they themselves knew how many copies their papers sold. It is just as likely, however, that they often modified that information when making it public. Informed, in 1897, that the owner of *al-Hilal* claimed to have 3,500 subscribers, Muhammad 'Abduh realistically observed: "If they count everyone whose name they put down in their register of subscribers, then he might have that number. But as for those who [actually] pay money, I doubt that they amount to thousands."[18] Published data was inflated to exaggerate the journalist's personal achievements, his political influence, or the paper's economic potential. At other times it was minimized for tax considerations (when taxation was levied according to the number of copies sold). Most often, however, it was concealed altogether. *"La presse est une femme,"* an Egyptian newspaper editor told a European inquirer in the 1920s. "What her age is to a woman, our circulation is to us. If a woman were to tell you her age, she would lie to you. If I were to tell you what our figures are, I should exaggerate through force of habit."[19]

As for outside observers, the best and most systematic of them were the foreign government offices in the region: mandatory survey departments, information sections of foreign consulates, and the like, which were interested in an accurate picture and had acquired some experience in procuring the necessary data. Their information is probably as good as it could be, although because of difficulties in obtaining it, it is often less than credible. Frequent discrepancies in their reports testify to the problems they faced in gathering data. Other observers, less well-placed, could do little more than speculate on the basis of such unreliable data as was provided by the papers and by hearsay, and offer guesses, educated or otherwise.

The general picture that emerges from the abundance of these largely speculative assessments resembles, unsurprisingly, a cloth full of holes, sloppily woven with divergent threads. To take an example of the kind of evidence that is available, Ya'qub Sanu' estimated that some 250,000 copies of his *Abu Naddara Zarqa'* were printed during the eventful period between March and May 1878, a patently inflated figure readily recalling the metaphor of the press as a woman. Other assessments of his newspaper refer to a weekly circulation of 50,000 for the same period; a total circulation of 50,000 for the period; a total circulation of 2,000 for the period; and a balance between all these figures of some 3,300 copies per issue during the said months, offered by a scholarly source.[20] To take an example of a different kind, a British Foreign

Office document of 1947 provided circulation data on Egyptian newspapers gathered by its Public Section, and contrasted it with figures claimed by the papers' publishers. While the Public Section put the combined daily circulation of three newspapers, *Sawt al-Umma* (Wafdist), *Al-Ikhwan al-Muslimin* (Muslim Brothers), and *al-Asas* (Sa'dist Party) at 18,000 copies, their publishers reported a total circulation of 130,000.[21] Because contradictions of this kind recur in the evidence all too often, the best that can be done, as has been suggested, is "obtaining as many informed guesses as possible and then balancing them up to make another guess."[22]

Tables 1 and 2 represent a sample of the estimates that appear to be most reliable. Reliability has been determined through comparison with other evidence on the state of the press in each country and period. Assessments that were obviously exaggerated or unreasonable — a very large number indeed — have been omitted. The data may be useful for indicating general trends, as individual figures are often likely to be inaccurate.

When the first state organs began to appear in the early nineteenth century, the governments issuing them required officials and civil servants to subscribe to them, normally by paying for the papers out of their salaries. Muhammad 'Ali exempted some of his officials from paying for his bulletin, but insisted that they receive and read it.[23] At that stage, distribution of the few hundred copies of each issue was made possible only by the state's initiative and financing. These official organs, with their meager circulations, published in Istanbul, Cairo, and Mount Lebanon, were the only periodicals that existed until the second half of the nineteenth century and remained so in most places until the end of the century. The public's disinterest in such papers did not result solely from the fact that they represented the voice of the authorities. When an Englishman, William Churchill, tried to publish the first nonofficial paper in Istanbul in 1840, he quickly found himself giving it away in the streets free of charge, for nobody would buy it. Failing to elicit sufficient public interest in this novelty, he was forced to shut it down after a while.[24]

The emergence of an Arab educated elite during the second half of nineteenth century engendered interest in news and in the instructional material that Arabic periodicals began to disseminate from the late 1850s onward. If the lists of the newspapers' agents are any indication, the geographical distribution of this readership may have been quite broad. Journals like *Hadiqat al-Akhbar*, *al-Jawa'ib*, *al-Jinan*, and *al-Muqtataf* were reportedly read from Fez to Baghdad, from Beirut to Aden, and from Cairo to Bombay, as well as in Europe.[25] The number of copies sold, however, seems to have been skimpy. The figure of 400 subscribers that *Hadiqat a-Akhbar* claimed for itself in 1858, and the assessment that *al-Muqtataf* sold some 500 copies per issue in the 1870s — both of which appear to be fairly sound — attest to a very small

Table 1. Circulation of Individual Arabic Newspapers, 1822–1947

Period	Country	Newspaper	Circulation	Comments	Source
1822(?)–1828	Egypt	al-Jurnal al-Khidiwi	100	official; irregular	Jayyid, *Tatawwur*, 29–30
1828–1840s	Egypt	al-Waqa'i' al-Misriyya	600	official; irregular	Jayyid, *Tatawwur*, 35
1858	Lebanon	Hadiqat al-Akhbar	400 subscribers	semiweekly; also sold on street	Krymskii, 487
Late 19th c.	Syria	Suriya; al-Furat	1,500 each	official; irregular	Iliyas, I, 180
Late 19th c.	Syria	Dimashq, al-I'tidal	500 each	weekly (both)	Iliyas, I, 180
1880s	Egypt	al-Muqtataf	500	monthly; circ. worldwide	Rae, 222
1880–1882	Egypt	al-Mahrusa	2,000	daily	Cole, 123
1880–1882	Egypt	al-'Asr al-Jadid	800	weekly	Cole, 123
1880–1882	Egypt	al-Tankit wal-Tabkit	3,000	weekly	Cole, 123
1889	Egypt	al-Mu'ayyad	800	daily	Zakhura, 542
1892–1894	Egypt	al-Mu'ayyad	2,000	daily	Salih, 115
1892	Egypt	al-Muqtataf	3,000	monthly; circ. in Egypt & abroad	Rae, 222
1892	Egypt	al-Muqattam	2,500	daily; circ. in Egypt & abroad	Rae, 222
1896	Egypt	al-Mu'ayyad	4,000	daily	Zakhura, 542
1896	Egypt	al-Mu'ayyad	12,000	brief peak, caused by scandal	Zakhura, 542–43
1896	Egypt	al-Akhbar	2,800	daily	Subhi, 103
1899	Egypt	al-Mu'ayyad	6,000	daily	Hartmann, 12
1900–1908	Egypt	al-Liwa'	14,000	daily	Salih, 115
1901	Egypt	al-Manar	300–400	monthly	Adams, 180
1903	Egypt	al-Sayyidat wal-Banat	1,100	monthly	Baron, *Women's*, 91
1903	Egypt	al-Muqattam	3,000–4,000	daily	Goldschmidt, 318
1903	Egypt	al-Liwa'	1,500–2,000	daily	Goldschmidt, 318
1908	Egypt	al-Liwa'	29,000	brief peak, at Mustafa Kamil's death	Salih, 116
1909	Iraq	al-Iqaz	1,000	weekly	Faydi, 71
1910	Syria	al-Muqtabas	2,000	combined figure for the monthly and daily (1,000 each)	Iliyas, I, 180–81

Year	Country	Title	Frequency	Circulation	Source
1911	Egypt	al-Jarida	daily	4,200	Kazziha, 379
1914	Egypt	al-Mustaqbal	weekly; street sales only	600	Musa, *Tarbiyya*, 157
1919	Egypt	al-Ahram	daily	20,000	F0371/3721/156659
1919	Egypt	al-Muqattam	daily	10,000–12,000	F0371/3721/156659
1919	Egypt	*Misr*	daily	12,000–14,000	F0371/3721/156659
1919	Egypt	al-Akhbar	daily	4,000–6,000	F0371/3721/156659
1919	Hejaz	al-Qibla	semiweekly; sold mostly abroad	5,000	*al-Qibla*, 11 Dec. 1919
1926	Yemen	al-Iman	weekly	800	Obermeyer, 180
1927–1928	Egypt	al-Ahram	daily	30,000	F0371/13880/8570
1927–1928	Egypt	al-Muqattam	daily	25,000	F0371/13880/8570
1927–1928	Egypt	al-Balagh	daily	10,000	F0371/13880/8570
1927–1928	Egypt	al-Siyasa	daily	10,000	F0371/13880/8570
1927–1928	Egypt	al-Siyasa al-Usbu'iyya	weekly	20,000	F0371/13880/8570
1927–1928	Egypt	al-Balagh al-Usbu'i	weekly	10,000	F0371/13880/8570
1927–1928	Egypt	al-Musawwar	weekly	20,000	F0371/13880/8570
1927–1928	Egypt	al-Kashkul	weekly	10,000	F0371/13880/8570
1928	Egypt	Ruz al-Yusuf	weekly	20,000	Fatima al-Yusuf, 130
1929	Palestine	Filastin	daily	3,000	*Blue Book*, 1929, 159
1929	Palestine	al-Karmil	3 times a week	1,000	*Blue Book*, 1929, 159
1929–1931	Syria	al-Mudhik al-Mubki	weekly	2,000	Iliyas, II, 448
late 1920s	Lebanon	al-Ahrar	daily	6,000	Muruwwa, 268
late 1920s	Iraq	Habazbuz	weekly	10,000	Sadr, 57
1930	Yemen	al-Iman	daily	1,500	Obermeyer, 180
1935	Palestine	Filastin	daily	2,000	Arnon-Ohanna, 201
1935	Palestine	al-Difa'	daily	3,500	Arnon-Ohanna, 201
mid-1930s	Lebanon	al-Nahar	daily	3,500	Sa'ada, *Nahda*, 258
1936–1939	Syria	al-Ayyam, al-Qabas	dailies	6,000–8,000	Iliyas, II, 352
1937	Egypt	al-Misri	daily	20,000	F0371/22006/2805

(continued)

Table 1. Circulation of Individual Arabic Newspapers, 1822–1947 (*Continued*)

Period	Country	Newspaper	Circulation	Comments	Source
1937	Egypt	al-Ahram	45,000–50,000	daily	F0371/22006/2805
1937	Egypt	al-Muqattam	8,000–10,000	daily	F0371/22006/2805
1937	Egypt	al-Balagh	14,000–16,000	daily	F0371/22006/2805
1937	Egypt	Ruz al-Yusuf	3,500–4,000	weekly	F0371/22006/2805
1937	Egypt	al-Musawwar	24,000–26,000	weekly	F0371/22006/2805
1939–1945	Egypt	al-Ahram	over 10,000	daily	Wynn, 392
1941	Syria	al-Qabas, al-Nidal	4,000	daily	Rifaʻi, II, 143
1944	Lebanon	Bayrut	4,000	daily	F0371/40353/A4667
1944	Lebanon	al-Nahar	3,000	daily	F0371/40353/A4667
1944	Syria	Alif Baʼ	2,300	daily	F0371/40353/A4667
1944	Syria	al-Ayyam	2,200	daily	F0371/40353/A4667
1944	Syria	al-Qabas	2,200	daily	F0371/40353/A4667
1944	Syria	al-Inshaʼ	2,200	daily	F0371/40353/A4667
1947	Egypt	al-Ahram	80,000	daily	F0371/62993/8141
1947	Egypt	al-Misri	70,000	daily	F0371/62993/8141
1947	Egypt	al-Balagh	8,000	daily	F0371/62993/8141
1947	Egypt	al-Siyasa	1,000	daily	F0371/62993/8141
1947	Egypt	Akhbar al-Yawm	90,000	weekly	F0371/62993/8141
1947	Egypt	Akhir Saʻa	40,000	weekly	F0371/62993/8141
1947	Egypt	Ruz al-Yusuf	20,000	weekly	F0371/62993/8141
1947	Egypt	al-Ithnayn	120,000	weekly	F0371/62993/8141
1947	Palestine	Filastin	3,000–4,000	daily	Shimʻoni, 410
1947	Palestine	Filastin	5,000–6,000	Saturday edition	Shimʻoni, 410
1947	Palestine	al-Difaʻ	6,000–10,000	daily	Shimʻoni, 410
1947	Palestine	al-Sirat al-Mustaqim	under 1,000	daily	Shimʻoni, 411

Table 2. Total and Average Circulations of Arabic Newspapers by Country, 1881–1947

Period	Country	Details	Circulation	Comments	Source
1881	Egypt	total circulation	24,000		Cole, 124
1890	Egypt	total subscription for periodicals	97,789	monthly subscription by mail	Artin, *Instruction*, Annex F
1897	Egypt	total no. of subscribers	over 20,000	excluding street sales	*al-Hilal*, October 1897, 131
1908–1914	Iraq	average per paper	500–1,000		Rafa'il Batti, 33
1910	Syria	average for leading papers	1,000–1,500		Iliyas, I, 180–81
1910	Egypt	total circulation	100,000		*al-Hilal*, May 1910, 489
1914	Egypt	total circulation	70,000–80,000		Malul, 447–48
1914	Syria	total circulation	9,000–12,000		Malul, 448
1914	Lebanon	total circulation	32,000–39,000		Malul, 449
1914	Palestine	total circulation	4,500–5,500		Malul, 449
1919–1920	Syria	average per daily newspaper	500–1,000	dailies	Iliyas, II, 351
1920–1935	Syria	average for leading dailies	1,000–3,500		Iliyas, II, 351
1920–1945	Syria	average for nondailies	500–800		Iliyas, 390
1920s–1930s	Iraq	total circulation	10,000		Fa'iq Batti, *al-Sihafa*, 53
1926	Yemen	total circulation	800	*al-Iman* (Yemen's only paper) weekly	Obermeyer, 180
1927–1928	Egypt	total for leading dailies and weeklies	180,000		F0371/13880/8570
1929	Palestine	total for leading papers	12,700		*Blue Book*, 1929, 159
1930	Syria	total circulation	33,000	including several French papers	French Government, *Rapport*, 1930, 11
1930	Lebanon	total circulation	68,000	Arabic and French papers	French Government, *Rapport*, 1930, 11
1930	Yemen	total circulation	1,500	*al-Iman* (Yemen's only paper) daily	Obermeyer, 180
1935–1936	Syria	average for leading dailies	4,000		Iliyas, II, 352
1935–1936	Syria	average for second-rank dailies	1,000–2,000		Iliyas, II, 352; Rifa'i, II, 118
1939–1945	Syria	average for dailies	1,000–2,500		Iliyas, II, 352
1947	Egypt	total for leading dailies	200,000		F0371/62993/8141
1947	Egypt	total for leading weeklies	360,000		F0371/62993/8141

reading public prior to the last third of the nineteenth century: conservatively, several hundred readers throughout the region; maximally, 2,000 to 3,000 readers.

The events that swept over Egypt during the last quarter of the century generated vigorous growth in the demand for newspapers. When Sanu's *Abu Naddara* appeared in the late 1870s, it was received by an eager public whose "mind was in ferment," as a contemporary observer noted. The paper was therefore "sold in immense quantities. It was in every barrack, in every Government-office. In every town and village it was read with the liveliest delight."[26] While the meaning of "immense quantities" is difficult to assess, the eagerness stirred by political change, and the accelerated progress of education under Isma'il, no doubt contributed to a more rapid expansion of the potential audience than previously. By the last decade of the century, the leading papers in Egypt had a daily circulation of 4,000 to 6,000, mostly within the country itself (special events could cause the figure to double briefly), while many other papers sold several hundred, or even 1,000 to 2,000 copies a day. By the eve of World War I, the total circulation of daily newspapers in Egypt was probably 80,000 to 100,000 copies.

Elsewhere in the region the figures prior to the war were smaller. Except in Lebanon, experiments in private journalism were limited until 1908, nor was there much public demand for newspapers. Papers arriving from Cairo, Alexandria, Beirut, and Istanbul were read in the cities of the Fertile Crescent and the Arabian Peninsula by the educated few, a number that may not have exceeded several hundred in total. Although the Young Turk revolution generated an incentive for publishing papers and a greater sense of involvement by the public, even then circulation remained small both because of the small literate population and because interest was still limited. By the eve of World War I, the number of newspaper readers in the cities of the Fertile Crescent had grown to quite a few thousand, perhaps up to 12,000 in Syria, and half that number or less in each of Palestine and Iraq. "My journal enjoyed an unmatched circulation in the conditions prevalent at the time," recalled the Iraqi politician and journalist Sulayman Faydi, who in 1909–1910 published the weekly *al-Iqaz* ("Awakening"). "It had a circulation of 1,000 copies per week." Even this modest circulation was not confined to a readership in Iraq, for the paper had subscribers "in India and Muhammara, Kuwait and Bahrain, Aden and Musqat, Jidda, Singapore, and elsewhere."[27] The readership in the handful of towns of the Arabian Peninsula before World War I must have been still smaller. Only Lebanon, the birthplace of the private press, had a relatively large readership, despite mass emigration by its most educated sector. Newspaper circulation there before the war may well have reached 32,000 to 39,000 copies, as estimated by a contemporary journalist.[28]

If Arabic-speaking society had largely preserved its old values prior to World War I, changing circumstances thereafter generated more public involvement, or at least growing curiosity. The war itself provided an impetus: "In spite of . . . the annual Moslem fast of Ramadan, and although the whole of the country population was engaged on the harvest, there was only a slight decrease in the attendance in the reading rooms," a British propaganda officer reported from Palestine in June 1918. "General interest in the news has certainly increased."[29] Once the war ended and restrictions on publication were lifted, press circulation began to increase markedly. Throughout the region the reading public, small as it was, read more newspapers than books, and journals served as the main venue for public debate of the major issues of the day. The number of newspaper buyers in Egypt apparently reached close to 200,000 in the late 1920s and perhaps up to 500,000 by the end of World War II, while in Syria, Lebanon, Palestine, and even Iraq, it reached tens of thousands. The figures were smaller in the states of the Arabian Peninsula and the newly established Emirate of Transjordan—apparently a few thousand at most by the end of the period.

Such appraisals, however crude, clearly reflect the small size of the newspaper-buying sector of society at every stage. It is safe to assume that at no time prior to the second half of the twentieth century were newspapers bought by more than 1 to 2 percent of the population in Syria, Palestine, and Iraq (and even less in the Arabian Peninsula and Transjordan); 3 to 4 percent of the population in Egypt; and 7 to 8 percent of the population in Lebanon. According to an assessment by UNESCO, by the mid-twentieth century the circulation of daily newspapers was 25 copies per 1,000 inhabitants in Egypt, 19 per 1,000 in Syria, 12 in Jordan, 10 in Iraq, and 1 to 2 in Saudi Arabia. In Lebanon, the country with the largest proportion of readers, 76 out of 1,000, or 7.6 percent of the population, bought newspapers.[30] The newspaper-buying public constituted not only a small fraction of society, but a small fraction of its literate segment as well. In Egypt in 1897 the "over 20,000" who subscribed to newspapers and journals constituted only 5 percent of the literate public, as counted in that year's census; thirty years later, the estimated total circulation of 200,000 represented only some 10 percent of the reading public. By 1947 the proportion of newspaper buyers (about half a million) may have increased slightly, but only to 11 to 12 percent of the estimated literate public (4.3 million). The rate was somewhat higher in Lebanon, but markedly lower in other parts of the region. Thus, the great majority of those who could read, along with those who could not, were outside the range of newspaper and periodical circulation.[31]

That most of the literate population did not purchase newspapers was attributable to several reasons. Part of the population was probably still uninterested in what the papers had to offer. Others, who may have been interested, were unable to afford a copy. Still, the number of copies sold may not be the best yardstick for measuring the size of the public exposed to the press. Those who had access to the press without actually buying newspapers were far more numerous than the small groups described above. Whether unwilling or unable to pay for newspapers, the literate as well as other parts of the interested public did not necessarily remain uninformed.

Popular Exposure to the Press

The reading habits of a society are seldom documented. Viewed as a trivial activity, one of many routine practices that do not merit recording, the act of reading is depicted mostly indirectly. Nor are the readers' responses to what they read usually documented, unless they care to express it in writing or some other way. Modes of reading and reactions to what is read differ from one society to another and change over time within the same society. Without recorded evidence, it is difficult to reconstruct the ways in which people read in the past, even in one's own society. Yet, an evaluation of how readers assimilated and responded to written texts is essential to an understanding of the development of writing, religious or secular, literary or journalistic, for the readership influences the writer in many ways. This influence is particularly important in periodical writing, which to a large extent depends on an ongoing dialogue, open or tacit, with the audience. Incomplete knowledge of the readers' side of this dialogue impedes our understanding of the development of the written medium.[32]

Reading as it is now known throughout much of Western society — regular perusal of mostly secular texts that are mass-printed and sometimes disposable after use, performed mainly as an individual rather than a collective act, visually rather than vocally — is relatively novel even for Western society itself. The pursuit of reading was different up until the late eighteenth century, confined to a small number of primarily religious writings, and performed collectively and aloud. The changeover to the modern mode occurred with such cultural and economic developments as the expansion of education, advances in printing, and the decline in the price of texts, which made them increasingly affordable to the public.[33] In Arabic-speaking society, such developments began later and proceeded more slowly.

The entrenched tradition of oral communication of information in Arab society was the result of both the low literacy level and a reverence for the written word that relegated reading to an elite. However, illiteracy may not have been only a cause of the tradition of oral communication but also a result of it, or, more precisely, an outcome of the fact that the spoken word was a medium that was so compatible with the cultural values of the society. Texts were written so as to be transmitted to an "audience" in the literal sense of the term — a listening, not reading, public. The people listened to the *imam* and the *khatib* convey re-

ligious messages and discuss their contemporary implications; heard
the instructions of the authorities from the *munadi*; were entertained by
story-tellers; and sent their children to receive an education that consisted of reciting verses orally, more often than not without any textbooks. The scarcity and high cost of written texts were in part responsible for these habits, but the reverse was apparently also true: The
prevalence of these traditions discouraged the production of written
texts. When Arabic books and periodicals began to be printed, they
were incorporated in the manner to which society had long been accustomed: They reached the greater part of their audiences orally, by
being read aloud. While this phenomenon was hardly conducive to the
development of mass printing of periodicals or of any other kind of
literature, it did help spread the messages of such texts, even among
those who were unable to read, in the centuries-old manner.

The small group of men who had acquired modern education
were naturally the first to change their habits of acquiring knowledge.
Trained by European-inspired methods, they quickly adopted the practice of reading secular material regularly. European books in the original and in Arabic translation became available in Muhammad 'Ali's
Egypt as part of his modernization efforts. The Syrian Scientific Society, founded in Beirut in 1847, had a library organized by missionaries,
and more libraries were later established elsewhere in the country.[34]
Commercial notices on the printing and sale of modern books, appearing in the early journals in the 1850s and 1860s and more frequently
thereafter, evidenced lively intellectual activity among the small educated community. During the last quarter of the nineteenth century,
"reading rooms" (*ghuraf al-qira'a*) opened in Egyptian and Lebanese
towns, making available not only books but also magazines and newspapers. An advertisement in an Egyptian newspaper in August 1876
announced the opening in Alexandria of a "public office for the reading
of all kinds of cultural books (*al-kutub al-adabiyya*) as well as all Arabic,
Turkish, and European newspapers."[35] By then, members of the educated class in Egypt had benefited from the khedivial library, used by
hundreds of readers since 1870, as well as from the Egyptian Geographical Society library, founded five years later, and from a number of
other public reading facilities. Libraries and reading rooms later
opened in towns of the Fertile Crescent as well. "The Reading Room is
well frequented," a British intelligence report from Jaffa noted in 1918,
"and, owing to the tact of the director, an Egyptian Sheikh, it has
become quite a meeting place where conversation is indulged in over
cups of coffee."[36] The new intellectuals applied a modern approach to
written material, eagerly absorbing new political, cultural, and scientific concepts and benefiting from them in ways unknown to their fore-
bears.

How did they actually read? Testimonies on reading habits during
the pre-World War I period are mostly by foreign visitors to the area

who, struck by observing practices long-forgotten in their own culture, found it of interest to describe them. For later years, there is, in addition, oral evidence by Arabic-reading contemporaries based on their personal recollections. According to these sources, those who could afford it subscribed to periodicals and newspapers that were delivered by mail and read them at home at their leisure, a pastime that became popular in Egypt and Lebanon during the last quarter of the nineteenth century, especially among the well-to-do, with the introduction of gaslight to their homes. Sons and daughters who were sent to the new schools and acquired the ability to read joined their educated parents or became readers for the family themselves. Other readers borrowed copies of newspapers from friends and relatives, or read them in libraries and reading rooms. Newspapers, besides being mailed to subscribers, were also sold in the street by hawkers, often "barefooted newspaper boys in their blue or white robes and grubby turbans" who ran shouting through the streets, squares, tram stations, and cafes.

> During my long sojourn in Egypt [a Syrian journalist recalled in 1918], I used to see newspaper sellers coming out with their journals, detecting the people's thirst for them as swiftly as lightening and distributing their papers all over. They did not collect their fee until after they had completed their round, then returned to receive the money from the merchants in the marketplace and from those sitting around in the public cafes.[37]

Cafes were popular and convenient locations for reading newspapers, sometimes more convenient than home. Many readers whose curiosity was greater than their ability to buy a paper would come there, pay the trifling sum for a cup of tea or coffee, and read all the daily newspapers, and sometimes other periodicals (or, as one foreigner put it, "read the barman's paper"). Anytime one passed a cafe, a British visitor to Cairo noted in 1911, "there are numbers of tarbushes to be seen both outside and inside. A few people may be playing dice or dominoes. But the mass are reading newspapers and talking politics."[38]

Reading newspapers, then, was not necessarily an individual act of receiving information. Again, tradition, and the public places that offered wide accessibility to newspapers, created a pattern of reading papers as a collective experience. Reading aloud, an old practice that converted a text of any kind to the property of a circle of listeners, was extended to journals. The thinker and journalist Rashid Rida related how he first became acquainted with al-'Urwa al-Wuthqa—the journal published by Jamal al-Din al-Afghani and Muhammad 'Abduh—while listening to articles read aloud from it by Egyptian political refugees in his hometown near Tripoli: "The famous Shaykh Muhammad 'Abd al-Jawad al-Qayati took [the paper], held one of those olive oil lamps in his hands, and began to read in an accentuated tone, as if he were a preacher. He paused every few sentences to give vent to the profound emotions which possessed him, and did not leave the paper until he reached the end."[39] The phenomenon was widespread. "We often see servants, donkey breeders, and others who cannot read gather around one who reads while they listen. The streets of Cairo and of other towns in the region are full of this," a local spectator related around the turn of the century.[40] Foreigners in Egypt often described the habit of townspeople "listen[ing] to the reading of newspapers and magazines," or, if they themselves were the objects of aggressive criticism in the press, complaining of "the diatribes which are read to them daily in the villages" and "the violent nonsense which is poured daily into their ears."[41] Such congregations took place in the streets, the marketplace and, in the larger towns, the cafes, the traditional gathering place for entertainment and the exchange and discussion of information. Foreigners encountering the phenomenon sometimes formed the impression that "Arabs are inordinately proud of their voices."

> They love an audience. Those who are literate often need glasses, but are too vain to wear them. It therefore not infrequently happens that some Demosthenes is found reading to a group of myopic satellites who should buy their own copy of the paper.[42]

In small towns that lacked the convenient institution of the cafe, other public locations were used for the purpose. In the towns of Syria, a German visitor in 1914 observed "people eagerly reading newspapers in the street, the railway station, the houses, and shops."[43] In the Hijaz during the Ottoman-Italian war of 1911, "when a person happened to obtain a copy of what they used to call al-ajans [news agency report] . . . he would sit on a bench in one of the shops, put his glasses on, and start reading aloud. The people would crowd around him, listen attentively, and punctuate every phrase with extensive supplications for the [Ottoman] state's victory."[44] During World War I, the British army in Palestine relied on a similar practice in disseminating its propaganda: "A paid reader is now employed here," an intelligence report from Beersheba noted in May 1918. He "goes round the cafés and market place, reading and explaining the news. The people here being . . . mostly illiterate, this appears the best way of interesting them."[45]

One literate person equipped with a single copy of a newspaper could thus convey its contents to many others. The educated read to their illiterate friends in public places and to their families at home. For women, who prior to the twentieth century seldom left home, the family reading was the only way to become aware of the news.[46] Another aspect of the same phenomenon, likewise a common habit, was the exchanging and sharing of newspapers. A reader who bought a journal would lend it to his friends or trade it with someone who had bought a different paper, or a group would get together to purchase a single copy. When the Syrian Salim al-Hamawi's weekly *al-Kawkab al-Sharqi* came out in Alexandria in 1873, 20 friends of Syrian origin in al-Mahalla

al-Kubra joined together to pay one franc each for a 20-franc subscription. "They would await the train every Friday as one would await the
festival moon," the town governor related. "When the train carrying
the mail arrived, the literate one among them would go to the post
office, with the rest of them forming a long line behind him. One of
them would then inquire, shouting at the top of his voice: 'Has the
Kawkab arrived?'"[47] A group of young Sunnis in Baghdad in the late
1870s organized the same kind of collective effort to purchase a single
subscription of al-Muqtataf.[48] Forty years later, in 1918, a similar phenomenon was depicted as still "quite common" in Syria: "Every four or
five men use one journal, which one of them purchases and reads,
walking along the road, while the others listen. Or, the one who paid
for it (an exorbitant sum!) reads while the others wait until he is
through and then circulate it among themselves."[49] In Iraq around
the same time, one newspaper described as common the practice of
"snatching" papers from readers in public places in order to read them,
as well as the practice of newspaper hawkers "renting" their papers to
customers who buy a copy, read it, and resell it to the hawker for half
the price.[50] Newspaper owners, understandably, often complained of
such practices, which undermined their efforts to increase circulation.
How can the journalist make a living, the owner of the Palestinian
al-Quds lamented in 1913, "if every subscriber circulates his copy among
another 50 readers?" Iraqi newspapers repeatedly denounced those who
engaged in these practices, running front-page notices such as "Damn
he who rents a paper from the distributor," and "Enticing the distributors to lend out their papers for reading is a disgrace."[51]

Old traditions adapted to serve modern needs thus helped overcome the limitations of illiteracy and poverty, facilitating the communication of the content of the press to large groups of people. Information
contained in journals was imparted orally even when no text was actually read to the listener. This reflected the viability of traditional modes
of face-to-face communication in the nineteenth and on into the twentieth centuries, which complemented the modern modes of conveying
news.[52] Interest in up-to-date news was more pronounced in urban
areas, where papers were readily obtainable, than in the countryside,
where the majority of the region's population resided but where demand for newspapers was lower. It would also be reasonable to assume
that the oral transmitting of news had a greater effect on men, who
were free to circulate in public places, than on women, who were not.
Ultimately, however, it is impossible to estimate how many more people were exposed to the message of the press than those who actually
bought newspapers. Sources depicting the phenomenon refer variously,
and impressionistically, to a single issue being read "by 10 people," "by
an average of 5, and a maximum of 15, or more," "by 50 people," or
"by 10, or scores or people." The assessment that "reading aloud multi-
plied the size of a periodical's audience many times" is both valid and

undocumentable.[53] Undoubtedly, the size of the audience that had access to the press was larger, even much larger, than circulation figures for the newspapers indicated.

Since direct access to the press was largely determined both by the ability to read and the ability to buy a newspaper, in countries where literacy was higher and economic conditions better, reading tended to be less collective and more individual. Similarly, news consumers in the cities were more likely to shift from listening to reading than their counterparts in the countryside. Yet, if the practice of reading aloud to an audience gradually decreased in parts of the region, it certainly did not disappear, and continued well into the second half of the twentieth century, sustained by pervasive poverty and illiteracy. It was perpetuated by the introduction of radio in the 1930s, a medium that enhanced the collective consumption of news. Not dependent on literacy, yet not quite affordable to most people in the region, radios in public locations were to replace the newspaper reader in enlightening audiences long accustomed to listening.

Press and Readership

Journalists in the Middle East, as elsewhere, viewed their role as responding to popular needs and expectations. Cultural periodicals were dedicated to edifying society and expanding its intellectual horizons, prompted by "the country's need and our sense of duty toward our beloved homeland," according to a typical statement by a literary publication at the turn of the century.[54] Political newspapers professed to enlighten their readers about domestic and world developments while also articulating the popular quest for independence and freedom, acting as "a banner of truth for compatriots and a standard for those who struggle," and bringing the "people's wishes, desires, complaints, and grievances" to the government's attention.[55] Journals designed for specific sectors—women, religious minorities, professional groups—were likewise committed to articulating the views and feelings of their readership.

But was there a process of dialogue between newspapers and readers that allowed the writers to learn the views and aspirations of those they had undertaken to serve? The question of mutual communication between writers and readers of any text is always complex, particularly when it comes to the press. While newspaper editors may gauge reader reaction through surveys, readers' letters, and, to some extent, an analysis of circulation patterns, the researcher interested in readers' reactions must make do with much less, especially in dealing with the press of the past. What exists, first, are letters to the editor published after selection, modification, even fabrication. In addition, there are inferences to be drawn from evidence of the paper's popularity, likewise a problematic source, as has been shown. There are also occasional testimonies by readers and observers. All of these sources together are barely sufficient for reconstructing reader reaction, still less for assessing the impact of readers' responses on writers and editors. What is attempted below, therefore, does not purport to be more than tentative observations.

If the habit of reading newspapers developed slowly among Arabic-speakers, the notion of responding to a newspaper actively by addressing letters to the editor was still slower to evolve. Traditionally, the exchange of views in writing, primarily though not solely on religious questions, was common: People wrote to the community's spiritual leaders for guidance and received written responses, and members of the educated elite engaged in often-heated written exchanges on a variety of cultural and philosophical issues. In a sense, therefore, intellectuals who first ventured to write letters and comments to the editors on such matters, and to debate with each other in the pages of periodicals, were as much continuing a tradition as breaking new ground. Still, the shift from the old format of dialogue to the new was not of necessity smooth, as the new medium entailed demands of a different sort. One typical obstacle was that many of those exposed to the press, even when able to read, could not write properly, which was reflected in repeated pleas by the early journals for those readers who made contact with them to write "in intelligible Arabic idiom, in clear and legible handwriting," for editors often had difficulty deciphering the letters.[56] More significant was the fact that political affairs had normally been precluded from the traditional written exchanges, for obvious reasons. Writing to the press on such affairs, therefore, was a complete novelty.

Cultural periodicals were the first to engage their readers in an active written exchange on scientific, historical, literary, and various other issues. Some of the leading journals of the late nineteenth century, notably al-Muqtataf, al-Hilal, and al-Jami'a al-'Uthmaniyya, encouraged readers to direct queries on such topics to the journal and published readers' letters in the earliest volumes. "People say that the moon influences the growth and fruitfulness of trees—is there any truth in that?" was a typical reader's question in al-Muqtataf's first volume, to which the editors responded in the negative. "Since your respectable journal is also historical," was another typical question, this time addressed to the editor of al-Hilal, "could you kindly enlighten us about the very idea of history, who invented it, how it developed, what is its importance, and all other things related to it"; the reader was referred to an article appearing in the same issue, "The Historical Science and Its History."[57] By 1897, five years after al-Hilal had begun publication, it claimed to be receiving about 100 readers' letters a month.[58] Each issue contained a few of these letters, published with the editor's reply, reflecting lively interaction between the paper and its readers, albeit on a modest scale. Farah Antun's al-Jami'a al-'Uthmaniyya, launched in 1899, likewise started a section devoted to readers' letters within three months of its establishment, in which Antun replied to questions on historical and cultural matters. He too claimed to be receiving "plenty" of letters, among them notes of support for the journal.[59] Women's journals, begun in Egypt in the 1890s, often had similarly active relations with their constituencies — largely though not exclusively women — who sought guidance and support and debated their specific sectorial interests in an otherwise unfriendly environment.[60] The letters published by all of these journals in the early decades of the press — to the extent that they were authentic — seemed to indicate that these publications were doing well both in rousing their readers' curiosity and in satisfying it.

Interaction with the readership in the political newspapers, especially the dailies, was far more limited at first. Prior to the twentieth century these papers seldom published, or discussed, readers' correspondence. One looks in vain for readers' letters in the Egyptian *al-Ahram* or the Lebanese *Lisan al-Hal*. Perhaps this was because both editors and readers were accustomed to regarding political matters as flowing one way — from the source of news or opinion to the audience, not vice versa. If the editors did receive readers' letters — a fact occasionally alluded to in such remarks as "many readers have suggested that . . . " or "we have been repeatedly implored by our subscribers to . . . " — they generally avoided quoting or discussing them specifically. The impact that any such reader response may have had on a newspaper is, therefore, impossible to gauge.

By the early twentieth century, however, this attitude of the newspapers had begun to change, as papers in Egypt and Lebanon began to open their columns to readers' comments and discussion. Newspapers there from the first decade of the century published readers' letters advocating political causes, complaining about poor performance by certain officials, praising other officials, and airing personal grievances — all, of course, in line with the paper's basic policy. Sometimes the published letters elicited responses by other readers and a dialogue developed. To take an example at random, the Egyptian *al-Mu'ayyad* of 8 February 1909 published readers' letters reacting to an article that the paper had run previously; responding to another reader's view that had been published in an earlier issue; and lamenting the resignation of a certain official. To take another example, the Lebanese *al-Mufid* of 9 April 1911 reproduced a reader's letter lauding the governor of Damascus, and three letters of criticism — of the central government's language policy (a controversial political issue at the time), of the management of the Tyre town council, and of the behavior of the Beirut bazaar merchants. By the eve of World War I readers' correspondence was being published regularly in certain newspapers in these two countries, and the practice spread further after the war, there and elsewhere. To illustrate, once again, the 18 May 1924 issue of the Egyptian *al-Liwa' al-Misri* published several letters by anxious readers airing their concern about the recent abolition of the caliphate; and the Syrian *Alif Ba'* of 1 January 1944 reproduced an exchange of letters between readers discussing the state of the Damascus market. On the whole, however, the phenomenon was limited. Most of the leading papers throughout the period under review did not feature readers' correspondence as a routine, perhaps because their editors still believed that political messages should only flow one way.

Another important, if indirect, barometer of the popular assimilation of newspapers was their circulation. In principle, a publication's large readership would indicate its success in articulating popular views and sentiment, a small circulation that it represents the views and tastes of few. Yet, because the popularity of a given paper is often determined by more than one factor, this measure may be more useful in evaluating broad trends than in assessing the public's response to a single journal. Broadly, the generally small circulation of Arab newspapers as well as the short life-span of most of them would seem to indicate that society was slow to accept the new medium as representative of its views and feelings, perhaps not so much because of any ideological or conceptual gulf between papers and readers as because of the very novelty of the medium itself, which required a far-reaching adjustment.

The Arab press reflected public sentiment most closely when it regarded itself, and was viewed, as leading the community's struggle against foreign domination and against local rulers who seemed to be serving foreign interests. The exceptional, if short-lived, popularity of Ya'qub Sanu''s newspapers in Egypt of the late 1870s and early 1880s may be ascribed to this cause: The paper's biting censure of government corruption and impotence in the face of Western encroachment accurately expressed widespread frustration. Similarly, the rise of nationalist and anti-British sentiment in Egypt around the turn of the century accounted for the popularity of such nationalistic dailies as *al-Mu'ayyad* and *al-Liwa'* and, sometime later, for the steep decline in circulation of the notoriously Anglophile *al-Muqattam*.[61] National sentiment was also responsible for the wide circulation of the Wafd papers in the interwar period — *al-Balaqh*, the weekly and daily *Ruz al-Yusuf*, and *al-Misri*; the rise in circulation of such newspapers in Syria as *al-Qabas* and *al-Ayyam* during the struggle against the French; and the popularity of the Palestinian *Filastin* and *al-Difa'*, the standard-bearers in the battle against Zionism and the British Mandate. The aversion to foreign domination, a highly emotional issue, was a dominant theme in intellectual and popular discourse. Newspaper editors hardly needed readers' letters to sense public feelings on this issue. As a high school student at the turn of the century, writer Salama Musa recalled, his soul had been "haunted" by Mustafa Kamil's *al-Liwa'* and, together with his friends, he had "rushed to buy it after classes."[62] Several years later, Musa and his colleagues, by then journalists, could scarcely misjudge the sentiment of the public within which they had grown. Similarly, when the province of Alexandretta was about to be torn away from Syria by the French authorities in 1937 and transferred to Turkish sovereignty, the local paper al-'Uruba ("Arabism"), which strongly protested the move, became highly popular among the local inhabitants. "Every Arab was buying it, even if he could not read," its editor Zaki al-Arsuzi recalled. "The newspaper-hawkers would stop children on their way to school, asking them to read out the paper for them."[63] At times such as those, the press evidently did respond to popular sentiment.

Other elements also appealed to the reading public. The wide circulation of papers such as the Egyptian al-Ahram from the beginning of the twentieth century, as well as al-Mu'ayyad and al-Muqattam during much of their existence, the Syrian Alif Ba', the Lebanese Bayrut, and the Iraqi al-Zaman cannot be attributed to the nationalist struggle alone, although they did often contribute to it. Rather, these journals were responding to another kind of reader demand—for detailed, prompt, and credible reporting. That such thorough and informative journals led in circulation demonstrated that reliable, nonpartisan reporting was needed and appreciated, more so during periods of war and crisis but at other times as well, no less than newspapers with a cause. The largest papers invested considerable resources in meeting this demand, acquiring a reputation for conscientious and dependable reportage. Yet another area in which the Arab press seemed to be meeting the readers' requirements or, more precisely, satisfying their taste, was in humorous and satiric writing. The success of journals such as Abu Naddara and al-Kashkul in Egypt, al-Mudhik al-Mubki in Syria, and Habazbuz in Iraq, to mention the most conspicuous among numerous such publications, as well as the impressive development of caricature in the Arab press since its beginnings, clearly reflected a demand for this genre.

The public responded to newspapers that expressed its communal feelings, provided it with reliable information, and appealed to its sense of humor by buying and reading such papers increasingly. This popularity may have signified growing approval of the press by the educated community. But was there consensual acceptance of the press among those who had access to it? Did not the fact that only a small minority of society availed itself of the press also attest—beyond obvious educational, economic, and logistic difficulties—to a certain degree of public disapproval? And, if so, did the press itself contribute to such aversion?

From the outset there were Arab journalists who functioned in such a manner as to undermine the readers' faith in the medium. Reportage that was repeatedly proven false, low professional and ethical standards, excessive reportage of partisan squabbling, dependence or suspected dependence on patronage by interested domestic and, worse still, foreign parties, and the use of offensive language all contributed to a poor image of individual newspapers that was often extended to the press as a whole. Evidence of such popular discontent is inevitably indirect yet quite convincing, coming as it does from some of the more conscientious Arab journalists themselves. They complained repeatedly about this lack of public trust in, and even revulsion from, the medium, accusing their colleagues of being "irresponsible," "unethical," and "incompetent," and of "abusing" the profession and damaging its image. "People turn away from papers . . . and do not read. They look to the press with contempt, realizing it is untruthful, delusive, corrupting, and harmful to them," lamented editor Muhammad Kurd 'Ali around the turn of the century, blaming this attitude on "incapable" people, "adventurers who dare to engage [in journalism] even though they themselves are unable to read newspapers and journals."[64] The people "disdain and scorn the press and regard it as rubbish," concurred Ahmad 'Arif al-Zayn of *al-'Irfan* in 1910. "They consider journalists to be engaged in a base occupation." He similarly ascribed this negative image to the poor performance of journalists who, rather than try to enlighten the uneducated, "bicker, quarrel, and contend with each other, seeking to expose each other's blemishes."[65] The public therefore looked down upon both newspapers and journalists, regarding the latter as "merchants of vain talk and jabberers," convinced that "when all other ways of profit are blocked before the chatterer and the blabber, he would turn to journalism in order to make a profit."[66]

The shady behavior of some journalists seemed to confirm the public view that the press was incompatible with higher values and that journalism was not a respectable occupation. In a 1904 *cause célèbre*, the marriage of 'Ali Yusuf, owner of *al-Mu'ayyad*, to the daughter of the prominent Sayyid 'Abd al-Khaliq al-Sadat was annulled by Egypt's supreme Shar'i court on the grounds that Yusuf's profession made him unworthy of marrying into the social elite. The 'ulama' who formed the court had their own grudges against the innovation of the press, but they were also reflecting popular sentiment in condemning Yusuf's occupation as "despicable," for it involved "petty spying on people's misdeeds and disseminating lies among the community." Reportedly, there was widespread public approval of the court's verdict, which was regarded as a victory for society's proper values and morals.[67] This mistrustful attitude on the part of the public remained very much in evidence throughout the region during the interwar period, perhaps best epitomized by the disdainful popular expression *kalam jara'id* ("newspaper talk").[68] A survey conducted in several Arab states at mid-century confirmed that the popular image of the press was still poor in many places, sometimes so much so that it prompted the more serious journalists to repeat a demand voiced by their colleagues a generation earlier for government intervention in order to save the press from bankruptcy.[69]

The performance of journals and journalists during the first century of the Arabic press thus generated an ambivalent response by the readers. Alongside appreciation and praise for its nationalist role, especially in the struggle for independence, the press was also criticized, and sometimes reviled, for its low standards, even by those who thought that the idea of a newspaper was in itself admirable. The more sophisticated readers were able to distinguish between a small number of respectable papers, for which they had high regard, and the great mass of lesser publications whose owners failed to maintain acceptable norms.

7

Cultural Legacy and the Challenge of the Press

Printing and the Guardians of Old Values

In 1555, Ogier Ghiselin de Busbeck, ambassador of the Holy Roman Empire to the Ottoman court, noted with amazement how people in Istanbul took great care to pick up pieces of paper from the ground lest they bear the name of God and be stepped on.[1] By Islamic convention, the written word had a measure of holiness attached to it. Writing, always prefaced with mention of "God, the Merciful, the Compassionate," was meant to be performed deliberately, not casually. Arabic, the language of Allah and his Holy Book, was scrupulously guarded by men of the pen, the 'ulama'. While printing began to be used in European countries during the second half of the fifteenth century, and by the beginning of the sixteenth was the accepted method for disseminating information and scholarship, the Ottoman Empire refused to adopt the invention until much later. Its government feared, justifiably, that the mass production of printed texts would imperil its uncontested authority, while religious leaders abhorred the thought that it might result in the desecration of God's name and, no less important, of his language. Cultural values in the Islamic empire were remote from the idea of unauthorized writing and the mass production of texts. Jews in the empire were allowed to start their own presses in the late fifteenth century, but the permit was limited to printing in their own script only, not in Arabic script (which was also used for Turkish). It was not until the eighteenth century, in 1727, that an imperial decree permitted printing in Turkish and Arabic, and even then holy texts were excluded; they could appear in print only toward the end of that century.[2]

The Ottoman rulers decided at last to adopt the concept of a press, along with other innovations, as part of the effort to close the gap that appeared to be opening between the empire and some of the European powers. Yet this governmental decision could not bridge the gulf between society's traditional attitude to writing and new exigencies overnight. Three centuries after Busbeck's observations from Istanbul, and following a century of printing in the empire, Edward Lane recorded profound misgivings still harbored by Egyptian Muslims about the press. Noting that Egyptians "object to printing their books," he wrote:

> They fear some impurity might be contracted by the ink that is applied to the name of the Deity in the process of printing, or by the paper to be impressed with that sacred name, and perhaps with words taken from the Kur-an . . . and are much shocked at the idea of using a brush composed of hog's hair (which was at first done here) to apply ink to the name, and often to the words, of God.[3]

The 'ulama', defenders of traditional values, were particularly suspicious of printing and continued to resist it as best they could. They were concerned about the dangers it posed to the faith and to the community's spiritual fabric, and no less to their own standing as spiritual leaders. As members of the religious establishment they were not, of course, unique in such opposition. Centuries earlier their Catholic counterparts had strenuously opposed the unrestrained printing of books and later periodicals, publishing an "Index of Prohibited Books" and employing the awesome machinery of the Inquisition to purge unauthorized texts. Like Muslims, they too felt that uncontrolled printing and unguided reading could inspire heterodoxy, for progressive ideas were diabolical ideas until proven otherwise. Likewise, they worried that print undermined, indeed destroyed, their monopoly over the written word by permitting lay people free access to sacred writings. Their opposition, too, was at once spiritual and political.[4] This resistance by the religious establishment was well founded, for mass printing would indeed play a central role in eroding the traditional basis of the old order on which their status was based, both in Christianity and in Islam. However, while their steadfast efforts to uphold the old values would hamper the development of printing and the press, they would ultimately fail to prevent it.

Ottoman sultans shared some of the same motivations that prompted the 'ulama' to resist the proliferation of printing. They too felt an obligation to guard the sacred written word and were loathe to see it used profanely by those not necessarily qualified for the task. They were also aware of the political potential of unorthodox texts that would be disseminated through printing. It has been suggested that Ottoman rulers were worried lest the new invention result in enlightening their people, as "it is no secret that educated people object to injustice and it is more difficult to rule over them tyrannically."[5] Even if the Islamic rulers did not have such dark motives, clearly they feared free access by their subjects to such a potent instrument and dreaded the prospect of not being able to control it. Such concern is particularly understandable in view of the power attributed to words in this and other Semitic cultures, perhaps more so than in other societies: A statement was all but tantamount to an act, a blessing tantamount to a gift, a curse to actual harm.

When the French invaded Egypt in 1798, they brought with them not merely technological innovations but also new ideas, which they spread through printed proclamations. The contemporary Egyptian historian 'Abd al-Rahman al-Jabarti, a member of the community's spiritual leadership and spokesman for the profound faith in the power of the word, was particularly alarmed by the use of this device by the French. Viewing it as a highly dangerous weapon, he sought to combat it with an equally effective tool: a reproduction in full of the text of Bonaparte's first proclamation to the Egyptians, and a systematic exposition of its literary, grammatical, and lexical faults. Jabarti tried to show how that "miserable text" was full of "incoherent expressions and vulgar phrases," a tactic which, for him, was tantamount to dismantling the foreigners' most hazardous weapon. "May God . . . strike their tongues with dumbness," was his most fervent wish.[6]

Words, then, were potent both for attack and defense and had to be employed cautiously. Careless use of them in print for mass circulation was potentially dangerous and generally objectionable. Rifa'a Rafi' al-Tahtawi, the imam of the first Egyptian student mission to France during 1826–1831, was another exponent of this view. Tahtawi, a highly intelligent observer of European culture who readily discerned certain advantages in the French press, nevertheless retained the views of an 'alim. "In these papers (jurnalat) every Frenchman is permitted to praise and censure as he pleases." Such licence, Tahtawi felt, was not necessarily right: "Nothing in the world is so full of lies as these papers."[7] For him, as for Jabarti, the frivolous use of print could spell danger for the correct social, spiritual, and political order. Tahtawi, however, was open-minded enough to change his views and later, in the 1840s, he became involved himself in publishing periodicals and making an invaluable contribution to the modification of traditional attitudes in this area. But the great majority of his colleagues, the 'ulama', adhered to the old concepts and resisted the vice of publishing for many more decades.

In the last quarter of the nineteenth century, Husayn al-Marsafi, a prominent al-Azhar 'alim, sharply criticized the uncontrolled spread of printing and the proliferation of newspapers that, in his view, corrupted the community's values. Rather than guiding the people, he argued, newspapers deceived them through lying, exaggeration, futile argumentation, and preoccupation with trivial details. Like many of his colleagues, Marsafi advocated the imposition of control over the production of books and journals.[8] One of these colleagues, Sayyid

Nu'man al-Alusi, son of the Hanafi mufti of Baghdad, scornfully turned down an offer to subscribe to *al-Muqtataf* upon receiving the first issue in 1876. "The owners are ignorant of our language and its secrets, and I do not understand what they are gabbling about in their alien language," he fumed. "Their talk about the chemistry of glass and about the moon is contrary to that which we have learned from our forefathers. . . . Our ignorance is better than such corrupt knowledge which distorts our views and those of our ancestors," Alusi concluded. His Shi'ite counterpart and compatriot, Husayn al-Shaliji, responded in like manner to the subscription offer: "We, the Shi'ite community, do not read journals, whatever their trend and type, whether these printed sheets are political papers or modern scientific treatises."[9] Many, perhaps most, of the 'ulama' shunned the press, refraining from writing for it or reading it. More important, they inspired their disciples to do the same, labeling the journals *bid'a* (an objectionable innovation), the act of reading them as *haram* (forbidden act), and, sometimes, those engaged in them as *kuffar* (unbelievers).

What kind of impact did their view have on the attitude of the general public toward the press? In a community as profoundly religious as pre-modern Arab society, which regarded its spiritual leadership with such reverence, opposition to the press by the 'ulama' must have had considerable impact indeed. The religious leaders could effectively influence their followers through the traditional oral channels, primarily through the sermons in the mosques. A case in point is that of several Sunni youths in Baghdad around the end of the nineteenth century. Having learned of *al-Muqtataf*, they visited the Christian Deacon Francis Augustin Jibran, who subscribed to the journal, and questioned him about the contents of the paper. "My response to them," Jibran related, "was: Take the latest issue I received with you and read it. They perused it, one at a time, but did not dare take it with them," lest they be caught with such forbidden material in their possession. In time, the young men became bolder and pooled their money to buy a subscription. "They would come to me at the end of every month to take and read [the journal], but would tear it up into pieces thereafter so that nobody who objected to their reading it could see them with it," Jibran recalled.[10] Showing interest in a modern journal was obviously inconsistent with cultural mores and the principles transmitted in the mosque. "God rendered the buying of journals and subscribing to them reprehensible," explained a state functionary at the end of the nineteenth century, echoing the learned guardians, "for, as the holy *hadith* of al-Bukhari says, 'you should avoid gossip, wasting money, and asking too many questions.' Journals combine all three evils."[11] Repeated complaints by journalists that "adhering to the views [of 'ulama'] and holding them sacred," which was so popular, was hindering their livelihood indicate that this attitude was widespread.[12] It was more so in places remote from the center of press activity—more so in Iraq and

the Arabian Peninsula than in Egypt and Lebanon; more so in the
countryside than in the cities; more so at the outset of the emergence of
the press in any given region than later on.

A few religiously prominent individuals, however, adopted a different outlook early on, electing to make use of the power of the press
in order to spread their views rather than distance themselves from it.
This divergence, if not disagreement, among the spiritual leaders
would inevitably have an impact on their disciples' attitude to newspapers, helping to dissipate public antipathy toward them. When Rashid
Rida decided to start his journal, al-Manar, in 1897, he consulted with
Muhammad 'Abduh, then a qadi in the native tribunals and about to
become chief mufti of Egypt. 'Abduh commended him for his initiative,
gave him his blessing, and promised to do whatever he could to help.[13]
Rida, though a devout 'alim, whose paper became the voice of conservative Islam for nearly four decades, was sufficiently forward- looking to
employ the new medium in order to confront secularist influences and
disseminate his own principles. He was, in his own words, "an exception among the people of my country, especially the Muslims, in whatever concerns independence of thought and the free exploration of
religious, political, and social matters."[14] Yet, "independence" and "freedom" notwithstanding, Rida himself launched an assault upon the uncontrolled proliferation of journals in Egypt in the first volume of al-
Manar. The situation, he charged, attracted people unfit to engage in
writing, "men of sin and seduction rather than of spiritual guidance
and good advice," who turned the press into "a tool of abuse, vitupera-
tion, lying, falsehood, exposition of [personal] secrets, and deception."
Such individuals acted against the true faith and misled the faithful.[15]
Rida and his colleagues at al-Manar believed that they were rendering
the community an important service by conveying the truth through a
channel whose effectiveness was no longer in question, defending it
against those who employed the vehicle for abusive purposes.

This distinction between the medium, which was not inadmissable
as such, and its improper use by the nondevout made new and more
flexible thinking by some 'ulama' regarding the press. The distinction
was similarly made in a statement by Shaykh Ahmad Abu Khutwa,
head of the religious court that heard the famous case of 'Ali Yusuf's
marriage to Shaykh al-Sadat's daughter (a marriage, it will be recalled,
that was eventually annulled because of Yusuf's "inferior" occupation).
The problem, the shaykh observed, was not with the press itself but
with the person of 'Ali Yusuf, who lacked the necessary attributes to be
a journalist and hence must be regarded as involved in something less
respectable. The daily press, however, was designed to educate the
people, he suggested, and as such was "a most honorable" institution —
a striking definition coming from an establishment 'alim.[16] It is possible
that Shaykh Abu Khutwa had in mind an image of a press more ideal
than real, one fully compatible with, and in the service of, his own

traditional values. Such standards would have been high above those of a popular paper such as Yusuf's *al-Mu'ayyad*, even though its editor was known to be more religious than most journalists of the time.

About a quarter of a century later, in 1931, al-Azhar, the bastion of Islamic orthodoxy, initiated its own periodical, *Nur al-Islam* ("The Light of Islam"), thus adopting what had previously been labeled a *bid'a*. In fact, opposition to the press by al-Azhar's 'ulama' remained as firm as that of their predecessors. They still regarded journalism as "one of the most dangerous means" at the disposal of "the enemies of the true faith" for spreading their "false message and extolling wrongdo-ing." The opening article of the periodical noted that if in the past the evil writings of these enemies could reach only the few, the invention of the press had made it possible for their publications "to enter every valley, spread their wicked ideas on every hill," and "corrupt the hearts" of the believers. Al-Azhar, therefore, had resolved to do the logical and legitimate thing: use the enemy's weapon to defend Islam by "calling for good . . . and illuminating the right path." The journal's editor was even prepared to concede that "there is much good" in periodicals. Yet otherwise his philosophy was the same as Marsafi's and Alusi's during the previous century. In the event, al-Azhar's success in checking the spread of the press was hardly any greater than that of the nineteenth-century 'ulama'.

The aversion to newspapers and to the practice of journalism by the 'ulama' derived from their view of the press as unnecessary and hence unwelcome. This, however, was a matter of interpretation, and other interpretations were also possible. They began to be articulat-ed toward the end of the nineteenth century, regarding the press not as a harmful innovation but as a continuation of a legitimate tradition. Such, as will be recalled, was the view expressed by Sultan Mahmud the Second, who ordered the publication of *Taqvim-i Veqayi* in 1831 as a modern means of reviving an old function — that of the imperial historiographer.[17] This line of thinking was reflected in the religious Egyptian paper *al-I'lam*, which stated in 1885 that journals "are a branch of the study of history (*qism min 'ilm al-ta'rikh*) which [the ances-tral sages] recognized in their books. They reckoned that history is made up of the accounts of those who lived in the past, whether remote or recent." This shows that history consists of two kinds of news, the paper explained, past news and contemporary news, with journals be-longing to the latter category. For, "as is well known, the past only becomes past after it had been a present, and papers reporting current events thus become history after a while."[18] Sometime later, the Egyp-tian weekly *al-Zahir* reiterated this concept when it described newspa-pers as "records of modern history" (*sijilat al-ta'rikh al-jadid*), with the editor of a newspaper serving, therefore, as a historian (*mu'arrikh*) who enlightens his community in all that concerns current events, science, culture, and education.[19]

This approach was part of an overall effort by a group of intellectual leaders to reconcile the many foreign innovations introduced into society with traditional concepts. Unwilling to forego either realm, the intellectuals found themselves engaged in defining and redefining both, thereby underscoring the distance between themselves and their more conservative colleagues, for whom innovation as such was abhorrent. These attempts at squaring foreign ideas with ancient local custom often produced peculiar rationalizations, as in the case of legitimizing the press of today as tomorrow's history. Another aspect of this approach was a curious attempt by Arab historians of the press to trace the roots of Arab journalism in earlier periods. Chroniclers such as the fifteenth-century Maqrizi and Ibn Iyas and the eighteenth- and nineteenth-century Jabarti were labeled "journalists" (*suhufi*, or *katib sihafa*), and their works "*sihafa* in the fullest sense of the word." Even authors of works other than chronicles during the classical period, such as Ibn al-Muqaffa', Jahiz, and Ibn Hawqal, (in the eighth, ninth, and tenth centuries respectively), were described as journalists or "reporters" (*katib riburtaj*).[20] This compelling need to reconcile the present with the past was understandable in a society that for so many centuries had held up the era of the Prophet as the absolute ideal. The great majority of those actually engaged in journalism in the nineteenth and twentieth centuries, however, did not bother to address the dilemma, carrying on with their basically secular endeavor without any special regard for historical precedent.

Ultimately, the ambivalent attitude of the 'ulama' to the press had the effect of tempering public aversion to it on religious grounds. Had the religious leadership been firmly united in opposing the *bid'a*, and had they acted vigorously to dissuade their followers from exposing themselves to it, they probably could have posed a greater obstacle to it than was the case. But the position of the 'ulama' was equivocal, and with the passage of time many within their ranks not only tolerated, or even welcomed, the press but also took part in it themselves, setting an explicit example for their disciples. Political circumstances constituted an element in the decline of religious opposition, for the struggle against foreign domination was a cause that was shared by the 'ulama' and the press. Both articulated an anti-Western message and an appeal for national independence, complementing each other as channels for popular sentiment. Jamal al-Din al-Afghani, a symbol of Islamic opposition to European domination during the late nineteenth century, sought to meet the challenge of foreign domination with the most powerful weapon available, by publishing his own journal and encouraging his pupils to do so as well. His colleague and sometime publishing partner, Muhammad 'Abduh, did the same and was even more prolific, as did Rashid Rida and other prominent 'ulama', a trend that was carried on with the publication of a journal by al-Azhar itself. By then, religious opposition to the idea of newspapers had become history for all intents and purposes.

Newspapers and Traditional Literary Norms

The genre of journalistic writing, especially reportage of news, demands, above all, brevity and clarity to suit the transient nature of a newspaper's contents, the limitations of format, and short deadlines. The goal of mass circulation requires, moreover, the use of straightforward language that can be readily understood by all. This is particularly true of daily newspapers, devoted mostly to reporting and discussing the transitory issues of the day, but even periodicals of lesser frequency and scope demand linguistic succinctness. In the West, a journalistic style had evolved along with the development of the press that departed from literary conventions associated with other types of writing, one of many literary and linguistic developments that took place over a period of three or four centuries.

Traditional linguistic and stylistic norms in Arabic did not readily lend themselves to journalistic writing. Nor was the writing of Ibn al-Muqaffa', Jahiz, Ibn Iyas, and Jabarti, sometimes cited, misguidedly, as the "earliest Arabic journalists," a functional basis for the new undertaking. Multilayered and extraordinarily rich, this legacy no doubt offered a broad range of options. Arab writers who were engaged in the new venture experimented with different modes of writing inherited from the past, to which they were passionately attached, while seeking to mold a distinctive language for the press. The process, begun with the emergence of first Arabic periodicals, was only completed by the mid-twentieth century, and even then not everywhere.

The most obvious point of departure for a press style was the literary prose of classical *adab* — a generic term used to describe all fields of learning but also the more specific sphere of *belles lettres*. *Adab* prose, which in early Islam had been simple and direct, underwent a transformation later on that rendered it more ornate and in many ways more pleasing but also less functional. *Adab* came to be marked by associative language that evoked both immediate and distant images through direct and indirect allusions. In form it was characterized by high embellishment, quotations from the Qur'an and from poetry, and such features as *saj'* (rhymed prose) and *jinas* or *ijnas* (homophony, or phonetic conformity of words). The more it made use of figures of speech — *isti'ara* (metaphor), *tashbih* (simile), *tawriyya* (allusion) — and hyperbole, the better it was considered to be.[21] By the eve of the modern era, the literary norms of *adab* had come to be typified by a striving for formal and verbal perfection at the expense of clarity, with ambiguity not regarded as a weakness. The premise was that a message is transmitted more effectively if it is multicolored, with maximal variations in shading. Beauty and embellishment were of the essence. Such standards reflected the centrality of the Holy Book in the community's life, cited several times daily in prayer, a text that had as much virtue in its form and timbre as in its content, which was not always quite intelligible. The various features of this style, especially rhyme, indicated clearly that these texts were designed to be read aloud, and with proper intonation, rather than silently. Much genius and devotion was invested in developing these standards, which became a source of pride to speakers, and even more so to writers, of the Arabic idiom.

A literary style emphasizing form as much as substance was not the only source of inspiration for the new genre. The Arabic literary heritage also contained more direct and factual prose, of the kind that was used in chronicles and historical texts, geographic accounts, and administrative manuals. Although the authors of such works often aimed at making their prose clear and utilitarian, this genre too was influenced by the literary conventions that gave prominence to aesthetics, sometimes so much so that these works could be classified as *adab* at its best. The impact of this literary norm may be seen in the titles of many of these works, which are often rhymed and highly ornate, and sometimes allude to the book's contents only indirectly. The title of Jabarti's chronicle, *'Aja'ib al-athar fi al-tarajim wal-akhbar* (roughly, as one scholar suggested, "Wondrous Seeds of Men and Their Deeds") is a typical instance.[22] Nevertheless, the effect of the ornamental style on this type of writing was usually more limited than on other modes of writing. In principle, therefore, the chronicle style seemed suitable as a point of departure for the journalistic enterprise, especially as chronicles constituted an annual, monthly, or even daily record of events.

Neither *adab* nor the more technical, historical, or geographical works, however, were produced for mass consumption. Rather, they were written for the relatively small literate community that had access to collections of manuscripts and appreciated high literary style. They were seldom produced with the constraint of a deadline, and authors could afford to take time to polish their style to the desired degree so as to impress their customers. The demands of the periodic press, of course, were different. Periodicals were designed to be read by a much larger public, which could be reached through the modern technique of printing. This larger public conducted its daily discourse in a functional, unadorned vernacular, which offered another possible style source for the new medium, albeit a somewhat problematic source, as the spoken colloquial language had hardly ever been used for writing.

These linguistic sources — embellished *adab*, the more direct style of the chroniclers and geographers, and sometimes the spoken vernacular, along with the foreign example of journalistic language — formed the basis for a new style that was devised during the first, formative century of the Arabic press. Standards were gradually forged through trial and error to suit the pace, the format, and the other demands of the me-

dium. In the process, the press — more so than any other literary medium — contributed to the shaping of modern Arabic as a functional
language, the secularization of the language, and the molding of literary norms that would facilitate the popularization of literature. An
examination of this contribution to language and literature is beyond
the scope of this work, but the trial and error that were involved in the
process are relevant, as they mirror both the achievements and the
difficulties in the evolution of the press.[23]

Editors of the early journals seem to have conceptualized the medium as designed not only to impart new kinds of knowledge, but to
fulfill the traditional objectives of books as well — to enlighten and entertain by catering to the literary tastes of the audience. This view was
reflected in the common practice of publishing literary works in the
press, not only in cultural journals but also in periodicals devoted to
news and political analysis, including daily newspapers. Muhammad
'Ali's first printed organ, *Jurnal al-Khidiw*, a bulletin of administrative
information, was reported to have featured stories from the *Thousand
and One Nights* "for attraction and amusement."[24] Its successor, *al-Waqa'i'
al-Misriyya*, under Tahtawi's editorship, ran essays of a broadly cultural
nature, for example, a discussion of various forms of government and
a study of Ibn Khaldun's style. Later, the paper also published stories
and poetry from the Arabic heritage and adaptations of European
works. Private papers too adhered to this tradition. The Beiruti *Hadiqat
al-Akhbar* serialized excerpts from the history of the fourteenth-century
Syrian Ibn Shahna from its second issue (January 1858) onward, and
(from July of that year) from the chronicles of his compatriot, Abu
Shama, and other original and translated literary works. Abu al-Su'ud's
Wadi al-Nil also published chapters from classical Arabic works in the
late 1860s, starting with the account of the fourteenth-century traveler
Ibn Battuta, as well as translated fiction. Similarly, *al-Ahram* featured a
serialized history of the pyramids, from which its name was derived;
al-Muqattam ran an adaptation of Walter Scott's *Ivanhoe*; and Lutfi al-
Sayyid's *al-Jarida* published a rendition of Jules Verne's *De la terre à la
lune*.[25] In the same tradition, newspapers commonly included curious
anecdotes (*nawadir*, or *ghara'ib*), such as a story about a calf born with
two heads, published in *al-Waqa'i' al-Misriyya*; an item about a girl who
swam an amazing distance at great speed "as if she had steampower
under her armpits," which appeared in the first issue of *al-Ahram*; and a
report on a newspaper published by Eskimos, which appeared on the
front page of the Alexandria daily *Lisan al-'Arab*.[26]

Poetry (*qasa'id*), a literary genre that predated Islam, was also
incorporated into the new medium. The rules of poetry elevated form
over content and elegance over clarity even more than in rhymed prose.
Traditionally, texts of all kinds were prefaced by a poem, most often a
panegyric of the ruler or other influential persons. Similarly, prose of
all types was interwoven with poetic verses so as to render it more

elegant. These norms were transferred to the press during the early decades, most commonly in the form of glorifying the sultan and khedive on important occasions, as has been noted.[27] Poetry was also used instead of prose to convey certain kinds of messages, as when the author wished to express strong emotions better articulated in verse; such, for example, was a "Salute to the Arab Army" (*tahiyyat al-jaysh al-'Arabi*) printed on the front page of a Damascus newspaper to welcome Faysal's army in 1918. At other times it was employed without any special reason, simply to appeal to the reader's sense of beauty or to demonstrate the author's literary skill. Such appears to have been the case with a poem titled "Syria's Demands" (*matalib al-Sham*), published in rhyme in another Damascus paper in 1921, in which the editor implores the French governor, General Gouraud, to grant such prosaic requests as a pardon to criminals, a reduction in the price of lighting gas, and lowered postal fees for journals.[28]

This brings us to the most typical feature of the carry-over of traditional literary norms to the press, namely, in its reportage of news. In the early phase — that is, during the third quarter of the nineteenth century in Egypt and Lebanon, the pre-World War I period in Syria and Palestine, and the 1920s in Iraq and the Hejaz — writers utilized the classical style as a matter of course, making only minimal adjustments to suit the new format. Some of them were, in the words of a leading Egyptian scholar of the press, "quite unable to understand the difference between the language of books and that of journals."[29]

This approach was appropriate for journals of a cultural and literary nature. For example, Luis Khazin, owner of the Lebanese cultural monthly *al-Rayyis*, announced the appointment of his partner as editor of the journal in 1900 thus:

> We have appointed as chief author of its scientific pieces and editor of its literary ones, for correcting its phrases and selection of its words, the most learned editor and renowned writer, whose pearls of articulation adorn the bride of meaning, the honorable master Ibrahim al-Hurani.

The Arabic original is far more captivating and lyrical, even to an ear unaccustomed to the sound of Arabic.[30] This mode of writing, however, was not confined to literary publications alone. Writers used the traditional literary conventions of embellishment, rhyme, parallelism, metaphor, and simile in daily and weekly newspapers as well, subjecting reportage and analysis of current affairs to the demands of the form. News items, technical announcements, the occasional letters to the editors, even translations of items from the foreign press were composed in traditional style. Virtually every journalistic category reflected these standards. Rhyme was used on the front page of the first issue of *al-Waqa'i' al-Misriyya* to announce that the paper was printed "with the help of the Creator of the universe/ by the master of magnificent conquests in his printing press."[31] A letter by an Egyptian student to *al-*

Ahram, in 1876, started by noting: "Many people received with great delight/ the news of *al-Ahram*'s coming to light./ Its publication is, without hesitation/ one of the glorious events of this generation."[32] The letter continues on in rhyme, with additional characteristics of the ornate classical style. Similarly, a lengthy notice in *al-Jawa'ib* in 1868 announcing the publication of a book on the history of the Arabic-speaking countries described it as:

> marked by grace and virtue/ and devoid of any insolence and immoral issue./ It would help state leaders in their administration/ and lend army commanders courage and determination./ It would teach potentates caution/ and their subjects respect and devotion.[33]

The opening article in the first issue of a newspaper was often written in classical *adab* style, the writer evidently feeling a need to link the new with tradition. Thus Amin Shumayyil's *al-Huquq* ("Laws," or "Rights"), a sober weekly report of legal proceedings, was launched in 1886 with a statement phrased in ornate *saj'* that reads like a segment of medieval literature: "In this paper, *al-Huquq*, we shall strictly adhere/ to candor of speech and to being sincere," the editor pledged.[34] Such, likewise, was the rhymed introductory article in *al-Mu'ayyad* in 1889, a paper that would later pioneer the use of functional language. The journal undertook to present domestic news

> which warns and teaches/ propagates and preaches./ And since the inclination to gather news/ and the desire to explore views/ is of the nature of the human mind/ we would not neglect matters of commerce and of any other kind. . . . [35]

Rhyme was also commonly used in polemic exchanges, reflecting an old tradition with roots in pre-Islamic times, in controversies over issues of language and style as well as in political disputes. 'Abdallah al-Nadim, in his satirical weekly *al-Ustadh*, attacked the owners of *al-Muqattam* in 1893 in biting rhyme for their pro-British stance. For these journalists, he charged,

> employing vain calumniation/ is both a habit and an inclination./ They believe they help the English by lying/ and confuse people's minds by falsifying./ Deluding themselves they thus assist/ the Egyptian nation and the peoples of the East./ But once true facts become clear/ you will readily tell the hypocrite from the sincere.[36]

A decade later, the editor of the daily *al-Zahir* interwove rhyme into an attack upon the person of 'Ali Yusuf after the religious court's decision to annul Yusuf's marriage with Shaykh al-Sadat's daughter. "You have assaulted the community's values and [neglected] your duty to God and His Prophet," the paper declared.

> You have fallen from a lofty peak down to the abyss of defeat/ hopeless, stranded in mud, of which there is no retreat/ tied up in chains of horror, you will ever remain in the pit.[37]

Papers also used *saj'* in reporting the news. An account in *Wadi al-Nil* of a celebration held by the khedive in the 'Abdin palace to mark the beginning of the new year in 1870 portrayed the event with much color:

> Army officers were solemnly received/ along with high royal servants by the khedive./ Adorned with stately attire and decoration/ they marked the new year in festive jubilation./ They eventually left the place/ having enjoyed royal hospitality and grace.[38]

A newspaper in Baghdad in 1909 denounced the perpetrators of an attempted coup against the Young Turks in April of that year for seeking "to return the people to slavery after liberation/ to social injustice after equalization/ and, after justice, to inequity and oppression."[39] An article in *Hijaz* around the same time lamented the poor state of the country thus: "We have substituted science and education/ with ignorance and degradation/ . . . Our civilized state no longer exists/ for fate has transformed us all into beasts."[40] And *al-Istiqlal al-'Arabi* of Damascus described Faysal's Arab army in 1918 as having traversed "awesome mountains and green valley[s] with ease/ tremendous stretches of land, and the vast seas."[41]

Proud of the Arabic literary legacy and emotionally attached to it, many writers were reluctant to consider any alternative. A few, however, sensed that the requirements of journalistic writing rendered the classical style inadequate. Butrus al-Bustani, who belonged to the first generation of writers, while as appreciative of the aesthetic achievements of this heritage as any of his contemporaries, voiced frustration that it was unsuitable for the clear and accurate expression of ideas. "A language that has many expressions for one notion but lacks words for many other notions is, in fact, a poor language, not a rich one, and its speakers are poor, not rich," he argued.[42] Jurji Zaydan complained similarly that the accent on form in Arabic had "made it all but impossible to grasp the meaning [of a text], couched as it was in ambiguous images."[43] Arab historians would later concur that the language of the nineteenth century was "sick" and "frozen," devoid of vigor and clarity, "imprisoned in the quarters of al-Azhar, [whose guardians] hardly ever venture out into real life"—a "feeble" language (*rakika*), as it was commonly depicted.[44]

The literary norms of *adab* that had served as a starting point for journalistic writing were bound to give way to other standards, a development that occurred as a result of both external and domestic factors. The introduction and assimilation of the telegraph dictated a shift to a more concise and practical style and the gradual abandoning of nonfunctional embellishments. Messages received by cable were incorporated in the press unchanged, as editing them was scarcely feasible in the rush of producing daily newspapers. These dispatches, and reports based on them, had a major impact on the emergence of a straightforward mode of writing. The European press, which by the late nineteenth century was received in the region on a regular basis, also presented attractive models of functional language that were emulated. Newspapers in Alexandria (where telegraph was first introduced, in 1866) and Cairo, and Shidyaq's *al-Jawa'ib* in the Ottoman capital, pioneered this change in the 1870s and 1880s, followed by the Lebanese press, which drew a large proportion of its reports from them. The shift to daily newspapers was an important factor in this transformation, for the deadlines involved were incompatible with a complex style that required more time to compose. The most typical product of these changes was the *khabar*, or news-item, a concise piece of reportage describing an event or paraphrasing a long statement in brief. In a way *khabar* continued the tradition of classical chroniclers who often recorded events laconically. But the modern version was more dynamic in nature — a short information item extracted from a longer news report, abbreviated to fit the pace and format of a newspaper. Style and beauty were given up for practicality. Brief, simple, generally devoid of the writer's personal feelings, *khabar* was the solution to the challenge of reporting the myriad domestic and foreign events transmitted to the region. *Khabar* was largely responsible for the modification of Arabic prose.

The first significant attempts in this direction were made by Rifa'a Rafi' al-Tahtawi as early as the 1840s. As editor of *al-Waqa'i' al-Misriyya* during the 1840s and of *Rawdat al-Madaris* in the early 1870s, he made admirable efforts to detach his writing from the old literary style, abandoning *saj'* and developing a simpler and more direct reportorial mode. Showing unusual creativity, he aimed at devising a new vocabulary that would be faithful to the old norms yet utilitarian to suit the new medium. Tahtawi's achievements were impressive, but, since he was breaking new ground, they left much to be desired. His writing was still marred by overuse of metaphor and simile, serial synonymous expressions, and occasional lapses into rhyme, resulting in narrative that was often awkward and sometimes nearly unintelligible.[45]

The next generation of journalists — mostly, though not exclusively, secular-minded Lebanese Christians — made further strides in divesting themselves of traditional modes and devising a style more suitable to the medium. Ishaq, the Taqla brothers, Sarruf, Nimr, Sanu', and Nadim in Egypt, Salim al-Bustani and Khalil Sarkis in Lebanon, and Shidyaq in Istanbul were more extensively exposed to European prose than their predecessors, and more prone to conceptualizing in secular and scientific terms. Their writing, remote from the intricate fashion of classical *adab*, was reminiscent of the more direct style used by Ibn Khaldun and Jabarti, but shorn of the literary orna-

mentation that had adorned their works. Since a newspaper's objective
was to communicate with the public, the editors of al-Muqattam believed, "it must be written in a language at once comprehensible to the
simple people and acceptable to the educated. We shall therefore seek
to select correct and familiar words, simple phrases, and uncomplicated
expressions."[46] What was meant by "familiar" and "simple"? Sarruf,
Nimr, and most of their colleagues did not have in mind the spoken
language, a possibility that was advanced by certain journalists as a
vehicle for written dialogue with the public (Sanu°s newspapers were
the most celebrated example). This direction was generally rejected,
with most journalists retaining a writing style well above the level of the
colloquial vernacular, viewing their occupation as a distinctly intellectual activity that was related to society's literary tradition despite necessary stylistic innovations.

'Ali Yusuf, of the same generation, was once credited as "the first
to have made the ultimate distinction between pure journalistic writing
and pure literary (adabiyya) style."[47] But it was actually a collective
effort. Other writers around the turn of the century—Mustafa Kamil,
Ahmad Lutfi al-Sayyid, Farah Antun, Salim Sarkis, and Amin al-
Rafi'i—advanced the trend, bringing the journalistic style to a point
much closer to its level today than to Tahtawi's and Butrus al-Bustani's
style half a century earlier. Why bother to say "the sun has eclipsed,
and the moon has disappeared, and the mountains have perished, and
the seas have vanished," argued Antun in 1902, when "a great man has
died" would do as well?[48] An Egyptian newspaper in 1910 ran this
typically straightforward account:

> the Republicans (al-jumhuriyyin) are awaiting the return of Mr. Roosevelt
> with profound concern. As for the radicals (al-mutatarifin), they have
> expressed surprise at Roosevelt's writing to one of them, inviting him to
> come and negotiate with him upon [Roosevelt's] return. The Republi-
> cans, however, have announced their confidence in the former presi-
> dent's impartiality.[49]

By then, after several decades of the new style of writing, and with
the growing popularity of the medium, most journalists had done away
with ornamentation and used a functional style as a matter of course.

Yet another important element emerged, alongside the khabar, out
of the convergence of traditional standards and new demands—the
political essay, the maqal or maqala. This development reflects a fascinat-
ing aspect of the evolution of modern Arabic literature, worthy of
separate study. The notion of a political essay was a novelty, implying
discussion of a specific, well-defined topic in a comprehensive, succinct,
and lucid manner, as distinct from the lengthy and often incoherent
polemics of traditional prose. Writers of Ishaq's and Nadim's generation initiated the format in the 1870s and 1880s, but it was only toward
the turn of the century, with the consolidation of the large Egyptian

dailies, that this type of writing developed into a norm. Essays appeared regularly as editorials (*maqal iftitahi*) or as features, dealing primarily with political or politically related issues. The major issue of the period—foreign domination, which evoked nationalist struggles against the occupiers and their domestic supporters—was reflected in intense essays that advocated a variety of courses of action, often conflicting. The British presence in Egypt was one such issue, along with Young Turk pressure in the Arab provinces before World War I, the Jewish presence in Palestine, and, after the war, British and French control over large parts of the region. Passionate and increasingly daring essays became the backbone of the political press during those highly charged periods, relegating almost all other categories, including news reportage (*khabar*) to secondary importance. A good example is the first issue of Lutfi al-Sayyid's *al-Jarida*, in 1907, which carried an editorial on page one entitled "Nationalism in Egypt"; three articles on political, social, and economic issues on page two (a comparison between Egypt and the United States; the Egyptian middle class; and problems related to Germany); and local and international news and commercial matters only on the third and fourth pages.[50] Even where the *maqal* received less prominence, it continued to play an important role in shaping journalistic style.

The early political essays were often produced by writers who were steeped in the art of *adab* and who published novels, short stories, history books, and the like in the best *adab* style alongside their journalistic undertakings. These writers viewed their role in the press as a continuation of the old tradition of Arab literature, and while their articles for journals were phrased differently from their other works, the difference was slight and the boundary was not pronounced. More often than not there was a marked ring of *adab* in their press essays. In fact, the phenomenon of author-journalists, for whom the press was simply another avenue of literary expression, was born with the Arab press itself, beginning with such early writers as Tahtawi and the Bustanis, continuing with Muhammad 'Abduh, Rashid Rida, Muhammad Kurd 'Ali, and writers of their generation, and reaching a zenith after World War I with such leading Egyptian writers as Muhammad Husayn Haykal, 'Abbas Mahmud al-'Aqqad, and Ibrahim al-Mazini. These gifted writers invested as much effort in their press articles as in their other endeavors, honing the essay into an art form, adapting it to the demands of the medium, and turning it into an effective vehicle for debating the issues of the day. The author-journalists personified the essence of the transformation of literary norms: Solidly grounded in the old conventions, they explored, developed, and passed on modified principles for written discourse.

The *maqal* writers themselves represented only an interim phase in the transformation of literary norms. The next generation of essayists—not necessarily chronologically but in terms of metamorphosis in style

—were generally less familiar with, and less interested in, the legacy of *adab*. They were, however, no less committed to public debate through the vehicle of the essay, which had emerged as an effective tool. Some of the writers who joined the press at the end of the nineteenth century—the number increased markedly after World War I—regarded it primarily as a battleground where they could launch or join a struggle. As such its requirements differed from those of the past: An unadorned style and aggressive language were better suited to the purpose and there was no need, or time, for artistic linguistic formulations. In fact, with newspapers aiming at arousing the public to battle, a direct style seemed to be the most effective. This view eventually came to dominate the field of essay writing.

By the early 1920s, perhaps the majority of the editorial and other essay writers in the Egyptian press, and many of those in the other Arab countries, viewed the press as a vocation—a "profession and (political) mission" (*hirfa wa-risala*), to borrow Salama Musa's definition—rather than as a literary and cultural pursuit. The qualifications required to engage in it were, accordingly, different and on the whole more limited. By the following decade, writers of the previous literary generation, who had hitherto divided their efforts between writing novels and writing for the press, were abandoning the routine of political essay writing and shifting to other literary areas. Although they continued to write for the press, they no longer referred to their output as *maqal*. Instead, they depicted it in such terms as *sura* (image, replica), *lawha* (sketch), *yawmiyyat* (diary), and the like, to distinguish it from the journalistic pieces written by their more pugnacious colleagues.[51] Gradually *maqal*-writing became the domain of the pragmatic political publicists.

The development of modern *khabar* and *maqal* greatly advanced the style of Arabic journalistic writing. Although it evolved at different tempos in the various parts of the region, overall the Arab press had freed itself from the restrictions of unsuitable literary norms and had created more functional alternatives by the mid-twentieth century. On the whole the process was rapid, accelerated by the quick pace of developments in other domains. Yet many characteristics of traditional prose were still discernible below the surface of the modern journalistic style even as late as the mid-twentieth century. Arabic writers were no more prone than their counterparts anywhere to abandon their rich literary legacy beyond what was needed to adapt to the new medium. This unease with journalistic writing was reflected in a variety of nuances, especially in the area of vocabulary and terminology.

The Vocabulary of the Press

Premodern Arabic was a rich language with an elaborate lexicon and a vast structural capacity for self-expansion. Scientific, human, social,

political, or artistic notions were precisely and often elegantly expressed. Like every language, Arabic reflected the views and attitudes
of society, a reflection, in turn, of socioeconomic and political realities.
Words had connotations rooted in society's values, often of a conspicuous Islamic nature, with harmony between conception and expression.[52] Under the impact of modern developments, however, this harmony was lost, with the result that the language lost a good deal of its
expressive vigor.

Until late in the nineteenth century, and in some places until the
twentieth century, domestic social, political, or technological developments were fully and easily described and discussed in Arabic. Basic
concepts remained much as in the past: Governmental and administrative institutions, political procedures, social customs, the tools and
methods of agriculture, crafts and trade, the art of medicine—all had
their traditional, and satisfactory, terminology. While periodicals faced
problems in addressing such matters in a concise style, as has been
seen, the difficulty did not lie in vocabulary. However, once writers
were confronted with the formidable challenge of dealing with foreign
concepts to which society was newly exposed—a host of unknown ideas,
institutions, and devices—the extant vocabulary proved inadequate.
Before long, many of the alien concepts and devices themselves began
to be imported into the region at the initiative of rulers. Egypt and, to
some extent, Lebanon became a stage for experimentation with such
new political ideas as nationalism, representative assemblies, and constitutions during the last third of the nineteenth century, with other
areas in the region exposed to these ideas after World War I. Innovations in the fields of science and technology were also imported. All
these novelties necessitated linguistic modification in order to be depicted and discussed. In some areas the conceptual changes were so
basic that vocabulary had to be completely transformed. Ibrahim al-
Yaziji, a nineteenth-century master of classical Arabic, expressed
amazement at the turn of the century at the far-reaching changes that
had affected the language during the previous decade;[53] had he been
able to see into the future and glimpse the newspapers half a century
later, he would have been all the more amazed, and no doubt would
have had difficulty making sense of much that was contained in them,
for the language had continued to evolve dramatically. For writers of
Tahtawi's and Bustani's generation, which had preceded that of Yaziji,
the press of the twentieth century would have been largely unintelligible. Conversely, twentieth-century readers would find the language of
the early journals strange and at times incomprehensible.

It was not only journalists who faced the challenge of adapting the
language to new needs. Translators of European works into Arabic,
textbook writers in new (especially scientific) areas, and travel writers
describing phenomena abroad all confronted similar problems even
before the advent of the press. Yet the leading role in introducing

linguistic change was played by newspapers. Forced to contend with problems of terminology on a regular, sometimes daily, basis, they undoubtedly made the largest contribution to changing Arabic into a functional, articulate modern language.

The interaction between the process of linguistic change and the development of the press is highly illuminating. In many ways, the change in language epitomized the assimilation of the medium in the region, which involved relinquishing old literary modes or adjusting them to new criteria. The domain in which Arabic was least prepared for the task was science and technology, for obvious reasons. Journals that undertook familiarizing their readers with scientific concepts, for example *al-Muqtataf*, needed considerable resourcefulness to produce terminology that would convey these concepts intelligibly and accurately, especially in an age of such dramatic technological momentum. However, even in social, political, and cultural fields, with which most of the periodicals dealt, and for which there existed a rich vocabulary, the problems were complex. Overwhelmed by the plurality of new foreign ideas that were sometimes analogous to, but seldom identical with, their own, the arbiters of the language groped for ways to express them. They borrowed foreign words, forged new expressions, revived old ones, and altered the meaning of others, in a process that was anything but smooth. Inevitably, considerable ambiguity resulted, and the press went through a phase of fractured communication between writers and readers, with public discourse on these matters, accordingly, rather confused.[54]

Speakers of Arabic were not the first in the Middle East to face the linguistic challenge posed by foreign ideas. The Turks, rulers of the Islamic empire for centuries, who maintained diplomatic and other contacts with Europe, had been exposed to foreign ideas earlier and by the turn of the nineteenth century had devised certain linguistic formats to express them. Because of the lexical proximity between the two languages, and since many educated Arabs were also versed in Turkish, these Turkish expressions were used extensively during the early decades of the process of the modernization of Arabic. When *al-Waqa'i' al-Misriyya* appeared in Egypt in 1828, it was printed bilingually, in Turkish and Arabic, with the Arabic translated from the Turkish original for over a decade thereafter. However, Turkish itself had not entirely adapted to the reportage of foreign affairs, so that rendering it into Arabic produced awkward results. Two brief examples will suffice to illustrate the quality of this reportage. An account from March 1830 reads approximately thus:

> A *jurnal* [report] from England received in France has indicated that *lah ubuld* [Leopold (of Saxe-Coburg)], one of their leaders [*ahad kibarihim*], was appointed as ruler [*hakim*] over *ta'ifat al-rum* [the Greek community, Greece] with the help of a man named *duqa walintan* [the Duke of Well-

ington]. Thus *qabuz strya* [Capo d'Istria] was relieved of his authority over them on behalf of Russia.

In the same issue:

> A man named Malaqus, one of the *ufijiyalat* [officials] of Austria, was charged by the king of the Muslims [*malik al-muslimin*, the sultan] with purchasing a known number of uniforms worn by the cavalry of the king of Austria who are called *husad* [i.e., Hussar] for the use of the military horsemen now training in the art of war in Islambul [sic].[55]

While the facts are basically correct, the language is murky. Aside from the strange ring of the proper names, some of the other terms must have been enigmatic to the readers, or understood erroneously in the Arabic (and, no doubt, also the Turkish) version: *hakim, ta'ifat al-rum, duqa, ufijiyalat, husad*, and more. A conspicuous mark of this awkwardness was the reference to the Ottoman sultan in the second segment as "*malik* (king) of the Muslims" — a title translated from a foreign source which had a derogatory connotation in Islamic parlance and which the sultan would never have used for himself. The practice of making up the *Waqa'i'* in Turkish continued until 1842, when Tahtawi became editor, whereupon he changed the procedure by producing the bulletin in Arabic with Turkish translation.[56]

The problem of linguistic inappropriateness lasted even longer in the other Arab provinces of the Ottoman empire, where the official bilingual bulletins were almost the only available journals until the Young Turk revolution. The official journals in Syria, Iraq, and Palestine were written by Turkish officials whose command of Arabic was limited and who were more familiar with colloquial than with literary Arabic, so that they commonly introduced words and morphological elements from the Arabic vernacular into the written text alongside Turkish expressions. They also borrowed foreign terms liberally, a practice more common in Turkish than in Arabic. Personal titles such as *bashmudir, bashkatib*, and *cha'ush*; honorifics such as *dawlatlu, fakhamatlu*, and *sa'adatlu*; and terms such as *kiler* (warehouse), *khasta khane* (hospital), *mashrutiyya* (constitution), and *mamnu'iyya* (prohibition) — all Turkish or Turkicized Arabic expressions — appeared routinely in their reports on domestic and even international affairs. Words of European origin such as *qumandan* and *qumisiyyun, bulis* (police), *brins* (prince), *jandarma* and *suldat* (French *soldat*), *bawabir* (plural of *babur*, French *vapeur*, steamship), and *bandira* (Italian *bandiera*, flag) were also used often. In regions where other languages were spoken, such as Kurdish, Armenian, and Persian, words from these languages too were interwoven in the Arabic. The choice of terms and their morphological context was random, the syntax was chaotic, and the aesthetic aspect, so important in Arabic, was nonexistent. The outcome, to quote one Syrian historian, was "a school for linguistic barbarism and literary poverty."[57]

Contemporary readers reported that the Arabic text was sometimes decipherable only after checking and comparing it with the Turkish. "Should you examine one of these papers," commented an Iraqi linguist in 1911, "and wonder in which language it was written, you would be unable to tell. You may ask yourself, perhaps the author is speaking in Turkish, or Kurdish, or Persian, or Hindi, or colloquial Arabic, but the truth is that he speaks in all of these languages at once." Fortunately, a Syrian writer remarked, this press had a small circulation, or it would have corrupted the people's language.[58]

The poor linguistic quality of these early publications could hardly endear them to the small educated community, which had been taught respect and love for their literary heritage. Someone as discerning as Tahtawi, for example, viewed such standards as unacceptable. He sought to rid the language of such intrusions and replace them with proper Arabic expressions that would be equally effective. Yet he was overwhelmed by the quantity of new concepts, and was forced to improvise under pressure. Inevitably, his vocabulary too included words taken from the spoken vernacular, foreign terms, and Turkish words, along with the phrases that he invented so resourcefully. [59]

Tahtawi's pupils, most of whom were less gifted than he, did not always adopt his contributions and often favored the stock of older, less successful expressions. His efforts were followed up more systematically, however, by the Lebanese Christian journalists writing in their own country, in Egypt, and elsewhere, whose initiative during the last third of the nineteenth century coincided with the broader Arabic cultural and literary revival in Lebanon. Men like Butrus and Salim al-Bustani, Faris al-Shidyaq, and Ibrahim al-Yaziji, proud masters of the language and convinced of its capacity to adjust to the new challenges, committed themselves to the development of a functional vocabulary. This mission, involving as it did the forsaking of much that was time-honored, and innovation based on personal judgment and taste, generated debates and controversies, the most famous of which was the Shidyaq–Yaziji conflict over the best method to invigorate the language.[60] A particularly important role in the development of a new vocabulary was played by Lebanese emigrants in Europe from the early 1860s, joined by a group of Egyptian colleagues the following decade. Their knowledge of European affairs, which occupied a prominent place in the Arab press, and their experience in a society where journals were a popular commodity, along with their close involvement in the Arabic revival movement back home, made them valuable contributors to the new effort.

Newspapers from these early years offer plentiful testimony to the linguistic difficulties faced by writers and their attempts to overcome them. Fluidity of terminology was one characteristic of this experimental stage: A new concept would be designated by a variety of interchangeable words, sometimes identical but more often only partly overlapping in meaning, each of which, in turn, would be employed to express more than one notion. For example, the idea of an international conference (a novelty in the Arab experience), was referred to by one paper interchangeably as *jalsa* (literally, a sitting), *majlis* (a sitting place, or session), *jam'iyya* (a gathering or association), and *mujtama'* (a meeting place, an assembly). The same paper, however, also ascribed other meanings to the first two words: *jalsa* was used in the sense of a conference session, and *majlis* to describe the British Parliament.[61] Other contemporary sources used other words to denote the idea of an international conference: *diwan*, which likewise had several other meanings;[62] the borrowed term *kunfirans* — conference;[63] and *mu'tamar*, a neologism that first appeared in the late 1870s and eventually became the accepted term for the notion.[64] To pick another example, the novelty of a newspaper was at first designated by either of two words, both of European origin, which had entered Arabic via Turkish: *ghazita*, from the French *gazette* or Italian *gazetta*,[65] and *jurnal*, from the French.[66] The latter term, however, also served variably to denote a register, a message, an official announcement, or a police report, depending on the context. The two words that would eventually be accepted, interchangeably, as definitive — *jarida* and *sahifa* — were both classical terms connoting written texts, which began to be used in the 1860s and became popular during the following decade. But until they won the day, all four words were used simultaneously, along with other expressions that were tried from time to time, such as *waraqa khabariyya* (literally, information sheet), *yawmiyyat* (daily events), and *nashra* (a published item). Similarly, the distinction between a newspaper, devoted primarily to news, and a periodical of some other nature, which by the end of the nineteenth century would be denoted by two different words — *jarida* (or *sahifa*) and *majalla*, respectively — was blurred during the early decades of the press.[67]

Such elasticity of meaning, the appearance and disappearance of terms, the borrowing of foreign words, and the emergence of neologisms all marked the transient phase that the language was undergoing. There were also more technical signs of this transition: the common practice of explaining new and unfamiliar expressions by attaching better-known words in parentheses;[68] interpreting difficult terms in footnotes, even in newspapers;[69] and the resort to hendiadys, the use of paired of words with overlapping semantic ranges to denote an idea that neither word could denote alone.[70] These devices reflected not merely difficulties but a virtual crisis for a previously rich language that had suddenly become inadequate as a means of communication.

A particularly curious characteristic of this phase was the common tendency to seek solutions to the problems of modern conceptual expression in the traditional Arabic repertoire. Words with distinct traditional connotations, sometimes with a specifically Islamic coloration, were utilized to convey modern ideas, inevitably lending them irrelevant implications. In many cases this practice reflected (and no doubt engendered) confusion between the new notions and what was perceived, or at least presented, as their local equivalents. Thus, papers often depicted European nation-states as *milla* (a community defined by its religion);[71] the Pope as *khalifa* (caliph), or as *shaykh* of the Vatican;[72] constitutions as *shari'a* (Islamic holy law);[73] a European emperor as *sultan*;[74] Europe's feudal aristocracy as *ashraf* (notables claiming descent from the Prophet);[75] the French revolution as *fitna* (sedition);[76] the United States House of Representatives as a *shura* (a forum of consultants to the ruler);[77] the chapel of the Versailles palace as *masjid* (mosque);[78] and the Washington Monument in the American capital as a *ma'dhana* (minaret).[79] Obviously, the forced affixing of irrelevant contexts to new ideas could blur the sense of a text, while hardly being conducive to a precise rendition of the concept. This temporary absence of a utilitarian vocabulary imposed a heavy burden on the press during its early phase, inevitably impairing its assimilation.

By the onset of the twentieth century, the Arabic press in Egypt and Lebanon, as well as in Europe, seemed to be emerging from the nadir of the language crisis. Several decades of journalistic experience, and intensive exploration of linguistic possibilities, had produced the elementary vocabulary needed for a reasonably fluent communication between press and readership. Political, social, and scientific concepts that half a century earlier were barely known had acquired standard names and were discussed with increasing coherence. Many of the foreign ideas had become familiar, so that there was less need to interpret them. This is not to say that the transformation of the language had been completed, nor had all the obstacles to clarity and designative accuracy been removed — Egyptian and Lebanese papers of the early twentieth century were often marked by the old deficiencies, and there was room for much improvement. Yet from then on change would take place more slowly, in a more evolutionary rather than revolutionary process. By the eve of World War I, the language of the press in Egypt and Lebanon was more akin to what it would be 50 years later than to what it had been 25 years before.

Such was not the case in other parts of the region at that stage. Writers in Syria, Palestine, and Iraq, while familiar with the press outside, had little opportunity to implement the new linguistic standards. Similarly, the readership there in 1900 had remained in much the same place, in terms of linguistic awareness, as it had been in 1800. The press that emerged in these countries after 1908 started off from a low point linguistically, as in most other respects, and for a long while lagged behind the more experienced Egyptian and Lebanese press. Long decades of restrictive censorship and the massive influence of the Turkish language inhibited innovation. Furthermore, although the Young Turk revolution elicited a surge of journalistic activity, many of those who were attracted to the field had a limited education and an incomplete command of the language and issued papers that were poorly written, poorly produced, and ultimately ephemeral. Moreover, at that stage, most journals were still prepared with the close involvement and supervision of Turkish officials (who sometimes made the granting of a publication permit conditional upon the applicant's proficiency in Turkish). It was only after World War I that the language gradually shed the effects of these influences. Juzif Iliyas, in his study of style and language in the Syrian press, has shown how prewar norms continued to dominate much of the journalistic writing there well into the 1920s, with more modern and coherent vocabulary emerging only toward the end of the decade and especially during the 1930s. Iliyas attributes the timing of this development to the spread of education, as well as to the establishment of the academy of science in Damascus, which had as one of its goals the modernization of the language.[80] Similarly, scholars who have explored the Iraqi press after World War I have noted the poor level of the journalists' command of the language and the unstructured style of their reportage. "Such ignoramuses," one writer lamented, "humiliated the language."[81]

Still, the press in the Fertile Crescent and the Arabian Peninsula did not have to undergo the long process of learning and adaptation as had its Egyptian and Lebanese predecessors, for the pioneering work had already been done. The few years of relative freedom prior to World War I permitted closer contact between writers from the different parts of the region, and the better journalists in Syria, Iraq, Palestine, and Hejaz eagerly followed the trail blazed for them linguistically and in the other aspects of press activity, particularly by the Egyptians. The dramatic political changes following the war, the cultural developments that ensued, and the proliferation of newspapers accelerated the process of closing the linguistic gap. Even in places where it was new, and despite problems of cultural adaptation, the press was able to shift to a fluent journalistic vocabulary relatively quickly. Although there were differences in linguistic level between countries and between newspapers within each country, these differences were more a reflection of variations in skill on the part of individual writers than a deficiency in the language itself. By the eve of World War II, the Arabic press as a whole had successfully met the dual challenge of devising an effective journalistic style and developing a functional vocabulary to serve it.

8

The Economic Angle:
The Press as Merchandise
and as Enterprise

The written Arab press was born and evolved under difficult economic conditions. Throughout the first century of the private Arab press, both its creators and its readership were, on the whole, poor, and publishers, functioning in a subsistence economy, had little inclination for economic enterprise. Furthermore, the technological infrastructure necessary for gathering news and producing and distributing newspapers—telegraph, printing, transportation, and postal services—developed tardily. The public's interest in the new products and its ability to read them were equally slow to develop. The process whereby newspapers became a standard commodity was prolonged and arduous, with innumerable journals failing along the way. Only very gradually did journalism become a profession capable of sustaining its members.

The Press as Merchandise

How many of those able to read could afford to buy a copy of a daily newspaper or subscribe to a journal? A major problem in answering this question is the fact that newspaper prices during much of the period under study were hopelessly chaotic. For one thing, the currency picture was extremely confused, especially prior to World War I, when "few countries had as unserviceable a currency as the Ottoman Empire."[1] The values of Ottoman coins fluctuated frequently, and there were variations not only between provinces but often within a single province as well. Moreover, a variety of foreign coins were in circulation throughout the empire, and their exchange rates were subject to similar shifts. Accordingly, the prices of journals, like those of other commodities, were quoted in various currencies. An example at random is Muhammad Kurd 'Ali's daily *al-Muqtabas* of 1908, which announced its rates as follows: a copy cost 1 metalik; a line of advertising 2 qurush; an annual subscription 4 riyals in Damascus, 1 Ottoman lira in the other provinces, and 25 francs abroad.[2] Unstable conditions in the aftermath of World War I perpetuated the currency turmoil for several more years, notably in the Fertile Crescent countries. As late as 1928, that is, ten years after the disintegration of the empire, the Damascene *al-Qabas* still quoted the price of a subscription in Ottoman gold liras.[3] Another factor contributing to the confusion was the great divergence in prices of newspapers, especially during the early part of the period. Journals of equal frequency, format, and size varied in price markedly, reflecting the experimental stage of their economic development. Weeklies in Egypt in 1893, for instance, sold at prices ranging from as little as 15 qurush to as much as 77 qurush.[4] Moreover, in their search for the most economical way to run their papers, owners often changed their prices. For example, the annual subscription rate for the Cairo daily *al-I'lam* inside Egypt was 50 francs on 21 April 1885, 45 francs by 21 June, and a low of 20 francs in September of the following year, a price that remained stable for the following two years. A single copy sold for 1 qurush in 1885, 2 qurush in 1886 and once again 1 qurush in 1887.[5] Given this confusing reality, only a very general picture of broad price ranges at different times and places may be reconstructed. Yet the significance of even these rough figures renders the unrecorded variations in prices inconsequential, as will be seen.

Nearly all newspapers were sold to subscribers who received them at their door. Only a few — mostly the large news journals that appeared daily, several times a week, or weekly — were also sold on the street singly. Subscriptions for dailies evidently cost more than for weeklies or monthlies. *Hadiqat al-Akhbar*, begun in Beirut in 1858 as a four-page semiweekly, set a rather high fee of 120 qurush for an annual subscription; a decade later, the fee had not changed. The weekly *al-Jawa'ib* in Istanbul charged the same fee in the 1860s. When the weekly *Lisan al-Hal* came out in Beirut in 1877, it charged only 14 francs, or 56 qurush, for an annual subscription, which typified the rates that would prevail throughout much of the Fertile Crescent following the journalistic flowering of 1908. On the eve of World War I, newspapers in Syrian towns sold for 30 to 80 qurush, in the towns of Palestine for 40 to 50 qurush, in Iraq for 30 to 40 qurush, and in the Hejaz 50 qurush.[6] *Lisan al-Hal*, having become a daily, sold an annual subscription in the years prior to the war for 93 qurush. Prices in Egypt, with its more dynamic economy, had always been somewhat higher. When *al-Ahram* appeared in Cairo, at first as a weekly, in 1876, its domestic subscription fee was

23 francs (equivalent to about 95 Egyptian qurush, which was 10 to 15 percent higher than the Ottoman qurush). When it became a daily, in 1881, the cost was raised to 55 francs, or 225 qurush. During the prewar period, daily newspapers in Egypt sold annual subscriptions domestically at rates ranging from 100 Egyptian qurush (*al-Liwa'*, 1900) to 180 qurush (*al-'Alam* and *al-I'tidal*, which replaced *al-Liwa'*, 1910). Non-news periodicals of varying frequencies had a broader range of prices. An annual subscription for *al-Muqtataf* cost 100 qurush around 1900, for *al-Hilal* 80, for *al-Manar* 60, and for *al-Jami'a* 40 to 60 qurush.

A modest rise in subscription rates was recorded throughout the region following the war. Prices in the former Ottoman provinces of the Fertile Crescent were quoted in the new currencies that came into use, gradually replacing the Ottoman coins. Syrian and Lebanese dailies in the interwar period sold for an annual fee of 1.5 to 2 Ottoman liras, or 3 to 6 Syrian pounds (the Syrian pound being roughly equivalent to 0.5 Ottoman lira). A subscription for the Lebanese *al-Ahwal* was 1.25 Ottoman lira in 1929, and for *Bayrut* 5.5 Syrian pounds in 1936. *Al-Muqtabas* of Damascus was offered at 3 Syrian pounds annually in 1924, as was *al-Qabas* in 1931. In Palestine, annual subscriptions for semiweeklies normally sold for 1 Egyptian pound (*al-Ittihad al-'Arabi* 1925, *al-Yarmuk* 1926) and for dailies 1.5 pound (*al-Hayah*, 1931); in Transjordan for 75 to 150 qurush; and in the Hejaz a subscription for the semiweekly *Barid al-Hijaz* in 1924 was in the same range, 100 qurush. Newspapers in Egypt sold at rates similar to those prevalent before the war: An annual subscription for the Nationalist Party's *al-Liwa' al-Misri* cost 200 Egyptian qurush in 1923; for the Liberal Constitutionalists' *al-Siyasa* 150 in 1927; for the Wafdist daily *Kawkab al-Sharq* 180 in 1929; for *al-Ahram* 120 in 1933; and for the Wafdist *al-Balagh* 150 qurush in 1942—i.e., between 120 to 200 qurush for Egyptian dailies in the interwar period. Prices for leading non-news periodicals were in the range of 85 to 120 qurush during this period: *al-Muqtataf* continued to sell annual subscriptions for 100 qurush; *al-Manar* raised its fee from 60 qurush to 100 in the 1920s and 1930s; and *al-Hilal* oscillated between 100–120 in the 1920s, then dropped to 85 qurush in 1939 and 50 during the World War II years. New periodicals appearing at this time generally set their prices in a similar range.

Did the price of 100 to 150 qurush (roughly equivalent to 1 to 1.5 English pounds or 5 to 7.5 American dollars) for an annual subscription to a daily newspaper, or half that amount for a periodical on cultural matters, constitute a great expense for people in the Middle East between the mid-nineteenth and mid-twentieth centuries? According to Issawi (relying on British consular reports, and other sources), on the eve of World War I, following several decades of continuous rise, the average annual per capita income in the provinces of the Fertile Crescent was an estimated $42, and in Egypt about $50, or roughly 850 and 1,000 qurush respectively. The income of large segments of society—

peasants, unskilled workers, and semiskilled laborers providing simple services—was even lower.[7] A subscription to a daily paper would amount to a prohibitive 10 percent or more of this average, clearly out of the question for a population living on a subsistence budget. In Damascus in 1900, the sum of 50 qurush—the price of a six-month subscription to *al-Muqtataf*—could purchase a total of 10 pounds of wheat bread, 20 pounds of wheat flour, about 4 pounds of rice, 3 pounds of beef, 10 pounds of cooking butter, and 3 pounds of coffee.[8] In Cairo of 1924, 75 qurush—a six-month subscription to any of several daily newspapers—could purchase a total of 16 pounds of wheat flour, 5 pounds of beef, 1 pound of cooking butter, and two dozen eggs.[9] A subscription to a newspaper or a periodical, then, was hardly a realistic option for the overwhelming majority of the population. It was, in fact, a luxury, accessible to the well-to-do, a tiny class that had the available income to spend as well as the time and interest to read and be involved.

But what about purchasing single copies of those newspapers that were sold on the street? This was, of course, more affordable, and did not necessitate committing resources for a year or six months in advance. Prices per copy appeared attractively low. During the second half of the nineteenth century, papers in the Fertile Crescent were normally sold at 1 qurush a copy, the cost, for example, of *Lisan al-Hal* in Beirut in the 1870s and of *Dimashq* in Damascus in the 1890s. After 1908 there was a marked decline in prices, apparently due to the flooding of the market with new publications, and many papers in Syria, including *al-Qabas* and *al-Muqtabas*, sold for as little as 1 metalik (0.25 qurush). In Egypt, *al-Ahram* initially sold for 0.5 franc (2 qurush) per copy in 1876, but by 1882 had cut the price by half. Around the turn of the century, some dailies, including *al-Muqattam* and *al-Mu'ayyad*, sold for 1 qurush a copy, while others, such as the popular *al-Jarida*, *al-Liwa'*, *al-'Alam*, and *al-I'tidal*, charged only 0.5 qurush, and there were papers that were still cheaper (*Lisan al-'Arab* in Alexandria charged 3 milims, or 0.3 qurush, per copy, with the stated aim of gaining broad circulation).[10] These rates remained largely unchanged throughout much of the region during the first half of the twentieth century, a striking fact in view of the rise in prices of other commodities, as well as the rise in income levels. Up until World War II, dailies were sold in Egypt for 3 to 5 milims, in Syria and Lebanon for 3 to 5 Syrian qurush (equivalent to 6 to 10 Egyptian milims), in Palestine for 1 qurush, and in Iraq and Transjordan for 0.5 to 1 qurush.

Again, an assessment must be made as to whether a newspaper that sold for a half qurush or a qurush per copy was widely accessible to the population. In the Ottoman empire of the nineteenth century, one qurush was enough to provide food for an adult for one day. It could buy a pound of rice or 1.5 pounds of flour in Beirut in 1871, 2 pounds of broad beans in Beirut at the end of the 1870s, and a pound of bread in Damascus and Aleppo during the first decade of the twentieth century. It was, likewise, sufficient for buying two meals a day in turn-of-the-century Egypt. A family of five — slightly below the average family size — required 5 to 8 qurush daily for basic foodstuffs during the late nineteenth and early twentieth centuries.[11]

Only people whose income was markedly above the requirement for basic survival could afford to buy a newspaper even occasionally. This group was almost exclusively urban, leaving the bulk of the population in the Arabic-speaking countries, which was rural, outside the pool of potential buyers up until the mid-twentieth century. How much better was the situation in the cities? A survey of nineteenth-century Syria showed that the vast majority of wage-earning laborers, including masons, carpenters, craftsmen, and unskilled laborers, earned an average of under 10 qurush a day. Within this group, unskilled laborers often earned a wage that was below subsistence for a family — 3 to 4 qurush or less, while masons and carpenters could sometimes earn 12 to 15 qurush a day. The situation in Iraq was generally similar during this period, although certain craftsmen, such as shoemakers and tinsmiths, could sometimes earn as much as 22.5 qurush daily. There was, however, a gradual increase in income for skilled labor and, concomitantly, in standard of living during the nineteenth century, which accelerated after 1900. Masons, carpenters, and cooks earned as much as 30 to 60 qurush a day in the Fertile Crescent on the eve of World War I.[12] After the war, income continued to rise slowly. By 1943, according to one assessment, unskilled laborers in Egypt and Iraq still earned 3 to 5 qurush daily, in Syria 8 to 10, and in Palestine (where exceptionally rapid economic development took place) as much as 22 to 25 qurush a day. Skilled workers, however, could earn 20 qurush in Egypt and Iraq, 30 in Syria, and up to 60 in Palestine.[13]

If a daily income of 10 qurush or less left the breadwinner outside the pool of potential newspaper buyers, an income of 20 to 30 qurush at the turn of the century, or 30 to 60 qurush after World War I, probably allowed for the purchase of a newspaper once in a while or even regularly, especially as the prices of newspapers had remained nominally unchanged, and hence were decreasing in real terms. Under these circumstances, while the peasant population and the unskilled laborers in the cities, who comprised the bulk of the urban population, were not a part of the press market either in the nineteenth or in the twentieth centuries, higher-income groups were: skilled workers, successful merchants, state functionaries, and a small but growing group of modern professionals, including journalists,[14] along with the tiny wealthy class, all of whom were not only able to purchase newspapers but, comprising society's literate population, were able to read them and benefit from them as well. Still, all these groups combined formed a very small fraction of the entire community.

While public interest in the messages of the press grew, enhanced by the dramatic developments taking place in the region particularly from the turn of the twentieth century onward, this curiosity increased faster than the public's purchasing ability. As we have seen, a single copy of a newspaper was utilized to reach a wide audience through collective subscriptions, public reading and, most commonly, transmitting the contents orally to family and friends. These devices played a vital role in amplifying the voice of the press, expanding the circle of consumers manyfold, but from an economic point of view they produced an adverse result: Newspaper publishers needed buyers, not merely readers, in order to sustain their operations. The slow growth of the purchasing market because of poverty seriously hampered the development of the press as an economic enterprise.

The Press as Enterprise: Starting Up

Many people believe that nothing is easier than starting a journal and turning it into a prosperous business, Egyptian publisher Jurji Zaydan noted in 1903. Prompted by an urge for publicity, they launch a newspaper, which, Zaydan explained, was easier than embarking on any other occupation:

> He who wishes to become a carpenter, for instance, cannot do so without investing in acquiring the necessary tools and renting a place. He who wants to sell groceries, or tobacco, or wine, or anything else, likewise needs appropriate capital, which in all cases is more extensive than what is needed to print one's own thoughts in a paper. He [the prospective journalist] therefore moves to establish a newspaper, assuming that after publishing the first issue or two income will begin to flow in and subscribers will rush to pay him so as to cover expenses. Publishing the first issue of a weekly paper or a periodical requires no storage place nor any special equipment, but only the fees for printing and postage. Rarely would a person be unable to afford it.[15]

Papers founded on a shoestring were typical of the Arabic press from its onset until World War II, more so than the few large newspapers that were established as big business from the start. Starting up a paper and running it for a while seems to have been a relatively simple matter, demanding, as one foreign resident in Egypt observed, merely "a little capital, an editorial writer and a grievance."[16]

In principle, producing a journal involved four basic activities: gathering material (if the paper was mostly or partly devoted to news), writing and editing, printing, and distribution. While a basic setting was required to run the operation — preferably an office, a post office box and, where available, a telephone — an office was not absolutely necessary, at least not at the beginning. It was possible to write and edit at home, in a cafe, or at the printer's shop. If the owner was prepared to make do with the most minimal means, if he was ready to work hard, and if he was resourceful and gifted, he could handle all four stages single-handedly or with very little help, and with a minimal infrastructure. If the message he wanted to promote had enough popular appeal, he could even score a marked success.

The costly way of gathering material was to subscribe to one of the news agencies, where they existed, as well as to employ reporters and informers throughout the province or the country and outside it—a must for a daily newspaper. But for a publication starting more modestly as a journal of opinion, which might also feature news at a less than daily frequency, news gathering could be accomplished far more cheaply: A pair of scissors could be effectively substituted for news agencies and reporters and used to expropriate from other papers. Knowledge of a foreign language was a useful asset in this context, for it allowed for the exploitation of the international press in a similar manner. Publishing a journal of views only, which necessitated no gathering of news, was even simpler. If the owner of a new publication wanted to avoid the expenses of paid writing, editing, and translation — which in Egypt had developed into legitimate occupations by the early 1880s—he could write and edit by himself. The one unavoidable expenditure was printing, but costs could be kept down even in that area. It was not necessary to acquire expensive printing equipment; rather, the owner could rent the services of existing presses, which were relatively inexpensive throughout the region and became increasingly so as they proliferated with time. Distribution of the finished product could necessitate costs if the owner mailed it to subscribers or sold it on the street, which would involve a small fee to the vendors, but this expense, too, could be largely avoided if the owner were prepared to distribute the paper personally, or hire a bunch of street urchins for the task at a pittance. Undertaking so many duties single-handedly, while not easy, was not impossible. More than one journal started this way and succeeded.

With patience and resolve it was possible to start a journal and run it for some time with very limited financing in the region during the entire period under review. Adib Ishaq, anxious to respond to Jamal al-Din al-Afghani's call for activism in print in Egypt of the late 1870s, was said to have embarked on his first project—the weekly *Misr*—with a capital investment of no more than 20 francs, or 80 qurush. Similarly, his contemporary, 'Abdallah Nadim, founded his own paper *al-Tankit wal-Tabkit* with merely "a few pounds in his pocket."[17] Ishaq and Nadim approached the press not as a business but as a mission, sustaining themselves and their journalistic projects through other sources of income. A quarter of a century later, Farah Antun started up his journal, *al-Jami'a*, in Alexandria with "what little [he] could save from teaching and odd jobs on other journals."[18] This was a common pattern for many of the new journalists who had strong passions but few financial resources. Shaykh 'Ali al-Rimawi, founder of the weekly *al-Najah* ("Success") in Jerusalem in 1908, was a teacher and civil servant. Yusuf al-'Isa, who established *Filastin* around the same time, was likewise a government official, and Iliya Zika, the owner of *al-Nafir*, supported himself by teaching Arabic to Jewish students in Jerusalem.[19] The case of Mahmud Mahdi Istanbuli, a Syrian teacher who in the early 1930s started a journal for teachers, is typical. "Ever since my appointment as a teacher," he related in his memoirs, "I had been thinking of establishing a journal that would discuss the problems of teachers, ease their task, and keep them abreast of new developments in education."

> But wherefrom shall I get the money, the source of life? I had nothing but my meager salary, which was already heavily burdened with expenses, for I had to support a large family both in Damascus and in the village. In addition, I resided away from the center of production of books and printed texts. Yet, since I felt that founding the journal was a must, I tightened the belt still further for myself and my family, cutting my expenses, something which elicited frequent complaints from my first wife, God bless her soul. Eventually I succeeded in establishing the paper under the name *Majallat al-Mu'allimin wal-Mu'allimat* ("Journal of [male and female] Teachers").[20]

For the prospective publisher who was prepared to do the bulk of the work by himself, the main expenditures were for printing and postage. Piecemeal evidence on the cost of printing in the region seems to indicate that it was rather low throughout the nineteenth and early twentieth centuries. Most presses utilized primitive equipment and methods, as labor costs for setting type and folding the paper manually were so low that it did not pay to install more advanced and costlier machines. Young boys entered the printing plants as poorly paid "devils" and before long became expert typesetters. Poor lighting conditions rendered many of them near-sighted: "I do not see how some of them avoid scratching their noses on the letters that they choose," noted an observer. "Seeing them at work, one would be led to think that they select type by scent."[21] A press owner in Egypt leased his business in 1919 for two Egyptian pounds per month, including the printers' wages. Several years later, when Fatima al-Yusuf considered starting her weekly, a colleague calculated for her that printing 3,000 copies of a 32-page journal on good-quality paper would cost 12 pounds. As late as 1951, hand-setting an issue of a daily newspaper in various parts of the region cost an estimated $13.[22] Postage was another expense that could be burdensome. For an operation the size of *al-Hilal*, for example, with several thousand subscribers, many of them overseas, mailing costs could be as high as double the cost of printing.[23] This would increase the required investment if the owner aimed at circulation beyond his hometown.

Establishing a paper with its own printing press — a substantial advantage for the journal (and a potential source of other revenues) —

was, of course, more costly, but even in that operational costs after the initial investment were quite modest. In 1887, Lord Cromer, the British agent and consul-general in Egypt, assessed that a primary investment of 100 pounds would be needed to establish an Arabic paper in that country, a figure that apparently included the cost of printing equipment. Thereafter, he estimated, some 25 pounds monthly would be needed. Cromer was not far off the mark. Two years later, 'Ali Yusuf founded his daily al-Mu'ayyad with the exact sum cited by Cromer. Yusuf, who had remarkable talent and gusto but no money of his own, borrowed 100 pounds from a friend, with whom he formed a partnership. This sum sufficed to purchase printing equipment, form a news-gathering network, including news agency subscriptions, and start up an enterprise that eventually succeeded.[24] Rashid Rida, who at the turn of the century mocked Farah Antun for his poor management of his monthly al-Jami'a, namely that he spent as much as 40 pounds to produce a single issue, noted that such a sum would suffice to run al-Manar for a whole year. Around the same time the offices of Rida's journal were broken into and all the equipment and the stock of paper were stolen, whereupon Rida borrowed 50 pounds from a friend, which was sufficient to repurchase equipment and stock and keep the operation running.[25] In 1911, the founder of the weekly Filastin in Jaffa was able to start up the project—one of the most ambitious in Palestine at the time—with an investment of "70 French pounds" (equivalent to about 60 Egyptian pounds), which sufficed for purchasing an old printing press, renovating it, and starting running the journal regularly.[26] Another British appraisal, during World War I, estimated the cost of establishing an Arabic weekly for propaganda purposes in Egypt at 60 pounds, but quoted a much higher figure—200 pounds—as required for monthly operational costs, apparently reflecting the high wartime cost of paper and the exceptionally high fee the British paid writers.[27] Similarly, the British-sponsored plan in 1916 to set up a semiweekly in Mecca after the war—which resulted in Sharif Husayn's al-Qibla— envisaged total monthly expenses of 146 Egyptian pounds, including the purchase of paper, wrappers and ink, wages for four editorial workers and six print and composition workers, and postage for 1,500 copies per issue.[28] These British assessments seem to have been markedly higher than the actual costs involved in launching and operating papers by local residents of the region in peacetime.

Without investing in purchasing printing equipment, a periodical could be started as a business and operated for a while on a modest budget. Its linchpin would be the owner-editor himself, who would generally gather the material, write the paper, sometimes even set the type by himself, and distribute the finished product on the street. In her memoirs Fatima al-Yusuf, who founded her journal in 1925, depicted what it was like to start a paper in Egypt then, a picture that was probably typical of such ventures throughout the region. The journal started out in Yusuf's private home, a small two-room apartment in the upper floor of a building accessible by 95 narrow stairs, with a staff of three people — herself as owner, the editor Muhammad al-Tabi'i, and a manager, Ibrahim Khalil. After a while they rented a more convenient two-room basement office for two pounds a month. *Ruz al-Yusuf* then bought two used desks from the daily *al-Balagh*, which was selling off its old furniture, for a total of 120 qurush. Together with a table from Yusuf's apartment, the paper finally had three writing tables, one for each member of the team. The three founders led a spartan life, traversing large areas of the city on foot with their pockets packed with printing blocks, sharing poor man's broad-bean sandwiches for lunch. After some time, participating in a promotion campaign for smoking cheap Susa cigarettes, the three collected enough gift coupons to win a bicycle, which thereafter served the editor and the manager for trips to the press and other arrangements. At first the journalists worked without pay, the budget department consisting of a slim notebook in which the scanty expenses and incoming revenues were recorded.[29] Those of Fatima al-Yusuf's colleagues who, like herself, invested little resources and made a success of their venture, did so because of good business instincts and, most often, fortuitous timing.

While the great majority of Arab papers started as exceedingly modest economic endeavors, this was not the case for all of them. Some individuals and groups with substantial wealth launched journalistic projects as big businesses from the outset. Such were most of the large daily newspapers, which involved a considerable initial investment and high operational costs. The earliest example of such backing was Khalil al-Khuri's *Hadiqat al-Akhbar* in Beirut in the late 1850s, which was initially supported by a wealthy patron, Mikha'il Mudawwar, who bought the press for Khuri and subsidized the operation until it functioned on its own.[30] Khuri's journal, although devoted primarily to reportage, was, however, a relatively simple undertaking both logistically and economically, drawing as it did on local informants and the foreign press for news that it offered at weekly intervals to readers who expected nothing more.

In time, such standards became inadequate. Expanding international activity in the region and the quick communication of news through the telegraph dictated a faster pace of reporting, with the services of a news agency becoming a must. Manually operated printing machines, unable to meet new requirements of speed and quantity, ultimately gave way to more sophisticated and expensive equipment. The slow but continuous expansion of the reading public elicited an improvement in distribution methods, and the employment of distribution agents became an important item in newspaper budgets. In Cairo, distribution agents had become an integral part of the press scene by the turn of the century.[31] Producing a daily of several pages was no longer a realistic undertaking for a single person, however gifted.

Rather, it was a project for a team of specialists in the various stages of production who worked for wages. An additional factor that evolved from these developments and that had a profound impact on every venture in the field was competition. With the reading market limited throughout most of the period under review, the continuous introduction of new publications generated aggressive competition, which meant investing more resources in improving the product and promoting sales in order to survive and succeed.

All of these needs required resources on a scale quite unlike the trifling sums that could be saved from the salary of a teacher or government official who had to support a family. Such resources came from family wealth or, more often, from patrons: groups of friends who shared the journalist's views; political parties; religious communities; or governments, domestic or foreign, all of whom financed newspapers for a variety of reasons. In 1906 the *Jarida* group was formed in Egypt— a company of 60 "gentlemen of high social and official standing" and considerable wealth who put together a fund of 20,000 Egyptian pounds to establish a share company for publishing a newspaper bearing that name the following year.[32] This marked a new approach to the press: viewing it as big business that required organizational efficiency rather than the improvisational tactics of resourceful individuals. Mustafa Kamil, owner of *al-Liwa'*, followed suit in 1907, establishing a share company for publishing English and French editions of his nationalistic daily, as did 'Ali Yusuf with *al-Mu'ayyad* some time later. Other journals conducted as large companies or even corporations evolved during the course of the twentieth century.

Information on the finances of the larger projects—i.e., their expenditure on office space, equipment, news gathering, salaries, and distribution, as well as their profits—may exist in the archives of the relevant journals and in the private papers of their owners and editors, but it is largely inaccessible to the researcher. The few assessments in this area published hitherto can offer only a general and not entirely reliable picture. In Egypt, which led the way in commercial press activity, as in other aspects of the development of the medium, founding a competitive daily around the turn of the century probably required thousands, or perhaps (as the *Jarida* case would indicate) tens of thousands of Egyptian pounds. Mustafa Kamil established his press company in 1907 with 20,000 pounds in capital. Some time later, one source estimated the revenue from his *al-Liwa'* at 88,000 pounds, while that of *al-Ahram* and *al-Muqattam* was assumed to be even larger. When *al-Mu'ayyad* was reorganized as a share company in 1909, its initial capital fund was reported to have been 50,000 pounds. By the 1930s, the large Egyptian dailies were each worth hundreds of thousands of pounds. In 1951–1952, a fairly reliable survey estimated that establishing a competitive new daily would require an investment of some 300,000 Egyptian pounds, in addition to a modern printing plant.[33]

Elsewhere in the region, where the domestic infrastructure was less developed, the market smaller, and competition more limited, the required investment was probably markedly more modest. This type of ambitious journalistic project appeared throughout the region in the interwar years. Political parties and groups generously backed newspapers that expressed their views, championing specific causes. Several private papers, whose owners regarded them primarily as a commercial venture, also fit into this journalistic category, most prominently *al-Ahram* and *al-Muqattam* in Cairo, *Alif Ba'* in Damascus, *Filastin* in Jaffa, and *al-Zaman* in Baghdad.

An examination of one particular item in newspaper budgets — wages of writers and editors — may yield clues to the economic scope of these operations. Only papers operating as medium or large firms, as distinct from one-man projects, could afford to employ a staff and pay salaries, however meager. With the emergence of large dailies in Egypt during the last two decades of the nineteenth century, writing, editing, and translating became recognized occupations. Reporters, columnists, and translators (then mostly Syrian emigrés), earned 5 to 10 pounds monthly up until the early years of the twentieth century. Hafiz 'Awad, for example, was employed as a translator by *al-Mu'ayyad* in 1898 for a wage of 4 pounds monthly. Salama Musa, who joined the staff of *al-Liwa'* in 1909 as an essayist, was paid 7 pounds a month. 'Abbas Mahmud al-'Aqqad earned 6 pounds monthly as editor of *al-Dustur* around the same time. Senior editors earned more, apparently up to 20 pounds a month.[34] When the investment group established *al-Jarida* in 1907, it set much higher standards: Ahmad Lutfi al-Sayyid's monthly pay as editor in chief was 50 pounds, a figure that "shocked the Egyptian public, which henceforward began to view the journalist with great respect" and encouraged the paper's competitors to follow suit. A year later, when 'Abd al-'Aziz Jawish succeeded Mustafa Kamil as editor in chief of *al-Liwa'*, he received 40 pounds as his monthly pay. It also became customary at that stage to pay writers by the article, normally up to one pound for a 500-word piece.[35]

Wages such as Lutfi al-Sayyid's and Jawish's were reserved only for senior editors of large papers and for popular authors who were hired to write editorials or topical essays. When the daily *Ruz al-Yusuf* was founded in 1935, Mahmud 'Azmi's salary as editor in chief was 60 pounds a month plus 50 qurush for every 1,000 copies sold over the first 10,000 copies (a clause which may have added a few more pounds to his monthly pay). 'Abbas Mahmud al-'Aqqad, who until then was employed as editor at the daily *al-Jihad* for 70 pounds a month, was hired by *Ruz al-Yusuf* to write a daily editorial and a weekly literary supplement for a salary of 80 pounds.[36] Less senior writers received much lower wages. Najib Kan'an was hired in 1926 to write for *al-Ahram* for 15 pounds monthly. Toward the end of that decade, the weekly *Ruz al-Yusuf* employed Mustafa Amin — who would become one

of Egypt's most important journalists—without pay for 3 years, then
gave him a monthly wage of 8 pounds. Karim Thabit, another writer
on the staff, also earned 8 pounds monthly; Jalal al-Hamamsi earned 4
pounds; and Sa'id 'Abduh was paid one pound for every article of his
that was published in the journal. Clearly the income of young journalists was not very high on the scale of contemporary wages for skilled
workers, as examples cited earlier in the chapter have shown. The
range of rates in the field of journalism—50 to 80 pounds for senior
editors, 8 to 15 pounds for new journalists—was maintained in the
Egyptian press until World War II.[37] Evidence on wages in areas outside Egypt is scantier, but clearly the smaller scope of the industry
meant lower wages for writers and editors. Nassuh Babil, who in 1926
was hired as foreign editor by the Damascus daily *Suriya al-Jadida*, was
paid 2.5 Syrian pounds (equivalent to half an Egyptian pound). While
it is not clear whether this was his monthly pay or a fee per article, even
if it was the latter it was considerably less than the fee paid to his
counterparts in Egypt.[38]

Salaries constituted only one item—and not necessarily the heavi-
est one—in the expenditure books of big newspapers. To cover these
and the other expenses, three channels of generating income were available to the newspapers: advertising, circulation, and accepting financial
support from a variety of possible patrons.

Sources of Income: Advertising

There were marked variations in advertising norms within the region.
Some papers announced advertising rates regularly, although there is
no way of knowing whether the prices quoted were those paid in practice. Papers in Syria and Palestine during the early years of the twentieth century, and in Egypt and the Hejaz in the 1920s, informed potential customers more vaguely, that "advertising is extremely cheap,"
"the fee for advertising is to be negotiated with the management," or
"subscribers advertise for half the price" without further elaboration.[39]
Governments advertised extensively and often (but not always) paid for
it, but whether they paid the same rates as other customers is similarly
unknown. The variety of commissions involved in the advertising business further complicated the financial scene. Tom McFadden, who in
1951–1952 made the first systematic attempt to study and assess the
economic weight of advertising in the Arab daily press, was unable to
reconstruct a picture of any accuracy and had to content himself with a
brief general summarization.[40] Our discussion of the subject, therefore,
must aim at more modest objectives: examining the broad characteristics of advertising activity in the Arab press on the basis of data samples
that provide clues to the scope of this activity. This might help us
evaluate—again, in general terms only—the importance of advertising
to the field at large.

Mass advertising, an attribute of a market economy and of an industrial society, was limited in the Middle East until the mid-twentieth century, because economies were undeveloped and markets small. The two notable exceptions were, again, Egypt from the late nineteenth century onward and Lebanon after World War I, where lively commercial enterprise generated concomitant advertising. The promotion of products for sale was not a novel idea in the region, but prior to the introduction of printing it was not employed on a mass level. As soon as newspapers appeared, however, they began to be utilized for this: The earliest Arabic papers announced advertising fees and carried ads. The field was led at first by the papers themselves, which promoted the services of their own presses and the books they printed. Such announcements appeared in Egypt in the official *al-Waqa'i' al-Misriyya*, which publicized the Bulaq printing press as early as the 1830s; in *Hadiqat al-Akhbar* in the late 1850s; in *al-Jawa'ib* in the 1860s; and in *al-Jinan* in the early 1870s. Foreign businesses also utilized the new channel for similar ends. Early issues of *Hadiqat al-Akhbar* featured ads for books by publishers not only in Beirut and Cairo but also in Europe. There were also advertisements by private businesses, such as importers of consumer goods, physicians, and dentists. These early notices were presented inconspicuously, often without headlines, which sometimes gave them the appearance of news items, and they occupied a very small proportion — seldom more than 5 percent — of the newspapers' total space. Moreover, advertising rates were relatively low. For example, *Hadiqat al-Akhbar* sold a line of advertisement for 5 qurush in 1858; *al-Jawa'ib* charged 5 qurush per line for ads on the front page and 3 qurush on the back page in 1868; and *al-Zahra*, the Beirut literary weekly appearing in 1870, put the base rate at 2 qurush per line. Given the limited space devoted to commercial notices and the low rates, advertising could not have generated significant revenues at that early stage.

Promotional announcements for books and other items related to literary activity, such as public libraries and printing presses, occupied a large share of all advertising at first, which may be explained by the intellectual proclivities of the publishers and of the small newspaper-reading public. For example, the four-page issue of *al-Jawa'ib* on 23 June 1868 featured three advertisements on page four, all of which announced recently published books. The four-page issue of *al-Muqattam* on 3 May 1889 carried 16 notices on page four, of which nine dealt with books. Other ads in the issue promoted goods and services that for the most part targeted the well-to-do: translation offices, law firms, doctors' clinics, dentists, pharmacies, beauty salons, and the large European-owned department stores. There were also a few ads devoted to products and services of a more popular nature, such as medicines and craftsmen's shops, as well as miscellaneous notices such as that by someone "seeking to buy a cart fit for one horse."[41] Gradually ads became more diverse in content and more attractive in presentation, using graphic embellishments and varied typefaces, in Arabic, Latin, and Cyrillic script (the non-Arabic titles for the growing local community of foreigners). To pick, again, an example, page four of *Lisan al-Hal* of 1 November 1913 carried, among others, four large ads with graphic features for shoes, elegant clothes, pianos, and beer, announced in Arabic, English, French, and Greek.

An element that began appearing in press advertising in the 1880s, and that soon became of primary importance, was announcements by governmental agencies. Besides utilizing the press as a convenient means to reach the public, governmental advertising became a means of controlling and manipulating the medium itself. Announcements of the activities of state offices, legal notices, information on postal services and rates, and so forth, constituted a sizable proportion of the advertising in papers that the government favored. As newspapers and journals became active forces in political life, governments advertised in them selectively, thereby influencing their financial condition and sometimes determining their economic viability.

With commercial life in the Arab countries centered in Cairo and Alexandria in the late nineteenth century, foreign companies and their local branches, major actors in Egyptian commerce, were also dominant in advertising there. Local firms, expanding as well, also advertised increasingly. By the late 1880s, a phenomenon that would henceforth typify advertising in the press became apparent: the growing gap between large papers which, due to relatively broad circulation, attracted more advertising and thus further consolidated their economic base, and weaker papers that had only a meager share in the advertising market. Advertising by then had become a substantial component of the large Egyptian papers. *Al-Muqattam*, for example, from its very beginnings in 1889 filled the fourth page of each issue—that is, 25 percent of its space—and sometimes more, with both commercial ads and government announcements.[42] At the time, the paper charged 8 qurush per line of advertising on the fourth page, 10 qurush for the second and third pages, and 15 qurush for ads on the front page. With a page of some 50 lines in each of its 5 columns of paid notices—and sometimes more than a page—advertising must have been a major source of income for *al-Muqattam*, possibly the main source. Other journals set similar fees,[43] but most of them were less successful. *Al-I'lam*, for example, hardly had any advertising during the first months of its existence in 1885. Within six months it managed to attract only enough ads to fill a little more than a column out of three on its last page, at 0.5 franc (one qurush) per line. In fact, the paper was unable to fill a full page with advertising for four years. *Al-I'lam* was more typical of the scope of advertising activity in Egypt than *al-Muqattam*, for despite growing commercial initiative, printed advertising was still limited. A sense of how novel the idea still was even at the end of the century may be obtained from an article entitled "Advertising in Newspapers and Magazines" published in *al-Hilal* in July 1895. Assuming general ignorance on the subject on the part of his readers, editor Jurji Zaydan explained the basic principles of advertising as a means of increasing business profits in the most elementary terms. *Al-Hilal's* occasional call upon the business community to advertise in the journal met with meager response during its first three years, whereupon Zaydan embarked on a more aggressive persuasion campaign, which, however, still produced rather limited results.[44]

Commercial activity, and advertising, were even more restricted elsewhere in the region. Advertising fees in the Fertile Crescent were lower than in Egypt: the Beiruti *Lisan al-Hal* in 1877 charged 2 qurush (1.5 qurush for subscribers) for a line of advertising on the last page, and 3 qurush (2 for subscribers) on the other pages; the Damascene *al-Sham* in 1896 sold a line of advertising on the second page for 2.5 qurush and on the front page for 3 qurush; and the daily *al-Muqtabas* in 1908 charged 2 qurush per line on all pages. Foreign companies dominated the small field even more so than in Egypt. A typical example is the 18 August 1912 issue of the Jaffa semiweekly *Filastin*, which ran a banner ad by the French company Messageries Maritime, a shipping firm, along the bottom of the first two pages (an ad which, as the editor would later recall, brought him a modest 10 Egyptian pounds a year, or about 20 qurush per issue).[45] The last page of the four-page issue carried additional ads for a Danish beer and Italian and British insurance companies, as well as two local businesses (a dentist with an unmistakably foreign name and a Ramallah hotel). These five notices took up about two-thirds of the small-format page. Newspaper ads reflected a somewhat more active commercial life in Beirut, but a somnolent situation in the towns of Syria. Advertising in Iraq prior to World War I was more limited still, in effect almost nonexistent.[46]

Enhanced economic activity after the war as a result of foreign and local initiative boosted the scope of advertising considerably. A growing range of services and products were promoted — steamship companies, movie shows, cars and bicycles, radio receivers, expensive clothing, chocolate, whiskey — testifying to economic and technological progress and increased consumption. More local businesses gradually entered the field. Egypt remained the leader in this arena, with advertising in the Egyptian press comprising about 80 percent of the total volume of advertising in the Arab press of the region in the mid-twentieth century, according to McFadden's findings. Lebanon, with a smaller domestic consumer market but serving as a thriving center of regional commercial enterprise, also featured an animated promotional activity.[47] The gap between large papers with broad circulations and ample advertising revenues, and small papers with scanty incomes from both sources, remained as wide as before, or grew wider. Advertising was becoming the economic mainstay of the leading newspapers, and special advertising departments were set up where employees sometimes earned more than columnists.[48] *Al-Ahram*, one of the leaders, devoted about half its pages to advertising on the eve of World War II; the Lebanese *al-Ahwal* and *Lisan al-Hal* and the Iraqi *al-Istiqlal* about a third; and the Palestinian *Mir'at al-Sharq* about a quarter.

But the great majority of publications in the region had to make do with much less. They normally featured a handful of announcements, most of them still by foreign businesses exporting goods and services to the region, printed on the inner and back pages, and occupying 10 to 15 percent of the paper's space at most. For most newspapers — small- and medium-size publications — advertising throughout the region prior to World War II was limited and could not be more than a secondary economic factor. The limited purchasing power of the local market still constituted a major constraint on commercial activity and, consequently, on the development of advertising. For the most part, therefore, newspapers had to look to other sources in order to survive.

Sources of Income: Circulation

Newspaper income from circulation, it appears, should be easier to assess than advertising revenues. Knowing the circulation of a journal, even if roughly, ought to facilitate calculating its revenue by multiplying the number of copies sold by the published price per copy, or extrapolating revenue from subscription fee figures. Yet in this area too the picture is confused. Not only are circulation figures often badly deficient and highly speculative, but, in the case of journals that circulated through both subscription and street sales, there is no way of ascertaining the number of copies distributed by each method and thus what revenues were obtained. Even when reasonable assessments of circulation and cost per unit are available, such data might be merely theoretical, for there commonly were discrepancies between stated prices and the newspapers' ability to collect them. In fact, obtaining payment from customers was a difficult and costly task, especially in the earlier part of the period under review, but also later where smaller and weaker papers were concerned. Circulation income, therefore, remains largely obscure. Still, some of the factors that affected this income may be examined for clues to yet another important segment of the economic puzzle.

The earliest circulation technique in the region was through subscription, which remained a common method thereafter. The practice of selling papers on the street also began early, in Istanbul of the 1840s (where it was introduced by William Churchill, who published the first private paper), and in Isma'il's Cairo, where *al-Waqa'i' al-Misriyya* was sold by vendors in the 1860s. The sale of newspapers on the street became commonplace in Egypt in the late nineteenth century, and in the Fertile Crescent in the early twentieth. Besides being the quickest way of getting the news to the reader, it had economic advantages to both buyer and seller: Unlike a subscription, it did not require the reader to commit himself to a large sum in advance, while the newspaper received payment immediately and in cash. Many publications that were sold on the street were also available by subscription.

For non-news periodicals, circulation by subscription—through the mail or through direct delivery to customers' homes—was a more viable sales method. More than newspapers, which were often read in public, they were largely read at home. A substantial body of subscribers was essential to the survival of the periodicals, and various kinds of incentives to encourage subscriptions were devised. The Lebanese literary weekly *al-Zahra* pointed out in 1870 that at year's end subscribers could bind all issues together into "a kind of general encyclopedia" and thus have something of lasting value. The Alexandrian *Lisan al-'Arab* in 1894 offered a summary of the main news items published by other papers, "so that reading this journal would be tantamount to reading all the other papers in an abridged form." Other journals introduced the device of prizes. *Al-Hilal* announced a lottery (*yanasib al-Hilal*) for subscribers in 1898, the first prize being 100 francs plus bound copies of all of editor Jurji Zaydan's works (equivalent, the editor noted, to the cost of 10 years' worth of subscriptions). In addition, subscribers would enjoy other privileges: a 20 percent discount on all *al-Hilal* books, the right to publish one ad of up to five lines in the journal at no cost, and a 5 percent discount at Zaydan's brother's costume store. Similar attractions were offered in the twentieth century as well: Salama Musa's *al-Majalla al-Jadida*, in 1929, offered a bonus of three books to annual subscribers in Egypt and eight books to readers abroad who subscribed for two years; the Beiruti *al-Ahwal*, in the same year, announced a lottery for its subscribers that included prize money as well as such gifts as wine bottles and jars of medical elixir; and the Lebanese *al-Fawa'id*, in 1932, likewise offered prizes in "money and other valuable gifts."[49]

A promotion technique that originated in the region in the earliest period of the press involved sending out a large number of copies of the first issue, or the first several issues, of a new journal to prospective customers and individuals considered likely to encourage distribution. While the idea was presumably to acquaint them with the new publication, there was also a sharp marketing technique involved. The journal would note, normally on the front page, that recipients who did not return the introductory copy, or copies, would automatically be considered subscribers.[50] Most recipients did indeed return the introductory copies, unwilling to commit funds to an item that would be delivered in parts over a long period. As experience had repeatedly shown, new publications were often precarious ventures that could fold at any time. Moreover, an added political factor from the late nineteenth century onward increased the risk to the subscriber. The bolder papers were subject to closure and suspension by the authorities, which further deterred potential customers from subscribing in advance. The result was that the prospective buyer's skepticism, well-founded though it was, hurt the new products at the stage when they needed subscriber support most.[51]

Recipients of the first copy or two of a journal who did not return them had their names registered in the paper's list of subscribers and became indebted to the owner. Such tactics on the part of publishers were irritating, and individuals repeatedly complained about journals reaching them against their wishes, forcibly turning them into debtors. How is it possible, asked recipients of such publications in Egypt during the 1890s, that journals are sent to them free, while at the same time announcing that payment must be made prior to delivery? One editor responded flatly: Should the Egyptian papers follow the European example of forwarding copies only to those who had paid in advance, "there would be no journals in Egypt."[52] From the point of view of the new publishers, trying to get as many people as possible indebted to the paper made good commercial sense.

Indebtedness to a paper, whether by choice or involuntarily, was one thing. Paying up, however, turned out to be quite another. Repeated complaints in every country in the region, and throughout the entire period explored here, attest to the fact that collecting the fees owed by subscribers was a difficult chore. "I receive no money from Mount [Lebanon] nor from Tunis," Ahmad Faris al-Shidyaq, publisher of the broad-circulation al-Jawa'ib, complained in a letter to a member of his family in 1866.

> As for the rest of the agents, some of them delay payment while others only send a quarter or an half of what they owe. I have already lost some 70 francs to my agent in Algiers. . . . In Istanbul there are some 50 people, men of dignity and education, who receive al-Jawa'ib without paying anything.[53]

"The journalist is miserable in our country [Lebanon] and deserves pity," one newcomer to the field commented in 1909, for "he subjects his resources to loss and cannot obtain the subscription fees except through extreme difficulty."[54] Papers pleaded with their readers time and again "to send the subscription fees and cover the accumulating arrears," explaining that delays in payment compromised the paper's ability to function regularly. Al-Hilal informed its patrons in 1900:

> Examining our records, we have discovered that a large group of al-Hilal subscribers have not yet paid their dues for this year, and some of them not even the fees for last year, or the year before. . . . We shall wait patiently until the end of the year, then stop delivery of the paper to those who do not pay at least their debt of last year. We have written to a few of them, and we hope they will not force us to take further measures.[55]

The Jerusalem weekly *Sawt al-Sha'b*, in notices placed conspicuously in its masthead, similarly pleaded with its subscribers in the 1920s, appealing to their sense of national responsibility:

> Do not forget that by paying your modest subscription fees you serve your homeland and defend your national and patriotic rights, whether you are a merchant, a craftsman, or a worker. Do not forget that paying your lira to the paper is more effective than shooting your enemy's heart.[56]

The humorous Iraqi weekly *Habazbuz* echoed the essence of the same message in its own particular style: "We beg our honorable subscribers not to hurry in paying their subscription dues, for the paper has no need for money. 'Haste is the making of the damned devil.'"[57]

Al-Hilal, which by 1900 had built a solid economic base, could afford to forbear until its clients chose to pay. Whoever starts a paper, editor Jurji Zaydan explained, must have enough capital at his disposal to cover expenses for several years without any profit and expect no gains until the distant future.[58] Most papers, however, were economically too weak to function for years without subscription payments. When pleas to readers through the papers or through direct letters proved ineffective, owners went out personally or sent agents to collect the debts. Advance announcements of such tours, and appeals to the readers to cooperate with the collectors, were common in the Arab press in its early decades prior to World War I. Frequently, one journalist complained, agents had to visit subscribers 20 or 30 times before they paid. Some subscribers resorted to devious tricks: promising to pay and then denying that they gave their word, pretending to be ill or too busy to see the agent, and sometimes even berating and cursing him.[59] The need to employ collectors led to another problem: impostors posing as collectors trying to extract money from subscribers. Journals repeatedly advised their customers to make sure that the receipts they were given upon payment bore the signature of the paper's owner or his certified agent: "The paper will not accept any claim from anyone unable to produce a receipt signed and stamped by us or by our agent in a legible way," warned 'Abdallah al-Nadim's *al-Tankit wal-Tabkit* in 1881. *Al-Hilal* took the precaution of publishing the names of its agents, warning its readers that they alone were authorized to collect money on the journal's behalf.[60]

Why were customers who had actually agreed to subscribe so slow to pay? The most basic explanation for such recalcitrance was the general indigence of society throughout the region. In a state of general want, avoiding payment where the pressure was weakest was a natural inclination. Moreover, the willingness — sometimes zeal — of publishers to deliver their publications for periods of weeks or months before demanding payment facilitated postponement or avoidance of payment due. Another explanation may be found in the nontraditional nature of the arrangement of subscribing to a publication. Journals, unlike other more tangible goods, had an elusive and often transient value. Subscriptions, therefore, tended to be viewed by the public as open to renegotiation at any time:

> Our agent in Jaffa [the editor of the Palestinian *al-Munadi* noted in 1912] has notified us that a certain man, a shaykh, refused to pay, claiming he is an *adib* [man of letters] and that most papers are sent to him free. Another man has professed to be a friend of ours, so he does not expect to be required to pay. . . . A third has stated that, since we once failed to inform the public of the formation of a town council in his town, he would now pay nothing.

"We are amazed at that Jaffa shaykh who claims to be an *adib*," the editor continued. "How can he think that his *adab* exempts him from paying the fees of a journal which seeks to survive with the support of his likes, not with the support of the riffraff?"[61] Other publishers complained of customers who believed their subscription entitled them to all sorts of privileges regarding the paper, including a say in its policy and style. When they saw that their views did not prevail, they felt offended and backed down on their commitment or avoided payment.[62] Still, the *adib* from Jaffa, and others who offered similar reasons for nonpayment, were putting forward arguments that were not altogether incompatible with accepted social norms.

The consumer market, then, was not only small but also often inhospitable. Jurji Zaydan estimated at the turn of the century that recalcitrant behavior by subscribers cost newspapers 30 to 40 percent of their circulation revenues, a sum which if saved, he said, could have freed them from the need to seek other resources.[63] Whether or not this was entirely accurate, clearly such lack of cooperation on the part of consumers was a heavy burden for the young press. Publishers of the numerous papers that appeared annually throughout the region hoped to emulate the example of the few prosperous publications and succeed where so many of their colleagues had failed, ignoring, or not appreciating properly, the adversities that lay in store. Had newcomers been aware of their predecessors' troubles, an Egyptian journalist suggested around the turn of the century, they would have desisted from embarking on this course. The market obviously could not sustain more than a few of them. Inevitably, this journalist concluded, most of those who embarked on careers in the press ended them like the hypothetical publisher whose story he related in such telling detail:

> When papers begin to appear, their owners assume that within a few months they will begin to yield wealth. When the first issue is ready, they print thousands of copies and send them to every notable, announcing that they already have 2,150 subscribers. More people buy the first issue, out of curiosity, than subsequent numbers. The publisher's first day goes by pleasantly, and at night he dreams of wealth just as the cat dreams of

a mouse. His excitement mounts when he receives congratulatory wishes and when would-be agents approach him to sell his papers or be his correspondents. . . .

These new publishers have a honeymoon shorter than that of wedded couples. A few days later the copies [sent to prospective subscribers] begin to return from all directions, piles upon piles, carrying notices such as "unwanted," "the paper lies and we do not wish to read it," "we have enough papers without it," "we have no time to read it," and suchlike [responses] which discourage the publisher and dampen his excitement. All this, however, is just a prelude to his suffering. He comforts himself with the thought that hundreds of readers, not thousands, would suffice, and that anyway he has no need for those who do not accept his paper willingly. He assumes that those who did not return their copies are interested in it, so he does not pressure them to pay, not wanting them to think that he is pressed financially. He still believes he has 500 subscribers whose fees should cover the paper's expenses and even yield a 300-pound profit a year. . . . When eventually he starts asking for payment, he confronts refusals and excuses such as: "I have never received the paper," "I am not a subscriber," etc. He continues to write to them and to face the same refusals, and runs into difficulties that mount every month, until the paper dies out after its owner has lost a fortune.[64]

Sources of Income: Subsidization

Even without a precise, or an approximate, reconstruction of the financial setting in which the Arab press operated, the available evidence shows that the market situation was distinctly adverse. That both advertising and circulation revenues were too insubstantial to support the numerous papers in the field is further evidenced by the fact that many of them turned to outside sources of support. Subsidies by patrons—private, public, and governmental (local as well as foreign)—were in fact available, uninfluenced by the market situation yet capable of determining the economic fate of newspapers.

One type of support was benevolent assistance to nonpolitical publications by governments and private patrons who sought to encourage cultural projects that they considered worthwhile, a continuation of an age-old Islamic tradition. Such assistance was normally offered in the form of subventions paid regularly or periodically, or through the purchase of a block of subscriptions at sums that would ensure maintaining a journal on a modest level. Thus, for example, Khedive Isma'il assisted Salim al-Bustani in his literary effort in *al-Jinan*, in the 1870s, at the same time supporting his father, Butrus al-Bustani, in his multivolume encyclopedia project, *Da'irat al-Ma'arif*, by reportedly subscribing to 500 sets. Shibli Shumayyil's medical monthly *al-Shifa'* ("Medicine"), appearing in Cairo in 1886, was supported for some five years by the Egyptian Ministry of Health, which purchased bulk subscriptions (and when the ministry eventually canceled them, the publication closed down). Niqula Tuma's monthly *al-Ahkam* ("Legal Rules"), published in Cairo from 1888, was similarly assisted by the Ottoman Minister of Justice Jevdet, who decreed that the journal's contents become required reading at the imperial law school in Istanbul and ordered the purchase of a large number of subscriptions. Early in the twentieth century, Prince Muhammad 'Ali Pasha sponsored the woman's journal *Fatat al-Nil* by donating subscriptions to it to several girls' schools.[65] Publishers of new journals could hope to obtain such assistance, although they could not always rely on it. When the founder of a new pedagogic publication in Syria in 1931 requested a subsidy from the Ministry of Education, he was notified that such aid was provided to journals only after they had been published for a year. By then, the frustrated journalist noted, his paper would no longer need the help: It would have either expired or established itself on a firm footing.[66]

Another category of financial sponsorship was more widespread: assistance rendered for political considerations, to buy the voice of a publication or to silence it. Both local and foreign governments subsidized — indeed bribed — newspapers in every part of the region to adopt a friendly, or at least not a hostile, stance and to attack the government's opponents, as we have seen. Other interested parties — political groups, religious communities, individual notables, and ambitious state officials — financed the press for similar ends. So did also business firms and groups, seeking to advance economic interests. Assistance was given through regular or occasional subventions, as well as through payment for signed or unsigned pieces praising the patron or vilifying his adversaries, which were known as *maqalat ma'jura* ("rented articles"), or for economic publicity camouflaged as news. This phenomenon developed at the earliest stage of the emergence of the press and has remained a part of it ever since.

Subsidies constituted a major factor for the survival of many Arab papers, which functioned only, or primarily, due to outside financial backing. This element, however, was an unknown quantity, normally carefully concealed, especially when it was political in nature. Public knowledge of subsidization would both compromise the journalist's image and undermine the objectives of the patron, so that both recipient and donor were eager to keep their association secret. But while publishers rarely admitted to sponsorship, few of them denied the existence of the phenomenon, or its broad extent. Tom McFadden, exploring the finances of Arab papers in 1951–1952 as thoroughly as was possible, found out that "it was rare for an editor to say that his paper had to and did accept secret funds. However, the majority had no hesitation in applying the subject to other papers and citing examples." McFadden was able to produce rough estimates indicating that out of 110 dailies from several major Arab cities, at least 60 (55 percent) were clearly unable to survive on advertising and circulation and hence necessarily relied on hidden funds. Another 24 papers (22 percent) were in the vicinity of breaking even, and McFadden estimated that they, too, or at least some of them, were backed by subsidies. Of the other 26 papers (23 percent), a high proportion (11 papers, or 10 percent of the total) were in languages other than Arabic (and hence the economic variables involved may have been different from these considered here). Only 15 Arabic-language dailies, or 13 percent of all those examined, were found capable of surviving without subsidies.[67] This gross assessment may or may not be applicable to former periods, but given the history of poverty in the region and, consequently, of the press, it would be reasonable to assume that at any given time a large proportion — and quite likely most — of the publications throughout the Middle East were totally or in part dependent on subsidies.

All three categories of economic subsistence presented in McFadden's survey were represented to one extent or another in Egypt and Lebanon from the late nineteenth century onward and elsewhere after World War I. Topping the economic pyramid was a small group of solidly based newspapers which, due to adequate start-up resources, good business acumen, and high professional standards, succeeded in avoiding or overcoming initial pitfalls and became large firms. Success was perpetuated through continuous circulation growth, which in turn also generated growth in advertising revenues. Such economically viable publications covered their expenses, supported large staffs, brought in good returns on investments, and sometimes even made their owners wealthy.[68]

The other two groups — newspapers that broke even and newspapers that were clearly unable to hold their own — were far larger, with the latter category being particularly widespread in the poorer countries of the Fertile Crescent. They consisted of medium- and small-size publications which, facing great financial difficulty, were prone to accept patronage when offered. Individuals, groups, or institutions — McFadden reported at mid-century — seeking to influence public opinion by secretly supporting the press, "shop around among the papers and the papers shop around among them, and the lines get so crossed and so entangled . . . "[69] These papers could not play an independent political or social role as they might have had they been self-sufficient, and often served as tools in the hands of their benefactors.

There was also a fourth category of economic subsistence, not included in McFadden's survey, made up of newspapers that were too weak to survive in the extant market conditions but that failed to elicit support from patrons — those which, as Lord Kitchener once noted, "eke out a miserable existence with unpaid staffs and rents in arrears. They appear, disappear, and appear again spasmodically."[70] Most of them expired quickly. For example, of 42 daily newspapers that appeared in Beirut during the first half of the 1920s (1920-1925), only 11 (26 percent) survived by the end of the decade; in Baghdad, only 4 out of 39 (10 percent) survived; in Damascus, 2 out of 21 (10 percent); and in Cairo, despite a period of economic momentum, only about a quarter (32 out of 120) survived.[71] Throughout the history of Arab journalism, the number of periodicals that disappeared soon after they were launched exceeded by far those that had a more durable existence in any of the categories discussed.

The straitened economic circumstances of the region were not the only obstacle that the Arab press had to contend with, and, given the severity of political, cultural, and educational constraints, may not even have been the most difficult. But the harsh economic environment did constitute a major impediment to journalistic progress. It foiled the majority of attempts at establishing newspapers and periodicals, and constricted those that did manage to persevere. It also impaired journalists' ability to address the serious issues of the day, especially in the political sphere, and caused them to be easily manipulated. This economic dependency, which inevitably compromised their freedom of expression, also compromised the authenticity of their message and, consequently, their public credibility. Poverty, therefore, undermined the functioning of the press as merchandise and as enterprise at once. Although impossible to quantify, the impact of the region's prevalent indigence on the emergence and progress of the Arab press was undoubtedly far-reaching.

9

The Craft of
the Arab Journalist

The definition of the journalist's craft is less precise and less obvious, generally, than that of many other vocations, such as the lawyer, physician, teacher, or pharmacist. Unlike these other professionals, journalists are not required to undergo a prescribed course of study, acquire particular skills, pass tests, or become certified in order to practice their craft. Indeed, the institutionalized teaching of journalism — significantly, as an academic pursuit, not a professional requirement — began in the West centuries after the advent of the vocation itself: toward the end of the nineteenth century in some places in the United States, and only in the twentieth century in Europe. Whom, then, should we call a journalist? In defining this occupation, perhaps we should not go beyond stating, loosely, that it involves the production of texts for the publishing of periodicals, leaving the precise boundaries of the profession to be determined by the context of the time and place under review.

The elusiveness of the definition is further compounded in the Middle Eastern context, where journalism developed as a variation distinct from the European prototype in the social and political roles it filled. The act of pronouncing one's opinions publicly and in print, especially on political matters, was a novelty in Arab society and a deviation from traditional values. It entailed, potentially at least, undermining the position of rulers and other important figures of authority, such as state officials and 'ulama', and often involved serious conflicts with them. More than just a new occupation, journalism represented a new outlook in Arab society (as did other modern vocations, such as law, or teaching, in their secular versions). By introducing new habits and techniques, journalists became active agents in a process of cultural transformation, even though not all of them were aware of the far-reaching implications of their pursuit. One group, however, must be excluded from this description: those involved in publishing journals for religious institutions, such as al-Azhar, who, rather than challenging the old order, utilized the new medium to defend it.

The evolution of journalism in the Arab countries is a broad subject that merits a study far more extensive than the limits of this discussion permit. However, the attraction of the field, the reasons most newcomers to it withdrew quickly in frustration, and the process by which Arab journalism gradually changed from an amateur occupation to a profession have bearing on the other issues explored in this work and deserves consideration here.

Lure and Frustration

The Egyptian historian Ibrahim 'Abduh, in his book on the luminaries of the Arab press,[1] places the khedives Muhammad 'Ali and Isma'il at the head of a list of 18 leading figures in the profession during the nineteenth and early twentieth centuries. His choice makes sense. The two Egyptian rulers, along with officials in their service, were responsible not only for importing the medium into that society, but also for laying the foundations for the new calling. The more creative among these officials, such as Rifa'a Rafi' al-Tahtawi and 'Abdallah Abu al-Su'ud, demonstrated in their writing the attractive potential inherent in this occupation. Others, who experimented with journalism privately around the same time and shortly thereafter, although having objectives different from those of the pasha's officials, also drew attention to the allure of the new occupation. Khalil al-Khuri, Butrus and Salim al-Bustani, Ahmad Faris al-Shidyaq, Ya'qub Sarruf, Faris Nimr, Salim and Bishara Taqla, and Rushayd al-Dahdah, who were drawn to the press under the inspiration of a foreign example, pursued journalism successfully in the 1860s and 1870s and showed that it was possible to publish opinions on public affairs and have an impact without antagonizing the government beyond an acceptable point, produce a salable commodity, and even make a living out of it—in other words, to turn writing on current affairs into a career. By the last quarter of the nineteenth century, these private publishers, along with state publishers, had established a new occupational option for society's educated sector.

The success—sometimes quite spectacular—of a small number of journalists, and their public standing as authentic and fearless spokesmen of popular sentiment (in particular, opposition to foreign domination), lent respectability to the vocation. Certain journalists attained this kind of public regard in the nineteenth century, and their number grew from the turn of the twentieth century onward. Prominent individuals in other fields gained added fame by publishing columns in the press. Writers such as Mustafa Kamil, Ahmad Lutfi al-Sayyid, Amin Al-Rafi'i, Sa'd and Fathi Zaghlul, Muhammad Husayn Haykal, 'Abbas Mahmud al-'Aqqad, Mahmud 'Azmi, 'Abd al-Qadir Hamza, and Muhammad al-Tabi'i in Egypt, Muhammad Kurd 'Ali, the Rayyis cousins, Nassuh Babil, and Yusuf al-'Isa in Syria, Jibran and Ghasan Tuwayni, and Muhyi al-Din al-Nusuli in Lebanon, Rafa'il Batti and Tawfiq al-Sam'ani in Iraq, and 'Isa al-'Isa in Palestine turned the press into an institution with which the educated public could identify, and journalism into a craft worthy of appreciation. Journalists who made personal sacrifices for public causes, such as the press martyrs of Syria and Lebanon during World War I, enhanced this positive view.

Despite cultural conventions, and material and political difficulties, people in the Middle East were attracted to journalism in ever-growing numbers, as reflected in the frequent emergence of new publications throughout the region from the mid-1870s onward. Thousands of newspapers and periodicals appeared between that time and the mid-twentieth century. Historian Philip di Tarrazi documented a total of 3,023 Arabic periodicals established up to the end of 1929, of them 2,490 that appeared in the Arab countries of the region under study and in Ottoman Turkey.[2] This phenomenon continued later on as well, with hundreds of additional Arabic periodicals launched during the 1930s and 1940s, especially in Egypt, Lebanon, and Syria. "Every day young men knock on the doors of newspaper and periodical managers, asking to join the profession," a leading journalist reported from Egypt in 1931.[3] Elsewhere this activity was more limited, but everywhere, even in the periphery of the region, new journalistic initiatives attested to the lure of the press as a career.

From the start, journalism in the Arab countries was an arena open to anyone. The requirements prescribed by the state for those wishing to join the field and start a newspaper were minimal. The Ottoman Press Law of 1865 stipulated only a minimum age of 30 and no criminal record, with no requirements at all in terms of education, training, or financial obligations. The Ottoman law of 1909 added the requirement that a newspaper owner be able to read and write in the language of his publication, while an amendment in March 1912 added further the demand of primary (seven years) education and a money deposit, designed to guarantee the owner's abiding by the censorship laws. The press laws of the post-Ottoman Arab states, following more or less a standard pattern, were not significantly different. Establishing a newspaper required a license, which was made conditional upon citizenship, a minimum age (usually 20 to 25 years), the absence of a criminal record, and financial guarantees. Some laws also demanded a "good reputation" (Egypt 1931 and 1936, Iraq 1933 and 1934), and a high school education was a requirement in certain other cases (the Transjordanian 1928 amendment to the Ottoman Press Law, the Saudi

Press Law of 1929, Iraq's laws from 1933 and 1934).[4] The requirement
of financial guarantees constituted a serious hurdle, as the sums involved were normally high — for example, 200 Ottoman golden liras for
a newspaper in the Arab provinces in 1912, 300 Egyptian pounds for a
daily in Egypt in 1931. But other than that, the conditions were mild:
The demands concerning education, when imposed, were modest,
given the fact that journalism was by definition an occupation of the
educated. More important, while publishers had to meet certain conditions in order to obtain a license, journalists who simply wanted to
write for newspapers could do so without meeting any requirements
whatsoever. By and large, then, the press was a no man's land governed
by very few rules.

The appeal of the new occupation to the many would-be journalists was multifaceted, with the motives universally familiar. One widespread motive, trivial yet not to be underestimated, was the quest for
personal publicity, enhanced by the exciting possibilities that the medium had to offer in this respect. Capable of spreading a person's name
much further than in the past, printing and mass circulation appeared
to be easily available to all. A great many of those who entered the
profession were no doubt driven primarily by just such an urge, though
seldom did any of them admit it. This desire for self-advertisement was
often coupled with the conviction that the public would benefit from
the views that the writer put forward.

For many journalists, the passion to write was kindled at an early
age when they were enthusiastic subscribers to periodicals, often foreign. "I started reading Arabic newspapers when I was 13 years old,
during my last years in elementary school" in the late 1880s, related
Muhammad Kurd 'Ali. At that young age, he subscribed to two Lebanese newspapers, *Lisan al-Hal* and *Bayrut*, and, having studied French
language and literature in the Lazarist school in Damascus, he subscribed to a Paris-based weekly, *L'Ami de la Campagne*, as well. "I read it
deliberately, not leisurely, sometimes reading an issue twice or more
before the next number arrived." He also read Turkish newspapers
published in Istanbul, "especially the literary and historical ones." At
the age of 15, he began submitting news reports and articles to various
newspapers, motivated by an urge for public involvement that was
stirred by the publications he read. The same motivation led him to
seek employment in the press some time later and eventually to establish newspapers of his own.[5]

Testimonies of this kind abound. Salama Musa, the Egyptian
writer, displayed similar proclivities in his youth. As a first-year student
in high school he used to "buy old and even new issues, despite their
high price, and devour them from cover to cover."[6] He too submitted
articles to the press as a young man, became a reporter and later
established newspapers of his own. A Syrian colleague, Nassuh Babil,
attested similarly that a passion for the press was born in him "since

infancy," when he first learned about "the impact of the press on the fate of nations and peoples" during the first decade of the twentieth century. Having made up his mind to become a journalist, after finishing high school, he started his career as a printer, and became the owner of a printing shop which, he hoped, would be his "ladder to the press." Later on, Babil became a correspondent for the prestigious Damascus daily *al-Ayyam*, a paper that he eventually came to own.[7]

Journalists often spoke of a desire to satisfy literary cravings as a major factor in their decision to start a newspaper. The prominent Lebanese *savant* Iskandar al-Ma'luf, who in 1911 founded the cultural journal *Majallat al-Athar* ("Journal of Past Works"), stated that he was motivated to publish it by "the lure of the craft and inclination of the soul." The Egyptian Najib Shaqra, a lawyer and founder of the weekly *al-Istiqlal* around the same time, noted in the journal's first issue that what he was seeking was "cultural fulfillment."[8] Both Ma'luf and Shaqra insisted that profit was not the object and that they were prepared to publish at a loss. Others who shared the same passion to write and to be published but were unable to establish their own papers were only too happy to have their pieces published in the press without pay. "We do not know an Arabic paper in Palestine which pays writers a fee for their contribution," noted a Palestinian author during the interwar period. "It is the writers who persistently beg the papers to publish their essays."[9]

Both Ma'luf and Shaqra also mentioned a more idealistic reason for choosing the profession: a desire to serve the community, the state, and the homeland. Virtually every opening statement of each new journal (and, for that matter, every journalist's memoirs) contained the cliche: a desire to serve the public good. Yet in spite of the commonplace usage of such formulas, there is no reason to doubt their sincerity. Many publishers were indeed impelled by a genuine desire to serve a cause, most commonly a political one. This motivation was central to the journalistic initiative of Jamal al-Din al-Afghani and his disciples on the eve of the British occupation of Egypt. Afghani, together with Muhammad 'Abduh, published *al-'Urwa al-Wuthqa* in Paris in 1884 "to defend the rights of the people of the East in general, and the Muslims in particular, and to draw the attention of the ignorant among them to that which is good for them."[10] Afghani and his followers pioneered the utilization of the new medium for political goals. Mustafa Kamil, a political activist who initiated a popular anti-British protest movement in Egypt around the turn of the century, made use of journalism as one of several instruments to serve his objectives by publishing *al-Liwa'*—"a standard of truth for our compatriots, a banner for those struggling for Egypt's progress."[11] Subsequently, newspaper publishing was adopted as a vital device by almost every political party and group in the region, and those who undertook to articulate their party's or group's views found themselves engaged in the field of journalism. Nonpolitical interests, such as religious minorities, women's concerns, and various professional groups, also drew their protagonists into the field.

Another kind of motivation was economic: the pursuit of journalism as a business interest. This attraction was enhanced by the ease with which a publishing project could be started in the Arab countries, with few resources and no special training. "People may be amazed at our initiative to launch this journal when so many periodicals abound," announced the owner of a new literary magazine in Beirut in 1932. "Our response to them is: It is a profitable merchandise. Had there been no plurality of views, there would be no market for these commodities. Our journal shall find a constituency, as did its numerous predecessors."[12] Although so candid an acknowledgement of material concern was not common, many publications throughout the region undoubtedly came into being precisely for such considerations. Newcomers were attracted by this deceptively easy option before discovering that it was far simpler to establish a paper than to sustain it. Some of those impelled by economic motives, however, relied not on the marketability of their publication but on another attractive option: hiring their columns to patrons, local or foreign, governmental or private—an option that was available in various forms from the very beginning of the Arab press until the mid-twentieth century and later. This kind of motivation had little to do with talent or the writers' personal convictions. Viewing their journals as commercial enterprises operating under tough market conditions, these publishers were guided by commercial norms rather than by the still-ambiguous ethics of journalism. Sometimes the owners wrote the columns themselves, according to the directives of their benefactors, at other times they hired writers to do this work. The hired writers, who usually possessed some literary gift, sold their talent for a fee, making a living out of their craft without necessarily sharing the patron's views.

Some of the publishers who entered the trade for material gains aspired from the start to establish big businesses. The pioneers of this group in the last quarter of the nineteenth century—such as the Taqlas with *al-Ahram* in Egypt and Khalil Sarkis with *Lisan al-Hal* in Lebanon—faced the double challenge of setting up the project as well as developing a market for this new commodity. Alert to changing cultural and political circumstances, they demonstrated that newspapers could not only survive but also thrive and even have a significant impact on social issues. Their prosperous enterprises became models for other entrepreneurs who sought similar achievements and sometimes succeeded. The success of these larger ventures, however, did not block the road for new, more modest journalistic undertakings. Slow economic development throughout the region, and the plethora of political forces anxious to hire publicists, perpetuated small-scale journalism as an appealing vocational option alongside the more ambitious enterprises.

If the expansion of the profession by the continuous addition of new members to its ranks attested to its ongoing attraction, the high expiration rate of newspapers and large-scale abandonment of the field showed that all too often the allure ended in frustration. One serious disadvantage in being a journalist was the low public image of the occupation, which remained so throughout much of the period under consideration. When Jurji Zaydan joined *al-Muqtataf* as an administrator in 1887, his father's reaction was, typically, strongly adverse. He wanted his son to study something more "decent," such as medicine or law.[13] Still an amorphous activity, journalism had none of the prestige of these other two professions, which were the preferred fields in the best of the region's educational institutions. Not only was journalism a nontraditional concern, and hence a suspicious innovation which the community's spiritual leaders denounced; to many, it was also an odd occupation, based on the sale of opinions and words, for which no special qualifications or training seemed necessary. It was widely believed that "if the gates of various [other] jobs were closed in the face of a young man, he could turn to the press for a career."[14] Men of letters often shared this view as well; as an Iraqi historian of his country's press noted, many "considered writing for newspapers too base an occupation to engage in—something that would discredit them."[15] Material hardship was another major factor in molding the popular image of the journalist as ill-fated. *Jurnalji*—the Turkicized French term commonly used to designate members of the vocation in Egypt and elsewhere prior to World War I and long after it—was a disdainful appellation which, in the words of one writer, connoted "vagrancy, poverty, and destitution" more than any other qualities.[16]

Economic difficulties were largely responsible for the disappointment shared by so many Arab journalists. A journalist's income was as notoriously low as was his public image. "I remember that in the year 1923 I needed to rent an apartment in Cairo," an Egyptian journalist related.

> I went to the place, examined it and agreed to rent it for a monthly fee of seven pounds. We began writing up the rental contract. But as soon as the landlady learned I was a journalist, she rose from her seat and exclaimed: "Where will a *jurnalji* get seven pounds a month to pay the rent?" She refused to sign the contract, and I could do nothing to make her change her mind.

Journalism, he reflected, was a miserable calling. With the income of journalists so meager, and with frequent harassment by the authorities, "the public in general came to view journalism as a dangerous occupation that led to imprisonment, a trade of those who had gone, or were about to go, bankrupt."[17] Even the lot of those who succeeded professionally was not always bright, and they sometimes ended their careers as penurious as they had started them. When Rashid Rida died, his friends and colleagues assumed he had left a legacy of "quite a few thousand pounds" after 37 years of the regular appearance of his monthly *al-Manar*, which, in addition to the books he had written, was read throughout the Islamic world. Rida's friends were amazed to discover that the house he had occupied "was built not to live in and be enjoyed but rather to store printing machines, letter boxes, trash of all kinds, and books," and was mortgaged for a thousand pounds.[18] Such depictions may have been overly bleak, but there is no doubting the general low regard for journalism and the consternation that it produced. Economic success and prestige were the exception. The rule was penury, causing many journalists "not to view their occupation as a mission for life, nor yet as a source of livelihood forever," but rather as a temporary station on a road leading elsewhere. Only those "who are haunted and blinded by the craft" remained, the Egyptian writer Salama Musa observed.[19] If this was so in Egypt, it must have been even more so elsewhere, where, as one Palestinian journalist complained, there was "neither public opinion to rely on, nor clear principles to support, nor yet open-mindedness to accept frank criticism," and this made the journalist's duty "extremely difficult and burdensome."[20]

The Egyptian novelist and essayist Ibrahim al-Mazini, who was successful and popular, offered a colorful description of the frustration that he and his colleagues often felt in journalism. "My experience of twenty years has taught me that [my efforts to] provide food for [people's] minds have been of no avail," he noted.

> Were I to start my life anew, I would not have engaged in journalism in Egypt. I would have preferred to sell *ta'miyya* (bean patties). I would have opened a shop, one like Abu Zarifa's, where I could sell *ta'miyya* and *ful mudammas* (stewed beans). Certainly, my situation would then have been better than it is now. I may even have outdone Abu Zarifa and his likes, who sell *ta'miyya* and *ful mudammas*, whose merchandise is more in demand in Egypt than literary products (*adab*), while they do not toil even as much as one hundredth of the literary man's toil. . . . I would have been able to serve my customers fresh *ta'miyya* and fine *ful*, so the name of al-Mazini would have become synonymous with *ta'miyya* and *ful mudammas* rather than be a brand name for the literary man who, in his *adab*, reaps nothing but constant distress, nor any satisfaction commensurate with his efforts.[21]

Mazini may have overstated his case, in his buoyant style, yet his frustration with the public's indifference to his cultural contribution through the press was genuine. Complaints like his over lack of professional satisfaction were voiced much less often than remonstrations about the material hardship involved in the vocation, but this frustration must have been experienced by others as well. Nonetheless, many, like Mazini himself, remained in the field, having been "haunted and blinded by the craft."

Toward Professionalism

Much as in the West, journalism in the Arab countries began as an amateur pursuit. The question of whether or when it became a "profession" depends on the standards applied in examining this occupation, as well as on how one defines profession. In a study entitled "The Rise of Professions and Professional Organization in Modern Egypt," Donald Reid suggested four criteria for measuring the professionalization of certain vocations in that country, including journalism: (1) the establishment of university-level training in the field, (2) the appearance of specialized journals for professionals, (3) the growth in number of those employed in the vocation, and (4) the establishment of a syndicate. These indices, Reid showed, are useful in exploring the development of the other professions that he examined: law, medicine, engineering, and teaching. When applied to journalism, however, they do not seem to have gotten him very far, as he himself acknowledged. The first criterion, in the case of Egypt, relates to a development that appeared at a late stage—in the second half of the 1930s—and teaches us little about the important stages that preceded it. The second criterion is scarcely relevant to journalism and was inapplicable to Reid's study. The third does not lend itself to precise measurement in this profession, and only the fourth proves to be of value in assessing professionalization. Indeed, in studying the evolution of the craft in Egypt, Reid ended up examining mainly organizational developments up until the formation of the press syndicate there in 1941 and touching briefly on the emergence of journalism departments in Egyptian universities from the late 1930s onward.[22] Any attempt to employ Reid's norms in studying the evolution of journalism elsewhere in the region prior to World War II would have been even less productive.

Since journalism in the Middle East, as elsewhere, differed from other vocations in its definability, the study of the development of journalism may require a more flexible approach. Rather than applying rigid tests to identify shifts from one stage to the next, we may use looser standards. It might be useful to follow the gradual progress from personal and individual initiative to institutional journalism and, concomitantly, the evolving differentiation within the trade (e.g., publishers, editors, columnists, correspondents, and administrative staff). Tracing the emergence of ethical awareness, and of rules of professional conduct, is another possible parameter. Finally, the development of organized methods of professional training, as well as professional organizations, which emerged late and were slow to evolve, might also be helpful in this exploration. None of these criteria, however, is precise

enough to define stages of development: In studying the history of
journalism, establishing accurate criteria or identifying precise stages
are, perhaps, unrealistic objectives.

"The main reason that the Arab press, especially in Syria, is in
such a miserable state," commented Nissim Malul, a Palestinian Jewish
journalist, in 1914, is that the newspaper publisher produces the entire
paper himself.

> He is the manager, the editor, the proofreader, the author of articles
> signed [by others], the one who puts the copies in their envelopes, and
> sometimes the one who carries them by himself to the *posta*. What, then,
> can be expected of a press whose entire editorial function is performed by
> a single person, who must be at once a political, social, economic, and
> scientific columnist, and must deal with all this at one and the same time
> with the rest of the paper's business, which ought to be completed on
> time?[23]

The image of the journalist as his own staff, a jack-of-all-trades
who performs all of the paper's editorial, administrative, and technical
duties single-handedly — a familiar feature of the European and American press in the seventeenth, eighteenth, and early nineteenth centuries — characterized Arab journalism into the twentieth century. In
some places it was the prevalent standard until well into the interwar
period. Ya'qub Sanu''s papers, published in both Cairo and Paris during the last quarter of the nineteenth century, epitomized this kind of
personal journalism: written in Sanu''s unique style (some of them
produced in his own handwriting), illustrated with his own cartoons,
carrying personal notices advertising his other services, and, most conspicuously, bearing the title by which Sanu' himself came to be identified, Abu Naddara. Salim Sarkis' *al-Mushir*, appearing in Cairo during
the 1890s, was another example of a highly personal publication. Written in the first person singular, it mirrored the owner's sentiments,
including personal comments incorporated in his reportage and quarrels with his personal enemies. In the summer of 1895, because of an
illness that kept him confined to bed for a month (during which, he
proudly noted, he carried on editing the paper), Sarkis was forced to
leave Cairo for convalescence in Alexandria. He would do his best to
assure that the paper continued to appear as usual, he promised his
readers, but his illness would preclude his responding to their letters.[24]
Changes in the personal calendar of the publisher-editor could upset
the publishing schedule even in a larger journal: *Al-Hilal* notified its
customers in 1900 that, "as the editor will occasionally be absent from
his work, we shall have to publish the journal this summer in double
issues at the middle of each month" (instead of the usual biweekly
schedule).[25] *Al-Hilal*, and other leading Arabic periodicals in the early
twentieth century, started as modest personal ventures that were managed with very little help, the team normally consisting of the owner

(*sahib al-imtiyaz*, or licensee) and one or two assistants. Toward the end of the nineteenth century, Ya'qub Sarruf of *al-Muqtataf* complained to a friend that he had to write and edit each of the journal's 100-page issues by himself[26] — a statement patently exaggerated but surely with an element of truth. Around the same time, Salim Taqla of *al-Ahram* noted that he "spent day and night working, body and soul. . . . I edited [the paper] and administered it, supervised [the work of] its employees, copied subscribers' addresses, and did most of the [other] work."[27] 'Ali Yusuf of *al-Mu'ayyad*, Khalil Sarkis of *Lisan al-Hal*, Najib Nassar of *al-Karmil*, and others described similar routines.[28]

Endeavors that would later grow into well-structured ventures supported by an extensive infrastructure and substantial resources were kept going at first by unending improvisation. Rashid Rida wrote the opening article for the first issue of *al-Manar* in 1897 "with a pencil, in the al-Isma'ili mosque." His contemporary Egyptian colleagues, mostly less orthodox, used to sit in the cafes of Cairo "in the squares of Bab al-Khalq and 'Ataba, 'Imarat al-Matatiya, and Khazandar," an Egyptian writer related. "There they wrote, negotiated with their agents and distributors, and bargained with those who wanted [to use their papers] to attack others."[29] Syrian journalists in the early years of the profession in that country often used the printshops that put out their papers as offices. "The paper's management is [located] in a special section of the Maronite press," noted *al-Nahar* of Aleppo in 1911, while at least two other newspapers listed the same address for their own offices that year—a common pattern.[30] Da'ud Bandali al-'Isa, the owner and editor of *Filastin*, depicted yet another facet of the work of the one-man publisher in the early days, describing how he used to go out to the towns and villages of Palestine riding a hired donkey, and to the nomad tribes of the desert on camelback, to collect back payments and to enlist new subscribers.[31] As late as 1927, Ibrahim Salih Shakir, publisher of the Baghdad daily *al-Zaman*, offered this description of his occupation:

> God bless your soul, oh 'Ali Yusuf! You published *al-Mu'ayyad* in Egypt during the age of darkness, writing and distributing the paper [all by yourself]. . . . In *al-Zaman* I follow in your footsteps: I draft the paper's various sections, including even local news, print it, and purchase the newsprint all by myself. I have no office, except for the cafes and hotels in which I sit and write *al-Zaman*. Yet I am not unhappy with my lot.[32]

Newspapers were closely identified with their owners in the early phase. If the owner fell ill, the paper suffered as well. Few publications survived after their owner's death. Accordingly, there was little functional differentiation in executing the various duties in a newspaper. At the same time, journalists were often involved in a number of papers simultaneously, as proprietors or editors. Under such pressing circumstances, those who took up the vocation were forced by material constraints to focus on survival rather than on social mission, professionalism, or ethics — concepts that were new even where the medium originated, in the West. Many of these early journalists did indeed enter the field in order to serve what they conceived as the community's needs by furthering enlightenment, combating tyranny and opposing foreign enemies, but such objectives were never defined *per se* as professional duties. The assumption was that society's basic ethical and moral rules were adequate for guiding newspaper writers, as they guided anyone involved in one kind or another of public activity. The question of professional training seemed equally irrelevant. Satisfied with their artful command of rhetoric, the early journalists felt no need for special instruction, nor did the new medium seem to impose any particular demands that would be above their qualifications.

By the mid-1880s, a different style of press activity began to appear in Egypt alongside the initial one. It was introduced by newspapers that aspired to become larger enterprises, especially those that, devoted primarily to reportage, sought to emulate Western achievements by adopting their techniques in news-gathering, management, and marketing. Part of this development was functional differentiation not merely between editorial, technical, and administrative staffs but also within each of these branches. The advent of political parties eager to finance newspapers, on the eve of World War I, prompted the formation of equally large, or larger, press organizations in Egypt and later in Syria and Lebanon, some of which produced more than just one publication. The appearance of party organs contributed to differentiation in yet another way, by turning politicians into part-time publicists who thereby added a new component to the professional profile of the journalist.

The shift into this new phase was slow, and for many years the new style evolved parallel to the old personal style of journalism. Economically there was only limited room for large press institutions: a handful in Egypt — perhaps half a dozen in the interwar years — two or three each in Syria and Lebanon, and one or two in Iraq and Palestine. "Journalism" in these larger enterprises meant something quite distinct from what it denoted in the old, more personal variation: A journalist was now a specialist within the system that produced the paper, rather than constituting the system itself.

This change in function was accompanied by a change in professional awareness, ethical attitudes, and regard for training and organization, resulting not so much from the functional modifications themselves as from another development. The unregulated entry of would-be journalists into the field and their frequent misuse of the medium prompted several concerned writers to demand that rules be laid down for the new profession. Criticism of abuse of the press by journalists for selfish ends was first voiced by colleagues in Egypt around the mid-1890s. Writers censured their "irresponsible" associates for failing to realize that journalism entailed certain ethical obligations.

Some of them even called upon the authorities to regulate the practice of journalism by law.[33] By the turn of the century, the need for a code of ethics was discussed extensively in the Arab press. There was considerable discontent with the situation which, according to Rashid Rida, invited "unfit people" to join the profession, people who had "intruded into this respectable calling without any preparation and damaged its reputation."[34] This dissatisfaction represented an incipient perception of journalism as an occupation with its own obligations and rules, even if these were as yet undefined.

What would make a person "fit" for the task, and what kind of preparation should he get? All the journalists who expressed themselves on this subject were in agreement that not everybody could be a journalist, and that certain qualifications were required. Muhammad 'Ali Hamid Hashishu, a writer from Sidon, pointed out in 1909 in the Lebanese *al-'Irfan* that a potential journalist must be wise and perspicacious, familiar with the realities of his community, its ills and the remedies for them. He must be a symbol and a leader for the people in his personal conduct, principles, and ethics, as well as an articulate writer and a master of style so as to hold his readers' attention.[35] Ahmad Shakir al-Karmi, editor of the Egyptian *al-Kawkab*, wrote in a similar vein in 1919:

> Those practicing journalism must have complete knowledge of the state of the community, its ethics and habits. They ought to concern themselves with its needs and desires, and become acquainted with the things which it likes and hates. Once they accomplish all this, they may approach the press assuredly. . . . Otherwise they are doomed to failure regardless of how well versed they are in arts and sciences.[36]

The Syrian Kurd 'Ali was even more demanding. Preceding all else, he stated, a journalist must have as good a command of the Arabic language as the best Arab writers; mastery of one or two foreign languages, so as to allow him to draw on the foreign press; familiarity with the sources dealing with the various subjects on which he may wish to write; proficiency in both religious and secular law, Islamic history, and especially the history, economy, and society of the country about which he writes; and familiarity with the history, evolution, and current realities of other peoples. "A perfect acquaintance with all of these issues is a minimum for the prospective journalist," Kurd 'Ali maintained.[37] Emile Zaydan, in a lecture on the journalist and his duties in 1931, stipulated that "only a born journalist who has the special character for it" could be a successful newspaper writer, although training was also indispensable for molding the journalist's professional personality. In addition, a journalist must be broadly educated, for "the readers of today are not those of yesterday, and he who does not give the press its due invites failure and defeat." Other vital qualifications, according to Emile Zaydan, included resourcefulness, creativity, and courage, as well as proficiency in the rules of journalistic writing.[38]

Such views were more idealistic than practical. Pinpointing the flaws of Arab journalism and presenting an ideal model of a journalist were no doubt important indications of professional awareness. But how could fitness be ascertained? Some writers called for legislation that would establish qualifying tests, such as existed in other professions.[39] Others recommended a program of study, a need that was recognized and discussed as early as the end of the nineteenth century. "Journalism has become a profession in Europe, an independent pursuit which people acquire in schools like other trades and crafts. . . . How we are in need of such a school in Egypt!" noted Jurji Zaydan in 1896. A Lebanese colleague echoed the plea a decade later, calling for "opening a school for the training of journalists and teaching them the skills of writing properly. Then society will benefit from constructive articles."[40] The organized study of journalism had just begun in the West then (the first full university department of journalism was founded at the University of Missouri in 1908, while in Europe such departments appeared only after World War I). In the Arab context, however, the notion of the press as a field of study was remote at that stage and certainly not practical. In 1923, in a symposium on "the present and future of the Arab press" conducted by *al-Hilal*, the idea of establishing an institution for training journalists elicited less than enthusiastic reactions by four leading Egyptian newspaper editors who were asked to comment. Only two, Mahmud 'Azmi and Amin al-Rafi'i, thought that such a school was indeed necessary. A third, Da'ud Barakat, conceded that establishing a school for journalists would be "a step as useful as the establishment of any scientific and professional institution," but maintained that "writing is a product of training and practice, not of studying or teaching." The fourth, Ahmad Hafiz 'Awad, was even less forthcoming:

> I see no need for opening a university department or a special institution for training journalists. Men of the press everywhere have had their education in the field of practice. The traits of a journalist, like those of a poet, are inherited, not acquired.[41]

Three years later, in 1926, another journalist noted that although it was important to train people employed in the press in various skills, he would not go so far as "anticipating the establishment of schools for teaching the basics of journalism as they have done in the United States and have begun doing in London." Applying the idea in Egypt, he felt, was still premature.[42] Another decade would elapse until the idea of a school for journalists would be taken up as a practical option, at the initiative of Egyptian Prime Minister 'Ali Mahir. Seeking to woo the press, Mahir announced his intention in March 1936 of starting a program of evening courses in journalism at Cairo University. Mahir's government fell before the plan could be realized (he would implement it upon his return to the premiership in 1939), but meanwhile a program was started in 1936 at the American University in Cairo, the first of its kind in the region.[43] In other Arab countries such organized studies were begun only in the second half of the twentieth century.

While discontent with the state of the craft was articulated clearly, ideas for solutions were far less precise and were seldom implemented during the period under review. This was so not only with regard to the institutionalized study of journalism but also in terms of the formulation of a code of ethics. Setting rules for professional conduct entailed the establishment of some kind of organization. But efforts at forming press associations in Lebanon, Egypt, and Syria in the twentieth century foundered, largely due to organizational incompetence and political controversies. A "press committee" (*lajna suhufiyya*) founded in Beirut in 1911 was designed to promote cooperation among members of the trade and "clear the press of Beirut of personal abuses and divisive publications." In formulating its objectives the committee touched briefly upon ethical matters and even fixed punishment for "papers committing the offense of personal assault." Soon thereafter, however, the committee was dissolved, to be followed by the establishment and disbanding of a series of other journalists' associations and syndicates in Lebanon, all seemingly preoccupied with organizational issues and personal conflicts at least as much as with questions of professional ethics.[44] An appeal for the formation of a press union in Egypt was apparently voiced as early as 1896 by Bishara Taqla, and in 1900 a group of journalists convened in Cairo to work out an organizational framework, but without much success. Repeated efforts to form such bodies over the next 40 years all produced short-lived results. Only in March 1941 was a syndicate established that proved to be more durable.[45] Syrian journalists made similar organizational efforts from 1929 onward, but a lasting syndicate was not established until 1942.[46] In all these efforts, the journalists' divisiveness apparently outweighed their motivation to collaborate. Thus, in pre-World War I Egypt, disagreement over whether the union should accept newspaper owners only or editors and columnists as well resulted in a division into two separate, but short-lived, unions.[47] Recurrent controversies between owners and employees, and between senior editors and other journalists, as well as estrangement between unions in different cities everywhere in the region, resulted in fragmentation and the formation of competing associations. Under the circumstances, consensually accepted ethical codes were necessarily slow to evolve.

Judged by the criterion of the development of systematic organized training and professional associations, Arab journalism as a whole remained at an elementary stage until World War II. However, two other criteria—the shift from personal to institutionalized journalism, and the slow but unmistakable emergence of ethical awareness—indicate the considerable progress made in the field throughout the region. These two processes gradually edged Arab journalism from its rudimentary, preprofessional early phase to a more sophisticated stage in which its practitioners had a clearer sense of professional mission. Given the diversity in rates of development throughout the region, the rudimentary phase did not disappear, but continued to exist alongside the more advanced systems. In general, however, there was a trend toward the consolidation of journalism as a recognized vocation with its own rules, requirements, and objectives, which gradually led, in turn, to an improvement in the status of journalists themselves. The fact that accomplished writers and recognized political leaders engaged in journalism as well also helped enhance the image of the profession. Salama Musa, writing in the mid-1950s about the "despised" popular status of journalism in his country, used the past tense throughout his article to indicate that this state was a matter of history by then.[48] As a prominent Egyptian journalist who had gained esteem during the interwar period, Musa had witnessed the shift in popular attitude toward his field firsthand. This change also occurred more slowly elsewhere.

Kurd 'Ali, Yusuf, Musa, Istanbuli

Certain obvious traits were shared by Arab journalists despite the wide range in time and place covered by this study. Not coincidentally, these were also the traits that characterized the reading audience as well: Arab journalists came from the small, literate segment of society, a self-evident fact. The nature of the occupation and its indebtedness to Western inspiration made it likely, furthermore, that those involved in it were exposed, at least to some extent, to knowledge of the West and hence were prepared to engage in a nontraditional pursuit. They were overwhelmingly male, with a handful of women in the Egyptian and Lebanese press only. In addition, members of minority communities were represented in the vocation in proportions that greatly exceeded their ratio in society. They were prominent in the field not only in Lebanon, where the majority of journalists both before and after the formation of the republic were Christians, but also elsewhere. In Egypt, about a third of all newspapers published until 1929 were founded by Christians, mostly Syrians and Lebanese but also native Copts, who remained prominent thereafter. In the Fertile Crescent Christians, though small in number, were likewise highly visible. Such noted figures as Salim 'Anhuri and Butrus Mu'awwad in Syria; Najib Nassar, the 'Isa brothers, Jurji Habib Hananya, and Bulus Shihada in Palestine; Rafa'il Batti and Tawfiq al-Sam'ani in Iraq; and Khalil Nasr in Transjordan illustrate the point.

Beyond these general attributes lay a vast variety of specific characteristics of the Arab journalist resulting not only from the geographic diversity and the lengthy time span under consideration, but also from the accelerated rate of change, especially in the cultural sphere, experienced by this society during the period. The Egyptian press, Donald Reid observed, "produced every shade of journalist from the secularized apostle of communism to the most rigid Islamic traditionalist. All they had in common was the use of a modern medium of communication."[49] This was so in other parts of the region as well. A representative profile of the Arab journalist, therefore, cannot be produced. But a glance at the careers of several members of the profession can illuminate aspects of the journalist's experience during the first century of the private Arab press.

The colorful career of Muhammad Kurd 'Ali (1876-1953) of Syria contained many features shared by Arab colleagues in various periods and places.[50] He was born in Damascus to a family that was not wealthy, but his father managed through hard work to acquire some landed property and provide his children with an elementary and high school education. Intellectual curiosity impelled the teenage Kurd 'Ali to immerse himself in reading both local and foreign newspapers and to submit articles to the press. At that stage, however, he did not expect to become a journalist, a vocation as yet unknown in the Syrian provinces, he relates in his memoirs. But he continued to write, and at the age of 20 was asked by the publisher of the local semiofficial weekly *al-Sham* to become editor of the paper. There he first encountered Hamidian censorship, which, both arbitrary and rigid, inhibited the development of journalism throughout the Fertile Crescent. He also had another instructive experience — an attempt to hire his pen in exchange for an imperial decoration, which, he related, he turned down so as not to compromise his freedom. In 1901, at the age of 25, he visited Cairo, where the Lebanese owner of the private semiweekly *al-Ra'id al-Misri* promptly enlisted him as editor. He served in that position for ten months, until a plague in Egypt forced him to return to Damascus.

Kurd 'Ali returned to Egypt in 1905 with a clear objective in mind: to establish a scientific and literary monthly. "I immigrated to Egypt, as did several other Syrian liberals," he recalled, "due to the growing pressure in the Ottoman provinces in the late days of Sultan 'Abd al-Hamid the Second."[51] Resourceful and practical, he approached 'Ali Yusuf, owner and editor of *al-Mu'ayyad*, with a proposal: He would write as many articles for *al-Mu'ayyad* as Yusuf would like, in return for the use of Yusuf's press to print his own journal. Yusuf, who was aware of Kurd 'Ali's talent, proposed instead that he edit a new weekly that Yusuf intended to publish. But Kurd 'Ali stuck to his original plan and launched *al-Muqtabas* on his own shortly thereafter, in February 1906. Apparently in economic need, he soon became involved in another paper, the daily *al-Zahir*, first as translator from French and then as editor-in-chief. Sometime later the paper went bankrupt, whereupon Kurd 'Ali joined *al-Mu'ayyad* as editor. By then he had gained firsthand knowledge of the state of the Arab press and joined the criticism of its performance and of abuses by many of his colleagues. More broadly, he repeatedly drew his readers' attention to the ills of society highlighted by the encounter with modernity and called for reform (*islah*), showing himself to be above all a popular educator. His interest in public enlightenment was reflected in the ambitious scope he envisioned for *al-Muqtabas*, which, according to the title page, aspired to address itself to "*pédagogie, sociologie, économie, littérature, histoire, archéologie, philologie, ménagerie, hygiène, bibliographie, civilisation arabe et occidentale.*"[52]

The Young Turk revolution altered the circumstances that had prompted Kurd 'Ali to emigrate to Egypt, and in late 1908 he returned to Damascus, transferring the monthly *al-Muqtabas* with him. Unlike the situation in Cairo, where his journal vied for the small audience of educated readers with several other publications, some of them more attractive, in Damascus *al-Muqtabas* was unique. Before the end of the year, Kurd 'Ali started a daily newspaper by the same name — the first daily in Damascus. The period that followed was not easy politically, and Kurd 'Ali tasted "a little that was good and a lot that was evil," in his words. His papers appealed to the small, younger, educated sector and to liberal-minded intellectuals, but was sharply criticized by "several ultraconservative shaykhs." There were also material difficulties — the limited reading market in Syria as well as technological limitations — which were reflected in the stark format of his monthly journal, especially in contrast to corresponding Egyptian publications. Kurd 'Ali financed his publications with income from private property, and possibly with secret aid from the French consulate as well.[53] A daring publicist, he soon attacked the new Committee of Union and Progress government for its aggressive Turkification policy, incurring its wrath. At first the authorities tried to bribe him into silence, but failing that penalized his papers with shutdowns, harassed him by threats and physical attacks, and even hired an assassin to do away with him. This hounding prompted Kurd 'Ali to flee Syria repeatedly, with consequent interruptions in the publication of his papers between 1909 and 1914. However, with the arrival of Ottoman General Jemal Pasha in Damascus, a major change took place. Jemal became fond of Kurd 'Ali, cultivated a friendship with him, and even helped him financially in putting out his daily. Whether from political conviction or calculated tactics, Kurd 'Ali abandoned his political crusade against the Ottoman authorities. Moreover, he actively cooperated with Jemal, became one of the editors of the Ottoman propaganda organ *al-Sharq* in 1916, and even agreed to retire from the daily *al-Muqtabas* so as not to jeopardize the Ottoman organ, putting his brother Ahmad in charge in his stead.[54] Kurd 'Ali, "hitherto one of the greatest oppositionists . . . [now] submitted to the hangman who executed the country's freedom fighters," a Syrian historian noted years later.[55] Identified with the Ottoman regime, he moved to the safety of Istanbul in 1917 once the Ottoman forces began to retreat.

The rest of Kurd 'Ali's life story touched upon the press only marginally and from a different perspective. Returning to Damascus at the invitation of King Faysal of Syria, apparently in early 1919, he resumed publication of *al-Muqtabas* and followed the old militant line. The paper supported Faysal's indigenous Arab government and opposed the presence of the advancing French. But Kurd 'Ali's interests shifted to other matters. He left the management of the paper to his brother once again and turned to scholarship and administration, becoming one of the founders, and president, of the Arab Scientific Academy in Damascus in 1920. He then immersed himself in writing a four-volume history of the city, *Khitat al-Sham*. In 1928 he became minister of education in Taj al-Din al-Hasani's government. Meanwhile, *al-Muqtabas* was run by his brother Ahmad and, after the latter's death, by Nassuh Babil, whom Kurd 'Ali hired as editor. Kurd 'Ali, a member of the government, found himself under attack by a newspaper that he himself owned. He invited Babil to his office in order to request him to tone down his criticism, advising him: "My experience has taught me, my dear friend, that moderation is often better than excess. Be moderate, be moderate!" Not surprisingly, Babil refused to temper his attacks, whereupon the minister ordered the paper closed indefinitely.[56] Muhammad Kurd 'Ali, by then a prominent establishment figure, had traveled a long road since his days as a bold critic of the government.

Kurd 'Ali's rich career in the press contained many elements that were common to other Arab journalists: the intellectual bent; the precocious proclivity for journals and for contributing to them; joining the staff of a local paper and encountering the pressures of censorship; emigration for political and intellectual reasons; involvement in the production of several periodicals simultaneously; founding a journal, running afoul of the establishment and paying a personal price for it; and becoming part of the educational effort to enlighten the public in the arts and sciences and in their own legacy. Other components of Kurd 'Ali's career—the eventual adjustment to government demands and cooperation with the authorities, serving in the government, and confronting the press as a representative of the state—were less typical, although by no means exceptional.

Shaykh 'Ali Yusuf (1863–1913) of Egypt embodied another type of Arab journalist: the devout Muslim who never strayed far from his traditional moorings and who was rooted in his native language and culture, but who was perceptive and ambitious enough to use the press as a powerful tool to advance his community's cause. Yusuf joined the field around the time his country came under British occupation, and, deeply influenced by this event, devoted his press activities to fostering nationalistic sentiment and generating popular opposition to the foreign presence. Born to a poor family in the Upper Egyptian village of Balsfura, he received a basic education in the village school. In 1881, at the

age of 18, he sailed down the Nile to Cairo, seeking to expand his
horizons. He enrolled at al-Azhar, hoping to become a teacher but
knowing that if he failed in his studies he could always make a living by
reciting verses from the Qur'an at funerals. Yusuf studied theology,
grammar, and logic, and was exposed to history and poetry. In the
process he allowed himself to become interested in literary and political
periodicals — al-Azhar's conservative atmosphere notwithstanding —
and began submitting literary pieces to them. He seems to have become
so fascinated with the medium that he abandoned school before gradua-
tion, apparently in 1886, and found employment as an editor with
Salim Faris al-Shidyaq's daily *al-Qahira*, and soon thereafter as editor of
the vociferously anti-British *Mir'at al-Sharq*.

But Yusuf was anxious to start his own paper. After waiting six
months for a license from the Government Publications Office, he
borrowed money from one of his al-Azhar colleagues, Ahmad Madi,
and in February 1887 launched the literary weekly *al-Adab*. About two
years later the journal attracted the attention of Prime Minister Mustafa Riyad Pasha, who, upset by British policies, was prepared to assist
local activists committed to combating the foreigners. When Sarruf
and Nimr established the pro-British daily *al-Muqattam* in March 1889,
Riyad was ready to back an organ that would combat their message.
The precise circumstances of the association between Riyad and Yusuf
are not entirely clear, but it is obvious that Riyad, along with several
other anti-British activists, played a key role in Yusuf's switch from
literary to political journalism in the winter of 1889. Riyad cut the red
tape involved in obtaining a publishing license, while Yusuf's previous
backer, Ahmad Madi, lent him money again and became a partner as
well in the new enterprise, *al-Mu'ayyad*.[57]

A villager who had spent eight years immersed in intensive cultural activity in the capital, Yusuf became an owner and the editor of a
promising political daily at the age of 26. *Al-Mu'ayyad* soon became the
organ of the evolving Egyptian nationalist movement, attracting such
writers as Mustafa Kamil, Muhammad Farid, Ahmad Lutfi al-Sayyid,
Qasim Amin, Sa'd Zaghlul, and Isma'il Sidqi, all of whom debated
their country's destiny in its columns. Generating public interest both
in Egypt and abroad, the paper became the country's best-selling periodical in the 1890s, with a circulation of 6,000 to 8,000 toward the end
of the decade. Yusuf himself was the driving force of the enterprise, his
talent and commitment more than compensating for his lack of familiarity with Western concepts and languages. Within two years, in the
fall of 1891, he parted company with Ahmad Madi, who, Yusuf felt,
was "incited by the paper's foes" — possibly bribed by the British.[58] *Al-
Mu'ayyad*, however, also had quite a few allies: a group of anti-British
nationalist activists, most prominently Mustafa Kamil, who wrote for
the paper regularly from 1895 and even filled in for Yusuf temporarily
as editor when he was on a tour abroad in 1898; Muhammad 'Abduh,

the chief mufti of Egypt, who was a close friend of Yusuf's; and above all Khedive 'Abbas Hilmi, who resented the highhanded policy and style of Cromer, the all-powerful British consul, and with whom Yusuf formed close personal and political ties. Yusuf's friendship with the khedive grew stronger over time and seems to have taken precedence over other considerations, earning *al-Mu'ayyad* a reputation as a khedivial mouthpiece. Yusuf, however, saw no contradiction between his friendship with 'Abbas Hilmi and his ideological causes: Both men harbored anti-British sentiments and both were anxious to rid Egypt of the foreign presence. The British reacted by trying to limit Yusuf's range of activity, depriving him of official sources of information (which they generously provided to their allies at *al-Muqattam*), instructing all officials in government offices not to cooperate with him, and punishing those who did.[59]

'Ali Yusuf reached the peak of his career as a journalist and public figure in his early thirties. His newspaper enjoyed unchallenged leadership in the field, catapulting him into politics, in 1902, as a member of *al-jam'iyya al-'umumiyya* (General Assembly), Egypt's quasi-parliamentary body. *Al-Mu'ayyad* was a leader in technological development as well, the first newspaper to introduce an advanced rotative electric printing machine in 1906 (an event that was marked by a large public celebration).[60] Yusuf continued to uphold his intense political convictions until close to the turn of the century. In 1898, following the incident of a near-confrontation between British and French troops in Fashoda—which ended in a British-French understanding—the khedive came to the conclusion that his aggressive anti-British policy was futile and decided to abandon it. Yusuf followed suit, adopting a more moderate line toward the British, which cost him his ties with some of the nationalists. Mustafa Kamil, critical of Yusuf's moderation, split from him and in 1900 established his own paper, *al-Liwa'*, which gradually replaced *al-Mu'ayyad* as spokesman for the nationalist Egyptian Islamic movement. Similarly, Ahmad Lutfi al-Sayyid founded *al-Jarida* to project his views. By 1907, the year in which Egypt's first three political parties were formed, including 'Ali Yusuf's Constitutional Reform Party, he had come to represent only one among several trends in the country's nascent nationalist movement. Yusuf continued to write for another five years, but in 1912 he quit journalism in favor of a prestigious position as head of the Wafa'iyya (sufi) order. A year later he died at the age of 50.[61]

The story of 'Ali Yusuf and *al-Mu'ayyad* was typical of a pattern in which journalism served as a means and the newspaper as a weapon in political combat. In addition, Yusuf's biography included two episodes that, while unique, illuminated important aspects of the assimilation of journalism in society.

The first of these came to be known as *qadiyyat al-tilighrafat*, "the Telegraphs [i.e., telegrams] Affair." In 1896, during Colonel Kitchener's military campaign in the Sudan, conducted mainly with Egyptian troops under British command, secret reports on the progress of the fighting were wired from the field to British headquarters in Cairo. *Al-Mu'ayyad* managed to obtain some of the reports dispatched from May to July, which cited military difficulties and casualties among the Egyptian troops, and published them together with sharp criticism of British military strategy. The authorities suspected an employee at the telegraph office of leaking the classified reports to the editor, but Yusuf, when interrogated, insisted on his right as a journalist to keep his sources of information confidential. Both men were taken to court. The case constituted a focus of public attention for several months, during which the circulation of *al-Mu'ayyad* increased markedly (reportedly doubling during the trial itself). Most of the press supported Yusuf and condemned the government's infringement on freedom of expression, while the public at large was, apparently, similarly upset with the official position.[62] In the end, the court acquitted Yusuf for lack of evidence, but convicted the telegraph official and sent him to prison; a court of appeal later acquitted him as well.[63] The affair was unusual in several respects, primarily in setting a precedent in the encounter between freedom of expression and the government's political interests. That a journalist had not been forced to reveal how he had obtained state secrets was another exceptional development, which could have taken place only during the brief interval when the authorities in Egypt under British tutelage were lax with the press. The resourcefulness Yusuf showed in getting hold of the information, publishing it, and defending his right to do so in court, was in itself quite extraordinary. Furthermore, in so doing, Yusuf stood up for a principle that was still unintelligible to most of his compatriots. If there was anything predictable about this affair, it was the broad popular support that Yusuf enjoyed, not so much for the liberal principle that he boldly defended as for his nationalistic spirit in defying his country's oppressors.

The other episode, briefly referred to in a previous chapter, involved 'Ali Yusuf's marriage to Shaykh al-Sadat's daughter, Safiyya, in 1904. Yusuf already had a wife, a woman of humble origins, whom he had married before embarking on his career as a journalist. Since then, however, he had become a celebrity: the first Egyptian to own a large newspaper that reflected popular sentiment, a confidant of the khedive and other leading personalities, and a member of the General Assembly, his chest adorned with prestigious state medals. Yusuf wished, therefore, to take a second wife whose standing befitted his changed position. His choice was the daughter of Shaykh 'Abd al-Khaliq al-Sadat, head of one of the country's most venerated families. As was customary, Yusuf approached the father, but, encountering procrastination over a period of several years, married Safiyya in secret. Outraged, the father went to court, suing for the annulment of the marriage on the grounds that Yusuf was unfit to marry into an aristocratic family for two reasons: his common origins, and his occupation in the press, "the most despicable vocation, one of shame and disgrace." Many other pejorative depictions of Yusuf's trade were articulated as well during the trial and the appeal, both of which ended in a ruling that the marriage be dissolved. It was claimed that "journalism was a contemptible profession in itself, prohibited by the Islamic faith" because it was based on such illicit acts as "petty spying" and dissemination of lies.[64] Significantly, public opinion was far from unanimous, and while there was considerable sympathy for Yusuf and support for his position, there was also a widespread feeling that the court's ruling against the marriage was consonant with revered traditional values. Apparently, the popular esteem for Yusuf's contribution to the national struggle, the high regard for his professional achievements, and his rise in public standing were insufficient to tip the balance in his favor when measured against traditional values. The roots of journalism were still considerably weaker, and its public standing far more precarious, than those of timeworn attitudes.

Half a century later, in a retrospective essay on the tribulations of Egyptian journalism, writer Salama Musa recalled the story of Yusuf's marriage to illustrate the low status of the profession and its practitioners at the turn of the century.[65] Musa (1887–1958), who grew up in pre-World War I Egypt, had witnessed many of the events and was subject to many of the influences that had shaped 'Ali Yusuf's career, but his sociocultural background, personal proclivities, and the rapidly changing political environment after the war resulted in a career distinct in many ways from that of his earlier compatriot. A Copt, he was born in the Delta town of Zaqaziq, where he received his basic education first in a traditional institution and then in a modern school opened by the Coptic community. His family, unlike Yusuf's, was well-to-do, and this allowed the young Salama options without economic pressure. Arriving in Cairo in 1903 to acquire a high school education, he attended a British-run school, which proved to be an unpleasant experience for him, because of what he described as the arrogant manner of the British teachers. But the city itself, then witnessing a period of rapid change, was an exciting place and offered many rewards. The press was becoming a major forum for the intensified political and ideological debate of the time, and Musa, together with many of his young friends, was captivated by the spirited views conveyed by the newspapers, above all by Mustafa Kamil's *al-Liwa'*. Musa grew to become an avid follower of the press, influenced most of all by three publications, by his own account: *al-Muqtataf*, *al-Jami'a*, and *al-Jarida*, all of which were more secular than *al-Liwa'*—an advantage in Musa's view.[66]

In 1907, upon completing his studies, Musa felt a need to expand his cultural horizons in Europe and went to France, where he spent two years exposed to new ideas that eventually would lead him to revolt against the conventions of Egyptian society. In Paris, at the age of 22, he wrote his first journalistic article — on Nietzsche's philosophy — which was published in al-Muqtataf.[67] In 1909, after a brief interval in Egypt, Musa went to London, where he stayed for four years of gratifying social and intellectual activity. In the winter of 1910–1911 he again returned home for a brief stay, during which he joined the staff of the Nationalist Party's al-Liwa'. He wrote articles on domestic and foreign politics for the daily, earning 7 pounds a month and, more important, acquiring "good journalistic practice." There he shared an office with Farah Antun, a hero of his youth, who had just returned from New York after four years of largely unsuccessful experimentation with journalism.[68] Antun was attempting to revive his old journal, al-Jami'a, but, like many of his colleagues, was forced by economic necessity to write for other newspapers as well. Musa, by contrast, had no such constraints and could readily afford to return to London after a while, to carry on with his intellectual edification. His departure from journalism, however, was only temporary, for the press remained "a bewitching phantasm" in his mind.

Back in Cairo in 1913 after his extensive intellectual adventure, Musa launched his own paper, the modernist secularist weekly al-Mustaqbal ("The Future"), in May 1914, which he edited jointly with another Christian modernist, Dr. Shibli Shumayyil, a Syrian emigré. The journal, reflecting youthful enthusiasm, was produced long before experience and political circumstances "extinguished the fire of zeal" in him and made him a more sober writer. Al-Mustaqbal sold a respectable 600 copies weekly "not counting the many devoted subscribers." It was a deliberately provocative publication that gave Musa a reputation as a controversialist and — as far as the government was concerned — a troublemaker.[69] Soon, however, World War I erupted and Musa was forced to close down the journal after 16 issues, because of the financial and political pressures of the war. He was invited to edit Iliyas Ziyada's small-circulation daily al-Mahrusa, which he did for several months, but then he retired to his home in Zaqaziq, irked by writing under the heavy hand of wartime censorship, and remained unemployed until the end of the war.

Musa's experience at al-Liwa' and al-Mahrusa laid the groundwork for his later incursions into political journalism. The "bewitching phantasm" of the press that overtook him in his youth continued to exert a hold on him for the rest of his career. Yet, as Musa himself realized early, he was more of a thinker, with a creative intellect, than a newspaperman. Although he felt at home in the press, and made it the primary channel for articulating his views, he simultaneously published many books on social, economic, and cultural issues — he was one of the more eloquent exponents of socialism in the region — produced studies in psychology, translated novels, and wrote several of his own. Some of these works were serialized in journals either before or after publication in book form. "My journalistic life in Egypt has been cultural in the extreme," he observed,[70] pointing to a distinction between his own writing and the usual type of political journalism, which tended to deal exclusively with current affairs. Despite his intensely individual style, Musa represented a significant group of Arab intellectuals, mostly Egyptians, for whom periodicals were a major, but not exclusive, medium for political and ideological debate.

With the end of World War I, Musa returned to the capital, seeking new access to the press. He was employed for a while as a teacher and worked as an editor for both the literary monthly *al-Hilal* and the pro-Wafd daily *al-Balagh*. In 1923, at the age of 36, he received his first major editorial appointment as editor-in-chief of *al-Hilal*, a forum that suited his intellectual bent. The 1920s were years of lively public debate among thinkers and writers on the issues of communal identity and orientation, and Musa played a prominent role in this milieu as a committed advocate of territorial Egyptian nationalism and Pharaonicism. He expressed his views consistently in the journal he edited as well as in other periodicals of the time such as *al-Siyasa al-Usbu'iyya*, *al-Rabita al-Sharqiyya*, and *al-Fajr*.[71] In 1925 he added to his responsibilities in *al-Hilal* the assignment of managing editor of *Kull Shay'* ("Everything"), a nonpolitical weekly magazine. Editing and writing for these papers, Musa acquired a name as one of the country's ablest essayists. But after a while he seems to have felt a need for a new challenge. He left *al-Hilal* in 1929 in order to establish his own journal, or rather two journals: He launched the monthly *al-Majalla al-Jadida* in 1929, and the weekly *al-Misri* the following year, both as forums for the discussion of contemporary ideological and political issues. But in 1930 Isma'il Sidqi, who had no liking for such debates, ascended to power as prime minister. Sidqi replaced the relatively liberal constitution with a more restrictive one and suspended many journals and newspapers, including Musa's. Musa resorted to the usual tactic of publishing similar papers under titles "rented" from licensed owners — about a dozen such publications in all — until Sidqi's Press Law of June 1931 put an end to this option as well and, moreover, facilitated Musa's brief imprisonment that year for his views. Thereafter he joined the staff of the Wafdist *al-Balagh*, carefully limiting his writing to social, economic, and literary matters, until a change of government in 1934 enabled him to renew publication of *al-Majalla al-Jadida*. He continued to edit it, as well as a weekly by the same name, until 1942, preaching a modernist secularist ideology even after many of his friends had reverted to a more conservative line, then in fashion. He also wrote editorials on Egyptian nationalism and Coptic civil rights for the Coptic daily *Misr*.[72]

Musa continued to be occupied with similar initiatives for the rest of his life, motivated by a sustained conviction in his views and a preparedness to fight for them. For a while, during World War II, he served as editor of a bulletin published by the Ministry of Social Affairs, viewing this work as "an opportunity to engage in edification toward modernism and social guidance," although the pay was only 20 pounds a month.[73] He also tried, without success, to obtain a license for a daily newspaper. After the war he continued to write regularly for *Misr* and various other newspapers and to publish books. At his death in 1958 he was associate editor of the popular weekly *Akhbar al-Yawm*.

Muhammad Kurd 'Ali, 'Ali Yusuf, and Salama Musa all had successful careers in the press, having realized their aspirations to write, publish, and leave their imprint on the events of their time. At the same time, their careers were marked by the characteristic trials and tribulations of the private Arab press during its first century. Typically, all three journalists became involved in politics, which often meant personal risk. They also had to contend with the discouraging commercial reality of operating a periodical, a challenge they met with the help of other sources — private wealth in the case of Musa, the support of a patron in the cases of both Kurd 'Ali and of Yusuf. All three left ample evidence of the details of their careers, shedding light on what it meant to be an Arab journalist — or, more precisely, a prosperous Arab journalist — in their time and place.

But the careers of a large number of other Arab journalists are not represented in the profiles of Kurd 'Ali, Yusuf, or Musa. These include the early Lebanese writers, whose goal was enlightenment, and who had no connection with political writing; individuals with writing skills who became hired political journalists expressing the views of patrons; politicians who put together newspapers hastily to serve *ad hoc* political ends and disbanded them just as fast, most typically in Iraq; journalists throughout the region who launched minuscule ventures with the hope of growing larger, then abandoned them in defeat; and journalists in the periphery, such as in Arabia and Transjordan, where a primitive infrastructure and an unresponsive audience precluded any lofty aspirations. All these, and more, were vital components of the multi-faceted milieu of Arab journalism quite distinct from those represented by the three figures examined above, but, for lack of recorded testimony or extant examples of their publications, their histories are difficult or impossible to reconstruct. Little is known of what it meant to be an "ordinary" or "marginal" journalist, although the great majority of Arab newspapermen were just that.

One brief record, published in Syria during the interwar period, sheds some light on this aspect of the picture. Mahmud Mahdi al-Istanbuli, a teacher and sometime journalist, was born in Damascus on the eve of World War I. His youthful memories were shaped by the dramatic events of the foundation of the Syrian state and its subjugation to the French mandate. His entry into primary school was delayed until he was 11 or 12 years old because his father, a small merchant, needed his help in running the business. Once enrolled, however, the young Istanbuli proved diligent and industrious. While still a student, he became an outspoken critic of the French authorities. Upon completing his studies in 1929, he was licensed as a teacher and found employment in the village school of al-Tall just north of Damascus. Istanbuli had the soul of an educator. "While my friends were preoccupied with having a good time, making money, and buying houses," he related "I was possessed, ever since my appointment to the job, with the thought of publishing a journal that would discuss the problems of the family of teachers, encourage them, and enlighten them on the most modern methods in education." He was also motivated by a patriotic drive "to unite all teachers under one roof . . . in order to combat [French] imperialism through a journal of guidance." Istanbuli approached "many knowledgeable people" in Syria and tried to enlist their aid, but all he heard was warnings that his idea was destined to failure and loss. Undeterred, he decided to launch the project with his own meager resources by tightening the family budget, which was based largely on his income as a salaried teacher.[74]

Istanbuli's 40-page monthly *Majallat al-Mu'allimin wal-Mu'allimat* appeared in April 1931. Early reactions were mixed, and while some readers were appreciative, others mocked him. Sadly, he recalled, he received only one letter of support "which brought remedy to my troubled soul. Had each of us lent his support and encouragement as much as he could to those who shoulder the burden of operating useful projects, the state of our Arab community would have been quite different." The periodical ran into considerable difficulties from the start, as the total number of teachers in Syria, the journal's potential market, was then less than 1,000. Istanbuli's request for financial support from the minister of education was rejected, although the minister promised assistance after the journal had proven viable for a period of a year. Optimistic and persevering, he continued to publish the paper single-handedly. In the summer of 1933 Istanbuli was summoned by the French high commissioner's headquarters and was interrogated on the functioning of his paper. "May we know what are the revenues and expenses of your journal?" a French officer inquired, to which Istanbuli replied in the negative, explaining: "I am not a merchant. I am not concerned with the business of gaining and losing money, for I am resolved to carry on with my duty whether I gain or lose!" Thus "the French adviser came to know the reason behind the persistence of the journal, namely, faith in the cause and utmost devotion to it."[75]

Later that year, a group of teachers approached Istanbuli with a proposal that he turn his project into a share company in which they would participate, which he accepted. The editing of the journal was assigned to a member of the group, a change which had a positive effect on its circulation. In Istanbuli's words, the journal became "a salutary beacon in Syria and the other Arab countries." More realistically, it managed to survive. Meanwhile, Istanbuli occupied himself with other kinds of pedagogic activity, especially writing much-needed textbooks.

Early in 1935, another group of teachers started a competing educational journal, *al-Shu'la* ("The Torch"), which, in Istanbuli's opinion, was weak and hopeless. The Ministry of Education, however, adopted the new publication and proposed to Istanbuli that he merge his paper with it. He refused, on the basis that the involvement of "too many people in producing one paper would undermine effective [management] and would lead to its collapse. In addition, the vital element of competition, so beneficial to the family of teachers, would be lost." Standing up to the ministry's director general, Istanbuli announced his preparedness "to be expelled to the remotest end of the country yet retain [his] view," but his high-principled stand was to no avail, for his colleagues, fearing the consequences, refused to cooperate with him. The two journals were merged under a new name in October 1936, and Istanbuli's paper ceased to appear. In the event, the new journal disappeared two years later.[76] These developments put an end to Istanbuli's short career as a journalist, and he devoted the rest of his life to other activities.

If little is known about the journalistic endeavors of Mahmud Mahdi al-Istanbuli—no more than he himself chose to tell us in his memoirs—the careers of the overwhelming majority of nameless Arab journalists remain even more obscure. We thus know little about what it meant to be an "ordinary" Arab journalist during the formative century of the profession. What does, however, emerge clearly from Istanbuli's biography, and from many anecdotal references to journalists' experience throughout the region, is the harsh reality they all faced in the markedly inhospitable Middle Eastern environment, which allowed only a few to survive professionally and fewer still to achieve success.

During most of the period under study, Arab journalists faced the challenge of defining their vocation and establishing respectability in a milieu that tended to regard them with suspicion, as they represented an alien idea. Certain leading figures attained these goals by dint of their talent, conviction, perseverance, and ability to articulate popular sentiment persuasively, especially in times of struggle against foreign enemies. But the performance of most others—less gifted, less devoted, or less honest—only served to confirm popular mistrust of the new occupation. Journalism as a profession was assimilated by Middle Eastern society slowly, reflecting the general condition of the press there—in certain ways an essentially marginal institution, but in other ways a valuable device for dealing with the formidable challenges of modernity.

Conclusion

"The Arab press, compared with its Western counterpart, is but a newborn baby just opening his eyes before a very old, worldly-wise and experienced man," the noted Egyptian journalist, Jurji Zaydan, observed in 1895. Is it not odd, Zaydan wondered, "that this baby should aspire to attain such goals as the old man had not achieved except after decades of trial and error?"[1] During the half-century that elapsed thereafter, the Arab press made significant strides, overcoming the major diseases of infancy and reaching maturity in the region's main centers of journalistic activity — Egypt and Lebanon — by World War II. Elsewhere in the region, while still struggling with certain initial difficulties, it displayed impressive stamina that would lead to eventual consolidation.

The press struck roots in Arab society and became one of the most successful institutions introduced into the region during the modern era in its durability and continuing improvement. Official bulletins, a new device in the government's hands from the first half of the nineteenth century, became a standard tool for the routine communication of announcements to the people, first alongside, and gradually instead of, the traditional state-operated channels. Still more remarkable was the successful assimilation of the private press, which became a permanent feature of the region's political, social, cultural, and literary life. Against adverse odds, the nonofficial press displayed striking vitality, drawing inspiration and vigor both from society's traditional values and from the successful foreign model. As a new institution, the Arab press played a modest role in the region's history during this period, although at certain times and places it had an important impact on political and social developments, and at least in one sphere, the modernization of literary norms and of the language, its contribution was pivotal. In the process, the industry built up a growing constituency of eager customers who became habituated to reading — or listening to the reading of — newspapers. Likewise, the new profession of journalism, when conscientiously practiced, elicited considerable public esteem for its members.

By the mid-twentieth century, the best products of Arab journalism—
notably, once again, the leading newspapers of Egypt and Lebanon—
had become among the world's finest.

By 1945, the Arabic press had gained substantial experience in the
advocacy of political and economic causes and had achieved satisfactory
standards of reportage and editing, a functional vocabulary, and many
technological advances. But there were also many problems. A foreign
observer remarked in 1948 that "an American editor-printer resur-
rected from the 1830s and dropped into a modern Cairo newspaper
shop could feel very much at home. . . . The American visitor would
step into a shop still using hand-set type; still wedded to partisan, if
not vitriolic, journalism; and accustomed to salaries and newspaper
standards long since abandoned at home."[2] There were other problems
as well, such as an immature ethical code—a burdensome flaw—and
insufficient managerial know-how. More significantly, in 1945 the
press was still a medium of limited utility throughout much of the
area, primarily because of widespread illiteracy, the persistence of old
political and cultural conventions, and pervasive poverty. Consequently, traditional channels of oral communication continued to be
used extensively, often more so than newspapers. In this respect, the
Arab press appeared to be only starting out, a product and a mirror of
the partial transformation that Arab society had undergone during the
previous century and a half.

With the departure of European forces from the Middle East following World War II, there was a general feeling in the region that
a major obstacle had been removed from the path of progress and
improvement. The states of Egypt, Syria, Lebanon, Iraq, and Jordan,
hitherto subject to foreign control of one form or another, were now
free to reorder their national priorities, stabilize their political and
economic systems, and invest their energy in such constructive efforts
as expanding their educational infrastructure and eliminating illiteracy.
This meant an opportunity for the press to consolidate its position in
the community by playing an active role in these developments and,
potentially, to raise its professional standards in the process.

In the event, however, developments took a different course. The
newly independent states were soon shaken by a series of military coups
whose leaders, disillusioned with the old order and unwilling to wait for
evolutionary change, resolved to open a new chapter of history by
reorienting their society's ideological and political direction by fiat. The
new regimes that came to power maintained that they represented "the
people" in a quest for sociopolitical justice and international respectability. To that end they claimed a monopoly on truth, prohibiting the
voicing of views other than their own and taking control of all means of
communication, including the press. This was generally achieved in
two stages: initially, by muting criticism in print while simultaneously
launching organs sponsored by the regime; and, as these measures

proved inadequate, "nationalizing" the press and turning it into a branch of government, thereby instituting what the Egyptian thinker Luis 'Awad termed "the regime of monologues."

The spirit of journalistic struggle that had marked the prerevolutionary era, the aggressive but vigorous vocabulary of the press, and the sense of mission within the profession were all wiped out. The government's message was carefully phrased by officials in the newly established information ministries before being passed on to the newspapers. It was the state that appointed and dismissed editors (loyalty being valued above talent), paid journalists' salaries, and above all issued editorial guidelines. The government selected the causes and defined the targets for the battles of the press. Aware of the limitations of the written word in a largely illiterate society, the new rulers invested heavily in developing the electronic media as effective means of public instruction and control, with negative results for the press. In many ways the press regressed to its starting point, becoming little more than official bulletins extolling state leaders, fighting the state's domestic and foreign verbal propaganda battles, and "educating" the public according to dictates from above. The press became an echo rather than a voice, and journalists, little more than bureaucratic functionaries, were forced back into docility, their role confined once again to recording "the true nature of events and . . . the real purport of the acts and commands of the government," as defined by the Ottoman *Taqvim-i Vekayi* back in 1831.[3]

In countries where no such revolutions occurred—Jordan, Saudi Arabia, and the Gulf states—governments continued to rule along traditional lines, allowing the press to operate within clearly defined boundaries. Newspapers in these countries were usually allowed to remain in private hands, or to be owned jointly with state agencies, rather than being absorbed into the bureaucracy. Still, much like the press in the revolutionary regimes, they were expected to follow the authorities' lead, especially on issues of political consequence, show complete loyalty to the government, and avoid independent political initiative. To ensure this, the government continued to utilize the tried and true tools, which remained as effective as ever: licensing, prosecution, and punishment, on the one hand, and subsidization or the withholding of it, on the other. But normally there was little need for harsh measures: The journalists themselves conformed, usually out of genuine, deeply ingrained respect for authority, but sometimes out of fear as well, seldom seeking to cross the tacitly agreed-upon lines. Writers in these countries were somewhat freer than their colleagues in the revolutionary states in choice of topics and style, but government control, and the journalists' own compliance, generally ensured that this gap never grew too wide.[4]

Two of the countries whose press was explored in this study do not fall into either of the two categories discussed above in terms of their post-1945 development. One was Arab Palestine, which after the termination of the British mandate in 1948 did not exist as a state, its population dispersed among several countries in the region. Its newspapers either died out or were incorporated into the Jordanian press. The other country was Lebanon, an atypical Middle Eastern community in more ways than one. Lebanon's pluralistic sociopolitical makeup and the absence of an authoritarian government allowed the growth of an independent and highly diverse press — a unique development in the area. Journalism continued to be regarded by its Lebanese practitioners above all as a business, with newspapers putting themselves at the service of various political interests, domestic as well as regional, for a fee. The post-World War II Lebanese press served as an outlet for inter-Arab disputes, in contrast to the surrounding tightly controlled settings. The 1975–1976 civil war and subsequent violent events dealt this Lebanese viability a serious blow, but the Lebanese papers that survived the turbulence continued to enjoy a considerable degree of liberty, assured by the absence of a strong central government. Anarchy, it turned out, functioned much the same way as licensed political pluralism in terms of its effect on freedom of expression.

A question arises as to what extent the review and analysis presented in this study are helpful in understanding later developments in the evolution of the Arab press. A learned answer, of course, would be possible only after a systematic exploration of those later trends. Yet, at the risk of stating the obvious, it may be said that grasping the sense of the developments during the early years is essential for a proper assessment of what happened subsequently. Not only did the early period serve as a historical prelude to the one that followed, but, more significantly, many of the political, economic, and cultural forces that shaped the growth of the press as an institution in Arab society prior to the mid-twentieth century remained and continued to influence it subsequently as well. To a large extent they still influence it even today.

Notes

Introduction

1. G. L. Lewis, "Fathname," *EI²*.

2. Borthwick, pp. 299–303; B. Lewis, "Propaganda."

3. Jabarti, *'Aja'ib*, I, p. 618. Jabarti reports similar occurrences nearly daily. For a discussion of the role of the *munadi*, see Rifa'i, I, p. 14; El-Zine, p. 97; Emin, p. 18.

4. El-Zine, pp. 90–98.

5. *The Daily Universal Register*, 1 January 1785, pp. 1–2.

6. Ghassani, p. 67; B. Lewis, *Muslim Discovery*, p. 303.

7. Tahtawi, p. 150.

Chapter 1

1. Both publications were issued regularly until the end of the French occupation in the fall of 1801. For a discussion of the French information policy in Egypt, see Salah al-Din al-Bustani, *suhuf Bunabart*, where the entire collection of the two journals is reproduced. In a more condensed form, see idem, *The Press*.

2. Tarrazi, I, pp. 48–49, quoting Jabarti, *'Aja'b*, IV, p. 238. See likewise Samahan, pp. 108–10. Tarrazi did not discuss the fate of al-Khashshab's original accounts in Arabic. In a later volume he modified his statement—see note 3 below.

3. Zaydan, *Ta'rikh adab*, IV, p. 17; Tarrazi, IV, p. 214. In this volume, published 20 years after the book's first volume, Tarrazi modifies his previous information and states that *al-Tanbih* was, in fact, the same as *al-Hawadith al-Yawmiyya*. Charles-Roux (p. 141), Vatikiotis (p. 182), Muruwwa, (pp. 148–49), and Lewis et. al., "*Dj*arida," *EI²*, all subscribed to the reports about the actual publication of such a paper.

4. See Heyworth-Dunne, *Introduction*, pp. 100–1; 'Abduh, *Ta'rikh al-tiba'a*, pp. 89–97; Wassef, pp. 109–19. All three authors strongly doubt, and the latter two effectively disprove, the actual existence of such papers. See also Sadgrove, pp. 36–41.

5. Hasani, pp. 49–50; Rafa'il Batti, p. 10; Tunji-Hafiyan, p. 45; Ibrahim, p. 55; Tikriti, p. 53.

6. The exceptions were two printing presses owned by Europeans and one

owned privately by an Egyptian, all of which operated with great difficulty. See Sabat, *Ta'rikh al-tiba'a*, pp. 165–67, 188–92.

7. Sabat, *Ta'rikh al-tiba'a*, p. 170.

8. Sabat, ibid., pp. 135–88; al-Shayyal, *Ta'rikh al-tarjama . . . fi 'asr Muhammad 'Ali*, pp. 195–200 and Appendices I-III; Heyworth-Dunne, "Printing," pp. 325–31; Perron, "Lettres."

9. 'Abduh, *Ta'rikh al-waqa'i'*, pp. 29–34; idem, *Tatawwur al-sihafa*, pp. 23–27; Sadgrove, pp. 48–50.

10. Heyworth-Dunne, "Printing," p. 330.

11. *Al-Waqa'i' al-Misriyya*, 3 December 1828, p. 1, quoted in Jayyid, p. 31.

12. Jayyid, p. 35.

13. Jayyid (pp. 37, 43) calculated that a mere 2.87 percent of all *al-Waqa'i'* news items between 1828 and 1841 dealt with such foreign issues.

14. Ibid., p. 35. In later years this proportion increased somewhat (ibid., pp. 49, 57), but "practical" reporting continued to occupy the bulk of the paper's space.

15. *Al-Waqa'i' al-Misriyya*, issue no. 28, quoted by 'Abduh, *Ta'rikh al-waqa'i'*, pp. 75–76, who also quotes another curiosity of a similar nature on pp. 74–75.

16. 'Abduh, *A'lam*, p. 12 (quoting 'Abdin documents).

17. See, e.g., Sami, *Taqwim*, II, pp. 438, 579; Sabat, *Ta'rikh al-tiba'a*, pp. 169–70.

18. 'Abduh, *A'lam*, pp. 10–17; idem, *Ta'rikh al-waqa'i'*, pp. 41–44.

19. 'Abduh, *Tatawwur al-sihafa*, pp. 38–41.

20. *Al-Waqa'i' al-Misriyya*, No. 49 (September 1829), quoted by 'Abduh, *Ta'rikh al-Waqa'i'*, p. 66.

21. *Al-Waqa'i' al-Misriyya*, No. 47 (August 1829), quoted by Jayyid, p. 39.

22. Jayyid, pp. 43, 54.

23. Ibid., p. 54.

24. For a detailed discussion of the *Waqa'i'* under Tahtawi, see al-Shayyal, *Ta'rikh al-tarjama . . . fi 'asr Muhammad 'Ali*, pp. 139ff.; Hamza, *Adab al-maqala*, I, pp. 109ff.; Jayyid, pp. 46–55. For Tahtawi's career, see Ahmad Badawi, *Rifa'a al-Tahtawi*; Hourani, *Arabic Thought*, pp. 68–83.

25. 'Abduh, *Tatawwur al-sihafa*, pp. 32–34; Jayyid, pp. 86–88.

26. Jayyid, pp. 77–82, reproducing the front page of the first issue.

27. Vatikiotis, pp. 70ff.

28. 'Abduh, *Tatawwur al-sihafa*, pp. 271–73, 356. The non-Arabic press in Egypt and the other countries of the region is beyond the scope of this study. For Egypt's foreign-language press during this and later periods, see Munier; Rae, pp. 215–20.

29. Quoted in 'Abduh, *Ta'rikh al-waqa'i'*, p. 111, and see also pp. 105–21; idem, *A'lam*, pp. 20–21; Jayyid, pp. 60–77.

30. For details on these publications, see Tarrazi, I, p. 67; II, pp. 68–70; Jayyid, pp. 83–92; 'Abduh, *Tatawwur al-sihafa*, pp. 42–51; Hasan and Dasuqi, *Rawdat al-madaris*. A paper titled *Le Moniteur Egyptien* had already existed in 1833–1834 in Alexandria, published at the initiative of the foreign community there. It was supported by Muhammad 'Ali, who apparently sought thereby to counter the hostile propaganda against him in *Le Moniteur Ottoman*, backed by the sultan. Both the Ottoman and Egyptian *Moniteurs* were short-lived (for the

Egyptian, see Sabat, *Ta'rikh al-tiba'a*, pp. 162-63; Rae, p. 213 [quoting John Bowring's report]; the Ottoman is discussed later on in this chapter). Isma'il revived *Le Moniteur Egyptien* in 1873 as part of his international public relations effort. In 1883, under British occupation, the *Moniteur* changed its name to *Le Journal Officiel*, and was later unified with the *Waqa'i'* to become *al-Jarida al-Rasmiyya* ("The Official Gazette"), published in both Arabic and French.

31. Lagarde, pp. 271-76; Slade, pp. 273-75; Ubicini, I, pp. 246-47; Gerçek, pp. 10-21; Emin, pp. 26-29; Davison, pp. 17-18.

32. Davison, ibid.

33. De Kay, pp. 404-5.

34. Orhonlu, pp. 36-39 (includes a reproduction of a page from the paper's first issue); Emin, p. 30.

35. Orhonlu, ibid.; Gerçek, pp. 32-33; Berkes, pp. 126-27. Little is known about these non-Turkish versions and still less about the distribution of the Arabic edition.

36. For lively contemporary accounts, see De Kay, pp. 401-6; Ubicini, I, pp. 247-53; White, II, pp. 218-19. Also Emin, pp. 31, 34-36; B. Lewis, *Emergence*, pp. 95-96; Berkes, pp. 126-27; Davison, pp. 18-19. The *Taqvim* continued to appear until the collapse of the empire after World War I.

37. For a discussion of these developments, see Chapter 2. For details on *al-Ra'id al-Tunisi*, see Tarrazi, I, pp. 64-66.

38. For text of the 1865 law in Arabic translation, see *Kanz al-ragha'ib*, V, pp. 56-59. See also Cioeta, pp. 168-69.

39. Hamza, *Adab al-maqal*, I, pp. 139, 191; Jayyid, pp. 93-94.

40. *Taqvim-i Vekayi*, first issue, quoted in Orhonlu, ibid.

41. For a detailed description and discussion of the two papers, see Iliyas, I, pp. 35-37; 148-64; 167-98, passim. Several months before the end of Ottoman rule in Syria, in May 1918, the government issued another official paper by the name *Çöl* ("Desert") in Dayr al-Zur, which was short-lived. See ibid., pp. 164-65.

42. Tarrazi, I, pp. 73-74; II, p. 40; Sa'ada, *al-Sihafa*, p. 328; Krymskii, pp. 571-72.

43. Modest beginnings in printing had been initiated by individuals and missionaries before the arrival of Midhat. See Sabat, *Ta'rikh al-tiba'a*, pp. 284-85.

44. For more details, see Abu al-Sa'd, pp. 9-12; Rafa'il Batti, pp. 12-15, 17-18; Hasani, pp. 25, 49-50.

45. Iliyas, I, p. 156.

46. Abu al-Sa'd, pp. 56, 131-42. For the similar situation in Syria, see Iliyas, I, pp. 159-60.

47. E.g., Iliyas, I, pp. 148ff., 173ff., 188-90; Abu al-Sa'd, pp. 10-12, 169-70.

48. Tarrazi, II, p. 4.

Chapter 2

1. Tibawi, "The American missionaries in Beirut"; Krymskii, pp. 256-79, 285-92, 393-96, 540-43; Sabat, *Ta'rikh al-tiba'a*, pp. 44-65; Zaydan, *Ta'rikh adab*, IV, pp. 67ff. (surveying the cultural and scientific societies in Syria and Lebanon); *al-Jam'iyya al-Suriyya*, passim (pp. 17-100 contain the full contents of

the society's first yearbook). The terms "Lebanon" and "Lebanese" are used here for the land and people of what is the present-day state of Lebanon. Though somewhat anachronistic, these terms correspond best to the area where the developments under discussion took place.

2. This first press, founded in 1610, was equipped with Aramaic type only. The first press with Arabic letters was established in Lebanon in 1733. Sabat, *Ta'rikh al-tiba'a*, pp. 34–42.

3. *Jeride-i Havadis* ("News Register"), published by William Churchill from 1840. See Gerçek, pp. 35ff.; White, pp. 219–22; B. Lewis, *Emergence*, pp. 146–47.

4. Krymskii, pp. 220–33; Zaydan, *Tarajim*, II, pp. 126–31; *al-Hilal*, 1 December 1899, p. 146, and 1 January 1900, pp. 234–35. Hasun engaged in further journalistic activity in Europe, and in 1876 published a paper in London bearing the same name as his first venture (see further below).

5. The best biography of Shidyaq is Sulh's, in which an extensive discussion of *al-Jawa'ib* appears on pp. 85–128. For briefer biographical summaries, see Zaydan, *Tarajim*, II, pp. 74–83; Tarrazi, I, pp. 61–64, 96–99; Hourani, *Arabic Thought*, pp. 97–99.

6. Quoted in Sulh, p. 96.

7. Tarrazi, I, p. 61; 'Abduh, *A'lam*, p. 23.

8. C.M. Doughty, quoted in Hourani, *Arabic Thought*, p. 99.

9. For the distribution of *al-Jawa'ib*, see Tarrazi, I, p. 61; Hamza, *Adab al-maqala*, I, pp. 195–96; Sulh, pp. 98–99, 102. Selections from the paper were published in Istanbul between 1871 and 1880 in a seven-volume series entitled *Kanz al-ragha'ib fi muntakhabat al-jawa'ib*. Shidyaq moved to Cairo in 1883, where he died four years later. His son, Salim Faris, continued to publish the paper in Cairo for a while under the name *al-Qahira*.

10. "Khutba fi adab al-'Arab," in *al-Jam'iyya al-Suriyya*, p. 115.

11. For a detailed discussion of Khuri's career and his paper, see Krymskii, pp. 481–505; Tarrazi, I, pp. 56–57, 102–5.

12. E.g., *Hadiqat al-Akhbar*, 31 May 1858, pp. 3, 4; 14 June 1858, p. 4; 22 June 1858, p. 4; 13 September 1858, p. 4; 11 October 1858, pp. 2–3.

13. *Hadiqat al-Akhbar*, 5 July 1858, pp. 2, 3; 23 September 1858, p. 3.

14. Krymskii, p. 487.

15. Tarrazi, I, p. 58.

16. See, e.g., the correspondence between Shakib Arslan and Jurji Zaydan, *al-Hilal*, 1 December 1899, pp. 146–47 and 1 January 1900, pp. 234–35. In the latter issue of *al-Hilal*, Arslan presents a rather convincing case as to why the paper cannot be properly labeled a state organ.

17. Tarrazi, I, pp. 53–54.

18. Details in Tarrazi, I, pp. 66, 69; II, pp. 18–21.

19. *Al-Bashir* was preceded by a short-lived Jesuit weekly in January 1870 called *al-Majma' al-Fatikani* ("Vatican Congregation"). Details in ibid., II, pp. 10–11, 44.

20. *Nafir Suriya*, 29 September 1860 through 22 April 1861. Eleven issues are extant at the Beirut University library. Tibawi, "The American missionaries," pp. 170–71, mentions "a dozen issues," and Tarrazi, I, p. 64, indicates 13. See also Hourani, *Arabic Thought*, pp. 101–2. For other ephemeral publications in Lebanon during the 1860s, see Tarrazi, I, pp. 66, 68–69, 71–73.

21. Bustani, *Khitab*, p. 11. For a more detailed description of cultural activity in Lebanon at that time, see Krymskii, pp. 539–47.

22. *Al-Jinan*, January 1870, p. 1.

23. Tarrazi, II, p. 22; Jurji Zaydan in *al-Hilal*, 15 October 1898, p. 128. *Al-Junayna* appeared on the days that *al-Janna* was not published, so that together they provided daily news coverage.

24. On Shalafun and his papers, see Tarrazi, I, pp. 68, 120–21; II, pp. 8–9, 22–24, 51–52. On Sabunji, ibid., II, pp. 71–81; Zolondek; Kramer.

25. See lists in Tarrazi, IV, pp. 4–6, 106–8.

26. For more details, see Nashabi; Tarrazi, II, pp. 25–27, 99–101; Krymskii, pp. 608–9.

27. "Awwal ta'til idari fi al-sihafa al-yawmiyya," *Awraq Lubnaniyya* (Beirut), III, 2 (February 1957), pp. 65–68; Zolondek, p. 102 and note 3 on p. 110.

28. 'Abd al-Sayyid, *Sulwan al-shaji*; Krymskii, pp. 575–77.

29. Krymskii, pp. 230–31. See also Tarrazi, I, p. 62, where other writers with whom Shidyaq quarreled are mentioned; II, pp. 77–78; *al-Hilal*, January 1929, pp. 305–6. A famous controversy in the early 1860s was carried on between Shidyaq's *al-Jawa'ib* and a paper called *Birjis Baris*, which was published in Paris by another former Lebanese, Rushayd al-Dahdah. See Tarrazi, ibid., and al-Ibyari, *al-Najm al-thaqib*. On *Birjis Baris*, see below.

30. E.g., Tarrazi, II, p. 26.

31. *Hadiqat al-Akhbar*, 7 June 1861, p. 1.

32. *Lisan al-Hal*, 18 October 1877, p. 1; Ghalib, pp. 90–91.

33. See e.g., Sulh, pp. 92–93.

34. See note 23 above.

35. For a more elaborate discussion of these aspects, see Chapter 8 below.

36. *Al-Zahra*, 1 January 1870, p. 3.

37. Philipp, *The Syrians*, pp. 78–85 and passim; Abu Zayyid, *al-Sihafa al-'Arabiyya al-muhajira*, pp. 13ff., 39ff.; Reid, *Odyssey*, pp. 19–22, 27; Issawi, "Economic development and liberalism," p. 283.

38. Heyworth-Dunne, *Introduction*, pp. 383–90.

39. Vatikiotis, p. 468.

40. For details, see 'Abduh, *A'lam*, pp. 19–27; idem, "Sahm Misr"; 'Inan, pp. 260–62.

41. Jayyid, p. 61.

42. For a biography of Abu al-Su'ud, see Hamza, *Adab al-maqala*, I, pp. 145–50; 'Abduh, *A'lam*, pp. 99–103. More details on both papers and their editors appear in Hamza, ibid., pp. 145–74; Jayyid, pp. 95–107.

43. For details, see Hamza, *Adab al-maqala*, I, p. 160; Tarrazi, I, p. 78; II, p. 277; 'Abduh, *A'lam*, pp. 103–4. Muwaylihi later acquired a distinguished reputation as editor of several papers in Egypt and Europe. See Hamza, ibid., III, pp. 21–66; *al-Hilal*, 1 April 1906, pp. 383–87. Jalal became known primarily as translator of La Fontaine's *Parables* and plays by Moliere.

44. Quoted in Tarrazi, III, p. 48. See also pp. 49–50.

45. See *Mithal al-Ahram*, a two-page notice published in Alexandria on 15 July 1876 to announce the forthcoming publication of the paper.

46. Quoted in 'Abduh, *Jaridat al-Ahram*, pp. 23–25. For a biographical sketch of the Taqlas, see Niqula Yusuf, pp. 446–56.

47. A list of the agents — 10 in Egypt and 16 elsewhere — appears in *al-Ahram*, 5 August 1876, p. 4.

48. For details see Jayyid, pp. 132–38, 182–87.

49. The one exception was in 1879, when it was briefly suspended for criticizing Isma'il's financial policy; Tarrazi, III, p. 51.

50. Biographical material on Ishaq may be found in Hamza, *Adab al-maqala*, II, pp. 56–59; Tarrazi, II, pp. 105–9; 'Abduh, *A'lam*, pp. 116–24; Niqula Yusuf, pp. 457–64; Kedourie, "The death of Adib Ishaq." In addition to the papers mentioned in the text, Ishaq edited *al-Taqaddum* (Beirut, 1874, 1882) and published another paper named *Misr* (Cairo, 1881). According to Tarrazi, he also served briefly as editor of *Thamarat al-Funun* in Beirut before moving to Egypt.

51. Details in Jayyid, pp. 162–66, 188–94; Niqula Yusuf, pp. 464–69; Kudsi-Zadeh, pp. 179–82.

52. Details in Jayyid, pp. 141–47. For a more detailed discussion of the role of the press during this period, see Schölch, pp. 108–14.

53. There is a vast literature on Sanu' and his contribution to Egypt's literary and journalistic life and to the Egyptian theater. For a concise account, see 'Abduh, *A'lam*, pp. 50–67. Gendzier provides a fuller study of Sanu', but it seems to contain inaccuracies (cf. Schölch's remark on pp. 334–35, note 100 in his book). Sanu''s activities in Europe are discussed briefly in the text later on. The name of his paper should be more strictly transliterated as *Abu Nazzara*, but it appears here in the form used by Sanu' himself.

54. For his biography and more details, see Hamza, *Adab al-maqala*, II, pp. 105–93.

55. For details, see Schölch, pp. 177ff.

56. *Sada al-Ahram* was suspended in February 1878, *al-Watan* and *al-Tijara* in February 1879, *Mir'at al-Sharq* in August and September 1879, and *al-Mahrusa* in January 1880; *Misr*, *al-Tijara*, and *al-Waqt* were closed down in November 1879, and *al-Hijaz* in November 1881.

57. Discussion of the 1881 law appears in Ramadan, pp. 23–27, 50–62.

58. Poujoulat, p. 50.

59. Additional biographical and other details may be found in Salim al-Dahdah, pp. 456–61, 489–90; Tarrazi, I, pp. 60–61, 100–1; Krymskii, pp. 214–19, 512. Abu Zayyid, in his *al-Sihafa al-'Arabiyya al-muhajira*, p. 27, mentions another paper, entitled *al-Mushtari* (another name for Jupiter), which Dahdah published in Paris in 1867.

60. Details appear in Tarrazi, I, pp. 77–78, 105–10; II, 247–48.

61. For biographical and other details, see references in note 24 above.

62. Details in Krymskii, pp. 622–25.

63. Gendzier, pp. 69–70; Jerrold, pp. 218–20.

64. *Misr al-Qahira*, 24 January 1879, p. 1.

65. Quoted in Hourani, *Arabic Thought*, p. 226; see also pp. 109–10. For an extensive discussion of Sanu''s, Ishaq's, and 'Abduh's activities in Paris, see Louca, pp. 121–78.

Chapter 3

1. The calculations are based on Tarrazi, IV, pp. 4–10, 106–10, 162–90, 214–24. The Young Turk revolution in August 1908 is used as the cutoff for

that year. While Tarrazi's lists are by no means devoid of errors, the data is sufficient for the purpose of comparison.

2. Dufferin to Granville, 6 February 1883, in British House of Commons, *Sessional Papers 1883*, Vol. 83, No. 38, p. 50.

3. See 'Abduh, *Tatawwur al-sihafa*, pp. 134–47. 'Abduh, in trying to refute the "distorted" image of Cromer's period as an era of freedom, cites several examples to show how Cromer's administration hampered the functioning and progress of the press. The image that emerges from his depiction, however, seems to be somewhat distorted in the opposite direction. See also Salih, pp. 100–7; Tignor, p. 299; Kelidar, "The political press," pp. 8–10.

4. Hamza, *Adab al-maqala*, VI, p. 221; similarly, Salih, p. 102.

5. Cromer, II, p. 220.

6. For details on Syrian occupations in Egypt, see Philipp, *The Syrians*, pp. 91–92, 96–100. Philipp also calculated that about 20 percent of all the papers published in Egypt from 1800 to 1914 were founded by Syrians.

7. Farag, "The Lewis affair." See also Faris Nimr's retrospective review in *al-Muqtataf*, 1 May 1936, pp. 561 ff.

8. Rae, p. 222.

9. *Al-Muqtataf*, May 1896, p. 326.

10. Musa, *Tarbiyya*, p. 42. For a biography of Sarruf, see *al-Muqtataf*, August 1927, pp. 192–99. This and several subsequent issues of *al-Muqtataf* (until June 1928) carried obituaries of Sarruf and discussions of his achievements. For Nimr's biography, see Tarrazi, II, pp. 138–42, and for that of Shahin Makaryus see Zakhura, pp. 417–32.

11. For his biography, see Philipp, *Zaydan*.

12. Ibid., pp. 160–61, from Zaydan's autobiography.

13. *Al-Hilal*, 1 July 1895, p. 840.

14. Quoted in Philipp, *Zaydan*, p. 40.

15. Tarrazi, IV, pp. 276–86.

16. For Rida's biography and ideas, see Adams, pp. 177–204; Hourani, *Arabic Thought*, pp. 224–44, 298–306.

17. *Al-Manar*, Vol. I (1897–1898), second printing (1909), pp. 4–5.

18. *Al-Ahram*, 2 January 1887, quoted in 'Abduh, *Tatawwur al-sihafa*, p. 148.

19. E.g., 'Abduh, *Tatawwur al-sihafa*, pp. 142–43, 148–49.

20. Quoted in Philipp, *The Syrians*, pp. 109–10.

21. 'Abduh, *Tatawwur al-sihafa*, pp. 150–51; Faris Nimr in *al-Muqtataf*, 1 May 1936, pp. 569–70. Shahin Makaryus, Sarruf's and Nimr's partner in *al-Muqtataf*, also joined them for a while in this new venture. See also Kelidar, "The political press," p. 6 and note 24 (quoting a British document). E. G. Browne, a knowledgeable source, recalled that government officials in Egypt under the British were forced to subscribe to *al-Muqattam*; Browne, p. 9.

22. Rae, p. 221.

23. E.g., *al-Muqattam*, 3 May 1889, in which both pp. 3 and 4 carry advertisements.

24. Rae, pp. 220–21.

25. *Al-Muqattam*, 1 August 1889, p. 1.

26. Philipp, *The Syrians*, p. 107. See also Musa, *Tarbiyya*, p. 36.

27. Yusuf's biography and his paper are discussed further in Chapter 9 below. They are the subject of Sulayman Salih's recent study. See also Hamza,

Adab al-maqala, IV, pp. 39–76 and passim; V, pp. 121–22; *al-Manar*, 30 October 1913, pp. 873–78; and Kelidar, "Shaykh 'Ali Yusuf."

28. Kurd 'Ali, *Mudhakkirat*, I, p. 58; Hartmann, p. 12; Swan, pp. 150, 154; Salih, pp. 108–10.

29. E.g., *al-Ra'y al-'Amm*, 31 October 1896, pp. 328–30; 27 February 1897, pp. 59–60.

30. *Al-Mushir*, 15 August 1895, front page and passim.

31. 'Ali Yusuf, quoted in Dasuqi and Dasuqi, p. 140.

32. *al-Hilal*, October 1897, p. 131.

33. Hartmann, p. 19.

34. Sir Eldon Gorst, memorandum on "The Press in Egypt," 16 September 1908 — FO371/451/31779. I am grateful to Professor Beth Baron for her help in procuring this document. See also Tignor, pp. 299–300; Kelidar, "The political press," pp. 11–13.

35. For Kamil's biography and a broader discussion of his journalistic work, see Murqus, especially pp. 13–69; Hamza, *Adab al-maqala*, V, especially pp. 79ff.; Rafi'i, *Mustafa Kamil*.

36. Musa, *Tarbiyya*, p. 32.

37. Al-Sayyid Marsot, pp. 220 ff.; Ahmed, pp. 58–84; Kazziha; Hamza, *Adab al-maqala*, IV, pp. 152–62; VI, especially pp. 95–102. See also, more concisely, Vatikiotis, pp. 225–30.

38. Tarrazi, IV, pp. 176–96, 222–40.

39. For details and text of the 25 March 1909 cabinet decision, see Ramadan, pp. 30–31, 65–68; also Lloyd, I, pp. 89–95; 'Abduh, *Tatawwur al-sihafa*, pp. 187–88.

40. *Al-I'tidal* ("Moderation"), 20 March 1910, p. 2. A day earlier, the party paper *al-'Alam* ("The Flag") was suspended for an attack on the British authorities.

41. Between 20 and 25 March 1910 the paper came out under the titles *al-'Alam*, *al-I'tidal*, *al-Sha'b*, and *al-'Adl*. See Rafi'i, *Muhammad Farid*, pp. 173–74; see also pp. 286, 322–23.

42. E.g., *al-Zahir* (Cairo), 12 November 1903, p. 1.

43. Sabat, *Ta'rikh al-tiba'a*, pp. 236–46.

44. Hartmann, p. 31.

45. For details, see 'Abduh, *Tatawwur al-sihafa*, pp. 195–200; Carter, pp. 10–15.

46. *Al-Istiqlal* (Cairo), 15 January 1902, p. 1. Likewise, *al-Mushir*, 8 November 1894, p. 1.

47. The figures are based on lists in Daghir, pp. 396–405. The Lebanese established 129 papers in Egypt, 29 in North America, 34 in South America, and 37 elsewhere during this period. See also Tarrazi, IV, pp. 6–40, 108–10.

48. For Kawakibi's biography and a discussion of his Aleppo papers, see Iliyas, I, pp. 49–52, 66–70.

49. Kurd 'Ali in *al-Muqtabas*, IV (1909), p. 410. For more details, see Iliyas, I, pp. 70–77; Kurd 'Ali, *Mudhakkirat*, I, p. 50.

50. Details on these publications appear in Iliyas, I, pp. 199–255.

51. Details appear in Hasani, p. 25. The Carmelites simultaneously published a French-language journal in Baghdad.

52. Hilmi, pp. 303–4.

53. This and the following figures are based on Tarrazi, IV, pp. 152–54, 360–62, 394; Iliyas, I, pp. 81–85, 177–79; Abu al-Sa'd, pp. 16–19; Yusuf Khuri, pp. 7–26.

54. *Al-'Irfan*, 5 February 1909, pp. 2, 134–35.

55. *Dimashq* front pages are reproduced in Iliyas, I, p. 305.

56. Reproduced in Ghalib, p. 21.

57. For details, see Iliyas, I, pp. 127–31, 135–36; Seikaly; Rafa'il Batti, pp. 20–37; Sinan Sa'id, pp. 17–18; Shamikh, pp. 50–58.

58. Tauber, "The press," pp. 163–65 and passim.

59. See, e.g., Rashid Khalidi, pp. 46ff.

60. Numerous examples of the phenomenon are cited in Iliyas, I, pp. 170–71, 298–355; Abu al-Sa'd, pp. 21, 156–57; Sulayman, *Ta'rikh al-sihafa,* pp. 139–40; Shamikh, pp. 51, 144.

61. *Al-'Irfan*, 5 February 1909, p. 134. Similarly, Iliyas, I, p. 181, quoting Kurd 'Ali; Abu al-Sa'd, p. 19; Sinan Sa'id, p. 19.

62. *Al-'Irfan*, ibid., p. 140; *Zahla al-Fatah*, 1 January 1910, p. 1; Iraqi newspapers quoted in Tikriti, pp. 64, 291.

63. Iliyas, I, pp. 179–82; Rafa'il Batti, p. 33; Shamikh, pp. 46–47; Malul, pp. 447–49.

64. Texts in Yusuf Khuri, pp. 154–71.

65. Kurd 'Ali, *Mudhakkirat*, I, pp. 62, 64–66; Tauber, "The press," pp. 173–75; Iliyas, I, pp. 129–33; Sulayman, *Ta'rikh al-sihafa,* pp. 48, 132–37; Muruwwa, pp. 171–72. For similar accounts, see Nu'aymi, p. 87 (a violent assault by soldiers on Khalil al-Badawi of *al-Ahwal*); Niqula Yusuf, p. 487 (an officially inspired attempt to assassinate Salim Sarkis around 1895).

66. Malul, p. 374.

67. Tauber, "The press," pp. 176–77.

68. Emin, p. 99. The same tactics were later employed by papers in Egypt during the monarchy. See Samahan, pp. 263–64.

69. Musa, *Tarbiyya*, pp. 156–57.

70. 'Abduh, *Jaridat al-Ahram*, pp. 529–45, containing lively descriptions of the functioning of *al-Ahram* during the war; idem, *Tatawwur al-sihafa*, pp. 205–6; Hamza, *Adab al-maqala*, VII, p. 58; Tarrazi, IV, 196, 226, 306.

71. Details in Amin Sa'id, I, pp. 58–92; Tauber, *The Arab Movements*, pp. 35–56. Zahrawi and the two Khazins were tried and executed on occasions other than those mentioned above.

72. Iliyas, I, pp. 120–22; Abu al-Sa'd, pp. 27–29. For typical examples of wartime papers, see *al-Balagh* ("The Message," Beirut) and *Bayrut*, February–May 1916; *al-Sharq* ("The East"), January 1917.

73. Cleveland, "The role of Islam," especially pp. 87–88, 93–99; Iliyas, I, pp. 120–22; Abu al-Sa'd, pp. 27–29.

74. Details in Shamikh, pp. 104–16; Palmer; *RMM*, XXXIV (1917–1918), pp. 320–28; Cleveland, "The role of Islam." Muhibb al-Din al-Khatib's name replaced that of the Sharif as editor from the second issue onward.

75. *Al-Qibla*, 11 December 1919, p. 2. According to the paper, about 5,000 copies were distributed, only several hundred of them in the Hejaz.

76. *Al-Qibla*, 15 August 1916, p. 1.

77. More details in Shamikh, pp. 116–20, 137–41; Sabat, *Ta'rikh al-tiba'a*, p. 310.

Chapter 4

1. Kamal, pp. 98–105.

2. *L'Égypte indépendente*, pp. 400, 415–56; 'Abduh, *Tatawwur al-sihafa*, pp. 340–42. Cf. the list in *Die Presse in Ägypten*, pp. 30–43 of the German text.

3. Philipp, *The Syrians*, pp. 152, 154–55; Reid, *Odyssey*, pp. 128–31.

4. Salama Musa, a Coptic Egyptian journalist, was one of the chief critics of this Syrian uninvolvement. See his *al-Sihafa*, pp. 5–16; Egger, pp. 170–71, 176–77; Gershoni-Jankowski, pp. 128–29.

5. Hamza, *Adab al-maqala*, VII, pp. 58–59, 134ff.

6. Musa, *Tarbiyya*, p. 155.

7. Amin, *Li-Kull maqal*, p. 84, and see also pp. 81–84.

8. Quoted by Jundi, *al-Sihafa*, p. 643, and see also pp. 640–43.

9. Full text and discussion in Shams, pp. 7–11. See also Chapter 5 below.

10. Subhi, p. 162; 'Abduh, *Ruz al-Yusuf*, pp. 212–14, 296–97. See also Jundi, *Tatawwur al-sihafa*, p. 288, where the author reproduces a partial but substantial list of journalists who were jailed for their writing.

11. 'Abduh, *Ruz al-Yusuf*, p. 118. The author lists all the punishments sustained by the journal on pp. 304–7.

12. Amin, *Li-Kull maqal*, passim; Shusha, pp. 304–8; Musa, *al-Sihafa*, p. 95ff.

13. Haykal-Mazini-'Inan, pp. 28–36; Amin, ibid., pp. 39ff.; Jundi, *al-Sihafa*, pp. 614–15, 620–28.

14. Sidqi, p. 58.

15. For a colorful instance of this practice, see Fatima al-Yusuf, p. 133.

16. *Al-Akhbar* in 1924, quoted in Hamza, *Adab al-maqala*, VII, pp. 141–42.

17. Quoted in Subhi, p. 99; Jundi, *Tatawwur al-sihafa*, pp. 287–88. Husayn was referring to the central role played by younger people in the anti-British revolt of March 1919.

18. For a comprehensive study of these trends and their exponents until 1930, see Gershoni-Jankowski.

19. "Report on Egypt for 1928–29," dated 26 August 1929—FO371/13880, p. 97; "Cairo papers" (August 1947)—FO371/62993. For further discussion, see Chapter 6 below.

20. Boyd, pp. 14–15.

21. Details in Samahan, pp. 119–23; Wynn, p. 394. See also Chapter 9 below.

22. Quoted in Iliyas, II, p. 15.

23. Iliyas, II, pp. 13–20, 349–51, 450–62, 509–15, 529, 538, 544–45, 552–53; Rifa'i, II, pp. 11–26.

24. Iliyas, II, pp. 347, 450ff.

25. Ibid., pp. 351–52; McFadden, p. 19. The figures for Cairo around 1950 were ca. 378,000 copies of daily newspapers for 2,100,000 inhabitants, for Damascus ca. 32,400 copies of dailies for 325,000 inhabitants. Rifa'i, II, p. 118, quotes 3,000 to 4,000 copies sold daily by the more serious papers in the mid-1930s, a reasonable assessment. For literacy and circulation, see Chapter 6.

26. Rifa'i, II, p. 44.

27. Iliyas, II, pp. 349–51; Rifa'i, II, pp. 28ff.

28. *Al-Jarida al-Rasmiyya* (Damascus), 24 March 1921, quoted in Khad-

dur, p. 145. See also the sections dealing with the press in the annual issues of France, Ministère des Affaires Étrangères, *Rapport a la societé des nations*; Babil, p. 88.

29. Details in Rifa'i, II, pp. 46ff. See also Babil, pp. 38–40, 62–65; Ar-suzi, IV, pp. 295–98; Philip Khoury, pp. 360–61, 363–64, 389; Iliyas, II, pp. 311, 349–51; Mardini.

30. *Al-Qabas*, 17 September 1928, p. 1.

31. Quoted in Rifa'i, II, p. 123. For a more extensive discussion of press-state tensions, see ibid., pp. 28–134; Iliyas, II, passim.

32. France, Ministère des Affaires Étrangères, *Rapport*, 1937, p. 7; 1938, pp. 9–10.

33. *Al-Qabas*, 17 February 1928, p. 1.

34. Rifa'i, II, p. 111.

35. Babil, p. 162.

36. Calculated according to Daghir, pp. 415–30. The proportion of periodicals published by Lebanese in their own homeland vis-à-vis the total output of Lebanese writers worldwide was markedly higher during this period than prior to World War I (see Chapter 3). Of the 265 papers published by Lebanese everywhere in the 1920s, 150 (57 percent) were printed in Lebanon. In the 1930s the rate was 86 out of 117 (74 percent). This trend—a subject for a separate study—seems to reflect not a return home of Lebanese writers but a shift of Lebanese abroad from journalism to other occupations (as, for example, was the case in Egypt; see Chapter 3).

37. Calculated according to Tarrazi, IV, pp. 16–40, 114–26.

38. France, Ministère des Affaires Étrangères, *Rapport*, 1935, p. 8.

39. F0371/40353/A4667.

40. Details in Muruwwa, pp. 259–77; Ghurayyib, pp. 97–106; Daghir, passim. On the Communist Party organs, see 'Akari, esp. pp. 9–28.

41. See, e.g., France, Ministère des Affaires Étrangères, *Rapport*, 1936, pp. 13–14.

42. *Bayrut*, 29 January 1937, p. 1. For the paper's suspension in November 1936, see France, Ministère des Affaires Étrangères, *Rapport*, 1936, p. 15.

43. France, Ministère des Affaires Étrangères, *Rapport*, 1927, p. 32; 1937, p. 9.

44. Hilmi, p. 303.

45. Details in Hasani, pp. 62–66; also Adhami, pp. 41–52.

46. Quoted in Rafa'il Batti, p. 77.

47. Details in Rafa'il Batti, pp. 55–80; Hasani, pp. 67–70.

48. Kedourie, "The kingdom of Iraq," p. 239.

49. Khadduri, p. 99, note 2. Khadduri and several other sources spell his name as Butti.

50. Details in Rafa'il Batti, pp. 93–119; Fa'iq Batti, *Sihafat al-ahzab*, pp. 14–40; Chadirchi, pp. 23–48, 53–68; Gailani, pp. 62–75.

51. The law was amended in 1933 and again in 1934, each amendment making it harsher. For the text of the 1934 version, see Hasani, pp. 13–24.

52. *Al-Istiqlal* (Baghdad), 18 April 1935, p. 1.

53. McFadden, pp. 47, 91–92.

54. For *Habazbuz*, see Sadr, pp. 53–73. For literary and professional journals until 1933, see Hasani, pp. 31–48.

55. Issawi, *The Fertile Crescent*, p. 30.

56. McFadden, p. 19. According to McFadden's estimates for mid-century, daily newspapers in Baghdad sold approximately one copy per 20 inhabitants (25,200 copies for 500,000 inhabitants), as against about 1 : 10 in Damascus and 1 : 5 in Cairo. Nor was radio, which started in Iraq as a government enterprise in 1935 or 1936 — broadcasting some five hours daily prior to World War II — very popular until after the war; see Boyd, pp. 106–7.

57. The one exception was *Lisan al-'Arab*, published in Jerusalem by the Lebanese Christian Ibrahim Salim al-Najjar, which appeared daily for about a year (1921–1922), then changed frequency to three times a week. For a detailed discussion of the Palestinian press of this period, see Yehoshu'a, *1919–1929*, passim; Porat, passim.

58. Among the exceptional newspapers were *Lisan al-'Arab* of Jerusalem and *al-Akhbar* and *al-Nafir* of Jaffa. See Yehoshu'a, ibid., pp. 56ff., 340ff., 411ff.

59. *Al-Quds al-Sharif*, 13 April 1920, quoted by Yehoshu'a, ibid., p. 128.

60. *Al-Ittihad al-'Arabi*, 30 May 1925, p. 1; 6 June 1925, p. 1.

61. Porat, pp. 242–43.

62. *Mir'at al-Sharq*, 18 September 1926, p. 1.

63. Figures for Palestine in *Blue Book*, 1929, p. 159 (this assessment includes only the larger papers, and hence the total should be increased by perhaps a quarter to a third to include all the Palestinian papers). Figure for Lebanon in France, Ministère des Affaires Étrangères, *Rapport*, 1930, p. 11.

64. On the eve of World War I, the Arab population of Palestine was assessed at some 600,000, with total circulation of Arabic papers estimated by Nissim Malul to be 4,500 to 5,500 copies. The 1931 census put the country's Arab population at about 860,000, while newspaper circulation two years earlier was assessed at 12,700. Population figures in Shim'oni, p. 415; circulation estimates in Malul, p. 449, and *Blue Book*, ibid.

65. *Al-Yarmuk*, 24 January 1926, p. 1. Cf. Sulayman, *al-Sihafa al-Filastiniyya wa-qawanin al-intidab*, p. 113.

66. *Filastin* was preceded by the Lebanese Christian George 'Azar's *al-Iqdam*, likewise a Jaffa-based newspaper, which shifted to daily publication several days earlier.

67. Figures for 1935 in Arnon-Ohanna, p. 201; for 1946 in Shim'oni, p. 410.

68. For examples of such fluctuations, see Shim'oni, pp. 406–8; Arnon-Ohanna, pp. 205–8.

69. *Al-Hayah* (Jerusalem), 22 January 1931, p. 1.

70. Sulayman, *al-Sihafa al-Filastiniyya wa-qawanin al-intidab*, pp. 74–79, 95–105, 120–21; texts of all laws and orders pertaining to the press in Appendices 1–10.

71. Yehoshu'a, *1919–1929*, p. 125; idem, *1930–1948*, pp. 95–96; Shim'oni, pp. 393–95, 408–9.

72. Yehoshu'a, *1930–1948*, p. 98.

73. For details, see Sharim, pp. 23–26, 82, where a copy of the paper is reproduced (some of the details concerning the number of issues and the dates of publication are confused). Details on other Transjordanian papers discussed below appear on pp. 13–51, 81–90. See also Muruwwa, pp. 347–51.

74. McFadden, p. 19. According to a survey by the Transjordanian Min-

istry of Education, 3,316 children attended school in 1922–1923, and 9,656 in 1939–1940; *al-Jazira al-'Arabiyya*, 20 December 1939, p. 1.

75. McFadden, ibid.

76. E.g., *al-Shari'a* in 1927; *al-Anba'* and *Sada al-'Arab* in 1928. See Sharim, pp. 81, 83; Muruwwa, p. 349.

77. See, e.g., *al-Jazira al-'Arabiyya*, November-December 1939, passim.

78. Details in Shamikh, pp. 124–27.

79. Details in Shamikh, pp. 149–79. *Sawt al-Hijaz* changed its name after World War II to *al-Bilad al-Sa'udiyya* ("Saudi Country"), then to *al-Bilad* when it became a daily.

80. Interview with 'Ali Hafiz, *Saudi Report*, 1 March 1982, pp. 6–7.

81. UNESCO, *World Communications* (1950), p. 170.

82. For details, see El-Zine, pp. 95–105; Obermeyer.

83. For details, see 'Izzat, pp. 295–99, 334–99.

84. *Saudi Report*, 1 March 1982, p. 6.

85. 'Abduh, *Jaridat al-Ahram*, pp. 626–32; idem, *Ruz al-Yusuf*, pp. 197–98; Rifa'i, II, pp. 135–42; Khaddur, pp. 227–29; Babil, p. 143; Yehoshu'a, *1930–1948*, p. 17; Walker, p. 168.

86. Longrigg, p. 284.

87. For details, see Rifa'i, II, pp. 138–51; Khaddur, pp. 243–46; Babil, pp. 63–64.

88. McFadden, pp. 36–37.

Chapter 5

1. Beaumarchais, p. 239.

2. Details in Cioeta, p. 168; Sinan Sa'id, p. 8.

3. Sabat, *Ta'rikh al-tiba'a*, p. 193; Cole, p. 223.

4. Text in *Kanz al-ragha'ib*, V, pp. 56–59. See also Ramadan, p. 147.

5. A detailed description appears in Cioeta.

6. Emin, p. 36; B. Lewis, *Emergence*, pp. 149–50.

7. *Hadiqat al-Akhbar*, issues 16–21, March-May 1858. See also Krymskii, pp. 492–93.

8. Quoted in Khaddur, p. 82.

9. Kurd 'Ali, *Mudhakkirat*, I, p. 51. For descriptions of Hamidian censorship and its impact in the Arab provinces, see *Lisan al-'Arab* (Alexandria), 10 August 1894, p. 1; *Yubil Lisan al-Hal*, pp. 10–11; Rifa'i, I, pp. 111–57; Iliyas, I, pp. 55–59; Rafa'il Batti, pp. 138–40; Sinan Sa'id, pp. 9–16. For a balanced discussion of the topic, see Cioeta.

10. *Al-Quds*, 5, 18 September 1908, quoted in Sulayman, *Ta'rikh al-sihafa al-Filastiniyya*, pp. 62–63; Yehoshu'a, *1908–1918*, pp. 10–11; *RMM*, VI (November 1908), pp. 570–71. A similar case quoted in *al-Muqtataf*, 1 May 1936, p. 564.

11. *Al-Manar*, Vol. I (1897–98), p. 658. Similarly, Salih, pp. 21, 70 (relating 'Ali Yusuf's difficulties in obtaining a license in Egypt in 1886).

12. Sarkis, as his grandson related, explained to the vali that such use of press equipment would make it impossible for him to use it thereafter, for "he would be unable to cut paper for Arabic texts in which the name of Allah appears frequently, or for holy books, after the blood of that damn villain had

defiled it," whereupon the vali backed down on his demand. The story appears in Ghalib, p. 96.

13. Sulayman, ibid., p. 48; similarly, Khaddur, pp. 77–78.

14. 'Abd al-Hamid, pp. 221–22.

15. 'Abduh, *Mihnat al-sihafa*, pp. 22–24; Farah, pp. 168–69; Cole, pp. 223–25.

16. *Al-Tijara*, 1 June 1878, quoted by Subhi, p. 53 (the paper's date might be in error); cf. Jayyid, pp. 142, 174.

17. Story told by Yusuf Ibrahim Yazbak in Sa'ada, *al-Sihafa*, pp. 324–27.

18. Ramadan, pp. 50–61.

19. Quoted in Jundi, *Al-Sihafa al-siyasiyya*, pp. 67, 470.

20. Sidqi, p. 58.

21. Quoted by Rifa'i, II, p. 123.

22. 'Azm, III, pp. 69–70.

23. Williams, pp. 240–41.

24. Burgoyne, II, pp. 205–6.

25. For a detailed discussion of these clauses and their implications, see Ramadan, pp. 32–33, 72–77; Shams, pp. 7–11; Dasuqi and Dasuqi, pp. 60–66; 'Abduh, *Mihnat al-sihafa*, pp. 33–35. The constitution also allowed the king to declare a state of emergency, enabling him to close all printing presses and ban all publications that, in his judgment, jeopardized "the social order." Similar clauses, phrased in similar language, were also included in the Lebanese constitution of 1926 (Art. 13); the organic law of Transjordan of 1928 (Art. 11); the Syrian constitution of 1930 (Arts. 16 and 17); and the Iraqi constitution of the same year (Art. 12).

26. Ramadan, p. 73.

27. Fatima al-Yusuf, pp. 128–29. Other confiscations of issues of the journal recurred subsequently, with the authorities impounding them "only after all copies had been printed, to increase the material damage to the paper"; ibid., p. 132.

28. Haykal-Mazini-'Inan, p. 29. Similarly *al-Ahram*, 9 January 1935, p. 16.

29. Details in Jundi, *Al-Sihafa al-siyasiyya*, pp. 614–15, 620–28; Samahan, pp. 228–33; Shams, pp. 130–34; Ramadan, p. 208.

30. Hafiz Mahmud, pp. 56–57.

31. For details, see Rafa'il Batti, pp. 143–46, 150–61.

32. Details in Rifa'i, II, pp. 120–23; Babil, pp. 108ff.

33. Babil, p. 109. For a similar incident involving a violent attack on the journalist Najib al-Rayyis by a person acting on behalf of Syria's minister of education, Husni al-Barazi, see Munir al-Rayyis, II, pp. 141ff.; *al-Istiqlal* (Baghdad), 11 January 1935, p. 1.

34. The case of *Majallat al-Kuwait* is described in 'Izzat, p. 298. The Saudi press law of 1929 appears in Shamikh, pp. 181–89.

35. 'Abd al-Hamid, pp. 221–22.

36. 'Abd al-Hamid, ibid. See also Sinan Sa'id, pp. 12–13 (where the author provides data on sums spent by 'Abd al-Hamid's government on the foreign press) and p. 15; Farah, pp. 160–61.

37. Tarrazi, III, pp. 44–47; Hamza, *Adab al-maqala*, IV, pp. 83–84; 'Abduh, *Tatawwur al-sihafa*, pp. 217–18; Crabitès, p. 995.

38. See, for example, the pictures of Khalil al-Khuri, Butrus al-Bustani,

Salim Shihada, Luis Sabunji, Niqula Naqqash, Salim 'Anhuri, 'Ali Yusuf, and Tarrazi himself in Tarrazi, I, pp. 2, 90, 102, 133; II, pp. 71, 121, 199, 249; III, p. 17.

39. Kurd 'Ali, *Mudhakkirat*, I, p. 53. Similarly, Sayyid, *Qissat hayati*, pp. 82–83; Salih, p. 37.

40. Quoted by Jundi, *Tatawwur al-sihafa*, pp. 102–3.

41. Babil, p. 39.

42. Ghurayyib, pp. 8–9; Shamikh, pp. 186–87. The 1933 Press Law in mandatory Palestine contained a similar provision, but since the government was foreign and largely oblivious to the conduct of the local press, the situation there was different. See Sulayman, *Al-Sihafa al-Filastiniyya wa-qawanin al-intidab*, p. 168.

43. E.g., *al-I'lam*, 4 August 1887, p. 1; *al-Muqattam*, 27 May 1889, p. 1.

44. Fatima al-Yusuf, p. 222; 'Abduh, *Ruz al-Yusuf*, pp. 158–61. Salama Musa, owner of several papers during the 1920s and 1930s, complained of having been similarly penalized; Musa, *al-Sihafa*, p. 28.

45. Beaumarchais, pp. 237–38.

46. *Hadiqat al-Akhbar*, 1 January 1858, p. 1; *al-Nahla*, 11 May 1870, front cover and pp. 14–15; *al-Zahra*, 1 January 1870, p. 3; 'Abduh, *Jaridat al-Ahram*, p. 23.

47. These phrases, one author suggested, "lost their true significance in a society which dealt incessantly with manners, form and high-flown expressions"; Ghalib, p. 98. According to Ahmad Emin, every paper in the Ottoman Empire had "some old, experienced man" whose sole duty was to produce lines of praise for the sultan, to be incorporated in the texts. "Only on rare occasions, however, did even he have any amount of original writing to do. There were formulas in back issues fitting every possible circumstance and event in which the sultan might be involved. These were simply copied without any thought as to their meaning and sense"; Emin, pp. 81–82. See also Rafa'il Batti, p. 19.

48. *Al-Zahra*, 1 January 1870, pp. 2–3.

49. *Lisan al-'Arab* (Alexandria), 1 August 1894, p. 1; *al-Zahir*, 12 November 1903, pp. 1–2; *Anis al-Jalis*, 31 January 1899, p. 2. For additional typical examples of this practice, see: *al-Jinan*, January 1870, pp. 1, 3; *al-Nahla*, 11 May 1870, pp. 2, 3, 13, 16 (of the paper's 16 pages, fully three are devoted to such praise in verse); *Mithal al-Ahram*, 15 July 1876, p. 1; *al-Ahram*, 5 August 1876, p. 1; *Lisan al-Hal*, 18 October 1877, p. 1; *al-I'lam*, 3 May 1887, p. 1; 12 May 1887, p. 1; *al-Muqattam*, 14 February 1889, p. 1; 12 March 1889, p. 1; *al-Hilal*, 1 December 1892, p. 190 (reference to the journal *al-Manzum*); 1 April 1893, p. 384 (reference to *al-Nadim*); 1 October 1894, pp. 119–20 (reference to *al-Nur al-'Abbasi*); *al-Ra'is*, January 1900, p. 1; Hamza, *Adab al-Maqala*, III, p. 72 (quoting from *Misbah al-Sharq*); IV, pp. 80–81 (quoting from *al-Mu'ayyad*); V, p. 116 (quoting *al-Liwa'*).

50. *Al-Hilal*, 1 September 1895, p. 13.

51. Quoted in *al-Hilal*, 1 October 1894, p. 118.

52. *Al-Muqattam*, 14 February 1889, p. 1; *al-Hilal*, ibid. Similarly, the first issue of *al-Mu'ayyad*, 1 December 1889, p. 1.

53. Faydi in *al-Iqaz*, 8 August 1909, quoted in Rafa'il Batti, pp. 165–67.

54. *Misr al-Qahira*, 24 December 1879, quoted in Farah, p. 172.

55. Ishaq, *Durar*, p. 236.

56. *Al-Ahram*, 9 January 1935, pp. 15–16.

57. Maqdisi, pp. 90–91. The word for angel is *malak*, which may also be translated as messenger.

58. *Al-Mushir*, 17 July 1895, p. 344.

59. *Al-Hilal*, 1 September 1895, pp. 14–17, and the sequel in 1 October 1895, p. 95.

60. *Al-Manar*, I (1897–1898), pp. 659–60.

61. *Al-Diya'*, 15 September 1898, pp. 10–12. Similarly, Zaydan in *al-Hilal*, 15 December 1894, p. 313 ("in certain circumstances, permitting freedom is worse than restricting it"); Rida in *al-Manar*, I (1897–1898), pp. 660–61; Ibrahim al-Muwaylihi in *Misbah al-Sharq*, 14 April 1898, quoted in Hamza, *Adab al-maqala*, III, pp. 74–75; Kurd 'Ali in *al-Muqtabas*, I (1324/1906), p. 61; V (1328/ 1910), p. 344; Dasuqi and Dasuqi, pp. 90, 114–15, 118–19.

62. *Majallat Lughat al-'Arab*, December 1913, pp. 332–33, quoted by Abu al-Sa'd, p. 20. Similarly, Fa'iq Batti, "Tatawwur al-maqal," p. 19; Abu al-Sa'd, p. 20.

63. *Al-Qabas*, 12 September 1928, p. 1. Rayyis criticized the existing law, which protected only the prime minister against abuse, leaving the other ministers and everyone else undefended.

64. *Al-'Irfan*, 5 February 1909, p. 139.

65. Swan, pp. 149–50.

66. 'Aqqad, pp. 36–37, and similarly pp. 88–90. For several other examples, see Zaydan in *al-Hilal*, 15 October 1898, pp. 132–33; *al-Muqtabas*, I (1324/1906), p. 63; Musa, *al-Sihafa*, pp. 49–52; Fatima al-Yusuf, pp. 181–82; Crabitès, pp. 1050–51; Mahmud, p. 232; Subhi, p. 133; *al-Ahram*, 28 June 1938, pp. 1, 14. For similar references in the Syrian context, see Rifa'i, II, p. 115; Babil, pp. 316–19. Likewise Karmi, p. 52; 'Azm, pp. 71–72; Subhi, p. 57.

67. *Al-Ahram*, ibid.; McFadden, pp. 34–35.

68. McFadden, pp. 47–50, quoting Iraqi journalists. Similarly, Antun al-Jumayyil (former editor of *al-Ahram*), pp. 36–37.

69. Babil, pp. 316–17.

70. Ramadan, pp. 64–65.

71. Jumayyil, pp. 36–37.

Chapter 6

1. *Sawt al-Hijaz*, 1 February 1938, quoted in Shamikh, p. 202.

2. For varied assessments, see Heyworth-Dunne, *Introduction*, pp. 10–11; Issawi, *Fertile Crescent*, pp. 30–33.

3. Lane, pp. 66–69. See also Vatikiotis, pp. 90–91.

4. Shayyal, *Ta'rikh al-tarjama . . . fi 'asr Muhammad 'Ali*, pp. 200–1.

5. Bowring, pp. 106, 109.

6. *Al-Jam'iyya al-Suriyya*, p. 113.

7. Issawi, *Fertile Crescent*, p. 30; idem, "Asymmetrical development," p. 386; McFadden, p. 19 (quoting data from Arab governments and UNESCO sources).

8. Data from Artin, *L'Instruction*, pp. 152–62; Heyworth-Dunne, *Introduction*, pp. 383–90; Egyptian Government, *Census 1897*, I, p. xx; *Census 1917*, p. 565; Amin Sami, *Ta'lim*, pp. 113, 118 and Appendix I, Table A. See also Cole, pp. 113–15.

9. Issawi, *Fertile Crescent*, pp. 30–33; Adwan, p. 11; Faydi, pp. 57–59.

10. Issawi, *Egypt at Mid-Century*, pp. 64, 66–67, 74, 78, 89; Vatikiotis, pp. 470–71; Shim'oni, p. 389; Winter, pp. 910–14; McFadden, p. 19; UNESCO, *Comparative Statistical Data*, p. 10; Tibawi, *Islamic Education*, pp. 208–9, 211.

11. Crabitès, p. 992.

12. Quoted in Issawi, *Fertile Crescent*, p. 31.

13. Quoted in Baron, *The Women's Awakening*, p. 81.

14. Egyptian Government, *Census 1897*, I, p. xx; *Census 1917*, p. 565; Issawi, *Egypt at Mid-Century*, p. 64; Woodsmall, pp. 174–86.

15. Issawi, *Fertile Crescent*, pp. 30–33, 54; *al-Jazira al-'Arabiyya*, 20 December 1939, p. 1 (and see the serialized survey of Transjordan's education in previous issues throughout the month); Sinan Sa'id, p. 27; Woodsmall, pp. 133–34, 187–216.

16. Egyptian Government, *Census 1897*, I, p. xxi; Issawi, *Fertile Crescent*, p. 30.

17. Issawi, *Fertile Crescent*, pp. 30, 54; Egyptian Government, *Census 1907*, p. 114.

18. Rida, *Ta'rikh al-ustadh*, I, p. 1003.

19. Crabitès, pp. 1050–51. "All I may say," Crabitès observed, "is that a very young woman is not prone to hide her age. By the same token I opine that a newspaper with a large circulation would be proud to give accurate information." See similarly Smith, p. 334; McFadden, pp. 75–76.

20. Quoted in Gendzier, p. 64, and similarly p. 139.

21. FO 371/62993/N8141, "Cairo Press," August 1947.

22. McFadden, pp. 75–76.

23. Jayyid, p. 35; Rida, *Ta'rikh al-ustadh*, I, p. 175; Emin, p. 31; Iliyas, I, p. 179; Abu al-Sa'd, pp. 138–39. For a description of a similar practice in Isma'il's Egypt, where officials and others were compelled to subscribe to private journals because of the khedive's desire to support the private press, see *al-Hilal*, 1 October 1907, p. 32.

24. Krymskii, p. 487; B. Lewis, *Emergence*, p. 146. The paper, *Jeride-i Havadis*, was revived during the Crimean war.

25. E.g., *Hadiqat al-Akhbar*, 10 October 1861, p. 1; *al-Jawa'ib*, 21 April 1868, p. 1; *al-Jinan*, 1870, p. 24; 1872, p. 291; *al-Muqtataf*, October 1891, p. 1. See also Hamza, *Adab al-maqala*, I, p. 195; Hourani, *Arabic Thought*, pp. 98–99.

26. Jerrold, p. 219.

27. Faydi, p. 71.

28. Malul, p. 449.

29. WO 157/728/144888. I am grateful to Dr. Yigal Sheffy for his help in obtaining this and other War Office documents quoted in this chapter.

30. Data taken from UNESCO's *World Communication*, 1950, pp. 18–19; *Statistical Yearbook*, 1957, pp. 634–35; *Statistical Yearbook*, 1964, pp. 436–43. There is some discrepancy between the three sources in the data for 1950–52. By comparison, the figures in the West at that time were 573 per thousand in England, 342 in the United States, and 239 in France.

31. This assessment is based on literacy figures and the estimates of circulation figures presented earlier in this chapter.

32. For further discussion on this issue, see Darnton, "First steps toward a history of reading," in his *The Kiss of Lamourette*, pp. 154–87; Suleiman,

"Introduction," in Suleiman and Crosman, pp. 3–45; Gershoni, "The Reader."
For an illuminating consideration of this question in a Middle Eastern context,
see Baron, "Readers."

33. Darnton, pp. 132–33, 166, 168–69; Scribner, pp. 49–62; Chartier,
pp. 51, 225–33.

34. Hourani, *Arabic Thought*, p. 54; Zaydan, *Ta'rikh adab*, IV, pp. 68ff.,
126–27; Baron, *The Women's Awakening*, p. 85.

35. E.g., *Hadiqat al-Akhbar*, 2 August 1858, p. 4; 6 August 1859, p. 4;
al-Jawa'ib, 21 April 1861, pp. 1, 4; *al-Ahram*, 19 August 1876, p. 4. A similar
advertisement of the opening of such a library in Beirut appeared in *al-Jinan*,
30 March 1876, p. 181.

36. WO 157/727/144888, May 1918.

37. *Lisan al-'Arab* (Damascus), 21 October 1918, p. 4. See also Fyfe, p.
114; Hartmann, p. 18; Arsuzi, IV, p. 296; Rafi'i, *Mudhakkirati*, p. 8; Baron,
"Readers."

38. Emin, pp. 47, 132, 135, depicting the practice in the towns of Turkey
on the eve of World War I, which was certainly very similar to that in the Arab
provinces; Crabitès, p. 1050; Fyfe, pp. 113–14. For the cafe as a place of
entertainment and exchange of political views in Middle Eastern tradition, see
Hattox, pp. 101–3; Lane, pp. 386–420.

39. Rida, *Ta'rikh al-ustadh*, I, p. 303.

40. *Al-Hilal*, October 1897, p. 131. Cf. a similar description quoted in
Cole, p. 125.

41. Rae, p. 214; Eldon Gorst in FO 371/451/31779 (16 September 1908).

42. Crabitès, p. 1050.

43. Thomsen, p. 211.

44. *Al-Bilad al-Sa'udiyya* (Mecca), 30 January 1949, p. 3. Hirabayashi-El
Khatib (p. 360), in their study of rural Egypt in the mid-1950s, mention the
front stairs of the village grocery store as the location for similar congregations.

45. WO 157/727/144888. Similarly, WO 157/728/144888.

46. See descriptions in Cooper, pp. 167, 241; also Baron, "Readers."

47. Quoted in Tarrazi, III, pp. 49–50.

48. *Al-Kitab al-Dhahbi*, p. 132.

49. *Lisan al-'Arab* (Damascus), 21 October 1918, p. 4. Similarly, *al-'Irfan*,
5 February 1909, p. 137.

50. *Al-Raqib*, December 1909, September 1910, quoted by Abu al-Sa'd, p.
150.

51. *Al-Quds*, 30 September 1913, quoted by Sulayman, *Ta'rikh al-sihafa
al-Filastiniyya*, p. 141; *al-Raqib*, *Sada Babil*, quoted by Abu al-Sa'd, p. 151.
Similarly, *Lisan al-'Arab* (Damascus), ibid.; Babil, p. 144; 'Izzat, p. 57.

52. Cf. Mowlana, "Mass communication," pp. 58–68.

53. Baron, *The Women's Awakening*, p. 92. Cf. Cole, pp. 122–23.

54. *Al-Mawsu'at*, 15 November 1898, p. 1.

55. *Al-Liwa'*, 2 January 1900, p. 1.

56. *Al-I'lam*, 21 February 1885, p. 1. Similarly, *al-Jawa'ib*, 21 April 1868,
p. 1; *al-Tankit wal-Tabkit*, 6 June 1881, p. 16; *al-Zahir*, 12 November 1903, p.
1; examples from Syrian papers in the early twentieth century quoted in Iliyas,
I, pp. 304, 305, 307, 310, 312, 319.

57. *Al-Muqtataf*, I (1876), p. 256; *al-Hilal*, 1 March 1893, pp. 305–9.

58. *Al-Hilal*, 1 September 1897, p. 23.

59. *Al-Jami'a al-'Uthmaniyya*, 1 June 1899, p. 107; 1 August 1899, p. 186; 1 September 1899, p. 224. See also Reid, *Odyssey*, pp. 56–58.

60. For details, see Baron, *The Women's Awakening*, pp. 96–100.

61. FO 371/3721/156659.

62. See above, Chapter 3.

63. Arsuzi, IV, p. 296.

64. Kurd 'Ali, *Mudhakkirat*, III, p. 814; idem in *al-Muqtabas*, I (1324/1906), p. 63; V, (1328/1910), pp. 342–44; idem, *Khitat al-Sham*, IV, pp. 91–93.

65. *Al-'Irfan*, 12 January 1910, pp. 28–29.

66. Sulayman, *Ta'rikh al-sihafa al-Filastiniyya*, pp. 145–46, quoting pre-World War I Palestinian newspapers. Similarly, *al-Manar*, I (1897–1898), p. 660; *al-Hilal*, 15 October 1898, p. 132; *al-'Irfan*, 5 February 1909, pp. 139–41; Musa, *al-Sihafa*, pp. 17–21; Rifa'i, II, p. 115; McFadden, pp. 15–17.

67. Details in Hamza, *Adab al-maqala*, IV, pp. 111–22; Salih, pp. 45–59; Baha al-Din, pp. 63–85. See also Chapter 9 below.

68. E.g., Hafiz Mahmud, p. 231; Subhi, p. 13.

69. McFadden, pp. 15–17, 45, 46–48.

Chapter 7

1. Emin, p. 20.

2. The decree of 1727 was by Sultan Ahmed the Third on the basis of a *fatwa* (religious ruling) by Shaykh al-Islam, the chief religious authority, 11 years earlier. Details in Sabat, *Ta'rikh al-tiba'a*, pp. 21ff.; Emin, pp. 20–24; Berkes, pp. 39–41, 147; B. Lewis, *Emergence*, pp. 41, 50–51.

3. Lane, p. 283.

4. Jansen, pp. 46–59. For examples, see Grendler, *The Roman Inquisition*, esp. Chapter 3, and his article under the same title; Horatio Brown, esp. Chapters 13 and 14, and passim.

5. Sabat, *Ta'rikh al-tiba'a*, p. 21.

6. Jabarti, *Ta'rikh muddat al-Fransis*, pp. 7–17 of the Arabic text. A century and a half later, a Syrian writer demonstrated the same profound belief in the power of words. Rafiq al-Maqdisi, commending journalist Najib al-Rayyis' contribution to the national struggle, praised his editorials, "which cast up their volcanic ashes vigorously in the face of the mandatory authorities, its embers spreading all over their fortresses. Violent fear of that fiery pen seized them." Maqdisi, p. 55, and similarly Rifa'i, II, p. 44.

7. Tahtawi, *Takhlis*, p. 150; Shayyal, *Ta'rikh al-tarjama . . . fi 'asr Muhammad 'Ali*, p. 214.

8. Marsafi, pp. 30–32. See also Mitchell, *Colonizing Egypt*, pp. 131–34.

9. *Al-Kitab al-dhahabi*, p. 131.

10. Ibid, p. 132.

11. *Al-Manar*, I (1897–1898), p. 660.

12. *Al-'Irfan*, 12 January 1910, p. 28; *al-Kitab al-dhahabi*, pp. 129–34; *al-Muqtabas*, I (1324/1906), pp. 62–63; *Sawt al-Hijaz*, 1 February 1938, quoted by Shamikh, pp. 202, 204; Maqdisi, p. 89; 'Izzat, pp. 293–94.

13. Rida, *Ta'rikh al-ustadh*, I, p. 1003.

14. Ibid., p. 1001. Rida was referring in this passage to his native country, Syria.

15. *Al-Manar*, I (1897–1898), pp. 657ff.

16. Quoted by Salih, p. 153. According to Hamza, *Adab al-maqala*, IV, pp. 121–22, the statement was made by Shaykh 'Uthman Alfandi, the lawyer representing Shaykh al-Sadat. See also Chapter 9 below.

17. See p. 110 above.

18. *Al-I'lam*, 11 January 1885, pp. 1–2.

19. *Al-Zahir*, 12 November 1903, p. 1.

20. E.g., Muruwwa, pp. 75ff., 157–59; Subhi, pp. 20–22, 25; Jayyid, pp. 7ff. See also Rafa'il Batti, pp. 8–9; Hamza, *Adab al-maqala*, I, p. 6.

21. Schuon, p. 13 and passim.

22. Rendition by Crabbs, p. 43. A more literal translation would be "The Marvel of Traces in Biographies and Events."

23. There are quite a few studies on the literary and linguistic aspects of the evolution of the Arab press. Among the most systematic and useful are Hamza's eight-volume *Adab al-maqala*, and Khurshid's highly instructive study.

24. Jayyid, p. 30.

25. Hamza, *Adab al-maqala*, I, pp. 112–24; idem, *Mustaqbal al-sihafa*, pp. 42–93; Jayyid, pp. 49, 66, 96, 147; Krymskii, pp. 499–501; Iliyas, I, pp. 202–4; *al-Ahram*, 5 August 1876, pp. 2–3 and subsequent issues; *al-Muqattam*, 14 February 1889, p. 2 and subsequent issues. Similarly, *al-I'lam*, 11 January 1885 and subsequent issues (serializing the owner's own book, *Safwat al-I'tibar*).

26. For the story from *al-Waqa'i' al-Misriyya*, see Chapter 1 above; *al-Ahram*, 5 August 1876, p. 4; *Lisan al-'Arab* (Alexandria), 4 August 1894, p. 1.

27. See Chapter 5 above.

28. *Lisan al-'Arab* (Damascus), 5 October 1918, p. 1; *Abu Nuwas al-'Asri*, 25 June 1921, p. 1.

29. Hamza, *Mustaqbal al-sihafa*, p. 118.

30. "*Wa-intadabna li-ri'asat tahbir 'ilmiyyatiha, wa-tahrir adabiyyatiha, wa-taqwim 'ibaratiha, wa-intiqa' kalimatiha, janab al-'allama al-tahrir, wal-katib al-shahir, man tahallat bi-durr alfazihi 'ara'is al-ma'ani, al-ustadh al-fadil Ibrahim afandi al-Hurani.*" *Al-Rayyis*, January 1900, p. 2. The English rendition here, and in the quotation that follows, is of course only approximate.

31. "*Tubi'at hadhihi al-Waqa'i' al-Misriyya bi-'awni khaliq al-bariyya, bi-matba'at sahib al-futuhat al-saniyya, bi-Bulaq Misr al-mahmiyya.*" Quoted in 'Abduh, *Ta'rikh al-Waqa'i' al-Misriyya*, p. 71.

32. "*Yahiqqu li-kull muhibb lil-khayr al-'amm an yasurr min al-ittila' 'ala mithal jaridat al-Ahram, allati hiyya bi-la rayb min ajall maathir hadha al-'asr*"; *Al-Ahram*, 19 August 1876, p. 3. *Mithal al-Ahram* was a two-page notice that appeared in Alexandria on 15 July 1876 announcing the forthcoming publication of the paper.

33. "*Qad jama'a amarat al-fadl wal-nabaha, wa-khala' min kull khala'a wa-safaha. Wa-huwa ma yuksib arbab al-duwal tadbiran, wa-ru'asa' al-juyush shuja'atan. Wa-wulat al-umur tahdiran, wa-ra'ayahum haybatan wa-ta'atan.*" *Al-Jawa'ib*, 21 April 1868, p. 1.

34. "*Wa-hiyya al-jarida allati ja'alna laha al-huquq isman, wal-ikhlas fi al-qawl haddan wa-hikman.*" *Al-Huquq*, 6 March 1886, p. 1.

35. "[*Al-mubadara ila nashr al-hawadith al-dakhiliyya*] *min al-i'tibar wal-tahdhir, aw al-tarwij wal-tabshir, li-anna al-mayl ila iqtitaf al-akhbar, wal-gharba fi istitla'*

ma yakun min al-afkar, min wada'i' al-fitra al-bashariyya, ghayr tarika sha'n al-tijara al-dakhiliyya wal-kharijiyya." Al-Mu'ayyad, December 1889, reproduced in Hamza, *Adab al-maqala*, IV, p. 81.

36. "*Wa-iltazamu ma la yujdi min al-si'aya, allati hiyya lahum mabda' wa-ghaya. Zanin annahum yakhdimu al-inkliz biturrahatihim, wa-yushawwishuna al-afkar bi-muftarayatihim. Muwahhamin innahum yas'una fi salih al-umma al-Misriyya, bal al-umam al-sharqiyya. Wa-idha inkashafat al-haqa'iq, tabayyana al-mukhlis min al-munafiq." Al-Ustadh*, 23 May 1893, p. 922.

37. "*Qad saqatta min shahiq 'al ila hadid khafd, tatakhabbat fi awhal 'ar la yutaq lahu dahd, wa-tatawahhaq bi-salasil awjal la yastata' laha naqd." Al-Zahir*, 1904 (?), quoted in *al-Hilal*, January 1929, p. 310.

38. "*Fa-mathala bayna yadayhi dubbat al-'askariyya al-kiram, wa-kibar al-mustakhdimin al-malakiyya al-'izam. Labisin malabisihim al-rasmiyya li-qasd al-tahni'a liqudum hadhihi al-'am. Wa-'adu fa'izin min 'indihi bi-mazid al-bashasha wal-ikram.*" Reproduced in Jayyid, p. 99. For another example, quoted from a news report in Ibrahim al-Muwaylihi's *Misbah al-Sharq* at the turn of the century, see Hamza, *Adab al-maqala*, III, pp. 76–77. See also ibid., I, pp. 147–59, 166–75; Jayyid, pp. 105–7.

39. "*I'adat 'umum al-ra'aya ila al-'ubudiyya ba'd al-hurriyya, wa-ila taraffu' al-ba'd 'ala ba'dihim ba'd al-musawah, wa-ila al-zulm wal-jawr ba'd al-'adala." Al-Raqib*, quoted by Rafa'il Batti, p. 162.

40. "*Istabdalna al-'ilm wal-'irfan bil-juhl wal-khusran . . . hatta tawatna yad al-ayyam min sijl al-madaniyya ila sijl al-anam." Hijaz*, 24 November 1908, quoted by Shamikh, pp. 88–89.

41. "*Qata'at al-jabal al-'ajib wal-wadi al-khadib, wal-balad al-rahib wal-bahar al-raghib." Al-Istiqlal al-'Arabi*, 14 October 1918, quoted by Iliyas, II, p. 367.

42. Bustani's "*Khutba fi adab al-'Arab*," 15 February 1859, text in *al-Jam'iyya al-Suriyya*, p. 109.

43. Zaydan, *Ta'rikh adab*, IV, p. 243.

44. Hamza, *Mustaqbal al-sihafa*, p. 118; idem, *Adab al-maqala*, I, pp. 81–85; Iliyas, I, pp. 189–90; Gibb, p. 251.

45. For several examples, see Hamza, *Adab al-maqala*, I, pp. 112–25, 145–46.

46. *Al-Muqattam*, 14 February 1889, p. 1.

47. Hamza, *Adab al-maqala*, V, p. 6.

48. Quoted in Reid, *Odyssey*, p. 61.

49. *Al-'Alam*, 31 May 1910, p. 6.

50. *Al-Jarida*, 9 March 1907, quoted by Hamza, *Adab al-maqala*, VI, p. 92.

51. For a more extensive discussion of these issues, see Khurshid, pp. 119–35. Also Musa, *al-Sihafa*, pp. 71–74; Maqdisi, pp. 46ff.

52. For a discussion of the relationship between language and the political sphere in Islamic history, see B. Lewis, *Political Language*.

53. Yaziji, p. 2.

54. For a discussion of this process in the sphere of politics during the nineteenth century, see Ayalon, *Language and Change*. For an overview of these developments in both the nineteenth and twentieth centuries, see Somekh, Chapter 2.

55. *Al-Waqa'i' al-Misriyya*, no. 130, 13 Ramadan 1245/March 1830, p. 1.

56. Jayyid, pp. 40, 49. The Turkish edition was separated from the Arabic edition in 1847.

57. Iliyas, I, pp. 163–65, 188–93, 196–97, containing many examples reproduced by the author.

58. Anastas al-Karmili in *al-Zuhur*, quoted by Fa'iq Batti, "*Tatawwur al-maqal*," p. 30; Kurd 'Ali, *Mudhakkirat*, I, p. 50. Similarly, idem in *al-Muqtabas*, V (1910), pp. 161ff.; Tikriti, pp. 288–90; Abu al-Sa'd, pp. 11, 169ff., including many examples.

59. For examples, see Hamza, *Adab al-maqala*, I, pp. 148–59; Jayyid, pp. 99–101, 106–7.

60. See Ibyari; Yaziji; 'Abd al-Sayyid. A brief survey of the major controversies appeared in *al-Hilal*, January 1929, pp. 305ff. The dispute between Shidyaq and the two Yazijis — Nasif and his son Ibrahim — also involved some of the other leading writers of the time, including Butrus and Najib al-Bustani, Ibrahim al-Ahdab, and Ibrahim al-Hurani.

61. *Hadiqat al-Akhbar*, 10 May 1858, p. 1; 17 July 1858, p. 1.

62. E.g., *Birjis Baris*, 1 February 1860, p. 2 — *diwan nuwwab al-muluk*, a conference of royal delegates.

63. E.g., *al-Jawa'ib*, 19 January 1869, pp. 1–2.

64. *Muntakhabat al-Jawa'ib*, VI, p. 246; VII, pp. 106, 178, 194; *al-Nahla* (London), 1 July 1878, pp. 18–19; *al-Janna*, 23 July 1880, p. 2.

65. E.g., *al-Waqa'i' al-Misriyya*, no. 110 (1830), pp. 3, 4; *al-Jinan*, January 1870, p. 1; *al-Jawa'ib*, 9 November 1870, p. 3.

66. E.g., *Hadiqat al-Akhbar*, 1 January 1858, p. 1; *'Utarid*, 2 July 1859, p. 1; *al-Ahram*, 19 January 1879, p. 1. For additional examples and discussion, see Ayalon, "Sihafa."

67. Muruwwa, *al-Sihafa al-'Arabiyya*, p. 14; Subhi, p. 34. On the confusion between *sahifa* and *majalla*, see Ishaq, *Durar*, p. 228, and Iliyas, I, p. 170.

68. As, for example, in the depiction of the British House of Lords as *majlis al-a'yan (al-lurdiyya)*, roughly "the council of notables (lords)"; e.g., *al-Qahira al-Hurra*, 16 April 1887, p. 1.

69. E.g., *Birjis Baris*, 24 June 1859, p. 2, where, in discussing the Italian struggle for a republic, the editor refers to the latter as *mufawada*, then explains in a note at the bottom of the column that "*mufawada* is what Europeans call *ribublik*" and adds an explanation for his choice of this term.

70. As, for instance, in a reference to French republicans in 1870 as "those seeking *mashyakha* and *jumhuriyya*" (two neologisms that were used interchangeably to denote the novel and still vague notion of republic); *al-Jawa'ib*, 26 April 1870, p. 5.

71. E.g., *Wadi al-Nil*, 23 April 1869, p. 16; *Thamarat al-Funun*, 20 July 1875, p. 1. Only a few of the innumerable examples are quoted here. See further in Ayalon, *Language and Change*, passim.

72. E.g., *al-Jawa'ib*, 21 April 1868, p. 4; *al-Raja'*, 29 March 1895, p. 2.

73. E.g., *'Utarid*, 9 October 1858, p. 2; *al-Jinan*, 1885, p. 100.

74. E.g., *al-Jawa'ib*, 6 December 1870, p. 3; *al-Muqattam*, 6 April 1889, p. 1.

75. E.g., *Birjis Baris*, 7 July 1859, pp. 1–2; *al-Lata'if*, IV (1889–1890), p. 153.

76. E.g., *al-Bashir*, 17 September 1870, p. 21; *al-Jawa'ib*, 9 November 1870, p. 1.

77. E.g., *Birjis Baris*, 18 January 1860, p. 3; *al-Jawa'ib*, 15 December 1875, p. 3.

78. E.g., *al-Sada*, 20 April 1876, p. 1.

79. E.g., *al-Jinan*, 1885, p. 102.

80. Iliyas, II, pp. 363–72.

81. Fa'iq Batti, *al-Sihafa al-'Iraqiyya*, pp. 89–95.

Chapter 8

1. Issawi, *The Economic Development of Turkey*, p. 326. The author provides data on the rapid changes of currency during the nineteenth century on pp. 326–31. See also idem, *The Fertile Crescent*, pp. 520–24. In the late nineteenth and early twentieth centuries, the Egyptian pound, or gineh, was roughly equivalent to the English pound. The Ottoman pound (lira or mecidiye) was worth about 10 percent less than the English pound. The Ottoman pound was divided into 100 qurush, or piasters, and each qurush was worth 40 para. A metalik was 10 para, or 0.25 qurush. A riyal was worth 20 qurush. The French franc was roughly 4 qurush, and the U.S. dollar roughly 20 qurush.

2. *Al-Muqtabas*, 17 December 1908, p. 1.

3. For additional examples, see reproductions of front pages of Syrian papers in Iliyas, II, pp. 682ff. Also Khoury, pp. 85–86.

4. See examples in *al-Hilal* of that year, which published information in every issue about other journals appearing in the region. The subscription rate for *al-Ra'y al-'Amm* was 77 qurush per year, as against 15 qurush for *al-Iltifat*. See ibid., 1 May 1893, p. 132, and 1 September 1893, p. 30.

5. *Al-I'lam*, front pages of issues of 21 April 1885, 21 June 1885, 2 September 1886, 12 May 1887, 3 May 1888.

6. Iliyas, I, pp. 286–325; Yehoshu'a, *1908–1918*, p. 18; Sulayman, *Ta'rikh al-sihafa al-Filastiniyya*, p. 140; Shamikh, pp. 48, 53.

7. Issawi, *The Fertile Crescent*, p. 34, and tables on income by occupation on pp. 37, 89–91; idem, "Asymmetrical development," pp. 383, 399–400.

8. Calculated according to Issawi, *The Fertile Crescent*, p. 428.

9. *Al-Musawwar* (Cairo), 5 November 1984, p. 65.

10. *Lisan al-'Arab* (Alexandria), 1 August 1894, p. 1.

11. Issawi, *The Economic Development of Turkey*, pp. 332, 335–36; idem, *The Fertile Crescent*, pp. 427–29; Ghalib, pp. 45–46; 'Aqqad, p. 72.

12. Issawi, *The Fertile Crescent*, pp. 34–37, 89–91.

13. Shim'oni, p. 425.

14. Journalists fit into the category of skilled workers as measured by income: Reporters and non-senior editors in Egypt earned 5 to 10 pounds monthly (i.e., some 20 to 40 qurush daily) in the late nineteenth and early twentieth centuries, and possibly slightly more after World War I, while senior editors could make as much as 40 to 80 pounds monthly, or 200 to 400 qurush daily.

15. *Al-Hilal*, 15 December 1903, pp. 183–84.

16. Crabitès, p. 994.

17. Hamza, *Mustaqbal al-sihafa*, p. 31.

18. Reid, *Odyssey*, pp. 58–59.

19. Yehoshu'a, *1908–1919*, p. 23.

20. Istanbuli, pp. 7–8.

21. Crabitès, p. 1051. Similarly Musa, *al-Sihafa*, p. 20.

22. Baron, *The Women's Awakening*, pp. 67–68, quoting a British document; Fatima al-Yusuf, p. 108; McFadden, p. 23.

23. *Al-Hilal*, 15 November 1900, p. 125; 1 November 1903, p. 94. The minimum postage rate for journals in Egypt until 1900 was 10 para (0.25 qurush) for the first 50 grams and another 10 para for every additional 50 grams. Prices were brought down markedly that year to a rate of 1 milim (0.1 qurush) for the first 150 grams. See ibid.

24. A British document quoted in Baron, ibid.; Hamza, *Mustaqbal al-sihafa*, pp. 31–32; idem, *Adab al-maqala*, IV, pp. 42–44. See also Chapter 9 below. In 1882, Luis Sabunji, who established the Arabic-language newspaper *al-Ittihad al-'Arabi* in London, assessed the cost of producing the paper's first issue (1,000 copies) at 24-6-0 English pounds, and the next issue at some 15 pounds; see Kramer, p. 776.

25. Rida, *Ta'rikh al-ustadh*, I, pp. 107–9, 811.

26. *Filastin*, 21 March 1967, p. 4.

27. British documents quoted in Baron, *The Women's Awakening*, p. 68.

28. Fu'ad el-Khatib to Clayton, 19 July 1916 — FO882/14. I am grateful to Mr. Joshua Teitelbaum for his help in procuring this document.

29. Fatima al-Yusuf, pp. 111–12, 121–22, 140.

30. Krymskii, pp. 393, 485; Tarrazi, I, pp. 55–60.

31. Subhi, p. 88.

32. Kazziha, p. 379, quoting British documents.

33. Hamza, *Adab al-maqala*, V, pp. 112, 123–24; Murqus, pp. 28–31; Salih, p. 117; *L'Égypte indépendente*, p. 408; Mahmud, p. 13; Hamdi, pp. 36–37; McFadden, p. 21.

34. Hamza, *Adab al-maqala*, VI, p. 81; Subhi, pp. 55, 84; Jundi, *Tatawwur al-sihafa*, p. 201; Musa, *al-Sihafa*, p. 18; 'Aqqad, pp. 70–71. Journalists' salaries in Istanbul before 1908 were roughly on the same order: 12 Ottoman pounds ($60) a month for a senior editor, 9 ($45) for an experienced assistant editor, 5 ($25) for a translator, 2 to 6 ($10 to 30) for a correspondent; Reid, *Odyssey*, p. 37.

35. Hamza, *Adab al-maqala*, VI, 81; Goldschmidt, p. 323, note 3; Baron, *The Women's Awakening*, p. 67, quoting a British document.

36. Fatima al-Yusuf, p. 167.

37. Fatima al-Yusuf, p. 140; Subhi, pp. 104, 112, 125, 162; Mahmud, pp. 168, 203; Jundi, *Tatawwur al-sihafa*, p. 282, and see also Wynn, p. 394.

38. Babil, pp. 28–29.

39. Many examples in Iliyas, I, pp. 295ff.; *Filastin*, front pages of various issues from 1912; *Umm al-Qura*, front pages of issues from 1924.

40. McFadden, pp. 29ff., 75ff.

41. *Al-Muqattam*, 3 May 1889, pp. 3–4.

42. E.g., *al-Muqattam* of 3 May 1889, which contained ads on the entire fourth page and part of the third. Similarly, *al-Zahir* of 4 April 1906, where page 4 was entirely devoted to ads, in addition to ads on pp. 2 and 3.

43. E.g., *Lisan al-'Arab* (Alexandria) in 1894: 8 qurush per line on the front page, 6 on pages 2 and 3, and 4 on page 4; *al-Zahir* in 1903: 15 qurush per line on the front page, 10 on pages 2 and 3, and 8 on page 4.

44. *Al-Hilal*, 1 September 1892, p. 48; 1 July 1895, p. 840; 15 August 1895, pp. 926–31; 15 November 1900, p. 128.

45. *Filastin*, 21 March 1967, p. 3.

46. Abu al-Saʿd, pp. 151–52.

47. Advertising in the Egyptian press amounted to $2 million out of a total of $2.5 million, according to an assessment based on what McFadden termed "informed guesses." The rest was divided between the Lebanese press (approximately $250,000) and that of Syria, Jordan, and Iraq. McFadden, p. 81.

48. See, e.g., Mahmud, p. 168, where the author recounts the case of an Egyptian journalist, a graduate of the faculty of *adab*, who complained during the interwar period that his monthly wage of 15 pounds was lower than that of advertising department employees.

49. E.g., *Al-Zahra*, 1 January 1870, p. 3; *Lisan al-ʿArab* (Alexandria), 4 August 1894, p. 2; *al-Hilal*, 15 November 1898, p. 125; 1 October 1899, pp. 16–17; 1 October 1900, p. 32; *al-Majalla al-Jadida*, November 1929, first and last pages; *al-Ahwal*, 1 December 1929, p. 8; *al-Fawaʾid*, 8 February 1932, p. 1.

50. E.g., *al-Ahram*, 15 August 1876, p. 1; *al-Raʾy al-ʿAmm*, 14 November 1897, p. 305; *al-Muqtabas*, I (1324/1906), p. 1; many more examples in Iliyas, I, pp. 291ff. See also Reid, *Odyssey*, p. 46; Subhi, p. 102.

51. Musa, *al-Sihafa*, pp. 8–9; Iliyas, II, pp. 350–51.

52. *Al-Raʾy al-ʿAmm*, 13 March 1897, p. 69.

53. Quoted in Sulh, p. 99.

54. *Al-ʿIrfan*, 5 February 1909, p. 139.

55. *Al-Hilal*, 15 August 1900, p. 689; similarly 15 September 1900, pp. 726–27.

56. *Sawt al-Shaʿb*, 1 August 1924, p. 1.

57. Quoted in Sadr, pp. 61–62. Similarly *al-Ahram*, 14 November 1876, p. 1; *al-Jamiʿa al-ʿUthmaniyya*, 1 August 1899, p. 186; *al-Muqtataf*, 1 August 1903, pp. 666–68; *Hijaz*, 24 November 1908 and 23 May 1912, quoted in Shamikh, pp. 47, 86–87; *al-Quds*, 30 September 1913, quoted in Sulayman, *Taʾrikh al-sihafa al-Filastiniyya*, p. 65, and see also pp. 140–43; Baron, *The Women's Awakening*, pp. 69–70.

58. *Al-Hilal*, 15 December 1903, pp. 184–85.

59. *Al-Raʾy al-ʿAmm*, 14 November 1897, p. 306. Similarly Sulayman, *Taʾrikh al-sihafa al-Filastiniyya*, pp. 140ff.; Yehoshuʿa, *1908–1918*, pp. 19–21.

60. *Al-Tankit wal-Tabkit*, 16 June 1881, p. 16; *al-Hilal*, 1 December 1898, p. 160 (noting problems of this kind in Alexandria); 1 March 1900, p. 352; 15 June 1900, p. 576; 15 July 1900, p. 40. For similar examples, see *al-Iʿlam*, 17 January 1885, p. 1; *al-Raʾy al-ʿAmm*, 7 November 1897, p. 305; Iliyas, I, pp. 291, 299, 312; ʿAqqad, pp. 59–62. See also the report in *Lisan al-ʿArab* (Alexandria), 2 August 1894, p. 3, where the paper complains that some of its sales agents charge excessive rates for the paper and pocket the difference.

61. *Al-Munadi*, 2 July 1912, quoted in Sulayman, *Taʾrikh al-sihafa al-Filastiniyya*, p. 142.

62. E.g., *al-Raʾy al-ʿAmm*, 14 November 1897, p. 307; *al-ʿAfaf*, 13 January 1911, quoted by Baron, *The Women's Awakening*, p. 70.

63. *Al-Hilal*, 15 October 1898, p. 130.

64. *Al-Raʾy al-ʿAmm*, 14 November 1897, pp. 305–6.

65. Krymskii, p. 585; Tibawi, *The American Missionaries*, pp. 179–80; Jessup, p. 485; Tarrazi, III, pp. 75, 78; Baron, *The Women's Awakening*, p. 68; ʿAbduh, *Jaridat al-Ahram*, pp. 26, 38.

66. Istanbuli, pp. 9–10.

67. McFadden, pp. 28–31, and see the broader discussion in ff.

68. E.g., *L'Égypte indépendente*, p. 408. The survey cited *al-Ahram*, *al-Hilal*, *al-Muqtataf* (i.e., also *al-Muqattam*), *Misr*, and *al-Siyasa* among these wealthy institutions. One need only visit the large newspapers' "sumptuous" office buildings, the survey noted, to realize how wealthy these enterprises are.

69. McFadden, p. 29.

70. Kitchener in 1914, describing the Egyptian press, quoted in Baron, *The Women's Awakening*, p. 74.

71. Calculated according to Tarrazi, IV, pp. 16–20, 46–48, 80–82, 115–16, 128–30, 142–46, 198–208, 306–16.

Chapter 9

1. 'Abduh, *A'lam al-sihafa al-'Arabiyya*.

2. Tarrazi, IV, pp. 488–91 and passim.

3. Emile Zaydan in *al-Hilal*, March 1931, p. 698.

4. Sulayman, *Ta'rikh al-sihafa al-Filastiniyya*, pp. 155, 158, 171; Ghurayyib, pp. 8ff.; Samahan, pp. 228–30, 236–38; Rafa'il Batti, pp. 150–52; Sharim, pp. 126–27; Shamikh, pp. 184–85.

5. Kurd 'Ali, *Mudhakkirat*, I, pp. 50–55. See also below.

6. Musa, *Tarbiyya*, p. 41 and ff.

7. Babil, pp. 25–30, 62–65.

8. *Majallat al-Athar*, July 1911, p. 4; *al-Istiqlal* (Cairo), 15 January 1902, p. 3.

9. Ishaq Musa al-Husayni, *'Awdat al-safina*, p. 40. Similarly Malul, pp. 444–45.

10. Afghani-'Abduh, p. 230.

11. *Al-Liwa'*, 2 January 1900, quoted by Hamza, *Adab al-maqala*, V, p. 114.

12. *Al-Rayyahin*, 25 March 1932, p. 1.

13. Jurji Zaydan's letter to his father, 28 August 1887. I am grateful to Professor Thomas Philipp for his help in obtaining a photocopy of this letter. See also Philipp, *Zaydan*, p. 26.

14. Emile Zaydan in *al-Hilal*, March 1931, p. 698.

15. Rafa'il Batti, p. 35.

16. Musa, *al-Sihafa*, pp. 17–20; *al-Hilal*, January 1929, p. 308; March 1931, p. 698.

17. Musa, *al-Sihafa*, pp. 17–20. Similarly, for the image of the profession in Istanbul on the eve of World War I, cf. Emin, pp. 128–29.

18. *Al-Ahram*, 20 April 1936, pp. 9, 15.

19. Musa, *al-Sihafa*, p. 19.

20. *Al-Jazira*, 2 February 1925, p. 1.

21. Quoted in Jundi, *Tatawwur al-sihafa*, pp. 272–73.

22. Reid, "The rise of professions," pp. 27–28, 32, 48–51.

23. Malul, p. 444.

24. *Al-Mushir*, 17 July 1895, p. 2.

25. *Al-Hilal*, 15 May 1900, p. 508. Similarly *al-Muqtabas*, VI, 4 (May 1911), back cover.

26. Kurd 'Ali, *Mudhakkirat*, I, p. 52.

27. Quoted in Subhi, p. 102.

28. Hartmann, p. 13; Ghalib, p. 49; *al-Munadi*, 3 December 1912, quoted in Yehoshu'a, *1908–1918*, p. 14; Sinan Sa'id, p. 20.

29. Rida, *Ta'rikh al-ustadh*, I, p. 1005; 'Aqqad, pp. 88–89; Subhi, p. 55.

30. Iliyas, I, pp. 292ff.

31. Retrospective article in *Filastin*, 21 March 1967, p. 5.

32. *Al-Zaman*, 21 October 1927, quoted in Tikriti, pp. 182–83.

33. Jurji Zaydan, "al-Jara'id wa-wajibatuha wa-adabuha" ("The press, its duties and ethics"), *al-Hilal*, September 1895, pp. 9–17. See also Chapter 5 above.

34. *Al-Manar*, I (1897–1898), p. 660.

35. *Al-'Irfan*, 5 February 1909, pp. 135–36.

36. *Al-Kawkab*, 25 November 1919, reproduced in Karmi, p. 53.

37. Kurd 'Ali, *Khitat al-Sham*, IV, p. 94.

38. *Al-Hilal*, March 1931, pp. 697–704.

39. E.g., *al-Muqtabas*, 1328/1910, p. 344; Dasuqi and Dasuqi, pp. 118–19.

40. *Al-Hilal*, 15 July 1896, p. 852; *al-'Irfan*, 5 February 1909, p. 142. Similarly, *Umm al-Qura*, 25 June 1937, p. 1.

41. *Al-Hilal*, 1923, no. 11, pp. 95–108.

42. Khalil Thabit in *Al-Muqtataf*, May 1926, p. 491. The idea of establishing a school or a center for the study of journalism was again raised in 1932 by Taha Husayn, then dean of the Faculty of Arts in Cairo University, and this time won the approval of the press. See Hamza, *Azmat al-damir*, p. 152.

43. Kamal, pp. 64, 72–75; Samahan, pp. 119–23.

44. Muruwwa, pp. 466–70; Ghurayyib, pp. 111–15.

45. Reid, "The rise of professions," pp. 48–51; *al-Hilal*, 1923, no. 11, pp. 99–100; Muruwwa, pp. 470–72.

46. Babil, pp. 162–63.

47. *Al-Hilal*, 1923, no. 11, p. 99, and see also p. 103.

48. Musa, *al-Sihafa*, pp. 17ff.

49. Reid, "The rise of professions," pp. 25–26.

50. The discussion of Kurd 'Ali's career is based on: Kurd 'Ali, *Mudhakkirat*, I, pp. 50–68, 107–10; Iliyas, I, pp. 127–31, 136–39; II, 403–6, 457–59; Seikaly; Tauber, "The press," pp. 173–74.

51. Kurd 'Ali, *Mudhakkirat*, I, p. 61.

52. E.g., title page in issues of *Al-Muqtabas*, VI (1329/1911).

53. Seikaly, p. 127.

54. Ibid., pp. 107–8.

55. Iliyas, I, pp. 131, 139.

56. Babil, pp. 39–40; Kurd 'Ali, *Mudhakkirat*, I, pp. 62–63.

57. Salih, pp. 17–21, 69–70; Baha al-Din, pp. 65–66; Zakhura, pp. 537–39. On *al-Adab*, see Tarrazi, III, pp. 30–31.

58. Yusuf, quoted by Jundi, *Tatawwur al-sihafa*, p. 67; Salih, p. 78. Madi demanded back his initial investment of 100 pounds, which put the entire venture in jeopardy. Fortunately for Yusuf, Sa'd Zaghlul, who was a friend, and a few other comrades came to his rescue and paid Madi his share, enabling the paper to continue to appear, with Yusuf as sole owner.

59. See further in Salih, pp. 23–24, 34ff., 60–65, 74–77, 108–10.

60. Jundi, *Tatawwur al-sihafa*, pp. 68–69; Hamza, *Mustaqbal al-sihafa*, p. 32; idem, *Adab al-maqala*, V, p. 121; Tarrazi, III, p. 39 (citing a *qasida* composed to mark the event).

61. Salih, pp. 35–41, 110–14.

62. There were exceptions, e.g., *al-Ra'y al-'Amm*, an old adversary of Yusuf's, which attacked him for printing "stolen information." See issue of 31 October 1896, pp. 329–30.

63. Hamza, *Adab al-maqala*, IV, pp. 107–11; Salih, pp. 82–95, 115.

64. Hamza, *Adab al-maqala*, IV, pp. 111–22; Salih, pp. 45–59; Baha al-Din, pp. 63–85. Once the trial was over, Shaykh al-Sadat, his status vindicated, relented and agreed to the marriage, but the affair had a painful effect on Yusuf and reportedly left him a broken man.

65. Musa, *al-Sihafa*, p. 17.

66. Musa, *Tarbiyya*, pp. 29–49. As Egger's meticulous study of Musa's career shows, there are numerous contradictions and inaccuracies in Musa's autobiography (*Tarbiyya*), apparently a result of his having written it many years after the events themselves. E.g., Egger, p. 29, note 1; p. 37, notes 115, 118; p. 107, note 3; and passim.

67. "Nitsha wa-ibn al-insan," *al-Muqtataf*, June 1909, pp. 570–73.

68. Reid, *Odyssey*, pp. 122–26.

69. See Egger, pp. 55–60.

70. Musa, *Tarbiyya*, p. 152.

71. Gershoni-Jankowski, passim.

72. Musa, *Tarbiyya*, pp. 158–59; idem, *al-Sihafa*, pp. 65–67.

73. Musa, *Tarbiyya*, p. 159.

74. Istanbuli, pp. 6–7; Iliyas, II, p. 561. See also Chapter 8 above.

75. Istanbuli, pp. 10–12.

76. Istanbuli, pp. 12–17; Iliyas, II, pp. 561, 565–68.

Conclusion

1. *Al-Hilal*, 1 September 1895, p. 14.

2. Wynn, p. 392.

3. *Taqvim-i Vekayi*, first issue, quoted by Orhonlu. See also Chapter 1.

4. For a discussion of the two states of the press, see Rugh, Chapters 2–4. Rugh depicts the press of the former group of states as a "mobilization press" and that of the latter group as a "loyalist press."

References

Newspapers and Journals

(Years indicated are those explored for this study)

Abu Nazzara (Cairo and Paris), 1878–1890, 1898–1899.
Abu Nuwwas al-'Asri (Damascus), 1921.
Al-Ahram (Alexandria and Cairo), 1876–1945.
Al-Ahwal (Beirut), 1929–1930.
Al-'Alam (Cairo), 1910.
Alif Ba' (Damascus), 1944–1945.
A'mal al-Jam'iyya al-Suriyya (Beirut), 1852.
Anis al-Jalis (Cairo), 1899–1902.
Al-Arghul (Cairo), 1896–1897.
Al-'Asr al-Jadid (Alexandria), 1881.
Al-Balagh (Beirut), 1916.
Al-Balagh (Cairo), 1934–1939, 1942–1945.
Barid al-Hijaz (Medina), 1924.
Al-Bashir (Beirut), 1870–1871, 1878–1900.
Al-Bassir (Paris), 1881–1882.
Bayrut (Beirut), 1916.
Bayrut (Beirut), 1936–1937.
Al-Bayyan (Cairo), 1897–1898.
Birjis Baris (Paris), 1859–1866.
Al-Diya' (Cairo), 1899–1906.
Fatat al-Sharq (Cairo), 1906, 1910, 1925, 1927.
Al-Fawa'id (Beirut), 1932–1933.
Al-Fayyum (Fayyum), 1895.
Filastin (Jaffa), 1912.
Hadiqat al-Akhbar (Beirut), 1858–1868.
Al-Haqiqa (Beirut), 1916.
Al-Hayah (Cairo), 1899.
Al-Hayah (Jerusalem), 1930–1931.
Al-Huquq (Cairo), 1886.
Al-Hilal (Cairo), 1892–1945.
Al-I'lam (Cairo), 1885–1889.
Al-Insan (Istanbul), 1884.

Al-Iqbal (Beirut), 1916.
Al-'Irfan (Sidon), 1909–1925.
Al-Istiqlal (Cairo), 1902.
Al-Istiqlal (Baghdad), 1934–1935.
Al-I'tidal (Cairo), 1910.
Al-Ittihad (Paris), 1880.
Al-Ittihad al-'Arabi (Tul Karm, Palestine), 1925–1927.
Al-Jami'a (Alexandria), 1899–1903.
Al-Janna (Beirut), 1879–1884.
Al-Jarida (Cairo), 1909–1913.
Al-Jarida al-'Askariyya al-Misriyya (Cairo), 1865.
Jaridat Arkan Harb al-Jaysh al-Misri (Cairo), 1874.
Al-Jawa'ib (Istanbul), 1868–1884.
Al-Jazira (Jaffa), 1924–1926.
Al-Jazira al-'Arabiyya (Amman), 1939.
Al-Jinan (Beirut), 1870–1886.
Kashf al-Niqab (Paris), 1894–1895.
Kawkab al-Mashriq (Paris), 1882–1883.
Kawkab al-Sharq (Cairo), 1926–1928, 1933, 1937.
Al-Lata'if (Cairo), 1887–1896.
Lisan al-Hal (Beirut), 1877–1932.
Lisan al-'Arab (Alexandria), 1894–1897.
Lisan al-'Arab (Damascus), 1918–1919.
Al-Liwa' (Cairo), 1900.
Al-Liwa' al-Misri (Cairo), 1921–1925.
Madrasat al-Funun (Istanbul), 1882–1883.
Al-Majalla al-Jadida (Cairo), 1929–1938.
Majallat Lughat al-'Arab (Baghdad), 1911–1912, 1929–1931.
Al-Manar (Cairo), 1897–1935.
Al-Mawsu'at (Cairo), 1898–1900.
Mir'at al-Sharq (Jerusalem), 1926–1928.
Al-Misbah (Beirut), 1899.
Misr al-Fatah (Cairo), 1908–1909.
Misr al-Qahira (Paris), 1879–1880.
Al-Misri (Cairo), 1937–1939.
Al-Mu'ayyad (Cairo), 1900, 1907–1914.
Al-Mudhik al-Mubki (Damascus), 1929–1931.
Al-Mufid (Beirut), 1911–1913.
Al-Mufid (Damascus), 1919–1920.
Al-Muqattam (Cairo), 1889–1945.
Al-Muqtabas (Cairo and Damascus), 1906–1914.
al-Muqtataf (Beirut and Cairo), 1876–1945.
Al-Mushir (Alexandria), 1895–1898.
Al-Nahla (Beirut and London), 1870, 1877–1880.
Nafir Suriya (Beirut), 1860–1861.
Al-Nashra al-Usbu'iyya (Beirut), 1871–1873, 1877, 1885–1886, 1888, 1891–
     1900.
Nur al-Islam (Cairo), 1931.
Al-Nur al-Tawfiqi (Cairo), 1881–1889.
Al-Qabas (Damascus), 1928–1938.

Al-Qahira (Cairo), 1885–1886.
Al-Qahira al-Hurra (Cairo), 1886–1888.
Al-Qibla (Mecca), 1916–1924.
Al-Ra'is (Junya), 1900–1902.
Al-Raja' (Paris), 1895, 1898–1899.
Rawdat al-Madaris (Cairo), 1870, 1875–1877.
Al-Ra'y al-'Amm (Cairo), 1894, 1896–1897.
Al-Rayyahin (Beirut), 1932.
Al-Risala (Cairo), 1933–1939.
Al-Sada (Paris), 1876–1877.
Sawt al-Ahali (Baghdad), 1944.
Sawt al-Sha'b (Bethlehem), 1924–1927.
Al-Sha'b (Cairo), 1910.
Al-Sharq (Damascus), 1917.
Al-Siyasa (Cairo), 1922–1934.
Al-Siyasa al-Usbu'iyya (Cairo), 1926–1931, 1937–1938.
Al-Tankit wal-Tabkit (Alexandria), 1881.
Al-Thaghr (Basra), 1939.
Thamarat al-Funun (Beirut), 1875–1882, 1889–1897.
Al-Thaqafa (Cairo), 1939.
Umm al-Qura (Medina), 1935–1945.
Al-'Urwa al-Wuthqa (Paris), 1884.
Al-Ustadh (Cairo), 1892–1893.
'Utarid (Marseille and Paris), 1858–1859.
Wadi al-Nil (Cairo), 1868–1870.
Al-Wafd al-Misri (Cairo), 1938.
Al-Waqa'i' al-Misriyya (Cairo), 1828–1833.
Al-Yarmuk (Haifa), 1925–1928.
Zahla al-Fatah (Zahla), 1910–1911, 1922, 1924.
Al-Zahir (Cairo), 1903–1908.
Al-Zahra (Beirut), 1870.

British Archival Material

FO 371/, FO 882/ — Foreign Office documents
WO 157/ — War Office documents

Works in Arabic Cited in the Text

'Abd al-Hamid al-thani. *Mudhakkirati al-siyasiyya 1891–1908*. Beirut, 1977.
'Abd al-Rahman, 'Awatif. *Al-Sihafa al-Sahyuniyya fi Misr 1897–1954*. Cairo, 1979.
'Abd al-Rahman, Huda. "Asalib wa-mu'alajat al-sihafa al-nisa'iyya fi al-'Iraq qabla al-arba'inat," in Wizarat al-I'lam. *Dirasat fi al-sihafa al-'Iraqiyya*. Baghdad, 1972, pp. 74–86.
'Abd al-Sayyid, Mikha'il. *Sulwan al-shaji fi al-radd 'ala Ibrahim al-Yaziji*. Istanbul, 1872.
'Abduh, Ibrahim. *A'lam al-sihafa al-'Arabiyya*. Cairo, 1948.
———. *Jaridat al-Ahram, ta'rikh wa-fann 1875–1964*. Cairo, 1964.
———. *Mihnat al-sihafa wa-waliy al-ni'am*. Cairo, 1978.

————. *Ruz al-Yusuf, sira wa-sahifa.* Cairo, 1961.

————. "Sahm Misr fi al-sihafa al-sharqiyya," *al-Thaqafa*, 24 March 1942, pp. 377–80.

————. *Ta'rikh al-tiba'a wal-sihafa fi Misr khilal al-hamla al-Faransawiyya 1798–1801.* Cairo, 1949.

————. *Ta'rikh al-waqa'i' al-Misriyya, 1828–1942.* Cairo, 1983.

————. *Tatawwur al-sihafa al-Misriyya 1798–1981.* 4th ed. Cairo, 1982.

Abu al-Sa'd, 'Adnan 'Abd al-Mun'im. *Tatawwur al-khabar wa-asalib tahririhi fi al-sihafa al-'Iraqiyya mundhu nash'atiha hatta sanat 1917.* Baghdad, 1973.

Abu Zayid, Faruq. *Safahat majhula min 'asr al-tanwir al-suhufi.* Cairo, [1971].

————. *Al-Sihafa al-'Arabiyya al-muhajira.* Cairo, 1985.

al-Adhami, Mustafa Hashim. "Jaridat al-hukuma al-'Iraqiyya," in Wizarat al-I'lam. *Dirasat fi al-sihafa al-'Iraqiyya.* Baghdad, 1972, pp. 41–52.

al-Afghani, Jamal al-Din and Muhammad 'Abduh. *Al-'Urwa al-wuthqa wal-thawra al-tahririyya al-kubra.* Edited by Salah al-Din al-Bustani. Cairo, 1958.

al-'Akari, Dahir. *Al-Sihafa al-thawriyya fi Lubnan 1925–1975.* Beirut, 1975.

Amin, Mustafa. *Li-Kull maqal azma.* Cairo, 1979.

al-'Aqqad, Mahmud 'Abbas. *Hayat qalam.* Cario, 196-?

al-Arsuzi, Zaki. *Al-Mu'allafat al-kamila.* 4 vols. Damascus, 1972.

'Attara, Qustaky Ilyas. *Ta'rikh takwin al-suhuf al-Misriyya.* Alexandria, 1928.

"Awwal ta'til idari fi al-sihafa al-Bayrutiyya," *Awraq Lubnaniyya*, February 1957, pp. 65–68.

'Aziz Bik. *Al-Istikhbarat wal-jasusiyya fi Lubnan wa-Suriya wa-Filastin khilal al-harb al-'alamiyya.* Beirut, 1937.

al-'Azm, Khalid. *Mudhakkirat.* Beirut, [1972]. Vol. 3.

Babil, Nassuh. *Sihafa wa-siyasa. Suriya fi al-qarn al-'ishrin.* London, 1987.

Badawi, Ahmad Ahmad. *Rifa'a al-Tahtawi bek.* Cairo, 1950.

Batti, Fa'iq. *Sihafat al-ahzab wa-ta'rikh al-haraka al-wataniyya.* Baghdad, 1969.

————. *Al-Sihafa al-'Iraqiyya, miladuha wa-tatawwuruha.* Baghdad, 1961.

————. "Tatawwur al-maqal fi al-sihafa al-'Iraqiyya," in Wizarat al-I'lam. *Dirasat fi al-sihafa al-'Iraqiyya.* Baghdad, 1972, pp. 28–40.

Batti, Rafa'il. *Al-Sihafa fi al-'Iraq.* Cairo, 1955.

Baha' al-Din, Ahmad. *Ayyam laha ta'rikh.* Cairo, 1967. Vol. I.

al-Bustani, Butrus. *Khitab fi al-hay'a al-ijtima'iyya wal-muqabala bayn al-'awa'id al-'Arabiyya wal-ifranjiyya.* Beirut, 1869.

al-Bustani, Salah al-Din. *Suhuf Bunabart fi Misr (1798–1801).* 9 vols. Cairo, 1971.

al-Chadirchi, Kamil. *Mudhakkirat Kamil al-Chadirchi wa-ta'rikh al-hizb al-watani al-dimuqrati.* Beirut, 1970.

Daghir, Yusuf As'ad. *Qamus al-sihafa al-Lubnaniyya, 1858–1974.* Beirut, 1978.

al-Dahdah, Salim. "Al-Kunt Rushayd al-Dahdah wa-usratuhu," *al-Mashriq*, 1 May 1951, pp. 385–96; 15 May 1951, pp. 456–61; 1 June 1951, pp. 489–98.

Dasuqi, Yusuf and Muhammad Kamil Dasuqi. *Fi al-sihafa.* Cairo, 1929?

Faydi, Sulayman. *Fi ghamrat al-nidal, mudhakkirat Sulayman Faydi.* Baghdad, 1952.

Gahlib, 'Abd al-Rahim. *Mi'at 'am min ta'rikh al-sihafa: Lisan al-Hal.* Beirut, 1988.

al-Ghassani, Muhammad ibn 'Abd al-Wahhab. *Rihlat al-wazir fi iftikak al-asir.* Tangier, 1940.

al-Ghaytani, Jamal. *Mustafa Amin yatadhakkar*. Cairo, 1983.

al-Ghurayyib, Mishal. *Al-Sihafa al-Lubnaniyya wal-'Arabiyya*. Beirut, 1982.

Hamdi, Muhammad. *Al-Sihafa wal-tiba'a, mawsu'a 'ilmiyya fi al-mihnatayn*. Cairo, 194–?

Hamza, 'Abd al-Latif. *Adab al-maqala al-sahafiyya fi Misr*. 8 vols. Cairo, 1958–1963.

———. *Azmat al-damir al-suhufi*. Cairo, 1960.

———. *Mustaqbal al-sihafa*. Cairo, 1961.

———. *Al-Sihafa wal-mujtama'*, CAiro, 1963.

Hamza, 'Abd al-Qadir. "Sahibat al-jalala al-sihafa, a'zam quwwa taqud al-jamahir wal-hukumat," *al-Hilal*, XLII, November 1933, pp. 73–5.

Hasan, Muhammad 'Abd al-Ghani and 'Abd al-'Aziz al-Dasuqi. *Rawdat al-madaris, nash'atuha wa-ittijahatuha al-adabiyya wal-'ilmiyya*. Cairo, 1975.

al-Hasani, 'Abd al-Razaq. *Ta'rikh al-sihafa al-'Iraqiyya*. Second printing. Baghdad, 1957.

Haykal, Muhammad Husayn, Ibrahim 'Abd al-Qadir al-Mazini and Muhammad 'Abdallah 'Inan. *Al-Siyasa al-Misriyya wal-inqilab al-dusturi*. Cairo, 1931.

al-Hilal. *Al-Kitab al-dhahabi*. Cairo, 1942.

Hilmi, Ibrahim. "Al-Tiba'a fi Dar al-Salam wal-Najaf wa-Karbala'," *Majallat Lughat al-'Arab* (Baghdad), VII, January 1913, pp. 303–9.

al-Husayni, Ishaq Musa. *'Awdat al-safina*. Jerusalem [1945].

Ibrahim, Zahida. *Kashshaf bil-jara'id wal-majalat al-'Iraqiyya*. Baghdad, 1971.

al-Ibyari, 'Abd al-Hadi Naja. *Al-Najm al-thaqib fi al-muhakama bayn al-Birjis wal-Jawa'ib*. Cairo, 1279/1863.

Iliyas, Juzif. *Tatawwur al-sihafa al-Suriyya fi mi'at 'am (1865–1965)*. 2 vols. Beirut, 1982–1983.

'Inan, 'Abdallah. "Al-Sihafa fi 'asr Isma'il," *al-Katib al-Misri*, March 1947, pp. 260–63.

Ishaq, Adib. *al-Durar*. Beirut, 1975.

al-Istanbuli, Mahmud Mahdi. *Dhikrayat*. Damascus, 1378/1958.

'Izzat, 'Izzat 'Ali. *Al-Sihafa fi duwal al-khalij al-'Arabi*. Baghdad, 1983.

al-Jabarti, 'Abd al-Rahman. *'Aja'ib al-athar fi al-tarajim wal-akhbar*. 3 vols. Beirut: Dar al-Jabal, n.d.

———. *Ta'rikh muddat al-Fransis bi-Misr*. Translated by Shmuel Moreh. Leiden, 1975.

al-Jam'iyya al-Suriyya lil-'ulum wal-funun, 1848–1852. Beirut, 1990.

Jayyid, Ramzi Mikha'il. *Tatawwur al-khabar fi al-sihafa al-Misriyya*. Cario, 1985.

al-Jumayyil, Antun. *Sani'u al-jarida wa-wajibuna al-suhufi*. Cairo, 1938?

al-Jundi, Anwar. *Al-Sihafa al-siyasiyya fi Misr*. Cairo, 1962.

———. *Tatawwur al-sihafa al-'Arabiyya fi Misr*. Cairo, 1967.

Kamal, Mustafa. *'Ali Mahir basha, al-mathal al-a'la lil-umma wal-watan wal-sihafa wal-adab*. Cairo, 1938.

Kanz al-ragha'ib fi muntakhabat al-jawa'ib. 7 vols. Istanbul, 1871–1880.

al-Karmi, 'Abd al-Karim. *Ahmad Shakir al-Karmi, mukhtarat min atharihi*. Damascus, 1964.

Khaddur, Adib. *Al-Sihafa al-Suriyya, nash'atuha, tatawwuruha, waqi'uha al-rahin*. Damascus, 1972.

Khuri, Yusuf. *Al-Sihafa al-'Arabiyya fi Filastin, 1876–1948*. Beirut, 1976.

Khurshid, Faruq. *Bayn al-adab wal-sihafa*. Cairo, 1972.

Al-Kitab al-dhahabi li-Yubil al-muqtataf al-khamsini 1876–1926. Cairo, 1927.

Kurd 'Ali, Muhammad. *Khitat al-Sham*. Damascus, 1926. Vol. 4.

———. *al-Mudhakkirat*. 3 vols. Damascus, 1948–1949.

Mahmud, Hafiz. *Asrar suhufiyya*. Cairo, 1975.

al-Maqdisi, Rafiq. *Fann al-sihafa*. Damascus, 195-?

al-Mardini, Zuhayr. "Qissat nisf qarn min al-sihafa al-sakhira," *al-Dustur* (London), 27 February 1984.

al-Marsafi, Husayn. *Risalat al-kalim al-thaman*. Cairo, 1881.

Murqus, Yuaqim Rizq. *Sihafat al-hizb al-watani 1907–1912, dirasa ta'rikhiyya*. Cairo, 1985.

Muruwwa, Adib. *Al-Sihafa al-'Arabiyya, nash'atuha wa-tatawwuruha*. Beirut, 1961.

Musa, Salama. *Al-Sihafa, hirfa wa-risala*. Cairo, 1962.

———. *Tarbiyyat Salama Musa*. Cairo, 1962.

al-Nu'aymi, Hazim. *Al-Hurriyya wal-sihafa fi Lubnan*. Cairo, 1989.

al-Rafi'i, 'Abd al-Rahman. *Mudhakkirati 1889–1951*. Cairo, 1952.

———. *Muhammad Farid*. Cairo, 1941.

———. *Mustafa Kamil*. Cairo, 1950.

al-Rayyis, Munir. *Al-Kitab al-dhahabi lil-thawrat al-wataniyya fi al-mashriq al-'Arabi*. Beirut, 1967. Vol. 2.

al-Rayyis, Najib. *Nidal*. Damascus, 1934.

Rida, Rashid. *Ta'rikh al-ustadh al-imam al-shaykh Muhammad 'Abduh*. Cairo, 1931. Vol. 1.

al-Rifa'i, Shams al-Din. *Ta'rikh al-sihafa al-Suriyya*. 2 vols. Cairo, 1969.

Sa'ada, Jurj 'Arij. *Al-Nahda al-suhufiyya fi Lubnan*. Beirut, 1960.

———. *Al-Sihafa fi Lubnan*. Beirut, 1965.

Sabat, Khalil. *Ta'rikh al-tiba'a fi al-sharq al-'Arabi*. Cairo, 1958.

———. *Wasa'il al-i'lam, nash'atuha wa-tatawwuruha*. Cairo, 1976.

al-Sadr, Muhammad Mahdi. "Min sihafat al-hazl 'habazbuz'," *in* Wizarat al-I'lam. *Dirasat fi al-sihafa al-'Iraqiyya*. Baghdad, 1972, pp. 53–73.

Sa'id, Amin. *Al-Thawra al-'Arabiyya al-kubra*. Cairo, 1934. Vol. 1.

Sa'id, Sinan. "Hurriyyat al-sihafa hatta 'am 1917," *in* Wizarat al-I'lam. *Dirasat fi al-sihafa al-'Iraqiyya*. Baghdad, 1972, pp. 7–27.

Salih, Sulayman. *Al-Shaykh 'Ali Yusuf wa-jaridat al-Mu'ayyad*. Cairo, 1990.

Samahan, Mahmud. *Al-Sihafa*. Cairo, 1939.

Sami, Amin. *Al-Ta'lim fi Misr fi sanatay 1914, 1915*. Cairo, 1917.

———. *Taqwim al-Nil*. Cairo, 1928. Vol. 2.

Sarkis, Salim. *Ghara'ib al-maktubji*. Cairo, 1896.

al-Sawi, Ahmad Husayn. *Fajr al-sihafa fi Misr*. Cairo, 1975.

al-Sayyid, Ahmad Lutfi. *Qissat Hayati*. Cairo, 1962.

al-Shamikh, Muhammad 'Abd al-Rahman. *Nash'at al-sihafa fi al-mamlaka al-'Arabiyya al-Sa'udiyya*. Cairo, 1982.

Shams, Riyad. *Hurriyyat al-ra'y*. Cairo, 1947.

Sharim, Amina Bashir. *Al-Sihafa al-Urdunniyya wa-'alaqatuha bi-qawanin al-matbu'at wal-nashr 1920–1983*. Amman, 1984.

Shaykhu, Luis. *Al-Adab al-'Arabiyya fi al-qarn al-tasi' 'ashr*. 2 vols. Beirut, 1924.

al-Shayyal, Jamal al-Din. *Ta'rikh al-tarjama fi Misr fi 'ahd al-hamla al-Faransawiyya*. Cairo, 1950.

———. *Ta'rikh al-tarjama wal-haraka al-thaqafiyya fi Misr fi 'asr Muhammad 'Ali*. Cairo, 1950.

Shusha, Muhammad al-Sayyid. *Asrar al-sihafa*. Cairo, 1959.

Sidqi, Isma'il. *Mudhakkirati*. Cairo, 1950.

Subhi, Samir. *Fi dahaliz al-sihafa*. Cairo, 1982.

Sulayman, Muhammad. *Al-Sihafa al-Filastiniyya wa-qawanin al-intidab al-Baritani*. Nicosia, 1988.

———. *Ta'rikh al-sihafa al-Filastiniyya 1876–1976*. Vol. 1: *1876–1918*. Nicosia, 1987.

al-Sulh, 'Imad. *Ahmad Faris al-Shidyaq, atharuhu wa-'asruhu*. Beirut, 1987.

al-Tahtawi, Rifa'a Rafi'. *Takhlis al-ibriz ila talkhis Bariz*. Cairo, 3rd. ed., 1958.

Tarrazi, Philip di. *Ta'rikh al-sihafa al-'Arabiyya*. 4 vols. Beirut, 1913, 1914, 1933.

al-Tikriti, Munir Bakr. *Al-Sihafa al-'Iraqiyya wa-ittijahatuha al-siyasiyya walijtima'iyya wal-thaqafiyya min 1869–1921*. Baghdad, 1969.

al-Tunji, Muhammad and Ahmad Hafiyan. *Al-Tiba'a wa-risalatuha al-qawmiyya fi 'alamina al-'Arabi*. Aleppo, 1960.

al-'Utayfi, Jamal al-Din. *Hurriyyat al-sihafa wafqa tashri'at al-jumhuriyya al-'Arabiyya al-muttahida*. Cairo, 1971.

Wizarat al-I'lam. *Dirasat fi al-sihafa al-'Iraqiyya*. Baghdad, 1972.

Yehoshu'a, Ya'qub. *Ta'rikh al-sihafa al-'Arabiyya fi Filastin fi al-'ahd al-'Uthmani (1908–1918)*. Jerusalem, 1974.

———. *Ta'rikh al-sihafa al-'Arabiyya al-Filastiniyya fi bidayat 'ahd al-intidab al-Baritani 'ala Filastin, 1919–1929*. Haifa, 1981.

———. *Ta'rikh al-sihafa al-'Arabiyya al-Filastiniyya fi nihayat 'ahd al-intidab al-Baritani 'ala Filastin, 1930–1948*. Jerusalem, 1983.

al-Yaziji, Ibrahim. *Lughat al-jara'id*. Cairo, ca. 1900.

Yubil lisan al-hal al-dhahabi, 1877–1927. Beirut, 1928.

al-Yusuf, Fatima. *Dhikrayat*. Cairo, 1976.

al-Yusuf, Niqula. *A'lam min al-Iskandariyya*. Alexandria, 1969.

Zakhura, Iliyas. *Mir'at al-'asr fi ta'rikh wa-rusum akabir al-rijal bi-Misr*. Cairo, 1897.

Zaydan, Jurji. *Tarajim mashahir al-sharq fi al-qarn al-tasi' 'ashar*. 2 vols. Cairo, 1922.

———. *Ta'rikh adab al-lugha al-'Arabiyya*. Cairo, 1957. Vol. 4.

Works in Other Languages Cited in the Text

Aboul Fath, Mahmoud. *The al-Misri Case*. [Geneva?], 1954.

Abu Lughod, Ibrahim. "The mass media and Egyptian village life," *Social Forces*, October 1963, pp. 97–104.

Adams, Charles C. *Islam and Modernism in Egypt*. London, 1933.

Adwan, Nawaf. *Le livre et la lecture en Irak*. Paris, 1980.

Ahmed, Jamal Mohammed. *The Intellectual Origins of Egyptian Nationalism*. Oxford, 1960.

Arnon-Ohanna, Yuval. *Herev mi-Bayit*. Tel Aviv, 1981.

Artin, Yacoub. "Etudes statistiques sur la press égyptienne," *Bulletin de l'Institut Égyptien*. 1905, pp. 89–97.

———. *L'Instruction publique en Egypte*. Paris, 1890.

Ayalon, Ami. *Language and Change in the Arab Middle East*. New York and Oxford, 1987.

———. "Sihafa: the Arab experiment in journalism," *MES*, XXVIII, 2 (April 1992), pp. 258–80.

Baron, Beth. "Readers and the women's press in Egypt," *Poetics Today*, XV, 2. Forthcoming.

————. *The Women's Awakening in Egypt: Culture, Society, and the Press*. New Haven and London, 1994.

de Beaumarchais, Pierre A[ugustine] Caron. *The Barber of Seville and the Marriage of Figaro*. Trans. Vincent Luciani. New York, 1964.

Berkes, Niyazi. *The Development of Secularism in Turkey*. Montreal, 1964.

Boktor, Amir. *School and Society in the Valley of the Nile*. Cairo, 1936.

Borthwick, Bruce M. "The Islamic sermon as a channel of political communication," *MEJ*, XXI (1967), pp. 299–313.

Boustany, Salaheddine. *The Press During the French Expedition in Egypt, 1798-1801*. Cairo, 1954.

Bouvat, L. "Al-Kibla, journal arabe de la Mecque," *RMM*, XXXIV (1917–1918), pp. 320–28.

Bowring, John. *Report on the Commercial Statistics of Syria*. New York, 1973 (reprint of first edition of 1840).

Boyd, Douglas A. *Broadcasting in the Arab World. A Survey of Radio and Television*. Philadelphia, 1982.

Brown, Horatio F. *The Venetian Printing Press 1469–1800*. Amsterdam, 1969.

Browne, E.G. *The Persian Press and Persian Journalism*. A lecture delivered to the Persian Society on 23 May 1913. London, 1913.

Brugman, J. *An Introduction to the History of Modern Arabic Literature in Egypt*. Leiden, 1984.

Buheiry, Marwan R. (ed.). *Intellectual Life in the Arab East 1890–1939*. Beirut, 1981.

Burgoyne, Elizabeth. *Gertrude Bell: From Her Personal Papers*. London, 1961. Vol. 2.

Carter, B.L. *The Copts in Egyptian Politics 1918–1952*. Cairo, 1988.

Centre d'études de politique étrangère, Paris. Groupe d'études de l'Islam. *L'Égypte indépendente*. Paris, 1938.

Charles-Roux, F. *Bonaparte: Governor of Egypt*. London, 1937.

Chartier, Roger. *The Cultural Uses of Print in Early Modern France*. Princeton, 1987.

Cioeta, Donald J. "Ottoman censorship in Lebanon and Syria, 1876–1908," *IJMES*, X, (1979), pp. 167–86.

Cleveland, William L. "The role of Islam as political ideology in the first World War," *in* Edward Ingram (ed.). *National and International Politics in the Middle East. Essays in Honour of Elie Kedourie*. London, 1986, pp. 84–101.

Cole, Juan R.I. *Colonialism and Revolution in the Middle East. Social and Cultural Origins of Egypt's 'Urabi Movement*. Princeton, 1993.

Cooper, Elizabeth. *The Women of Egypt*. London, 1914.

Crabbs, Jack. *The Writing of History in Nineteenth-Century Egypt*. Detroit and Cairo, 1984.

Crabitès, Piérre. "Journalism along the Nile: the press in a country where editors often put politics before business," *Asia*, XXVII (December 1927), pp. 992–1052.

Cromer, Earl of (Sir Evelyn Baring). *Modern Egypt*. 2 vols. New York, 1908.

Darnton, Robert. *The Kiss of Lamourette. Reflections and Cultural History*. New York, 1990.

Davison, Roderic H. "How the Ottoman government adjusted to a new institution: the newspaper press," *in* Sabri Akural (ed.). *Turkic Culture: Continuity and Change*. Bloomington, Indiana, 1987, pp. 17–26.

De Kay, James Elsworth. *Sketches of Turkey in 1831 and 1832 by an American*. New York, 1833.

Egger, Vernon. *Salamah Musa and the Rise of Professional Classes in Egypt, 1909–1939*. New York, 1986.

L'Égypte indépendente, see Centre d'études de politique étrangère.

Egyptian Government. Ministry of Finance. Statistical Department. *The Census of Egypt, Taken in 1907*. Cairo, 190–?

———. *The Census of Egypt, Taken in 1917*. 2 vols. Cairo, 1920–1921.

Emin, Ahmed. *The Development of Modern Turkey as Measured by Its Press*. New York, 1914.

Farag, Nadia. "The Lewis affair and the fortunes of al-Muqtataf," *MES*, VIII (1972), pp. 73–83.

Farah, Caesar. "Censorship and freedom of expression in Ottoman Syria and Egypt," *in* William W. Haddad and William Ochsenwald (eds.), *Nationalism in a Non-National State, the Dissolution of the Ottoman Empire*. Columbus, Ohio, 1977, pp. 151–94.

Fyfe, Hamilton H. *The New Spirit in Egypt*. London, 1911.

al-Gailani, Ghazi Ismail. *Iraq's Journalism and Political Conflict 1956-1963*. Unpublished Ph.D diss., University of Iowa, 1971.

Gendzier, Irene L. *The Practical Vision of Ya'aqub Sanu'*. Cambridge, Mass., 1966.

Gerçek, Selim Nüzhet. *Türk Gazeteciliği*. Istanbul, 1931.

Gershoni, Israel. "The Reader's 'another production'. The reception of Haykal's biography of Muhammad and the shift of Egyptian intellectuals to Islamic subjects in the 1930s," *Poetics Today*, XV, 2. Forthcoming.

Gershoni, Israel and James Jankowski. *Egypt, Islam and the Arabs: the Search for Egyptian Nationhood, 1900–1930*. New York and Oxford, 1986.

Gibb, Hamilton A.R. "Studies in contemporary Arabic literature," *in* his *Studies on the Civilization of Islam*, edited by Stanford J. Shaw and William R. Polk. Princeton, 1982, pp. 245–58.

Goody, Jack (ed.). *Literacy in Traditional Societies*. Cambridge, 1968.

Gouvernement Egyptien. *Recensement général de l'Egypte, 1 Juin 1897–1er Moharrem 1315*. 3 vols. Cairo, 1898.

[Gouvernemt Française]. *Rapport à la société des nations sur la situation de la Syrie et du Liban*. Paris, annually, 1924–1939.

Grendler, Paul. *The Roman Inquisition and the Venetian Press, 1540–1605*. Princeton, 1977.

———. "The Roman inquisition and the Venetian press, 1540–1605," *Journal of Modern History*, XLVII, 1 (March 1975), pp. 48–65.

Groves, Anton N. *A Journal of a Residence at Baghdad During the Year 1830*. London, 1832.

Haim, Sylvia. "Salama Musa, an appreciation of his autobiography," *WI*, New Series, II, (1953), pp. 10–24.

Hartmann, Martin. *The Arabic Press of Egypt*. London, 1899.

Hattox, Ralph s. *Coffee and coffeehouses, the Origins of a Social Beverage in the Medieval Near East*. Seattle, 1985.

Heyworth-Dunne, J[ames]. *An Introduction to the History of Education in Modern Egypt*. London, 1938.

———. "Printing and translation under Muhammad Ali: the foundation of modern arabic," *Journal of the Royal Asiatic Society*, Part III (July 1940), pp. 325–49.

Hirabayashi, Gordon K. and M. Fathallah El Khatib. "Communication and political awareness in the villages of Egypt," *Public Opinion Quarterly*, XXII (Fall 1958), pp. 357–63.

Hourani, Albert. *Arabic Thought in the Liberal Age 1798–1939*. Oxford, 1970.

———. "Bustani's encyclopaedia," *Journal of Islamic Studies*, 1 (1990), pp. 111–19.

Issawi, Charles. "Asymmetrical development and transport in Egypt, 1800–1914," *in* William R. Polk and Richard L. Chambers (eds.). *Beginnings of Modernization in the Middle East*. Chicago, 1968, pp. 383–400.

———. "Economic development and liberalism in Lebanon," *MEJ*, Summer 1964, pp. 279–92.

———. *The Economic History of Turkey 1800–1914*. Chicago, 1981.

———. *Egypt at Mid-Century, an Economic Survey*. London, 1954.

———. *The Fertile Crescent 1800–1914. A Documentary Economic History*. New York, 1988.

Jansen, Sue Currey. *Censorship; the Knot that Binds Power and Knowledge*. New York, 1988.

Jerrold, Blanchard. *Egypt Under Ismail Pacha*. London, 1879.

Jessup, Henri Harris. *Fifty Three Years in Syria*. London, 1910. Vol. 2.

Kazziha, Walid. "The Jaridah-Ummah group and Egyptian politics," *MES*, October 1977, pp. 373–85.

Kedourie, Elie. "The death of Adib Ishaq," *in* his *Arabic Political Memoirs and Other Studies*. London, 1974, pp. 81–100.

———. "The kingdom of Iraq: a retrospect," *in* his *The Chatham House Version and Other Middle Eastern Studies*, London, 1970, pp. 236–85.

Kelidar, Abbas. "The political press in Egypt, 1882–1914," *in* Charles Tripp (ed.). *Contemporary Egypt: Through Egyptian Eyes. Essays in Honour of Professor P.J. Vatikiotis*. London and New York, 1993, pp. 1–21.

———. "Shaykh 'Ali Yusuf: Egyptian journalist and Islamic nationalist," *in* Buheiry, *Intellectual Life*, pp. 10–20.

Kenny, L.M. "East versus West in *al-Muqtataf*, 1875–1900," *in* Donald P. Little (ed.). *Essays on Islamic Civilization Presented to Niyazi Berkes*. Leiden, 1976, pp. 140–54.

Khadduri, Majid. *Independent Iraq, 1932–1958*. Oxford, 1960.

Khalidi, Rashid. "'Abd al-Ghani al-'Uraysi and *al-Mufid*: the press and Arab nationalism before 1914," *in* Buheiry, *Intellectual Life*, pp. 38–61.

Khalidi, Tarif. "Shaykh Ahmad 'Arif al-Zayn and al-'Irfan," *in* Buheiry, *Intellectual Life*, pp. 110–24.

Khoury, Philip S. *Syria and the French Mandate. The Politics of Arab Nationalism 1920–1945*. Princeton, 1987.

Kramer, Martin. "Pen and purse: Sabunji and Blunt," *in* C.E. Bosworth et. al. (eds.). *The Islamic World from Classical to Modern Times. Essays in Honor of Bernard Lewis*. Princeton, 1989, pp. 771–80.

Kronenwetter, Michael. *Journalism Ethics*. New York, 1988.

Krymskii, Agathangel Efimovich. *Istoria Novoi Arabskoi Literaturyi*. Moscow, 1971.

Kudsi-Zadeh, A. Albert. "Salim 'Anhuri (1856–1933), journalist, poet, and social critic," *in* Donald P. Little (ed.). *Essays on Islamic Civilization Presented to Niyazi Berkes*. Leiden, 1976, pp. 179–89.

Lagarde, L. "Note sur les journaux français de Constantinople à l'èpoque révolutionnaire," *JA*, 236 (1948), pp. 271–76.

Lane, Edward William. *Manners and Customs of the Modern Egyptians*. London, 1978.

Lewis, Bernard. *The Emergence of Modern Turkey*. Oxford, 1961.

———. *The Muslim Discovery of Europe*. New York, 1982.

———. *The Political Language of Islam*. Chicago, 1988.

———. "Propaganda in the medieval Islamic world," lecture in the Mortimer Raymond Sackler Series, delivered at Tel Aviv University, 18 January 1993.

———. et. al. *"Djarida," EI²*.

Lewis, Geoffrey L. "Fathname," *EI²*.

Lloyd, Lord. *Egypt Since Cromer*. 2 Vols. London, 1933.

Longrigg, Stephen Hemsley. *'Iraq, 1900 to 1950*. London, 1956.

Louca, Anouar. *Voyageurs et écrivains égyptiens en France au XIX⁰ siècle*. Paris, 1970.

Malul, Nissim. "Ha-'itonut ha-'Aravit," *Ha-Shiloah*, XXXI (1914), pp. 364–74, 439–50.

McFadden, Tom J. *Daily Journalism in the Arab States*. Columbus, Ohio, 1953.

Mirante, M. "La presse périodique arabe," *14th International Congress of Orientalists* (1905), Vol. III, Section I, pp. 196–205.

Mitchell, Timothy. *Colonising Egypt*. Cambridge, 1988.

Moreh, Shmuel. "Ya'qub Sanu': his religious identity and work in the theater and journalism, according to the family archive," *in* Shimon Shamir (ed.). *The Jews of Egypt*. Boulder, Colorado, 1987, pp. 111–29.

Mowlana, Hamid. "Mass communication, elites and national systems in the Middle East." Paper presented at the AIERI International Scientific Conference, Karl Marx University, Leipzig, September 1974.

———. "Mass media systems and communication behavior," *in* Michael Adams (ed.). *The Middle East, a Handbook*. London, 1970, pp. 584–98.

Munier, Jules. *La presse en Egypte*. Cairo, 1930.

Nasser, Munir. "The Middle East press: tool of politics," *in* Jane Leftwich Curry and Joan R. Dassin (eds.). *Press Control Around the World*. New York, 1982, pp. 187–208.

Nashabi, Hisham. "Shaykh 'Abd al-Qadir al-Qabbani and *Thamarat al-Funun*," *in* Buheiry, *Intellectual Life*, pp. 84–91.

"The native press of Egypt," *MW*, VII (1917), pp. 415–19; X (1920), pp. 184–91.

Obermeyer, Gerald J. *"Al-Iman* and al-Imam: ideology and state in the Yemen, 1900–1948," *in* Buheiry, *Intellectual Life*, pp. 176–92.

Orhonlu, Cengiz. "Türkçe yayinlanan ilk gazete 'Takvim-i Vekayi'," *Belgelerle Türk Tarih Dergisi*, March 1968, pp. 36–39.

Palestine [Mandatory Government]. *Blue Book 1929*. Alexandria, 1930.

———. *Blue Book 1930*. Alexandria, 1931.

Palmer, M. Reeves. "The Kibla: a Mecca newspaper," *MW* VII (1917), pp. 185–190.

Perron, A. "Lettres sur les écoles et l'imprimerie du pacha d'Egypte," *JA*, 4th Series, Vol. II (1843), pp. 5–60.

Philipp, Thomas. *Ǧurǧi Zaydan, His Life and Thought*. Wiesbaden, 1979.

———. *The Syrians in Egypt 1725–1975*. Stuttgart, 1985.

Poujoulat, Baptiste. *La verité sur la Syrie* (first published in 1861). Beirut, 1986.

Die Presse in Ägypten. Internationale Presse-Ausetellung. Cologne, 1928.

Rae, W. Fraser. "The Egyptian newspaper press," *The Nineteenth Century*, XXXII (July–December 1892), pp. 213–23.

Ramadan, Abdel Meguid Sadik. *Evolution de la législation sur la presse en Egypte.* Cairo, 1935.

Reid, Donald M. *The Odyssey of Farah Antun.* Chicago, 1975.

———. "The rise of professional organizations in modern Egypt," *Comparative Studies in Society and History*, XVI (1974), pp. 24–57.

Reinaud, M. "De la gazette arabe turque imprimée en Egypte," *JA*, 2nd Series, Vol. VIII, (1831), pp. 238–49.

Rosenthal, Franz. *The Muslim Concept of Freedom.* Leiden, 1960.

Rugh, William A. *The Arab Press.* 2nd. ed. Syracuse, 1987.

Sadgrove, Philip Charles. *The Development of the Arabic Periodical Press and Its Role in the Literary Life of Egypt (1798–1882).* Unpublished Ph.D diss., The University of Edinburgh, 1983.

al-Sayyid Marsot, Afaf Lutfi. *Egypt's Liberal Experiment: 1922–1936.* Los Angeles, 1977.

Schölch, Alexander. *Egypt for the Egyptians!* London, 1981.

Schuon, Frithjof. *Dimensions of Islam.* Lahore, 1985.

Scribner, Robert W. "Oral culture and the diffusion of reformation ideas," *in* his *Popular Culture and Popular Movements in Reformation Germany.* London, 1987, pp. 49–69.

Seikali, Samir M. "Damascene intellectual life in the opening years of the 20th century: Muhammad Kurd 'Ali and *al-Muqtabas*," *in* Buheiry, *Intellectual Life*, pp. 125–53.

Shim'oni, Yaacov. *Aravei Eretz Israel.* Tel Aviv, 1947.

Shoshan, Boaz. "On popular literature in medieval Cairo," *Poetics Today*, XIV, 2 (Summer 1993), pp. 349–65.

Slade, Adolphus. *Records of Travel in Turkey, Greece & c. and of a Cruise in the Black Sea With the Captain Pasha in the Years 1829, 1830 and 1831.* 2 Vols. London, 1832.

Smith, Henry Ladd. "The Egyptian press and its current problems," *JQ*, Summer 1954, pp. 331–36.

Somekh, Sasson. *Genre and Language in Modern Arabic Literature.* Wiesbaden, 1991.

Sommerland, Ernest Lloyd. *The Press in Developing Countries.* Sydney, 1966.

Steinberg, S. H. *Five Hundred Years of Printing.* Baltimore, 1955.

Storey, Graham. *Reuters.* New York, 1951.

Suleiman, Susan R. and Inge Crosman (eds.). *The Reader in the Text: Essays on Audience and Interpretation.* Princeton, 1980.

Swan, George. "The Moslem press in Egypt," *MW*, I (1910), pp. 147–54.

Tauber, Eliezer. *The Arab Movements in World War I.* London, 1993.

———. "The press and the journalist as a vehicle in spreading national ideas in Syria in the late Ottoman period," *WI*, XXX (1990), pp. 163–77.

Thomsen, P[eter]. "Verzeichnis der arabischen Zeitungen und Zeitschriften Palästinas," *Zeitschrift des Deutschen Palästina-Vereins*, 1914, pp. 211–15.

Tibawi, Abdul Latif. *American Interests in Syria 1800–1901.* Oxford, 1966.

———. "The American missionaries in Beirut and Butrus al-Bustani," *St. Antony's Papers*, No. 16 (1963), pp. 137–82.

————. *Islamic Education*. London, 1972.

Tignor, Robert L. *Modernization and British Colonial Rule in Egypt, 1882-1914*. Princeton, 1966.

Ubicini, M.A. *Letters from Turkey*. Translated from the French by Lady East-hope. 2 Vols. London, 1856.

UNESCO. Department of Mass Communication. *World Communications, Press, Radio, Film*. Paris, 1950.

————. *World Communications. A 200 Country Survey of Press, Radio, Television and Film*. Paris, 1975.

————. Office of Statistics. *Comparative Statistical Data on Education in the Arab States*. Beirut, 1967.

Vatikiotis, P.J. *The History of Modern Egypt, From Muhammad Ali to Mubarak*. 4th Edition. Baltimore, 1991.

Walker, Martin. *Powers of the Press: the World's Great Newspapers*. New York, 1982.

Washington-Serruys. *L'Arabe moderne étudie dans les journaux et les pièces officielles*. Beirut, 1897.

Wassef, Amin Sami. *L'Information et la presse officielle en Egypte jusqu'à la fin de l'occupation française*. Cairo, 1975.

White, Charles. *Three Years in Constantinople*. London, 1845. Vol. 2.

Williams, Francis. *The Right to Know. The Rise of the World Press*. London, 1969.

Winter, Michael. "Ma'arif," *EI²*.

Woodsmall, Ruth Frances. *Moslem Women Enter a New World*. New York, 1936.

Wynn, Wilton C. "Western techniques influence party newspapers of Egypt," *JQ*, XXV, No. 4 (December 1948), pp. 391–94.

El-Zine, M. Abdallah Yahia. *Le Yemen et les moyens d'information 1872–1974*. Algiers, 1978.

Zolondek, L. "Sabunji in England 1876–1891: his role in Arabic journalism," *MES*, XIV (1978), pp. 102–15.

Index

DATE DUE